Performance Practices
in the Classical Era

Also by Dennis Shrock

Music for Beginning Conductors:
An Anthology for Choral Conducting Classes

Performance Practices
in the Classical Era

as related by primary resources and as illustrated
in the music of W.A. Mozart and Joseph Haydn

DENNIS SHROCK

GIA Publications, Inc.
Chicago

Performance Practices in the Classical Era
as related by primary sources and as illustrated in the music of W. A. Mozart
and Joseph Haydn
by Dennis Shrock

G-7815
ISBN: 978-1-57999-799-1

www.giamusic.com

CONTENTS

INTRODUCTION

This book presents information from more than 100 Classical-era authors and composers about the performance of music during their time. Being contemporary to music during the years of its composition and first performance, the information is direct or primary, and as such, the instructions and commentaries presented here have not been subjected to the vagaries that affect communication from one person to another over decades or generations. Absent are the inevitable results of accounts from secondary sources (e.g., interpretations, re-interpretations, opinionated colorings, modifications to accommodate changes of fashion and taste, and dependencies on memory), which, however well-intentioned, alter original meaning or intent.

The primary sources cover a broad spectrum: 1) they represent the entire time frame of the Classical era from 1751 to the 1830s (and sometimes beyond to show that a particular performance practice continued into the beginning or even middle years of the Romantic era); 2) every decade of the era is represented, as well as most years within the decade (e.g., there are sources from every year of the 1770s and all but three years each of the 1760s, 1780s, and 1790s); 3) the sources come from all across Europe—most specifically Germany, France, Italy, England, and Spain—and also from the United States; 4) the subject matter of the sources encompasses virtually every type of performing medium and genre of composition common in the era, including the flute, oboe, bassoon, trumpet, kettledrum, violin, viola, cello, stringed bass, singer, a variety of keyboard instruments, and all types of vocal and instrumental music; and 5) the sources are in a diversity of formats, including instruction books (such as treatises, primers, or tutorial methods that are meant to educate), diaries that comment on performances of the time, prefaces to compositions by composers of the era, and dictionaries, letters, biographies, and essays.

The benefits of such a wide range and extensive amount of performance practice information are many: inclusion of quotations from the entire time frame of the era provides for a broad overview of the practices (for instance, one can take note of the limited or extensive practice of certain conventions and also the relative importance of practices over a long period of time); representing most years of the era illustrates the development of practices and provides for an awareness of consistency or change as the era progressed; inclusion of sources from multiple countries demonstrates the regional nature of practices, especially in regards to the peculiarities of specific countries, the adoption of practices from one country to another, and the relative similarities or congruities of basic concepts among many countries; combining quotations from sources written about specific performing media (instrumental and vocal) with sources written for different purposes (tutorials and criticisms) provides for a deep understanding of the practices and also for an awareness of the pervasiveness of particular performance conventions (for example, it is confirming to read the same basic information about flute playing, singing, and stringed instruments, and, similarly, it is elucidating to compare material from rudimentary instruction books meant for beginners with critiques of famous performers); and, finally, the incorporation of numerous quotations on each topic aids in the credibility of the quotations. With repetitions of identical or near-identical recommendations from a diversity of sources and countries across the era—with a concinnity of the material—today's musician can feel confident in the application of the practices.

Congruity and concinnity do not, however, imply rigid dogma or lack of flexibility. In many instances authors promote and encourage variability and freedom of interpretation, and most often the authors express notions of generality—concepts, ideals, and even rules that allow for the creative input of performers. These generalities are parameters within which performers are expected to operate; differences within the parameters are quite acceptable, even desirable. Only differences outside the parameters are inappropriate. Because of the latitudes recommended by the primary source authors, I believe that such terms as "authentic" and "right/wrong" as applied to performance practice are unsound and even harmful. These terms suggest categorical opinions that do not tolerate creative differences. Terms such as "appropriate" and "compatible" are better suited to the meanings of the primary sources and to achieving a balance between rule-oriented precepts and performer-creative involvement.

The material in this book is presented in a topic-specific manner, with all the primary source information related to a single subject or category presented chronologically and grouped together in one location. Consequently, the material of an author or source that covers multiple topics is divided, and the author or source may appear numerous times throughout the book, although always with new material. The categories represent the main performance practices of the era and are arranged according to their influence on one another. The subject of sound is first because it affects all the other subjects; if sound is appropriate according to primary source ideals and guidelines, other performance issues will be aided, while if sound is inappropriate, the other issues will be hindered. The category of tempo is, logically, second in that it impacts the degrees or qualities of subsequent categories—most especially articulation and metric accentuation. The category of expression is last, not only because it encapsulates all the other categories, but also because it brings the entire subject of performance practice full circle; the mood and character of expression help determine precise colorations of sound.

The quotations are preceded by a general description of the practice—a summarized narrative of its nature and an introduction to the primary source material. With commonly known categories such as vibrato and tempo fluctuation, the introductions are brief and without elaboration. However, with lesser-known categories such as meter influencing tempo and metric accentuation, the introductions are lengthy, and, for clear elucidation, they contain musical examples drawn from works by W. A. Mozart and Joseph Haydn. Each quotation is headed by the author's name, an English equivalent of the source of the quotation (e.g., flute treatise), the year of the source's authorship or publication, and the name of the chapter or section in which the quotation appears. (The original title of the source appears in the Bibliography.) All translations of the foreign-language quotations are mine, and the spelling of English-language quotations has been retained. Finally, the quotations in each category of performance practice are presented in paragraph form, thus presenting the specific practices in context and also providing for an awareness of each author's style of presentation.

The organization of material according to topics is meant to facilitate the identification, comprehension, and manifestation of performance practices germane to and common during the Classical era. With the book's encyclopedic design, therefore, performers interested in a specific topic (tempo or trills, for example) can conveniently access and digest relevant information, while conductors interested in a broader issue (overdotting or ornamentation) can reference material specific to those subjects. Students and scholars interested in the development of a practice or in the interrelationship of multiple practices can read the book more thoroughly.

The study of performance practice is really the study of notation; it is an inquiry into the meaning of written music so as to determine its precise intent and, therefore, its manifestation in performance. In this regard, performance practice is more than the usage of period instruments (instruments original to the time or reproductions of instruments based on original models). While period instruments provide colors that are different from modern instruments, and while the period instruments suggest certain limitations (such as volume) and techniques (such as the messa di voce effect created by a pre-Tourte bow drawn across gut strings tuned to a pitch lower than

A=440 HZ), present-day performers may still impart today's techniques into their playing, creating an effect more modern than historical. For instance, any instrumentalist can (and is likely to) play successive notes with present-day concepts of equal stress, thus obviating patterns of metric accentuation. Likewise, an instrumentalist can play all appoggiaturas short and thus strip a performance from the preferred dissonance that would be created by a long duration. Without the knowledge and understanding of what an instrument is supposed to accomplish, a player can unwittingly impose something inappropriate or assume something erroneous. Beyond this, it is dangerous and misleading to base performance practice on the utilization of period instruments because doing so gives such a practice inordinate importance. Choice of instruments was not paramount in the minds of Classical-era musicians. Style was much more important, and style can be understood through a knowledge of notation.

Notation is a language of communication between composer and performer. Accordingly, a performer must understand the meanings of the notational language in order to translate or transfer the notation into a performance that will realize the composer's intentions. The more a performer comprehends the meaning of the notation of a composer, the more the performer can manifest the composer's meaning and the more a composition can reveal its essence. To understand notation, then, is to have the opportunity to approximate music's art in its original state.

To understand notation is also to understand the term *come scripta* (as written), used by numerous people in present times to say that one should perform only what is notated—nothing more. If one comprehends the notation of the Classical era in terms of present-day meanings, then usage of *come scripta* is fallacious; one is not reading what is written, but instead what a misinformed person thinks is written (or not written). The term *come scripta* is appropriate only if one understands the notation as the composer understood it. For example, a meter signature today conveys information only about equations of beats into measures. During the Classical era, however, meter signatures conveyed that information as well as indications of tempo and metric accentuation. This multiple meaning was the *come scripta* of a meter signature; its notation communicated all this information to performers.

In addition to understanding meanings of notation that have been lost to later ages, performers must be wary of changing meanings. For instance, the term *vivace* today means "very fast." A performer, therefore, will assume that music marked with this term should be faster, often considerably faster, than music marked with *allegro*. However, the term *vivace* meant "vivacious" to musicians of the Classical era, with implications for an actual tempo comparable to or slightly slower than *allegro*. So, performers today must be wary of applying meanings retroactively; instead, performers should strive to gain meanings from their origins. Primary source information can aid in this process.

Performance practices are customs or common procedures. Separately, they are the specific ways in which performers actually realize elements of performance. Together, they are characteristics and mannerisms that make for a performing personality, one that, like looking at an object from all different sides, shows dimension and shape. In this regard, it is important to realize that the practices of the Classical era (as with any era) apply to all music being performed during that era. Consequently, music composed during the Baroque era—say 1720—being performed during the Classical era—say 1780—would be performed according to Classical-era (1780) conventions. The Classical-era performance practices promote ideals of elegance and gentility. From sound to expression, they are the means to capture the heart of a composer's creation, and also the means to allow all generations of performers and listeners to be fully enriched by the beauty the composer sought to create.

It is hoped that the presentation of such an extensive range of primary source material will provide the modern-day performer, student, and scholar with a comprehensive understanding of each performance topic, an understanding that will help to define the scope and limits, as well as the character and appropriate parameters of each performance practice. With the grouping together of numerous quotations addressed to diverse audiences (e.g., beginning and advanced singers, violinists, keyboardists, and composers), it is hoped that today's musician will view the basic universality of practices—the consistency of practices from one performing medium to another and from one compositional genre to another, and also the coordination of the practices into an overall ethic of performance. Players of keyboard instruments, for instance, can then relate better to string players and singers, and instrumentalists and vocalists can better understand and coordinate their separate efforts. The reinforcement of practices—early and late, across many countries, addressed to a variety of performers, and written in a variety of forms—all testify to the verity of the subject matter.

Chapter 1
SOUND

The constituent elements of sound—those elements that are involved in the direct formulation of an identifiable acoustical characteristic and those elements that were written about in detail during the Classical era—include aural quality (timbre), volume (dynamic levels), vocal registers (in particular, falsetto), vibrato, pitch, and instrumentation (the types and proportions of instruments and singers, including castratos). Timbre was most often discussed in terms of the idealized model of the human voice, with adjectives such as "sweet" used to characterize desired qualities of gentility and elegance. Discussions of volume reinforced the preferred qualities of refinement as authors extolled the virtues of subtlety and nuance and praised singers who sang softly and instrumentalists who played like singers. In like manner, authors discussed the extensive use of falsetto and its appealing qualities and lauded singers who could seamlessly meld the falsetto with the middle range of the voice. Vibrato, as it was defined, was narrower in pitch fluctuation than is customary today, and it was either to be employed in a limited sense, as an ornamental feature, or to be avoided; a number of authors who wrote treatises addressed to vocalists decried the use of vibrato altogether. The mention of pitch during the era confirms the fact that there was no standard (such as A=440 Hz) and that levels could vary from location to location by as much as the interval of a third. However, from physical data, it is assumed that the referential A was around 420 Hz, which is almost a half step lower than present-day pitch levels (A-flat=415

Hz). Finally, the particular qualities of Classical-era sound were colored by a practice of doubling or tripling wind and brass instruments in orchestras that contained a relatively large number of strings, the inclusion of a keyboard instrument in all orchestral performances, the placement of choirs in front of orchestras, and the use of castratos for both solo and choral performance.

As acknowledged during the era, the sound produced by the combination of the elements mentioned above is one of the most significant components and critical aspects of performance practice. It is significant because it is what most impacts the listener; it is the element of performance that is the most obvious—the feature of performance that most determines the aesthetic perception of an aural experience. Sound is critical because it sets the stage for all the other aspects of performance practice; it is a physical property, with parameters, that determines the degree to which the other elements can be accomplished or accommodated, and it helps or hinders these other elements, from tempo to articulation, phrasing to rhythmic alteration, and ornamentation to expression. Without appropriate sound, for example, recommended tempos may seem illogical, prescribed articulations of rhythms may not be feasible, phrasing spaces and altered rhythms may seem exaggerated, ornamentation may be labored, and expressive nuances may be obscured. With appropriate sound, on the other hand, tempos and phrasings may be logical to the point of revealing structural clarity to compositions, unlabored articulations may provide special qualities of spirit and elegance to performances, performers may have the capability and desire to add to music needed and desirable ornaments, and rhythmic alterations and other elements of expression may create pleasurable qualities of drama.

Present-day musicians may agree with the importance of sound and may appreciate the interaction of its constituent elements, but present-day musicians may also think that sound is mainly an indigenous quality of the construction of an instrument or the particular physiology of a voice; original instruments from the Classical era or more current reproductions produce sounds that are appropriate, and singers either do not make similar sounds or they approximate compatible sounds as best they can with their modern-day vocal techniques. While it is basically true that instruments produce sounds based upon their construction (e.g., violins with gut strings generally produce a messa di voce effect when played with pre-Tourte bows and Classical-era trumpets produce a sound that is considerably softer in volume and more mellow in quality than their modern counterparts), differences that may seem subtle are significant, and, as primary source quotations testify, players have a consequential impact on relative qualities of sound. Also, as seen in the first subheading of this chapter (The Vocal Model), primary source quotations provide unqualified support to the expectation that singers and instrumentalists of the Classical era should be united in their efforts to produce timbral ideals.

In addition to the challenges of unifying vocal and instrumental production, some of the elements of sound are difficult to grasp objectively and are, therefore, perceived and interpreted differently. For example, it is impossible to know the precise levels of idealized volume, even on period instruments; the production of falsetto may vary considerably from person to person; and a lack of vibrato in singers can be the result of poor vocal production and, therefore, can result in an unpleasant quality of tone. Furthermore, some of the elements of sound are challenging to implement in performance (e.g., the doubling or tripling of wind instruments in orchestrations and the locating of choirs in front of orchestras), and some elements, such as soft volume, may limit the appreciation of intended drama, given the extraordinarily loud levels of volume that are a part of today's world. However, these elements are only difficult to grasp and challenging to implement when considered individually. When considered collectively and when combined with other elements of performance practice such as recommended tempos, articulations, and metric accentuation, the elements are more easily realized. Sound, as a part of the overall fabric of performance practice, can be seen as both an initial factor (one that influences others) and as a culminating factor (one that results from the accomplishment of others).

The combination of both viewpoints is likely to aid modern-day performers in accomplishing the directives of Classical-era prescriptions and in reaching the aesthetic goals imagined by Classical-era composers.

THE VOCAL MODEL

Virtually all commentary from the Classical era regarding either the quality or production of sound expresses ideals related to the human voice. The numerous treatises on the playing of instruments assert unqualifiedly that sound should be modeled on the voice (e.g., Tromlitz states in his flute treatise that "the only model on which an instrumentalist should form his tone is a beautiful human voice"), and journals and memoirs about performances either praise or criticize instrumentalists for their relative success at emulating the voice (e.g., Hawkins, in his history of music, states that Giuseppe San Martini, who "was undoubtedly the greatest [oboe] player that the world had ever known," produced "such a tone as approached the nearest to that of the human voice of any we know"). Even players of keyboard instruments were advised to produce a singing tone (note the comment by C. P. E. Bach in his clavier treatise that keyboardists should listen to "artistic singing" and "think in terms of song").

The compatibility of instrumental to vocal tone is important in that compatibility reinforces the concept of a unified sound ideal within the era: all sounds, instrumental and vocal, were to be as similar as possible. Knowledge of this is helpful to present-day musicians because original or reproductions of period instruments have been used extensively in performances and recordings and are generally available to performers. Consequently, one does not have to guess at basic qualities of timbre; the specific qualities of instrumental tone and ranges of volume can be heard and therefore applied to singing. The Classical-era reference of voice to instrument can be reversed, and singers of today can model their vocal sounds, both according to volume and quality, on the sounds of Classical-era instruments.

Apropos of volume and quality, it is interesting to read quotes relating flute playing to vocal production. Quantz, for instance, compares the ideal flute sound to the chest tones of singers, and he further characterizes these flute and chest tones as masculine. To understand Quantz adequately, it is important to know that during the early part of the Classical era it was common to equate the chest voice with the full, or natural, voice, and to know that this full, natural sound of the voice was quite soft and sweet. Also, it is important to comprehend relative degrees of masculinity. Present-day concepts of chest tones and masculinity, which are far removed from the sounds of the flute (even the modern-day flute), need to be adjusted. Performers today need to conceptualize different meanings—ones that are based upon understandings of terminology and capabilities of period instruments, and also ones that will aid in the production of sounds approximating those of elegance and gentility idealized during the Classical era.

Geminiani, violin treatise (1751), Preface

The Intention of Musick is not only to please the Ear, but to express Sentiments, strike the Imagination, affect the Mind, and command the Passions. The Art of playing the Violin consists in giving that Instrument a Tone that shall in a Manner rival the most perfect human Voice; and in executing every Piece with Exactness, Propriety, and Delicacy of Expression according to the true Intention of Musick.

Quantz, flute treatise (1752), Chapter 4 "Of the Embouchure"

In general, the most pleasing tone quality on the flute is that which more nearly resembles a contralto than a soprano, or which imitates the chest tones of the human voice. You must strive as much as possible to acquire the tone quality of those flute players who know how to produce a clear, penetrating, thick, round, masculine, and in addition, pleasing sound from the instrument.

Much depends upon the flute itself, and whether its tone has the necessary similarity to the human voice. If it lacks this, no one can improve the tone quality, even with very adroit lips, just as no singer can make a poor natural voice beautiful.

——. Chapter 11 "Of Good Execution in General in Singing and Playing" *Paragraph 19*

Each instrumentalist must strive to execute that which is cantabile as a good singer executes it. The singer, on the other hand, must try in lively pieces to achieve the fire of good instrumentalists, as much as the voice is capable of it.

——. Chapter 16 "What a Flutist Must Observe if he Plays in Public Concerts" *Paragraph 30*

If a flutist has to play in concert with a vocal part, he must seek to match it as much as possible in tone quality and manner of execution. He must vary nothing except where imitations give the opportunity to do so.

C. P. E. Bach, clavier treatise (1753), "Introduction to Part One"

The true art of playing keyboard instruments depends on three factors so closely related that no one of them can, nor indeed dare exist without the others. They are: correct fingering, good embellishments, and good performance.

Owing to ignorance of these factors and their consequent absence from performance, keyboardists can be heard who after tortuous trouble have finally learned how to make their instrument sound loathsome to an enlightened listener. Their playing lacks roundness, clarity, forthrightness, and in their place one hears only hacking, thumping, and stumbling. All other instruments have learned how to sing.

——. Chapter 3 "Performance"

As a means of learning the essentials of good performance, it is advisable to listen to accomplished musicians. . . . Above all, lose no opportunity to hear artistic singing. In so doing, the keyboardist will learn to think in terms of song. Indeed, it is a good practice to sing instrumental melodies in order to reach an understanding of their correct performance.

**Avison, essay on musical expression (1753), Part 3
"On Musical Expression, as it relates to the Performer" Section 1 "On the
expressive Performance of Music in general"**

The *Organ* and *Harpsichord*, although alike in so many Respects that
the same Performer may equally show his Skill and Execution on both,
are in their respective Compositions and Manner of Performance widely
different: The former expressing the grand or solemn Stile [style], the latter,
those lively or trickling Movements which thrill in the Ear. . . .

When the full Organ is heard, no *Mixtures* or *Furnitures* etc. shall
predominate, but that the *Diapasons*, with their *Octaves* (Principals and
Flutes) may unite and fill the whole; so we may rank the *Violins* with their
Basses and *Double-Basses*, as the *Diapasons* and *Principles* of the Concert:
For in Fact they may be said to contain the very Strength and Spirit of
all Harmony; and have in them, not only the Expression of all the other
Instruments, but contain a prodigious Variety of many other noble Properties
peculiar to themselves, of which all the rest are utterly destitute. It is their
remarkable Distinction that no Concert can be formed without them, as
they unite and agree as well with every Instrument, as with each other, and
return every Advantage they receive. And, as the finest *instrumental Music*
may be considered as an Imitation of the *vocal*, so do these Instruments,
with their expressive Tone and the minutest changes they are capable of in
the Progression of Melody, show their nearest Approaches to the Perfection
of the human Voice.

**L. Mozart, violin treatise (1756), Chapter 5 "How by adroit control of
the Bow, one should seek to produce a good tone on a Violin and bring it
forth in the right manner"**

Who is not aware that singing is at all times the aim of every
instrumentalist, because one must always approximate to nature as nearly
as possible.

Hawkins, history of music (1776), Book 20, Chapter 194

Giuseppe San Martini was a native of Milan. He was a performer on
the hautboy [oboe], an instrument invented by the French, and of small
account, till by his exquisite performance and tone which he had the art of
giving it, he brought it into reputation. . . .

As a performer on the hautboy, Martini was undoubtedly the greatest that the world had ever known. Before his time the tone of the instrument was rank, and, in the hands of the ablest proficients, harsh and grating to the ear; however, by great study and application, and by some peculiar management of the reed, he contrived to produce such a tone as approached the nearest to that of the human voice of any we know.

Manfredini, defense of modern music (1788), "Conclusion"

There is general agreement about instrumental music, that it is in a lofty position now, and that ancient music did not achieve so much. But what else does this kind of music contain, if not vocal lines or melodies that are more spirited, more pleasing, and more meaningful than the ancient ones? They are melodies almost all of which derive from vocal music, whose follower and companion instrumental music has been and always will be. It is simply true that instrumental music is for the most part a copy and imitation of the vocal. When it doesn't sing, it doesn't express—that is, it says nothing and it is worth nothing at all. So while instrumental music has greatly improved, it first had to be made into vocal music, and whoever denies this can deny anything.

Türk, clavier treatise (1789), "Introduction"

The most important properties of a fine clavichord are: 1) it must have a strong, full, and at the same time, pleasant and singing tone, which does not die away immediately after the striking of the key, but rather continues to sound for the value of at least four to six eighth notes in a moderately slow adagio. . . .

If the student is to achieve a proper and good style of execution—and should he not achieve this?—then the teacher must play the piece he has assigned for him, at first very simply (without improvisatory ornaments), but with expression. I would only do this, however, when the student is able to play it with some facility, for otherwise he might learn it only by ear, using only his memory and not his understanding—*and this he should never do*. In addition, frequently listening to good music, excellent players, and particularly to sensitive singers, contributes greatly to the formation of taste. Whoever can study another instrument at the same time, for example, the violin or the flute, or also have lessons in singing, will make even greater progress in playing the keyboard.

With regard to proper execution, some teachers are too negligent in the beginning, for no matter how unevenly and tastelessly their students strum, they let it go by as long as they use the proper fingers and keep the time, etc. Indeed, in the first lessons one must not require certain subtleties of the student, but certainly a singing tone, a sustaining touch, and a variation of loud and soft tones, for at this point in some cases it is just as difficult for him to do things incorrectly as to do them correctly.

Tromlitz, flute treatise (1791), Chapter 6 "Tone and pure intonation"

Since tone is a principal component of good performance for instrumentalists as well as for singers, no effort at all should be spared to keep it as beautiful as one possibly can. Everyone knows that a hollow, dull, and wooden tone is incorrect, and is very detrimental to good delivery. Of course, singers must use the voice that Nature has given them; but even the best voice can be spoiled by forcing it through the nose and between the teeth, or obstructing its normal passage through the throat and mouth. But if an instrumentalist has a bad tone, it is his own fault, for a good sound is entirely the result of his skill, although it is true that a great deal also depends on the instrument. A bad instrument cannot produce a good tone. . . .

I say: the only model on which an instrumentalist should form his tone is a beautiful human voice; and as far as I am concerned, a human voice that is beautiful is one that is bright, full and resonant, of masculine strength but not shrieking, soft but not hollow; in short, for me a beautiful voice is full of timbre, rounded, singing, soft, and flexible.

Each instrument matches that voice with which it is most congruent: flute, oboe, and violin model themselves on a beautiful soprano and alto; viola, cello, and bassoon on a beautiful alto, tenor, and bass voice. Now since this tone quality is unquestionably to be found in its most perfect manifestation in the human form, so therefore the instrument that most closely approaches this tone must have the most perfect sound.

Streicher, remarks on the fortepiano (1801), "On tone"

It is very difficult, if not impossible, to agree upon what constitutes a really beautiful instrumental tone since everyone has a more or less different idea about it. For this reason, some prefer a *sharp, cutting* or *shrill* tone; others, on the contrary, prefer a *full, well-rounded* tone. Without offending anyone, however, it can be assumed that if the tone of the fortepiano is both to move and please the listener, it should, as much as possible, resemble the sound of the best wind instruments.

If the tone of a fortepiano is otherwise (a so-called 'silver tone,' which very soon, however, becomes an 'iron tone' if played too heavily), it is already on the verge of being *dry, thin or meager,* and is thus too far removed in resemblance to the human voice, or to those instruments which, through their fullness of sound, fill the ear with tone and strongly affect our feelings.

Spohr, musical diary (1860–1861), "Paris, January 30, 1821"

The accentuation of the last note of a phrase by increased pressure and a rapid upward sweep of the bow is common, more or less, to all the French violinists. . . . I cannot imagine how such a practice could have been generally adopted, for the effect is as if a speaker were to continually accent the short last syllables. If they [the French violinists] had modeled the phrasing of their cantabiles on human song—which I believe every instrumentalist should do—they would never have strayed into such byways.

**Czerny, composition treatise (1834),
Part III "On Vocal Compositions"
Chapter 1 "General Remarks on Vocal Music"**

In a state of perfection, the human voice produces the finest sound within the range of music, and no instrument can, in this respect, be compared with it. Besides, as it is inseparably united with poetry and its innumerable ideas, and consequently with language, it must also, in general, always form the predominant part of every vocal composition; all the rest serves only as an accompaniment, to impart a coloring to the thoughts expressed by it, and for the support of the melody, of which it is the mistress.

Tulou, flute treatise (1835), "Tone Quality"

What is a beautiful tone on the flute? It is a tone that most closely resembles the human voice. Now, in order to imitate the fullness, sonority, and mellow quality of the voice, the lips must be shaped in a favorable way.

SOFT AND SWEET IDEALS

Classical-era commentary about vocal models of tone includes idealized descriptive characteristics that are both instructional (i.e., how to produce tone) and evaluative (i.e., praises or criticisms of tone). The instructions generally advise performers to produce sounds that are soft and sweet ("sweet" being the most commonly used adjective to describe idealized timbre) and to avoid excessive loudness and abstain from producing tones that could be thought of as coarse. Evaluations, in like manner, criticize sounds that were loud and harsh and praise performances of sounds that were soft and gentle. As noted in an important singing treatise by Isaac Nathan, "Quality more than quantity of tone should be the chief consideration. A judicious singer, with even a weak voice, will frequently, from nice management, excite more pleasure than another whose magnificent volume of tone leads him to loftier flights."

It was especially important that notes in the high register or tessitura be sung or played softly. As stated by Giambattista Mancini, one of the great castratos and singing teachers of the late nineteenth century, "Great care must be taken by the student to attack high notes with the required sweetness and proportion in order that he can command his entire range to perfection."

A number of authors acknowledge that dynamic levels should be gauged to the size and nature of performance venues. Quantz, for instance, states that a singer "must know how to moderate the tone quality of his voice from the low register into the high and, in so doing, how to distinguish between the theater and the chamber." Nevertheless, softness was still the ideal in large spaces, as noted in the admonition by Charles Avison "to soften every rough and grating sound, . . . particularly in churches where the expansion is large and ample." Reinforcing this is the comment by Charles Burney in praise of a performance in Westminster Abbey: "Madame Mara had . . . the power of conveying to the remotest corner of this immense building the softest and most artificial inflexions of her sweet and brilliant voice."

While the idealization of a sweet tone production is understandable for a culture whose defining element was elegance, and while it is logical to assume that characteristics of gentility would pervade all aspects of life and art during the Classical era, gentility and elegance are challenging to manifest today when singers and instrumentalists are accustomed to producing dynamic levels that have increased significantly in volume. In addition, the environment of modern society has experienced dynamic levels and dramatic expressions that are considerably more exaggerated than those of the Classical era. The Classical-era person had no concept of loudness as it is experienced today or no knowledge of the dimension that dramatic expansion would achieve. For modern-day performers, therefore, it is difficult to have a sense of a Classical-era marking of *forte* or an expression of strength. Today's performers can easily feel that a sound is too soft or too weak if it does not meet current standards of loudness. However, gentility and elegance do not have to be in opposition to loud volumes and expressions of strength if relative values of volume and expression are incorporated and if performance is governed by an overriding concept of gentility and elegance. If this overriding concept is the case, then not only are volume and drama contained within appropriate parameters, but other ideals are also aided, from softness and sweetness to tempo, articulation, phrasing, and ornamentation.

Quantz, flute treatise (1752), Chapter 10 "What a Beginner Must Observe in his Independent Practice" *Paragraph 3*

One must blow the flute weakly in the high notes, in accordance with their proportions, and strongly in the low ones, especially in passages that consist of leaps.

——. Chapter 17 "Of the Duties of Those Who Accompany or Execute the Accompanying or Ripieno Parts Associated with a Concertante Part" Section 7 "Of the Duties that All Accompanying Instrumentalists in General Must Observe" *Paragraph 20*

The Forte and Piano must never be unduly exaggerated. The instruments must not be handled with more force than their constitution permits, since the ear will be most disagreeably affected, especially in a small place.

——. Chapter 18 "How a Musician and a Musical Composition are to be Judged" *Paragraph 11*

[A singer] must not express the high notes with a harsh attack or with a vehement exhalation of air from his chest; still less should he scream them out, coarsening the amenity of the voice. . . . He must know how to moderate the tone quality of his voice from the low register into the high and, in so doing, how to distinguish between the theater and the chamber, and between a strong and a weak accompaniment, so that his singing of the high notes does not degenerate into screaming.

Avison, essay on musical expression (1753), Part 3
"On Musical Expression, as it relates to the Performer" Section 1 "On the expressive Performance of Music in general"

Let the lover of Music call to Mind the delightful Effects they afford, when joined with the Organ to a Chorus of good Voices, particularly in Churches where the Expansion is large and ample, to soften every rough and grating Sound, and unite the Variety of Voices and other Instruments, that complete a grand and solemn Performance.

L. Mozart, violin treatise (1756), Chapter 2 "How the Violinist must hold the Violin and direct the Bow"

The bow is held in the right hand, at its lowest part, between the thumb and the middle joint of the index finger, or even a little behind it. . . . One may, at times, hold the bow with the first or second joint of the index finger, but the stretching of the index finger is at all times wrong; doing so causes the hand to stiffen because the nerves are taut and the bowing becomes labored and clumsy. . . . One must accustom oneself from the beginning to draw a long, uninterrupted, soft, and flowing stroke.

**Tartini, letter to Signora Maddalena Lombardini (1770),
"March 5"**

Your principal practice and study should, at present, be confined to the use and power of the bow, in order to make yourself entirely mistress in the execution and expression of whatever can be played or sung, within the compass and ability of your instrument. Your first study, therefore, should be the true manner of holding, balancing, and pressing the bow lightly, but steadily, upon the strings, in such manner as that it shall seem to breathe the first tone it gives, which must proceed from the friction of the string, and not from percussion, as by a blow given with a hammer upon it. This depends on laying the bow lightly upon the strings, at the first contact, and on gently pressing it afterwards, which, if done gradually, can scarce have too much force given to it, because, if the tone is begun with delicacy, there is little danger of rendering it afterwards either coarse or harsh.

Of this first contact and delicate manner of beginning a tone, you should make yourself a perfect mistress in every situation and part of the bow, as well in the middle as at the extremities, and in moving it up as well as in drawing it down.

**Burney, account of music in France and Italy (1770),
"Rome 7 October"**

I dined with the D. of D. [Duke of Dorset] and then went with his grace to ALBANO. . . . The D. took a band [group] of music [musicians] with him to Mr. Leighton's at Albano whose guests we were, and we had music all the evening, with delightful singing by Bacchelli, commonly called the Mignatrice. She has a very sweet voice with infinite taste—has a good shake [trill], great flexibility, and is more free from affectation of any sort than ever I saw in an Italian singer.

———. "Rome 12 October"

After dinner I went to Crispi's academia which was the best of all those I had heard at his house. I subscribed to his quartettos, 2 or 3 of which were played after the company was gone and pleased me much more than his sinfonies which are too furious and noisy for a room or indeed for any other place. He made me a present of his duo, which I heard and liked much the first night I saw him. There was a young man Signor *Ruma*, who played the violin in a very delicate and pleasing manner.

——. "Naples 18 October"

After dinner to the Franciscan's church again where there was a larger band than the day before, the whole conservatorio of the Pietà consisting of 120 all dressed in a blue uniform attended. The *sinfonia* was just begun when I arrived, it was very brilliant and well executed—then followed a pretty good chorus—after which an air by a tenor voice, 1 by a soprano, 1 by a base, 1 by a contr'alto and another by a different tenor, but worse singing I never heard before in Italy: all was unfinished and scholar-like, the closes stiff, studied and ill-executed; and nothing like a shake could be mustered out of the whole band of singers. The soprano forced the high notes in a false direction till they went to one's brain and the base singer was as rough as a mastiff, whose barking he seemed to imitate. A solo concerto on the bassoon too in the same incorrect and unmasterly manner, drove me out of the church ere the whole vespers were finished.

——. "Naples 19 October"

In the evening I went again to St. Francesco's Church and heard the performance of the scholars of another conservatorio, namely *Santa Maria di Loreto*. They appeared all in a white uniform with a black kind of sash. The singing was a little better, but the instruments hardly so good. The 1st air, after a smart *sinfonia* and chorus, was sung by an inoffensive tenor—then another by a soprano not quite so, after which a 3rd air by a base voice, the direct contrary of inoffensive, such a bawling stentor with a throat so inflexible sure never was heard before. The divisions were so rough and so strongly marked they became quite grotesk.

——. "Naples 31 October"

After dinner to the theater of S. Carlo to hear Jomelli's new opera rehearsal. . . . The subject I believe is Demofonte—the names of the singers as yet I know not, except Aprile the Ist man and Bianca the Ist woman who have both great merit. The former has rather a weak and uneven voice, not constantly steady as to intonation—but has a good person, a good shake, and much taste and expression. The latter has a sweet and elegant toned voice constantly in tune with an admirable portamento—I never heard any one sing with more ease or in a manner so totally free from affectation.

———. "Rome 18 November"

I went to [hear an oratorio] at St. Gerolamo della Carità, which had only 3 characters in it—the subject was the Judgment of Solomon—the tenor was admirable—had great taste and facility of execution—and one of the mothers, a castrato, had a sweet toned voice and sung in a very pleasing manner.

Mancini, singing treatise (1774)

The high voice is more difficult to master [than the low voice] because it is often strident by nature. Consequently, the student ought not to neglect to treat the high portion of the voice with due sweetness. Great care must be taken by the student to attack the high notes with the required sweetness and proportion in order that he can command his entire range to perfection.

A voice that is robust, crude, and strident has no other need than to become sweetened and purified. If one should say to a youth who has a robust voice, "Give all the voice," surely he will not be able to correct his fault. Indeed, the fault will be made greater, because one cannot thus correct the already bad quality, but rather increase it. In this case, then, one ought to decrease strength to achieve sweetening, which is especially needed on high notes.

Burney, account of music in Germany, the Netherlands, and United Provinces (1775), "Manheim"

Thursday, August 6th. In the evening I went to the public theatre in this town, where Zemire and Azor, translated into German, and accommodated to the pretty music of M. Gretry, was performed. . . . The girl who played the part of Zemire had not a great voice, but her manner of singing was natural and pleasing. She had a good shake, and never forced her voice, or sung out of tune.

———. "Nymphenberg"

At eight o'clock the Elector's band assembled, for his private concert. . . . The concert was begun by two symphonies of Schwindl. . . . The first song was sung by Signor Panzachi, who has a good tenor voice, a pleasing expression, and a facility of execution. . . . After this song, the Electress dowager of Saxony sung a whole scene in her own opera of *Talestri*. . . . She sung in a truly fine style; her voice is very weak, but she never forces it, or sings out of tune.

——. "Munich"

I went to the burletta of *Le Finte Gemelli* . . . set by Matteo Rauzzini. . . . The second singer of this company, Signora Manservisi, deserves to be mentioned; her figure is agreeable, her voice, though not strong, is well-toned, she has nothing vulgar in her manner, sings in tune, and never gives offence. . . .

Friday. I spent the greatest part of this morning with Signor Rauzzini; he was so obliging as to sing to me a great number of excellent songs, in different styles, among which there were many of his own composition. As to his abilities in singing, I think his shake is not quite open enough, nor did I then think his voice sufficiently powerful for a great theatre; but in all other respects he is a charming performer; his taste is quite modern and delicate; the tone of his voice sweet and clear; his execution of passages of the most difficult intonation amazingly neat, rapid, and free. . . .

Signora Mingotti made [a concert] for me, of the best musicians which she could get together upon short notice, whom I had not heard before. M. Kröner, whose performance I had only heard at Nymphenburg in full pieces, was first violin. There was M. Sechi, a very good hautboy [oboe], who, if I had not lately heard Fischer, would have charmed me: M. Rheiner, the bassoon, who, when in England, was so ill, that he was unable to play more than once in public, and whom I had not yet heard, was here tonight, and had quite recovered his health. His tone is sweet, and execution neat, and he must be allowed by every competent and impartial judge, to be a very able and pleasing performer. . . .

Signor Guadagni and Signor Rauzzini were both at this concert, and the latter, whom I had only heard before, in one song, with full accompaniments, was so obliging, as to sing a very pretty air of his own composition, and another admirable one, by Signor Sacchini, in the *Eroe Cinese*. In the execution of these airs, he manifested great and captivating powers: a sweet and extensive voice, a rapid brilliancy of execution, great expression, and an exquisite and judicious taste.

———. "Vienna"

Tuesday, September 1ˢᵗ. At half an hour past six this evening, I went to the comic opera of *Il Barone*. The music, composed by Signor Salieri, a scholar of M. Gasman. I did not receive much pleasure from the overture, or the two first airs; the music was languid, and the singing but indifferent. There were only four characters in the piece, and the principal woman did not appear till the third scene; but then she gave a glow to every thing around her; it was one of the Baglioni, of Bologna, whom I had heard both at Milan and Florence, during my tour through Italy. She is very much improved since that time, and her Voice is now one of the clearest, sweetest, truest, most powerful, and extensive I ever heard.

S. Burney, letter to her sister Fanny (1779), "20 November"

I went to [a rehearsal of] the pasticcio [Alessandro nell' Indie] and heard Pacchierotti in a beautiful cavatina "Se mai più sarò geloso," which is placed about the middle of the first act. . . . It is elegant, charming music, and admits of all those refinements and graces in which Pacchierotti so peculiarly excels. And he *did* sing it like a very angel. To *you* it will give little trouble to conceive the pleasure I felt at hearing his most sweet voice, and that in such sweet music.

Burney, account of performances in Westminster Abbey (1785), "Commemoration of Handel, First performance" Part III

ANTHEM. Composed about the Year 1719.
AIR AND CHORUS
"O sing unto the Lord a new song; O sing unto the Lord all the whole earth."

Madame Mara's voice and manner of singing in this plain and solemn air, so admirably accompanied on the hautbois [oboe] by Fisher, had a sudden effect on myself, which I never before experienced, even from her performance of more pathetic [expressive] Music. I have long admired her voice, and abilities in various styles of singing; but never imagined tenderness the peculiar characteristic of her performance: however, here, though she had but a few simple notes to deliver, they made me shiver, and I found it extremely difficult to avoid bursting into tears on hearing them. Indeed, she had not only the power of conveying to the remotest corner of this immense building, the softest and most artificial inflexions of her sweet and brilliant voice, but articulated every syllable of the words with such neatness, precision, and purity, that it was rendered as audible, and intelligible, as it could possibly have been, in a small theatre, by meer [sic] declamation.

———. "Second performance" Part I

AIR IN ATALANTA.
Composed 1736.
MADAME MARA.

This Air, which was originally set for the celebrated Conti, *detto Gizziello*, from Gizzi, a famous singer, and, afterwards, singing-master, of whom he learned his art, though it requires in the singer no uncommon extent of voice, pathos, or execution, yet, by the grace, elegant simplicity, and sweetness, as well as power of voice, with which Madame Mara sung this pleasing song, she fortified the great reputation which she brought into this country, and which she had realized, and so much increased, by her performance in Westminster-Abbey.

———. "Third performance" Part I

Handel's Overtures are generally analogous to the opening of the first scene of the Drama to which they belong, and may be called real prefaces or preliminary discourses to a book. In order therefore to suppress every idea of levity in so sacred a performance as the Messiah, he very judiciously finished the Overture without an Air. And the short symphony to the accompanied Recitative, or *Aria parlante "Comfort ye my people,"* (Isai. xl. I.) seems to such as are not acquainted with the Oratorio, a preparation for the light minuet, gavot, or jig, with which Overtures are usually terminated; but how exquisitely are judicious ears disappointed! Indeed, I am acquainted with no movement of the same cast, to the words of any language, which is more grateful and soothing than this. There is not a note, either in the principal melody or accompaniment, that is become vulgar, common, or unmeaning. Mr. Harrison, with his sweet and well-toned voice, did this Recitative and the following Air great justice, by delivering them with propriety and the utmost purity and truth of intonation.

Chapter One

RECITATIVE accompanied.

"And suddenly there was with the Angel a multitude of the
Heavenly Host, praising God, and saying."

These Recitatives, as delivered by the sweet voice and articulate pronunciation of Madame Mara, had an effect far beyond what might be expected from such few and simple notes, without air, or measure: they were literally made *"melting sounds,"* to every hearer of sensibility present. . . .

"Rejoice greatly, O daughter of Zion;
shout! O daughter of Jerusalem;
behold! thy king cometh unto thee.
He is the righteous Saviour,
and he shall speak peace unto the Heathen."

This brilliant and difficult Air afforded Madame Mara an opportunity of displaying some of her wonderful powers of execution, and shewed her in a very different light from any thing she had hitherto sung at the Commemoration; but so firm, sweet, and judicious, was her performance of every kind, and so delightful to the audience, that she never breathed a sound without effect.

———. "Third performance" Part III

The favorite Base song, *"The Trumpet shall sound,"* (I Cor. xv. 52.) was very well performed by Signor Tasca and Mr. Sarjant, who accompanied him on the trumpet admirably. There are, however, some passages in the trumpet-part to this Air, which have always a bad effect, from the natural imperfection of the instrument. In Handel's time, composers were not so delicate in writing for Trumpets and French-horns, as at present; it being now laid down as a rule, that the fourth and sixth of a key on both these instruments, being *naturally* so much out of tune that no player can make them perfect, should never be used but in short passing notes, to which no base is given that can discover their false intonation. Mr. Sarjeant's tone is extremely sweet and clear, but every time that he was obliged to dwell upon G, the fourth of D, displeasure appeared in every countenance; for which I was extremely concerned, knowing how inevitable such an effect must be from such a cause.

Türk, clavier treatise (1789), Part 4
"Concerning the Appropriate Use of Ornaments and Certain Other Means Which are Required for Good Execution, or Which Take Part in It to Some Extent" *Paragraphs 54 and 55*

A beautiful tone must be clear, full, supple, bright, and above all, agreeable; it follows that it should not be harsh at even the highest degree of loudness or unclear at a pianissimo. But since it is the purpose of music to express feelings of various types, then to these qualities of a beautiful tone must be added the expression of music's character. "The most beautiful tone" writes Sulzer, "is that tone which takes upon itself every mode of expression, and in all the shadings of *forte* and *piano* remains both clear and bright."

The achievement of a beautiful and singing tone must be a matter of the most extreme importance for the clavichord player. In this regard, I would particularly advise those who still do not have a good tone to play a number of notes of long duration often, striking the keys with only moderate strength and pressing them down only as long as is necessary for the tone to reach its maximum strength. . . . One accomplishes, through this practice, a very supple stroke, which is even required for maximum strength.

Streicher, remarks on the fortepiano (1801), "On tone"

It would not be difficult to cite all the rules which, when followed, produce good tone or, when avoided, produce a bad one. However, it will be of greater value to musical amateurs and make a deeper impression on them if these rules are illustrated by describing *two types of keyboard playing*.

Imagine, if you will, a true musical artist who is before us now playing the fortepiano publicly or socially. With a demeanor which shows that music gives *him* pleasure, he seats himself at his instrument and at the same time shows us through his bearing that he knows what constitutes good playing.

As he runs his fingers over the keys, the very first notes which escape his fingers are *so light, solid, neat, and so naturally beautiful* that no one is even aware of the artistry.

In running passages, the position of *the arms, the hand, and the action of the fingers themselves is extremely quiet.* No movement betrays trouble or strain. The keyboard, under his hands, is a soft, pliant mass from which he can shape tone as he wishes. Like the beautiful lines of a painting, all shades of increasing and diminishing notes melt into one another.

He plays with all the ardor of a masculine artist but his tone always remains beautiful, *because he seeks to play forte and fortissimo more through full-voiced harmonies than through individual notes.* His strong chords never resemble a piercing cry, which is appropriate only in symphonies or theatrical pieces. Even here he tries to produce tone less through hacking and chopping at the keyboard: rather he produces it through a *quick, efficient attack.* If, however, the greatest strength must be used, he prefers to achieve the effect through the use of the bass as a melodic voice, for then the instrument is not damaged, nor the ears of the listeners too offended.

In fast as well as slow passages, *his piano or pianissimo is always proper.* He knows that *when light notes are* produced *with the utmost exactness and certainty, this and this alone affords the listener the greatest delight,* so that he has no doubt as to what he has heard. *'Bravo,' 'beautiful,' 'excellent'* reward the pure feeling of the player immediately.

Allow me to introduce into this picture the opposite type of performer, who is indeed unworthy of imitation, but who will serve to illustrate mistakes which should be avoided.

A player of whom it is reputed, 'He plays extraordinarily, such as you have never heard,' seats (or rather *throws*) himself at the fortepiano. Already the first chords will have been played so that one asks oneself whether the player is deaf or believes his listeners to be so. Through the movement of his body, arms and hands, it seems he would have us understand how difficult the *work* is which he has undertaken. He operates in a fiery manner and handles his instrument like someone bent on revenge, someone who has his arch-enemy in his hands and, with sadistic pleasure, wants to torture him to death. If he wants to play *forte*, he has already so exceeded it at the beginning that he can produce no greater degree of volume. *He pounds so hard* that suddenly the maltreated strings are put out of tune; several fly in the direction of bystanders who hurriedly retreat to safety in order to protect their eyes. Over this note is a *sforzando*! Luckily the hammer as well as the string can withstand it. But hear how the tone grates, and how painfully it falls upon the ear. Ardent passion he transforms into rage and the gentler sentiments he expresses through indifferent playing. Here he plays at a higher volume; it is only natural that he makes the fortepiano shriek and howl in the expression of sorrow. In quick, joyful passages, keys, and hammers strike lamely.

Corri, singing treatise (1810), Vol. 1
"Dialogue, Introductory, Requisites for Vocal Music"

Scholar: What are the requisites, or gifts, necessary for a good singer. [?] Master [Teacher]: First, a singer ought to have a good ear. . . . Secondly,—The voice,—this is capable of great improvement, and, like metal or stone, may be polished to a high degree of perfection; it is not the extent or compass, nor the body of voice, which alone will constitute a good singer, but its proper and skilful [sic] management;—good quality, or sweetness of voice, however, is a very desirable possession.

Bombet, lives of Haydn, Mozart, and Metastasio (1817)

Although 377 stringed instruments accompanied the single voice [of soloists singing in Handel festivals held in Westminster Abbey at the end of the 18th century], such was the lightness of the effect, they did not overpower, or incommode it. From the great extent of the surface from which sounds emanated, they were diffused through the atmosphere, so as to completely fill it. No single instrument was heard, but all were blended together in the softest showers of harmony.

Parke, musical memoirs (1830)

1784. The Pantheon concerts commenced on the 29th of March, in which Madame Mara made her first appearance in England. Her sweet and powerful voice, her brilliant execution, and refined taste, surprised and delighted all who heard her, and the applause she received was immense. . . .

The second performance was at the Pantheon, on the evening of Thursday, May 27. . . . Madame Mara, in the air in "Atalanta, while I retire," by the beautiful sweetness and power of her voice, delighted every hearer. . . .

1785. The manager of the King's Theatre, who felt the loss of Pacchierotti, and who had made every endeavor to obtain efficient performers, presented to the public, on the 21st of January, the serious opera of "Demetrio," in which Signor Crescentini and Signora Ferrerese made their first appearance. The singing and acting of Crescentini, though by no means equal to Pacchierotti's, was at all times neat, and often brilliant. Ferrerese had a sweet voice, and sang with taste. . . .

1786. At Covent Garden Theatre Mrs. Billington, who had been performing with success on the Dublin stage, made her début on the London boards, on the 13th of February, as Rosetta, in the opera "Love in a Village." She sang . . . with such sweetness, taste, and brilliancy, the audience . . . bestowed on her unbounded applause. . . .

1787. At the King's Theatre a new comic opera, called "Giannina Berdoni," was performed on the 9th of January. The music was by Cimarosa. In this opera Signora Binini, a new *prima buffa*, appeared with success. Her voice was sweet, and she sang with great taste. . . .

1790. A curious musical contest took place during the preceding summer in Ireland, between Mrs. Billington and Miss George, who had a voice of such extent, that she sang up to B in alto perfectly clear, and in tune; this being three notes higher than any singer I ever heard. Mrs. Billington . . . sang her songs delightfully, particularly "Cease your funning" [from the Beggar's Opera], which was tumultuously encored. Miss George, who performed the part of Lucy, perceiving she had little chance of dividing the applause with the great magnet of the night, had recourse to the following stratagem: when the dialogue duet in the second act, "Why, how now, Madame Flirt," came on, Mrs. Billington gave her verse with great sweetness and characteristic expression, and was much applauded. Miss George in reply, availing herself of her extraordinary compass of voice, and setting propriety at defiance, sang the whole of her verse an octave higher, her tones having the effect of the high notes of a sweet and brilliant flute. The audience, taken by surprise, bestowed on her such loud applause as almost shook the walls of the theatre, and an unanimous encore was the result. . . .

1791. At a concert in Hanover Square the 7th of February, . . . Mr. J. Parkinson performed a concerto on the bassoon. [He] had great and neat execution, and his tone was remarkably sweet, having none of that nasal quality which . . . in the upper notes of the bassoon [can sound] like a hautboy laboring under a cold. . . .

1794. The King's Theatre opened for the season on the 11th of January, with a comic opera by Cimarosa, called "Il Matrimonio Segreto. . . ." Signora Casentini, by her tasteful style of singing, and her unaffected gentleness and ease, was extremely interesting. . . . The voice of Banti evinced sweetness, power, and flexibility. . . .

1796. Signor Viganoni made his first appearance the 14th of June, in a new comic opera called "Tesoro." Viganoni's voice, though not remarkable for power, was distinguished for its sweetness; and his style of singing was fanciful and elegant. He was greatly and justly applauded. . . .

1804. Fischer, the celebrated oboe player, died in the early part of this year. [His] tone was soft and sweet, his style expressive, and his execution was at once neat and brilliant. . . .

1816. The King's Theatre opened for the season on the 17th of January, with a new musical drama, called "Griselda, osia la virtu in cimento." In this opera Madame Fodor made her first appearance before a British audience. She displayed great sweetness of voice and delicacy of expression. . . .

1818. The Vocal concert, last year discontinued, was this season revived, and commenced at Hanover Square on the 6th of March. . . . Many new pieces were composed expressly for the undertaking. . . . This species of music, at the time this concert was instituted, was very fashionable, and was sung there so extremely *sotto voce*, that it was aptly termed whispering. It was however sung by first-rate singers. . . .

1820. At the King's Theatre Mozart's "Nozze di Figaro" was performed on the 11th of January, and on Saturday the 18th, Rossini's popular opera "La Cenerentola" was brought out. In this opera Signor Torri appeared for the first time. He displayed a sweet and flexible tenor voice, and sang with judgment. . . .

1826. The oratorios commenced at Covent Garden Theatre on the 30th of January, with Handel's "Messiah." Miss Paton sang "Rejoice" with uncommon sweetness and brilliancy. . . .

1829. On Wednesday the 7th of May the first of a series of new concerts commenced in the room of the King's Theatre, now styled the King's Concert Room. . . . Mr. Schmidt performed some variations on "Di tanti palpiti" on the trombone, by which he excited more surprise than he gave delight; for although he has by labour and perseverance achieved much, the tones of the trombone resembling more the music of the spears than the spheres, are better adapted to a military band than a concert-room.

1830. At Covent Garden Theatre a new musical adaptation of the hackneyed subject, "The Maid and the Magpie," was produced on the 4th of February. The music is entirely taken from Rossini's popular opera, "La Gazza Ladra," even to the overture. Miss Paton performed the character of "Ninetta." The English version of the celebrated cavatina, "Di piacer mi balza il cor," was sung by her with all that sweetness and brilliancy for which she is so eminently distinguished.

Nathan, singing treatise (1836), Chapter 5 "Tone or Sound"

Agreeable sounds to the ear are as genial as the sun to the flowers. A sweet-toned mellow voice is one of nature's best gifts; it soothes the spirit by its mellifluence, and immediately prepossesses those who listen in favor of the possessor; while the harsh and discordant voice jars on the ear, and irritates the nerves more forcibly than can be described. . . .

Pure tone is the most essential requisite in singing; it is the vehicle of every other beauty in the science; execution, elocution, and expression, are all subservient to tone, for without its aid they would be as nothing. Quality more than quantity of tone should be the chief consideration. A judicious singer, with even a weak voice, will frequently, from nice management, excite more pleasure than another whose magnificent volume of tone leads him to loftier flights. I will admit that in all songs of grandeur, the power of the latter is indispensable; it creates surprise, and is valuable in a theatre or concert-room; but the former may also be energetic, as well as impressive and elegant. A sensible singer will give his own character to whatever he may sing, and though (to avoid fatiguing his auditors by repeated monotony) he may vary in tone, he will still preserve that in mind which creates most effect on the feelings of those about him.

———. Chapter 6 "The Mouth"

It is when the mouth is in a smiling form, that the sweetest tones are produced, and indeed, were it otherwise, it would be better to forego a little volubility, when we gain a pleasing exterior by the sacrifice.

———. Chapter 9 "Expression"

A singer of celebrity, held in abhorrence by his brethren for the libertinism of his principles, was officiating in the synagogue as singer; when the high priest who had been the most vehement against him for his misdemeanors, was so struck by the sweetness of his voice and particular expression, that, forgetting where he was, he exclaimed in an audible voice, "Favoured of heaven, happiness must be thy lot hereafter, thy crimes are forgiven!"

There is a similar incident related of Mrs. Cibber, the celebrated actress, who, it is said, when in Dublin singing in the oratorio *Messiah*, so struck a certain bishop with the extreme sensibility of her manner, that he could not refrain from saying, loud enough to be heard by numbers round him, "Woman, thy sins be forgiven thee!"

Czerny, letters on playing the pianoforte (c.1837–1841), Letter I "First Rudiments of the Piano"

Miss Cecelia,

When I, some years ago, had the pleasure of being personally acquainted with your family, I discovered in you so decided a talent for music, that I am exceedingly rejoiced to hear that you are now really about to devote yourself to the delightful art of playing the pianoforte. Your memory, at that time, easily retained any agreeable melody which you heard; you manifested a natural feeling for time and musical expression; and, added to this, your delicate fingers and hands possessed all the natural qualities so necessary for playing the pianoforte—flexibility, quickness of movement, and lightness, without being either too weak or too stiff.

———. Letter II "On Touch, Tone, and the Mode of Treating the Pianoforte"

No property is more necessary and important to the player than a well-developed *flexibility, lightness,* and *volubility* of the fingers.

Garcia, singing treatise (1840–1847)

But frequently the charming softness, so pleasing in the high notes, is perversely turned into tormenting yells.

FALSETTO

Commentary during the Classical era about falsetto (a light, soft vocal production above the range of the natural, or full, voice) is especially helpful in further appreciating the ideals of gentility and elegance and in comprehending the degree of softness described in writings of the time. For instance, it is illuminating that commentators described the falsetto as being not much louder than the natural or full voice, which is sometimes called chest voice during the era, but not as a reference to the chest voice that would be in use today. For example, Quantz says, "the chest voice is the natural one used in speaking" and Isaac Nathan says, "the *chest voice*, called by the Italians, *voce di petto* [is also called the] *voce naturale*, the natural voice." Furthermore, Quantz says that the falsetto is "only a little weaker than . . . the natural voice," and Johann Samuel Petri says that the falsetto "is not differentiated appreciably from the chest voice." It is also interesting to note that singing in falsetto was common and desirable and that a composer such as Rossini clearly intended for certain high notes in his operas to be sung in falsetto.

With commentary about the particular appreciation of falsetto singing and its qualities of softness, present-day performers can better understand innate qualities of compositions and, therefore, can better utilize performance techniques that will realize intended ideals.

Quantz, flute treatise (1752), Chapter 4 "Of the Embouchure"

The octaves on the flute must not be produced by strengthening and doubling the wind, but by advancing the chin and lips. In this respect the flute again somewhat resembles the human voice. There are two kinds of voice, the chest voice and the falsetto or fistula voice. With the latter, in which the larynx is even more compressed than is ordinarily the case, you can, without straining yourself, produce several more notes in the upper register than is possible with the chest voice. The Italians and several other nations unite the falsetto with the chest voice and make use of it to great advantage in singing. Among the French, however, it is not customary, and for that reason their singing in the high register is often transformed into a disagreeable shrieking, the effect of which is exactly the same as that created when you do not cover the mouth hole sufficiently on the flute and try to force out the high notes by blowing more strongly. The chest voice is the natural one used in speaking, while the falsetto is artificial, and is used only in singing. It begins where the chest voice ends, and the tone quality . . . becomes only a little weaker than in the natural voice.

——. Chapter 18 "How a Musician and a Musical Composition are to be Judged" Paragraph 11

The chief requirements of an excellent *singer* are that he have a good, clear, and pure voice, of uniform quality from top to bottom, a voice which has none of those major defects originating in the nose and throat, and which is neither hoarse nor muffled. . . . In addition, the singer must know how to join the falsetto to the chest voice in such a way that one does not perceive where the latter ends and the former begins. . . . He must have firmness and sureness of voice, so that he does not begin to tremble in a moderately long hold, or transform the agreeable sound of the human voice into the disagreeable shriek of a reed pipe when he wishes to strengthen his tone.

Petri, musical guide (1767)

High basses become, through the falsetto, employable for singing the best tenor arias, which is no small advantage, at least in case of an emergency. But I must admit that only a few learn to use a good falsetto, which is not differentiated appreciably from the chest voice.

C. P. E. Bach, letter to Georg Wilhelm Kottowsky (1769)

An alto by the name of Ambrosius, who sings in the choir in Dessau, wants very much to come here. Be so kind and ask him in my name to let himself be heard before you, and report to me how old he is, if his voice is good, if he has a falsetto, if he sings in tune, if he has a good manner of singing, and if he is of good conduct.

Burney, account of music in France and Italy (1770), "Rome 5 October"

At 4 this evening Signor Santarelli made me a long visit in which we had an uninterrupted musical conversation which, on his part, was curious, historical, and full of anecdotes. . . . He has two daughters. The eldest is a scholar of Signor Santarelli and sings divinely with more grace, taste and expression than any female in public or private I have ever heard. She was so obliging as to sing 6 or 8 capital airs in different styles, and all charmingly, but her *fort* [specialty] is the pathetic [expressive]. She has a good shake [trill] and well toned voice, an admirable portamento with great compass, and high finishing in all she attempts. Indeed she does infinite credit to her master for he has contrived to unite the falset so with the real voice, that 'tis very difficult to say where it begins.

Tenducci, singing treatise (1782) "Rule 9"

Never force the Voice in order to extend its compass in the *Voce di petto* [natural voice] upwards, but rather cultivate the *Voce di testa* [head voice] in what is called *Falsetto* in order to join it well and imperceptibly to the *Voce di petta*. [If this is not done, there is the] fear of incurring the disagreeable Habit of singing in the Throat or through the nose—unpardonable Faults in a Singer.

Corri, singing treatise (1810), "Rules for the management of the Voice"

There are four sorts of Voices: Basso, Tenore, Contralto, and Soprano. The extent of the Natural Voice of either denomination is in general no more than one Octave and 2, 3 or 4 Notes beyond; altho' the Voice may contain above four Octaves, the part of the Voice below the Natural is in general indistinct, inexpressive and destitute of power, that part above the Natural is called the feigned or falsetto Voice, with which some effect of Pathos may be produced, but is not capable of energy: therefore the attention and practice of the Scholar [student] ought to be chiefly directed to the attainment of as much of the Natural Voice as he can possibly acquire, and this practice ought to be made with great care and prudence; extending a compass of Voice may be compared to stretching a piece of Leather, which if done violently at once will break, but if by gentle degrees, daily increasing the force and distance, it may be brought to stretch very far: The Scholar ought to begin the Exercises of the Voice from that Note which he thinks is the first of his Natural Voice, and from thence proceed to its Last Note. . . . After the Scholar has ascertained the compass of the Natural Voice, his great study should be to contrive to unite the Natural to the first Note of the Falsetto, to blend them with such nicety, that the union may be imperceptible.

A great defect in most Singers is the imperfect Manner of joining the Natural to the Feigned Voice, the sudden transition of which, frequently gives a shock to the Ear, abrupt, as the squeak of a little Boy, which is unbecoming the dignity of manhood to utter, or produces a similar effect, as playing at the same time with one hand on a Small, and with the other on a Grand Piano Forte. . . .

Singers ought . . . to measure the extent of the Song with the extent of the Voice, and pitch the Key accordingly, for every Composition is not calculated for every one's abilities; but should they have a particular wish or fancy to sing those pieces that are unsuitable to their extent of Voice, by which some part must be sacrificed, either the lower or higher Notes, I advise them rather to sacrifice the lower part of the Voice than risk having a break between the Natural Voice and the Feigned; should this transposition be ineffective, let the whole of these passages be taken in the Feigned Voice.

Parke, musical memoirs (1830)

1790. The proprietor of the King's Theatre . . . on the 26th of March [presented] entertainments of singing and dancing. . . . The principal singers he had retained were, Signor Tajano, Albertarelli, and David, the latter of whom possessed a clear and flexible voice, with an extensive falsetto, and an elegant expressive style.

1817. The performers at the King's Theatre this season, with the exception of Madame Fodor and Naldi, were all new. At the head of them were Madame Camporese, Madame Pasta, and Signor Crevelli. These three made their first appearance on the 11th of January, in Cimarosa's grand serious opera called "Penelope." Madame Camporese's voice was powerful and clear, and she sang with taste and feeling. The voice of Madame Pasta was finely regulated and flexible, and her style was full of expression. Crevelli's was a tenor voice of considerable power, with an extensive falsetto.

Nathan, singing treatise (1836), Chapter 6
"On the Human Voice, and its General Qualities"

The qualities of the human voice are commonly distinguished under three heads, according to the natural organs which appear most particularly concerned in its modulation and tones: - 1st, where the sound appears to issue almost entirely from the lungs, it is distinguished as a *chest voice*, called by the Italians, *voce di petto*; also, *voce naturale*, the natural voice: 2ndly, where the throat appears the chief organ connected with the production of sound, it is called a *throat voice*, termed in Italian, *falsetto*: and 3rdly, where the process of breathing seems more than usually connected with the nostrils, and the sound is accordingly modulated by their influence, it is termed a *head voice*, in Italian, *voce di testa*. There is a fourth kind of voice, which is but little appreciated, consequently rarely cultivated—and since I cannot trace any sponsors, either among the Italian, or English, who have given a name to this peculiar style, I shall call it the *feigned*. I am aware that the *falsetto* is considered a feigned voice; and certainly that voice must be feigned which is produced by artificial constraint, and that does not consequently seem to come forth naturally from the chest; but the quality of sound that I allude to is not that which is produced in the throat; and already distinguished under the name of *falsetto*; nor is it the *voce di testa*. It is a species of ventriloquism, a soft and distant sound produced apparently in the chest, and chiefly in the back of the throat and head—an inward and suppressed quality of tone, that conveys the illusion of being heard at a distance: It is as a sweet and soft melodious sound, wafted from afar, like unto the magic spell of an echo.

——. "On the Formation or Building of the Voice"

There is a break, more or less, in the voices of both sexes, but more particularly in that of the male, between the *Voce di petto* and *falsetto*; that precise part of the vocal organ where the *Voce di petto* forms this juncture with the *falsetto* is by the Italians called *Il Ponticello*, "the little bridge;" and singers who can with safety carry this *Voce di petto* over this little bridge may truly sing its praises. It should here be an object with the Singer to contrive to blend the two qualities of tone, at their junction, in such a manner, that the transition from one to the other may not be perceptible to the ear. This cannot be accomplished without the aid of the *feigned voice*, which may be justly considered the only medium or vehicle by which the *falsetto* can be carried into the *Voce di petto*. . . .

Let every note be begun in the feigned voice as softly as possible, by swelling gently, and immediately returning to the first piano: as the voice increases in power and quality let the swell be increased, yet with caution; the slightest irregularity or roughness being a sign that the singer has exceeded the development of which his organ is as yet capable. Any unsteadiness or tremor of voice is to be remedied by taking the note *softer*; a contrary course only serving to increase and confirm the defect. . . .

The greatest care must be paid to these remarks, in the cultivation of the higher tones of the voice: for as the natural compass of the *voce di petto*, of either denomination seldom extends beyond 8, 10 or 12 notes, all others are properly artificial, and must be assimilated to the original by the above method—any attempt to supersede which, by forcing the chest-notes, will certainly be attended by the ruin of the singer, and notes so acquired being harsh, are incapable of coloring, and liable to disappear altogether. The rule experience pronounces infallible is this: when the singer after having cultivated the lower tones, (which form the basis and give the character to his voice) arrives at the *break* or meeting of the registers *di petto* and *di testa*, let him proceed in the *feigned* voice alone; let him increase its power by swelling, and let him gradually unite it with the chest voice rather by its own enlarged volume than by any exertion of the latter—thus affected, the junction will be imperceptible, and once gained will never be lost. It is only by voices so formed, that the higher effects of the heart can be produced—or that the qualities so often lauded be realized.

Many persons, who do not appreciate the beauty of a judicious management of the *falsetto*, depreciate altogether the use of it: there are undoubtedly instances where it is not to be tolerated—the indulgence of it, for example, would be against all good taste and judgment in energetic passages, such as "Sound an Alarm"—particularly if displayed upon the last word—we should in that case certainly feel but little terror at an alarm announced to us by such an effeminate sound. . . . There are innumerable instances where the falsetto may in the like manner be exercised to great advantage; hence it is the abuse of the falsetto, not the judicious use of it that should be depreciated.

Schindler, biography of Beethoven (1840), "Third Period" Section 3 "1823"

The concert took place at noon on 23 May in the Great Redoutensaal. Of the Missa [solemnis] only the Kyrie was performed. The rest of the program consisted of the great overture with the double fugue, opus 124; the trio *Tremate, empi*, sung by the stars of the Italian opera, and the ninth symphony. . . . Henriette Sontag also sang brilliantly one of her favorite bravura arias by Mercadante. [In addition,] a special drawing card was to be a performance of the cavatina from Rossini's *Tancredi*, "Di tanti palpiti," written for the contralto but sung on this occasion by the idolized tenor of the Italian opera, Davide, who transposed the piece several notes higher and sang it almost throughout in a falsetto.

Rossini, account of an evening at Villa Rossini (1858), "1843"

Duprez [Gilbert-Louis Duprez (1806–1896), who debuted as Arnold in *Guillaume Tell* in 1837 and was popular for his so-called chest tone high C] was the first one to think of chafing the Parisians' ears by disgorging in *Guillaume Tell* that chest-tone C of which I had never dreamed. Nourrit [a leading tenor at the Paris Opéra] had been satisfied with a head-tone C, which was what was required. Then, during my stay in Paris in 1837 [really 1843], just after Duprez's resounding debut in *Guillaume Tell*, the impetuous tenor came to see me to invite me to hear him at the Opéra. "You come to see me instead," I told him. "You will produce your C for me alone, and I'll be more than flattered." I was staying with my friend Troupenas. Duprez hastened to come. With Troupenas present, he sang for me—magnificently, I must admit—several fragments of my opera. At the approach of the '*Suivez-moi,*' I experienced the kind of anxious discomfort that some people feel when they know that a cannon is about to be shot off. Finally, he burst forth with the C! Zounds, what an uproar! I rose from the piano and rushed to a vitrine filled with very delicate Venetian glass that decorated Troupenas' salon. 'Nothing broken,' I exclaimed, 'That's wonderful!' Duprez appeared enchanted by my remark, which he took for a compliment in my style. 'Well, then, Maître, tell me sincerely, does my C please you?' 'Very sincerely, what pleases me most about your C is that it is over, and that I am no longer in danger of hearing it. I don't like unnatural effects. It strikes my Italian ear as having a strident timbre, like a capon squawking as its throat is slit. You are a very great artist, a true new creator of the role of Arnold. Why in the devil abase your talent by using that humbug?' 'Because,' Duprez answered, 'Opéra subscribers are accustomed to it now; that C is my great success . . .' 'Well, would you like an even greater success? Unload them two at a time.'

Garcia, singing treatise (1840–1847), "The Head Register"

[Question]. What of the head register?

[Answer]. This register forms the purest and brightest portion of the soprano voice; but frequently the charming softness, so pleasing in the high notes, is perversely turned into tormenting yells that almost injure the ear of the listener.

CASTRATOS

Castratos were very much a part of the performance culture in the Classical era, especially in the eighteenth century. They appeared in significant numbers throughout Europe (Burney says that there were large numbers of them in cities throughout Italy and that the Conservatorio of S. Onofrio in Naples housed sixteen of them), and they performed frequently in opera houses, where they sang the leading soprano and alto roles—many composed specifically for them. W. A. Mozart, for example, composed the roles of Idamantes in *Idomeneo* (1781) and Sextus in *La clemenza di Tito* (1791) for castratos. They also participated with boys in cathedral and chapel choirs; Felix Mendelssohn commented on hearing them at the Sistine Chapel in 1831.

Burney's comments about the housing of groups of castratos and about the castration of boys seem to suggest that, although the practice of castration was clearly against the law, it was still very much tolerated and accepted. Indeed, there were notable castratos throughout the nineteenth century; Domenico Mustafà (1829–1912) sang in the Sistine Chapel choir and was its director from 1860 until 1898, and Alessandro Moreschi (1858–1922) sang in the choir from 1883 until 1913.

Burney, account of music in France and Italy (1770), "Milan 20 July"

Friday 20. This morning [I went] to hear a *messa* in *musica*, composed under the direction of Signor Monza, Maestro di Capella. His brother played the violoncello with much facility of execution, but not a very pleasing tone or taste. The first violin, Signor Lucchini, who leads at the Burletta: 2 or 3 castrati sung. . . . The Ist soprano was what we should call in England, a pretty good singer, with a pretty good voice; his taste neither original nor superior. The contr'alto, who was the second singer, was likewise *pretty* well. His voice pleasing and he never gave offence by the injudicious management of it.

Chapter One

——. "Naples 18 October"

It is forbidden to castrate boys in these schools [La Pietà, Santa Maria di Loretto, and S. Onofrio]—that they chiefly come from Leccia in Puglia, but are first tried here or elsewhere as to the likelihood of voice and then taken out by their parents for this barbarous purpose, but it is death by the laws to those who perform the operation and excommunication to all concerned in it, unless it be done, as is often pretended, on account of some disorders which may be supposed to require it and with the consent of the boy. . . .

But as to these previous trials of the voice, it is my opinion that this cruel operation is but too frequently performed without trial or at least without sufficient proofs of a dawning and improvable voice—otherwise there could never be found such numbers of them in every great town throughout Italy without any voice at all—or at least without one sufficient to compensate for the loss. Indeed all the *musici* in the churches at present are made up of the refuse of the opera houses, and it is a very rare thing to meet with a tolerable voice upon the establishment of any church in Italy.

——. "Rome 22 September"

[I went] to Mr. Beckford's concert, consisting of 12 of the best hands in Rome, led by Celestini—and 3 voices, [two of which are] Signor Crisofero of the Pope's chapel who sings very much in Guarducci's way and is little inferior to him in delicacy, Grassetto—a boy made a eunuch by his own choice against the advice of his friends in order to preserve his voice, which is a very pleasing one, and he is moreover in other respects a very promising singer.

——. "Naples 31 October"

This morning I went to . . . [the] conservatorio of S. Onofrio.... There are in this college 16 castrati, and these lye by themselves in a warmer apartment upstairs than the other boys for fear of colds, which might endanger or injure the voice.

Burney, account of music in Germany, the Netherlands, and United Provinces (1775), "Ludwigsburg"

I obtained an exact state of the present musical establishment of the Würtemburg court, stage, and church. The first *maestro di capella*, is Signor Boroni. The *soprano* voices are, Signora Bonani and Seeman, Signor Muzio and Signor Guerrieri, *castrati*; contralti, Rubinelli and Paganelli.

Parke, musical memoirs (1830), "1778"

The Italian opera this season again possessed a host of strength in Pacchierotti, who first appeared at the King's Theatre in the year 1778, and, notwithstanding this was his seventh season, his voice (a *soprano*) was as much admired as ever, and he was still considered a most accomplished singer, though I have frequently heard him hold a note for two or three bars below the pitch, and be enthusiastically applauded for it. . . . As a singer, Pacchierotti was the greatest favorite with the ladies since Farinelli.

On Saturday the 5th of April, Signor Marchesi and Ignora Giuliani made their first appearance in a new serious opera of Sarti's, "Giulio Sabino." Marchesi possessed a good and youthful figure; his voice (a *soprano*) was powerful, rich, and clear, and his style was elegant, and peculiarly his own. If his singing was a little too florid, his science and genius enabled him to display a continual variety which afforded high gratification.

VIBRATO

Vibrato, sometimes called tremolo and generally defined as a slight and regular fluctuation of pitch, was employed as a performance practice during the Classical era. However, it was not utilized pervasively (i.e., at all times), and, like other elements of performance practice, it was more limited in scope than is common in present times. As to its frequency of usage, vibrato was considered to be ornamental in nature and, therefore, used occasionally—mostly to decorate the apex of a long held note. As to its physical limitations, its pitch fluctuation was narrow; soft and light productions of tone, both instrumental and vocal, accommodated only a slight and gentle vibrato, and most commentators on the subject, including Leopold Mozart, who discusses vibrato at some length, suggest that it should be subtle. The two main Classical-era authors about the voice—Isaac Nathan and Manuel Garcia—decried its practice altogether.

Two other manifestations of vibrato are notably different from that in practice in modern times. First, vibrato, in terms of pitch fluctuation, was varied in speed. As recommended by many authors, including Francesco Geminiani, Leopold Mozart, Giuseppe Tartini, and Johann Georg Tromlitz, the speed could be slow, fast, or accelerated. (Note that Tartini's descriptions are almost identical to Mozart's.) Second, vibrato (called in German "Bebung") could be and was employed on the clavichord by gently rocking a finger back and forth while a key was depressed.

Geminiani, violin treatise (1751), "Of the Close Shake"

This [the Close Shake, or Vibrato] cannot possibly be described by Notes [musical notation] as in former Examples. To perform it, you must press the Finger strongly upon the String of the Instrument and move the wrist in and out slowly and equally; when it is long continued, swelling the Sound by Degrees, drawing the Bow nearer to the Bridge, and ending it very strong, it may express Majesty, Dignity, etc. But making it shorter, lower, and softer, it may denote Affliction, Fear, etc. and when it is made on short Notes, it only contributes to make their Sound more agreable [sic] and for this Reason it should be made use of as often as possible.

**Quantz, flute treatise (1752), Chapter 14
"Of the Manner of Playing the Adagio"**

If you must hold a long note for either a whole or a half bar, which the Italians call *messa di voce*, you must first tip [the flute] gently with the tongue, scarcely exhaling; then you begin pianissimo, allow the strength of the tone to swell to the middle of the note, and from there begin to diminish it to the end of the note in the same fashion, making a vibrato with the finger on the nearest open hole.

C. P. E. Bach, clavier treatise (1753), Chapter 3 "Performance"

A long, affettuoso tone is performed with a vibrato. The finger that depresses and holds the key is gently shaken. The sign of a vibrato appears in Example a. The best effect is achieved when the finger withholds its shake until half the value of the note has passed.

Figure 169

L. Mozart, violin treatise (1756), Chapter 11
"Of the Tremolo, Mordent, and some other improvised Embellishments"

The Tremolo . . . is an ornamentation which arises from Nature herself and which can be used charmingly on a long note, not only by good instrumentalists but also by clever singers. Nature herself is the instructress thereof, for if we strike a slack string or a bell sharply, we hear after the stroke a certain wave-like undulation of the struck note. This trembling after-sound is called tremolo, also tremulant.

Take pains to imitate this natural quivering on the violin. When the finger is pressed down on the string, one makes a small movement with the whole hand, which however must not move sideways but forwards toward the bridge and backwards toward the scroll. . . . For as, when the remaining trembling sound of a struck string or bell is not pure and continues to sound not on one note only but sways first too high, then too low, just so by the movement of the hand forward and backward must you endeavor to imitate exactly the swaying of these intermediate tones.

Now because the tremolo is not purely on one note but sounds undulating, so it would be an error if every note were played with the tremolo. There are performers who tremble consistently on each note as if they had the palsy. The tremolo must only be used at places where nature herself would produce it, namely as if the note taken were the striking of an open string. For at the close of a piece, or even at the end of a passage which closes with a long note, that last note would inevitably, if struck for instance on a pianoforte, continue to hum for a considerable time afterwards. Therefore a closing note or any other sustained note may be decorated with a tremolo. But there is also a slow, an increasing, and a rapid oscillation. They can be distinguished by the following signs.

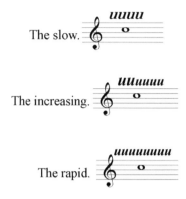

The larger strokes can represent eighth notes, the smaller sixteenth notes, and as many strokes as there be, so often must the hand be moved. The movement must, however, be made with strong after-pressure of the finger, and this pressure must be applied always on the first part or notes of every quarter note, and in rapid movement on the first part or notes of every half-quarter note. For instance, I will here put down a few notes that can very well be played with the tremolo, yea, which in truth demand this movement. They must be played in the third position.

Thus must one express the tremolo.

Thus does one make the movement.

In the two examples, in N.1. the strong part of the movement always falls on the note marked by the numeral (2), for it is the first part of the quarter or half-quarter note. In example N.2., on the contrary, the stress falls, for the same reason, on the note marked with the numeral (1).

The tremolo can also be made on two strings, and therefore with two fingers simultaneously.

Before beginning a cadenza, which at the end of a solo is improvised, it is customary to sustain a long note either on the tonic-note or on the dominant. On such a long sustained note an increasing tremolo can always be used. For example, at the close of an adagio, one can play thus:

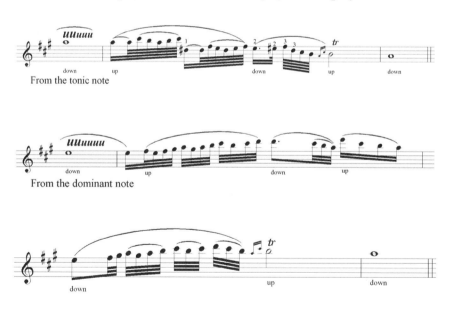

But the stroke must commence softly and gather strength toward the middle, in such fashion that the greatest strength falls at the beginning of the more rapid movement; and finally, the stroke must end again softly.

Tartini, ornamentation treatise (1771), "Concerning the Vibrato or Tremblement in French"

This kind of ornament is by its nature better suited to instruments than to the voice. Sometimes, when it occurs in a human voice, it is due to the nature of that voice.

The sound of harpsichord strings, of bells, and of open strings of certain good bowed instruments leaves in its natural wake an undulation in the air which has been animated by the vibrations of the tiny parts composing the metal, or by the continued vibration of the string set in motion by the bow in the case of a bowed instrument, and by the jack in the case of a harpsichord string. In imitation of this effect one can produce this vibration artificially on the violin, viola, and 'cello with a finger held on the string while the vibrato is impressed on the finger with the force of the wrist, without the finger leaving the string, despite its being lifted slightly. If the vibrato of the finger is slow, the undulation which is the vibrato of the sound will be slow; if it is fast, the undulation will be fast. One can accordingly increase the speed of the undulation little by little, by starting slowly and rendering it faster by degrees. An example will show this augmentation indicated with small semicircles, the relative sizes of which mark the slowness and the quickness and consequently the increased speed.

Example of a slow but equal undulation; [and] of one that is fast but equal:

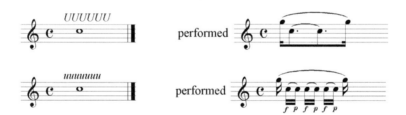

and of one that passes by degrees from slow to fast:

This ornament is never used on semi-tones, which ought to imitate not only the human voice but also the nature of perfect intonation to a mathematical point; that is to say, the intonation ought not to be altered at all on semi-tones. . . .

This ornament produces a very good effect on the final note of a musical phrase, if this note is not long. It benefits the tone and the *cantabile*. It produces the best natural tonal effect, because when one has struck for the last time a harpsichord string, or a bell, or an open string on a bowed instrument, the sound continues and maintains the vibrato naturally for some time.

It also has a very good effect on the long notes of any air in any meter whatsoever, when the notes are arranged in the following way:

This should always be equal and performed so exactly in time that the strong [pressure] of the vibrato occurs on the second of the two slurred notes marked with a 2 and the weak on the first marked with a 1, which is a general rule:

Finally, it has a very good effect on long notes played on two strings, as shown above. But it should be observed that in ordinary time (that is in 4/4 time) the strong [pressure] occurs on number 1, and the weak on number 2, whereas in triple time the strong occurs on number 2 and the weak on number 1.

The general rule is that the strong always occurs on the first note of the quarter, eighth, or sixteenth part of the measure.

Türk, clavier treatise (1789), "Introduction"

The true clavier or clavichord has, above most other keyboard instruments, the special advantages that one can execute the *Bebung* [vibrato] upon it, that it can bring out the various levels of strength and weakness available to other instruments in rapid alternation, and that one can consequently play with much more expression than is possible, for example, on the harpsichord.

A fine clavichord . . . must have a strong, full, and at the same time, pleasant and singing tone, which does not die away immediately after the striking of the key, but rather continues to sound for the value of at least four to six eighth notes in a moderately slow adagio, and allows the vibrato to be clearly heard.

Tromlitz, flute treatise (1791)

The tremolo is the variation of pitch on a long, sustained note, which can be uniform, or increasing and decreasing in speed. It is produced on the flute, on a long note, by alternately covering and opening the hole next to the last one closed with one finger, covering it a little, or half way, or covering another hole completely, depending on what the circumstance calls for. On the flute you do not do this with the breath, for it does not have a good effect, it whimpers, and whoever does it this way ruins his chest and his whole playing, for he loses his steadiness and therefore cannot hold a solid and pure tone. Whatever comes from his chest always quivers. It is not recommended to use this ornament too often. It can be used on sustained notes, fermatas, and on the note before a cadenza. In my opinion, very fast tremolos are an ugly frill. . . .

It is not possible to teach a set standard of how much the finger should cover the hole. As the tone must be held and sustained in doing the tremolo, the ear will easily be able to decide how much the extended finger which covers the hole should actually cover it, in order to vary the pitch alternately a little higher or lower; for some notes, only a quarter of the hole is covered, for others half or three-quarters, and for others the hole is completely covered. . . .

I remind you once again that you should not do the tremolo with the chest, because you could very easily become accustomed to the resulting quiver, and it would give a wretched performance. If, however, you wanted to have the chest help along, it would have to take place simultaneously with the movement of the fingers, for in raising the finger you would increase the airflow a little, and in putting it down you would decrease it, thereby making the tremolo somewhat stronger and clearer. Real beauty on the flute consists of a firm, crystalline, and even tone; although this is difficult to do on the instrument and is rarely achieved, you must try to acquire it, and thereby develop your chest to be firm and strong so that it does not quiver. I also remind you once again to use this ornament only rarely, so that it does not lose its good effect, for it will certainly be ugly if it appears too often.

Busby, musical manual (1828), "Vibrato"

Vibrato (Ital.). A term used in the Italian opera, to signify that at that note, or passage, to which it refers, the voice is to be thrown out, in a bold, heroic style.

Nathan, singing treatise (1836), Chapter 5 "Tone or Sound"

There are so many different toned voices, each arriving at perfection in its own excellencies and qualities, that it would be difficult to bestow the need of approbation on any one in particular; every tone that is equal without partaking of the nasal or guttural, that is devoid of tremor or harshness, that can gently sink into pathos where required, gradually melt on the ear into silence, like the soft sounds of an Aeolian harp, or swell into that majesty of tone which fixes the hearer in astonishment, is alike desirable.

Garcia, singing treatise (1840–1847), "Faults of Emission"

Guttural sounds, nasal sounds, tremolo, slurring. These are the most striking; others, such as flat, hollow sounds, or as shrieking, whining, weeping qualities of voice, we only mention in passing, as they are easily corrected. . . .

What is tremolo? The trembling of the voice. This intolerable fault ruins every style of singing. . . .

PITCH

There was no standardization of pitch during the Classical era. Pitch levels varied from community to community and from one performance location to another depending upon the construction of the instruments in use (especially organs), category of music (called "church" or "choir pitch" and "chamber pitch"), and comfortable ranges of singers. In order for performers to tune to each other and to achieve a common pitch for performance, stringed instruments adjusted their strings and wind and brass instruments had crooks or bits that were inserted or removed to lengthen or shorten the instrument and thus raise or lower pitch.

It is not assumed, however, that pitch levels were greatly different one from another. Chamber pitch is generally thought to be just one step lower than choir pitch, and pitch levels of organs of the time varied only by as much as a minor third. Alexander Ellis, in his *On the History of Musical Pitch* of 1880, provides compelling evidence to determine the relatively precise range of pitch in use during the Classical era. By measuring unaltered organ pipes, collecting tuning forks, and analyzing other data, Ellis shows that the pitch A was generally between 415 Hz and 430 Hz, and that the mean of these, 422.5 Hz, was the most common. Some of Ellis' evidence is as follows:

Gottfried Silbermann's famous 1754 organ in Dresden – 415 Hz

George Frideric Handel's tuning fork – 422.5 Hz

Mozart's pianos in 1780 – 421.6 Hz

Franz Anton von Weber's tuning fork – 424.1 Hz

The Dresden orchestra from 1815–1821 – 423 Hz

The Grand Opera in Paris in 1810 – 423 Hz

The Italian Opera in Paris in 1823 – 424.2 Hz

The London Philharmonic from 1813–1828 – 423.7 Hz

With the present-day standard of A equaling 440 Hz, A-flat is 415 Hz. This puts the general pitch level of music during the Classical era approximately a quarter of a step lower than the common modern pitch.

Quantz, flute treatise (1752), Chapter 1
"Short History and Description of the Transverse Flute"

In earlier times the transverse flute consisted of only a single piece, like the Swiss pipe still used today, or the so-called soldiers' cross-pipe, although it was an octave lower than the latter. But when in France the single key was added, to make the flute as well as other instruments more serviceable for music, it not only received a better exterior form, but was also, for the sake of greater convenience, divided into three parts, namely a head piece in which the mouth hole was found, a middle piece with six holes, and a foot piece on which the key was found. If the same pitch had prevailed everywhere, these three pieces would have sufficed. About thirty years ago, however, the flute was supplied with several interchangeable middle pieces, necessitated by the fact that the pitch to which we tune is so varied that a different tuning or prevailing pitch has been introduced not only in every country, but in almost every province and city, while even at the very same place the harpsichord is tuned high at one time, low at another, by careless tuners. Accordingly, the long middle piece with six holes was divided into two parts to make the flute more convenient to carry about in one's pocket; and to take the place of one of these two parts, namely the upper section, two or three others were fashioned, one shorter than another, so that they differed from one another by about a semitone. . . . When the instrument still could not be tuned correctly, one piece often being too low, the other too high, the upper middle piece had to be pulled out a little from the head piece. Since the difference between these middle pieces was still too great, however, and the middle pieces had to be drawn out further than the structure of the flute permitted, making it false, means were finally found to add still more middle pieces, each differing from one another by no more than a comma, or the ninth part of a whole tone. Six middle pieces now form an interval a little larger than a major semitone, which the construction of the flute permits with no detriment to true intonation; and if it is necessary, two more middle pieces can be added.

———. Chapter 17 "Of the Duties of Those Who Accompany or Execute the Accompanying or Ripieno Parts Associated with a Concertante Part" Section 7 "Of the Duties that All Accompanying Instrumentalists in General Must Observe"

The pitch regularly used for tuning in an orchestra has always varied considerably according to the time and place. The disagreeable choir pitch prevailed in Germany for several centuries, as the old organs prove. Other instruments, such as violins, double basses, trombones, recorders, shawms, bombards, trumpets, clarinets, &c., were also made to conform to it. But after the French had transformed the German cross-pipe into the transverse flute, the shawm into the oboe, and the bombard into the bassoon, using their lower and more agreeable pitch, the high choir pitch began in Germany to be supplanted by the chamber pitch, as is demonstrated by some of the most famous new organs. At the present time the Venetian pitch is the highest; it is almost the same as our old choir pitch. The Roman pitch of about twenty years ago was low, and was equal to that of Paris. At present, however, the Parisian pitch is beginning almost to equal that of Venice.

The diversity of pitches used for tuning is most detrimental to music in general. In vocal music it produces the inconvenience that singers performing in a place where low tuning is used are hardly able to make use of arias that were written for them in a place where a high pitch was employed, or vice versa. For this reason it is much to be hoped that a single pitch for tuning may be introduced at all places. It is undeniable that the high pitch is much more penetrating than the low one; on the other hand, it is much less pleasing, moving, and majestic. I do not wish to argue for the very low French chamber pitch, although it is the most advantageous for the transverse flute, the oboe, the bassoon, and some other instruments; but neither can I approve of the very high Venetian pitch, since in it the wind instruments sound much too disagreeable. Therefore I consider the best pitch to be the so-called German *A* chamber pitch, which is a minor third lower than the old choir pitch. It is neither too low nor too high, but the mean between the French and the Venetian; and in it both the stringed and the wind instruments can produce their proper effect.

**Tromlitz, flute treatise (1791), Chapter 1
"The flute and its character"**

While the pitch of all places is not the same, but sometimes varies up to a semitone higher or lower, it is necessary to have several middle joints correctly graduated higher or lower, in order to be able to play in tune everywhere. To be sure, this is not easily done with a flute having three middle joints. If the three middle joints are very close to one another, they do not cover a sufficient range, while if they are made farther apart in order to be able to tune higher or lower, they are not always just right.

Altenburg, trumpet and kettledrum treatise (1795)

Tuning Bits and Crooks

The so-called shanks are straight little brass tubes that lower the pitch of the trumpet. If one puts several of them attached to one another, the pitch will be still lower. Since the trumpet would be uncomfortable to hold if the tuning bit were too long, the longest ones are wound in the shape of a circle or bent into a curve, for which reason they are also called crooks. . . . The tuning bits and crooks are as varied as they are necessary and useful, differing partly in their size and length, partly, too, according to their use and effect. There are some that lower the pitch of the instrument by a whole tone, a half tone, a quarter tone, or I daresay even less, while [there are] some that lower it by two tones, a tone and a half, or a whole tone.

Choir and Chamber Pitch

In order to play in tune it is necessary for everyone to know the difference between choir and chamber pitch. It actually consists therein: that choir pitch, as far as the sound is concerned, is a whole tone higher than chamber pitch. Thus, the former sounds fresher and more thrilling, but it is somewhat troublesome for singers. [I might add that] organs as well as trombones &c. are usually in choir pitch. However, it is known that the old organs are usually in a higher pitch than the new ones. On the other hand, chamber pitch sounds more pleasant and more serious and is also more suitable for voices and wind instruments, and therefore almost all musical instruments are adjusted to it. The matter can be represented approximately as follows:

What is in chamber pitch: C, C$^{\#}$, D, E$^{\flat}$, E, F, F$^{\#}$, G, A$^{\#}$, A, B$^{\flat}$, B, &c.
is in choir pitch: B$^{\flat}$, B, C, D$^{\flat}$, D, E$^{\flat}$, E, F, G$^{\flat}$, G, A$^{\flat}$, A.

Tuning

Because nowadays chamber pitch has become almost universally established, both within the church and without (that is, in the chamber), all tuning is thus regarded according to chamber pitch except when certain chorales and songs of praise such as *Herr Gott, dich loben wir &c.* are sung with trumpets and kettledrums alone, without other musical instruments. In this instance only the trumpets and kettledrums are tuned to the organ, which is still usually tuned to choir pitch. However, in some places they have begun to introduce chamber-pitched organs. Where there is a pianoforte, the trumpet is tuned to it so that, for example, for a D trumpet, one asks to have the note D sounded [on the pianoforte], which should sound like a C on the trumpet. It can thus be clearly seen that there are about eight common keys, although several more of them might be possible.

If one wanted to play and be in tune in these [eight keys], one would also have to have eight trumpets of different sizes. However, so many are not really necessary, since by the addition of tuning bits and crooks a concert trumpeter needs only three trumpets (or at most four)—namely, the chamber-pitched D, F, and G trumpets.

However, if the tuning is still not accurate, one can easily assist oneself with very short tuning bits or with a little paper wound around the mouthpiece, so that the [mouthpiece] does not go in too deeply. It will also be [of] no small advantage if the mouthpiece has been accurately turned out all the way around so that it goes into the trumpet to the necessary depth, because it is always easier to lower the pitch than to raise it. It should also be mentioned that there are various other pitches according to which instruments are fashioned in a few foreign places, such as the Roman, Venetian, and French pitch. However, these will not be considered here.

Corri, singing treatise (1810), "Timbre"

Singers ought to measure the extent [range] of the Song with the extent of the Voice and pitch the key accordingly, for every Composition is not calculated for everyone's ability.

Spohr, musical diary (1860–1861), "Paris, 1820"

We have visited the Italian Opera several times and have had much artistic pleasure there. Yesterday, at long last, we saw *Don Giovanni*, which had been absent from the repertoire for some time. . . . Only two numbers prompted much applause, and it was expended on the singers rather than the composer.

These two numbers, each of which had to be repeated, were the duet between Don Giovanni and Zerlina, "La ci darem la mano," and Don Giovanni's Champagne aria. The first was transposed a half-tone up, to B-flat, and the latter raised a whole tone, both because of the weakness of Herr [Manuel] Garcia's lower register.

Schindler, biography of Beethoven (1840), "Third Period, Section 3, 1823"

If we cannot find in an ignorance of the rules setting forth the capability of the vocal organs the reasons for such unsingable handling of the voices in the *Missa* [*solemnis*,] where can we look? Some have claimed that when Beethoven was still able to hear, the orchestral pitch had been a half-tone lower than it is now, so that his whole being was conditioned to the lower pitch.

INSTRUMENTATION

The topic of instrumentation involves discussion of types and numbers of singers and instruments and of their logistical arrangements or placements in performances. Included in this discussion are considerations of singers and instruments used in church, the distribution of forces in choral/orchestral works, and basso continuo (also called thoroughbass).

The Baroque-era practice of using keyboard instruments as a part of virtually all vocal and instrumental ensembles continued throughout the Classical era, whether the ensembles played sacred or secular music or performed in churches, concerts halls, or theaters; at least one keyboard instrument (or another chord-producing instrument such as a theorbo) was a part of all ensembles. This includes, for example, the use of harpsichords in churches (note C. P. E. Bach's quote that "in all recitatives and arias in [church music] a harpsichord must be used") and pianofortes in performances of Mozart and Haydn symphonies (Parke documents Haydn as presiding "at the pianoforte during the performance of [the] twelve subscription-concerts in Hanover Square [London]" in 1791 and at "a grand concert [for] his royal Highness the Duke of York" in 1795). There were no specific pianoforte parts for Haydn or other keyboardists; players simply read from the full score or from cello or bass parts and, as was the practice during the Baroque era, realized chords appropriate to the harmonies and expressive content of the music. In the early years of the Classical era, the normal keyboard instruments were the organ and harpsichord, and they were often used in multiples and in combination with each other. Organs and harpsichords, for instance, were often played together in churches, and there were often multiple organs in churches and two harpsichords in theater orchestras. At the end of the era, the normal instrument was the pianoforte, which was generally used only in theaters and concert halls and not in combination with other keyboard instruments. The serpent, which is a wind instrument with a soft and mellow tone quality, and the bajón, an early form of the bassoon common in Spain, were frequently used in churches to accompany chant and to play the bass part of choral music.

Singers included boys, castratos, women, and men. Since women were generally excluded from singing in church, liturgical service music was generally performed by the combination of boys, castratos, and men. Boys and castratos often participated together in singing the treble parts of sacred music, and male altos (i.e., countertenors) and/or castratos sang the alto parts. The numbers of singers in choral ensembles varied greatly. Church choirs generally had from between eight and thirty-two singers, while festival ensembles numbered more than two hundred.

The typical orchestra in the early years of the Classical era consisted of strings, flutes, oboes, bassoons, and one or two keyboard instruments, with horns added from time to time and trumpets and timpani added for festival compositions. In addition, trombones were often used to accompany choral parts colla parte (i.e., the trombones would play from the alto, tenor, and bass choral parts). Clarinets were not generally utilized until the nineteenth century. The proportion of string to wind instruments in the typical orchestra is interesting. As Quantz specifies, there should be one wind player per part in combination with a string complement of between fourteen and seventeen players (four to five first and four to five second violins, two violas, two cellos, and two to three basses). However, the winds should be doubled, with two players per part, in combination with a string complement of twenty-one players. There should also be an extra keyboard instrument. As with choirs, the sizes of orchestras varied considerably in the Classical era. There are records of orchestras with one player per string part to orchestras with forty-eight first violins and twenty-four oboes. Documents of major opera orchestras list from thirty to forty string players. Adam Carse, in his *The*

Orchestra in the XVIIIth Century, calculates that the average orchestra had from four to six first and four to six second violins, two to three violas, two to three cellos, two double basses, and single players on each of the other instruments. The first and second violins were generally positioned across from each other, with the first violins to the left and the second violins to the right of the conductor.

The ratio of orchestral players to choral singers was generally two to one. This is to say that there were generally twice the number of players to singers. Haydn conducted performances of his *The Creation* in March of 1800 with sixty instrumentalists and a choir of twenty-four, and Salieri conducted performances in March of 1808 with sixty instrumentalists and a choir of thirty-two. The famous Tonkünstler-Societät performances of *The Creation*, conducted by Haydn, had an orchestra of 120 and a choir of sixty. This orchestra, by the way, was comprised of tripled winds; there were three players on each of the flute, oboe, clarinet, bassoon, and horn parts to balance eighteen players on each of the string parts. The small number of singers in proportion to the large number of instrumentalists could be accomplished in part because the choristers—as described by Johan Berwald in his description of a performance of Haydn's *The Creation* in 1799 (see the quotation at the end of this section) and as depicted (below) in a famous

painting by W. Wigand of a performance of Haydn's *The Creation* given at Old University in Vienna on March 27, 1808—were generally positioned in front of the orchestra. In performances such as the Handel festivals in Westminster Abbey in 1784, platforms were built to raise the orchestra above and behind the choir (see Burney's diagram).

Quantz, flute treatise (1752),
Chapter 17 "Of the Duties of Those Who Accompany or Execute the Accompanying or Ripieno Parts Associated with a Concertante Part"
Section 1 "Of the Qualities of a Leader of an Orchestra"

The leader must know how to distribute, place, and arrange the instrumentalists in an ensemble. Much depends upon the good distribution and placement of the instruments, and upon their combination in the proper ratio. In the orchestra pit of an opera house, the first harpsichord may be placed in the middle, with the broad end facing the parterre and the tip to the stage, so that the singers are visible to the player. The violoncello may be placed on his right, and the double bass on his left. The leader may sit next to the first harpsichord, on the right and slightly forward and elevated. The violinists and violists may form a narrow oval ring, beginning with the leader and continuing so that the violists have their backs to the stage and extend to the tip of the harpsichord, in such fashion that all may see and hear the leader. If, however, the pit is spacious enough to seat four people abreast, the second violins may sit, in two pairs, one behind the other, in the middle between the first violins and the violists, and sitting with their backs to the stage; the closer together the instruments are, the better the effect they produce. On the same side, at the end where the violinists stop, there still may be enough room for another violoncello and a double bass. The second harpsichord is placed on the left side of the first, parallel to the stage and with its tip turned toward the first, but so that room may still be found behind it for the bassoons, unless you wish to put them on the right side of the second harpsichord, behind the flutes. Another pair of violoncellos may be placed next to the second harpsichord. On this, the left, side of the pit, the oboes and hunting horns may sit in a row with their backs to the listeners, like the violins on the right side; the flutes, however, are posted in a diagonal line next to the first harpsichord, so that they turn their eyes toward the harpsichord, and the lower ends of their flutes toward the parterre. In some places, however, where there is an empty space between the pit and the listeners, the flutes are placed with their backs to the parterre, and the oboes are stationed in a diagonal line between them and the second harpsichord. The oboes produce an excellent effect, especially in tutti sections, serving as a filler, and their sound justly deserves a free outlet, one which the flutes also enjoy if no one stands close behind them and if the players turn a little to the side. . . . The theorbo may find a comfortable place behind the second harpsichordist and the violoncellists. . . .

In a composition for a large ensemble, performed either in a hall or in some other large place where there is no stage, the tip of the harpsichord may be directed towards the listeners. So that none of the musicians turns his back to the listeners, the first violinists may stand in a row next to the harpsichord, with the leader on the right of the keyboard player, who has the two bass instruments playing on either side of him. The second violins may come behind the first, and behind them the violas. Next to the violas, on the right, place the oboes in the same row, and behind this row the hunting horns and the other basses. The flutes, if they have solo parts to play, are best placed at the tip of the harpsichord, in front of the first violins, or on the left side of the harpsichord. Because of the weakness of their tone, they would not be heard if they were to stand further back. Singers also may take the same place; if they were to stand behind the keyboard player and read from the score, they would not only hamper the violoncellists and double-bass players, but would also obstruct their own breathing and stifle their own voices if poor sight forced them to bend over.

In a small chamber ensemble the harpsichord may be placed by the wall on the left of its player, but far enough removed from it so that all the accompanying instruments except the basses have room between him and the wall. If only four violins are present, they and the violists may all stand in one row behind the harpsichord. If, however, there are six or eight violinists, it would be better to place the second violins behind the first, and the violas behind the second violins, so that the middle parts do not stand out above the principal part, for this produces a poor effect. The soloists, in these circumstances, can take their places in front of the harpsichord, in such a way that they have the accompanists in view to the side.

He who wishes to perform a composition well must see to it that he supplies each instrument in the proper proportion, and does not use too many of one kind, or on the other hand, too few of another. I shall propose a ratio which, to my thinking, will satisfy all requirements in this regard. I assume that the *harpsichord* will be included in all ensembles, whether large or small. With *four violins* use *one viola, one violoncello,* and *one double bass* of medium size. With *six violins,* the same complement and *one bassoon. Eight violins* require *two violas, two violoncellos,* an *additional double bass,* larger, however, than the first, *two oboes, two flutes,* and *two bassoons.* With *ten violins,* the same complement, but with an *additional violoncello.* With *twelve violins* use *three violas, four violoncellos, two double basses, three bassoons, four oboes, four flutes,* and in a pit *another keyboard* and *one theorbo. Hunting horns* may be necessary in both small and large ensembles, depending upon the nature of the piece and the inclination of the composer.

With this distribution in mind it will not be difficult to order even the largest ensembles in the correct ratios, if the increases from four to eight, from eight to twelve, &c., are properly noted. Since the success of a composition depends as much upon an arrangement of the instruments in the proper proportions as upon good execution, foresight in this matter is particularly important. Many compositions would be more effective if the distribution of the parts were arranged properly. For how can a composition sound well if the principal parts are drowned out and suppressed by the bass or even the middle parts? The former should stand out above all the others, and the middle parts should be heard least of all.

——. Section 3 "Of the Violist in Particular" Paragraph 11

Since one viola, if a good and strong instrument, is sufficient against four or even six violins, the violist must moderate the strength of his tone if only two or three violins play with him, so that he does not cover the others, especially if only one violoncello is present and no double bass. The middle parts, which, considered in themselves, provide the listener with the least pleasure, must never be heard as strongly as the principal parts. Hence the violist must decide whether the notes he is to play are melodic or simply harmonic. The former he must play with the same strength as the violins, the latter a little more softly.

——. Section 6 "Of the Keyboard Player in Particular"

The general rule of thorough-bass [playing the basso continuo part on a keyboard instrument] is that you always play in four parts; yet if you wish to accompany well, a better effect is often produced if you do not bind yourself very strictly to this rule, and if you leave out some parts, or even double the bass an octave higher with the right hand. For just as a composer is neither able nor compelled to set a three-, four-, or five-part instrumental accompaniment to all melodies, lest they become unintelligible or obscure, so not every melody allows an accompaniment of full chords upon the keyboard; hence an accompanist must govern himself more by the individual case than by the general rules of thorough-bass.

A piece with full harmony accompanied by a large body of instruments also requires a full and strong keyboard accompaniment. On the other hand, a concerto executed by a few instruments already requires some moderation in this respect, particularly in the concertante [solo] passages. You must then pay attention to whether these passages are accompanied by the bass alone or by additional instruments; whether the concertante part plays softly or loudly, and in the low or high register; whether it has a sustained and singing melody, leaps, or passage-work to execute; whether the passage-work is played quietly or with fire [etc.]. . . .

In a trio the keyboard player must adjust himself to the instruments that he has to accompany, noting whether they are loud or soft, whether or not there is a violoncello with the keyboard, whether the composition is in a *galant* or elaborate style, whether the harpsichord is loud or soft, open or closed, and whether the listeners are close by or at a distance. The harpsichord is obtrusive and quite loud close by, but at a distance it is not as loud as other instruments. If the keyboard player has a violoncellist with him, and accompanies soft instruments, he may use some moderation with the right hand, especially in a *galant* composition, and still more if one part rests and the other plays alone; with strong instruments, however, and with a piece that is harmonically full and elaborate, and also if both parts play at the same time, he may play with fuller chords.

The greatest discretion and restraint are required in a solo . . . . The accompanist is to be censured if he uses the right hand too actively or if he plays melodically with it, or arpeggiates, or introduces other things in opposition to the principal part at the wrong time, or if he does not express the Piano and Forte at the same time as the soloist, but instead plays everything without sentiment, and with the same volume. . . .

On a harpsichord with one keyboard, passages marked Piano may be produced by a moderate touch and by diminishing the number of parts; those marked Mezzo Forte, by doubling the bass in octaves; those marked Forte, in the same manner and also by taking some *consonances* of the chord into the left hand; and those marked Fortissimo, by quick arpeggiations of the chords from below upwards, by the same doubling of the octaves and the consonances in the left hand, and by a more vehement and forceful touch. On a harpsichord with two keyboards, you have the additional advantage of being able to use the upper keyboard for the Pianissimo. However, on a *pianoforte* everything required may be accomplished with the greatest convenience, for this instrument, of all those that are designated by the word keyboard, has the greatest number of qualities necessary for good accompaniment, and depends for its effect only upon the player and his judgment. The same is true of a good clavichord with regard to playing, but not with regard to effect, since it lacks the Fortissimo.

The tone of each instrument may be produced in different ways, and the same is also true of the harpsichord, although it might appear that on this instrument everything depends not on the player, but on the instrument itself. Experience shows, however, that if two musicians play the same instrument, one produces a better tone than the other. . . .

In the Adagio the accompanist must neither arpeggiate nor play melodically with the right hand, unless the soloist has sustained notes or rests. He must not allow the accompanying parts to become more prominent than the bass. In an Adagio in common time, he may strike each eighth note with the right hand. But in an Arioso in which the bass has a quicker movement, whether in eighth notes, sixteenth notes, or triplets of either species of notes, it is not necessary to strike chords with the right hand for each note; it sounds better to allow one note to go by in equal notes and two in triplets, provided that the passing notes have no figures of their own above them. . . .

In a recitative sung from memory it is much easier for the singer if the accompanist anticipates the singer's first notes at each caesura, and, so to speak, puts them into his mouth for him by striking the chord with a quick arpeggiation, in such fashion that, where possible, the singer's first note lies in the upper part; immediately afterwards he should strike separately several of the following intervals that appear in the vocal part (see Tab. XXIII, Fig. 5).

Fig. 5

Avison, essay on musical expression (1753), Part 3
"On Musical Expression, as it relates to the Performer" Section 2 "On the expressive Performance of Music in Parts"

Having said so much with regard to the expressive Performance of Music in general, I shall now conclude with a few Hints that may be of Service in the Performance of full Music: Especially of such *Concertos* as have pretty near an equal Share of *Air* and *Expression* in all their Parts.

The first material Circumstance which ought to be considered in the Performance of this Kind of Composition, is, the Number and Quality of those Instruments that may produce the best Effect.

And, 1st, I would propose, exclusive of the four principal Parts which must be always complete, that the Chorus of other Instruments should not exceed the Number following, *viz.* Six *Primo*, and four *Secondo Repienos*; four *Repieno Basses*, and two *Double Basses*, and a *Harpsichord*. A lesser Number of Instruments, near the same Proportion, will also have a proper Effect, and may answer the Composer's Intention; but more would probably destroy the just Contrast, which should always be kept up between the *Chorus* and *Solo*: For in this Case the Effect of two or three single Instruments would be lost and over-powered by the Succession of too grand a *Chorus*; and to double the *Primo*, and *Secondo Concertino*, or *Violoncello* in the *Solo*, would be an Impropriety in the Conduct of our musical Oeconomy [order], too obvious to require any Thing to be said on that Head [subject]. It may be objected, perhaps, that the Number of Basses, in the above Calculation, would be found too powerful for the *Violins*: But as the latter Instruments are so clear, sprightly, and piercing, and as they rather gain more Force by this Addition, they will always be heard: However, if it were possible, there should never be wanting a Double Bass; especially in a Performance of full Concertos, as they cannot be heard to any Advantage without that NOBLE FOUNDATION of their Harmony. As to Wind-Instruments, these are all so different in their Tone, and in their Progressions through the various Keys, from those of the stringed kind, besides the irremediable Disagreement of their rising in their Pitch, while the others are probably falling, that they should neither be continued too long in Use, nor employed but in such Pieces as are expressly adapted to them; so that in the general Work of Concertos, for Violins, etc. they are almost always improper; unless we admit of the *Bassoon*, which, if performed by an expert Hand, in a soft and ready Tone, and only in those Passages that are natural to it, may then be of Singular Use, and add Fullness to the Harmony.

C. P. E. Bach, clavier treatise (1753),
"Introduction to Part Two"

The Organ, harpsichord, pianoforte, and clavichord are the keyboard instruments most commonly used for accompaniment. . . .

The organ is indispensable in church music with its fugues, large choruses, and sustained style. It provides splendor and maintains order. However, in all recitatives and arias in this style, especially those in which a simple accompaniment permits free variation on the part of the singer, a harpsichord must be used. The emptiness of a performance without this accompanying instrument is, unfortunately, made apparent to us far too often. The harpsichord is also used for arias and recitatives in chamber and theatrical music.

The pianoforte and clavichord provide the best accompaniments in performances that require the most elegant taste. Some singers, however, prefer the support of the clavichord or harpsichord to the pianoforte.

No piece can be well performed without some form of keyboard accompaniment. Even in heavily scored works, such as operas performed out of doors, where no one would think that the harpsichord could be heard, its absence can certainly be felt. And from a position above the performers, all its tones are clearly perceptible. . . .

The best accompaniment, one which is free of criticism, is a keyboard instrument and a cello.

C. P. E. Bach, letter to Johann Gottlieb Gleditsch (?) (c.1760)

18 church pieces by the ducal Capellmeister in Meiningen Herr Johann Ludewig Bach. Most are with 2 oboes, 2 violins, viola, 4 voice parts and continuo. . . . All 18 pieces consist of (1) a clean score in the hand of my late father; (2) all parts written out with doubled violins and three continuo parts, among which a transposed organ bass is always present, because of the chamber pitch.

Haydn, preface to *Applausus* (1768)

Since I cannot be present myself at this *Applaus* (sc. *Applausus*), I have found it necessary to provide one or two explanations concerning it execution, *viz.*: . . . . I would ask you to use two players on the viola part throughout, for the inner parts sometimes need to be heard more than the upper parts, and you will find in all my compositions that the violin rarely doubles the bass. . . .

If you have to copy two sets of violin parts, the copyist should see that they do not turn their pages at the same time, because this takes away a great deal of strength from an orchestra with only a few musicians. . . .

In the soprano aria the bassoon can be omitted if absolutely necessary, but I would rather have it present, at least when the bass is *obbligato* throughout. And I prefer a band with 3 bass instruments—'cello, bassoon and double bass—to one with 6 double basses and 3 'cellos, because certain passages stand out better that way.

Burney, account of music in France and Italy (1770), "Milan 18 July"

This morning I heard the whole service after the Ambrosian manner, was introduced to the Maestro di Capella, Signor Jean Andrè Fioroni, who invited me into the orchestra, shewed me the service they were to sing printed on wood in four parts, separate, cantus – altus – tenor – bassus – out of which after the tone was given by organist Signor Jean Corbeli they *all* sung, namely I boy, 3 castrati, 2 tenors and 2 basses, under the direction of the Maestro di Capella, without the organ.

———. "Rome 30 September"

Went this morning to S. Peters to hear Mass where I staid [sic] 2 hours and had a delightful contemplative lounge—from hence to Signor Santarelli, with whom I spent 2 hours more very profitably. He had looked out several very curious things to show me, among which 2 MS [manuscript] volumes of extracts from curious authors and anecdotes. . . . There is no organ or other instrument ever used in the chapel. The singers are 32: 8 trebles – 8 contr'altos – 8 tenors and 8 bases. These are all in ordinary—there is likewise a number of *extras* ready to supply the places of those who are sick, absent, and infirm, or dead—so that the number of singers is on common days never less than 32 and on festivals nearly doubled. They are all in a kind of purple uniform.

——. "Naples 17 October"

After dinner to music at the Franciscan's church—where the 3 conservatorios were to furnish music and musicians for a great festival of 8 successive days, morning and evening. . . . The band was very numerous, consisting of above 100 voices and instruments, in a long occasional gallery totally covered with gold and silver gilding.

——. "Naples 7 November"

Signor Fabio, the 1st fiddle of the opera of S. Carlo, dined with us and brought his violin. [He is] a coarse player, tho' a fat good natured man. He sung several buffo songs and accompanied himself very well on his fiddle and after dinner he had a 2nd who came to accompany him in one of Giardini's solos etc.—I got from him the number of hands employed in the great opera orchestra: 18 1st and 18 2nd violins, 5 double bases and but 2 violoncellos, which I think has a bad effect, as the double base is played so coarsely throughout Italy as to produce no musical sound nothing but meer [sic] noise.

——. "Rome 11 November"

I went to the Chiesa Nuova to hear an oratorio in that church where that kind of drama first took its rise. There are two galleries—in one an organ and in the other a harpsichord—in the former the service was begun by the vespers in 4 parts a la Palestrina—then the Salve Regina à voce sola.

Burney, account of music in France and Italy (1773), "Lisle"

As I made no considerable stop till I reached this city, the capital of French Flanders, I here began my enquiries, and first tried to discover the manner of performing the Gregorian chant, which subsists throughout France in all cathedrals and collegiate churches. It is oftener performed without the organ than with; and though there are organs in every large church in this town, and throughout the kingdom, I find that they are only used, as in our parish churches, on Sundays, and at great festivals. . . .

In the French churches there is an instrument on each side the choir, called the *serpent*, from its shape, I suppose, for it undulates like one. This gives the *tone* in chanting, and plays the base when they sing in parts. It is often ill-played, but if judiciously used, would have a good effect. It is, however, in general overblown, and too powerful for the voices it accompanies; otherwise, it mixes with them better than the organ, as it can augment or diminish a sound with more delicacy, and is less likely to overpower or destroy by a bad temperament, that perfect one, or which the voice only is capable.

Burney, account of music in Germany, the Netherlands, and United Provinces (1775), "Ghent"

At the great church of St. Bavo, two *serpents* and a double base accompany the chant, when sung in parts, even when the organ is not played.

——. **"Antwerp"**

There are three organs in this church [Notre Dame Cathedral], one very large, on the right hand side, at the west end of the choir, and a small one in a chapel on each side of the broad aisle. . . . The chanting here, as in other churches of this country, is accompanied by the double base and *serpent*. . . .

At the Dominicans church, there are two organs, which are esteemed the best in the town. . . . On Sunday, 19ᵗʰ at seven o'clock I attended the first mass. There were a few violins, two bassoons, and a double base placed with the voices in the organ loft, over the west door of the choir; but before these were employed, a considerable part of the service was chanted in *Canto Fermo*, with only a *serpent* and two bassoons in accompaniment. . . .

At nine o'clock high mass began and continued upwards of two hours. . . . Before the service . . . the canons and boys marched in procession round the church, with each a lighted taper in his hand, chanting the psalms, in four parts, with the two bassoons and *serpent* above-mentioned.

——. **"Brussels"**

Attending high mass at the collegiate church of St. Gudula . . . I again heard the performance of a considerable band of voices and instruments; and I was glad to find among the former two or three women, who, though they did not sing well, yet their being employed, proved that female voices might have admission in the church, without giving offence or scandal to piety, or even bigotry.

——. "Ludwigsburg"

At the Würtemburg court . . . there are eighteen violins . . . six tenors, three violoncellos, and four double bases; the principal organists are, Frederick Seeman, and Schubart; for hautbois: Alrich, Hitfch, Blesner, and Commeret; flutes: Steinhardt, a very good one, and Augustinelli; three horns; two bassoons.

——. "Vienna"

The first time I went to the cathedral of St. Stephen, I heard an excellent mass, in the true church style, very well performed; there were violins and violoncellos though it was not a festival. The great organ at the west end of this church has not been fit for use these forty years; there are three or four more organs of a smaller size in different parts of the church.

——. "Alost"

The voices in the church at Alost are accompanied with six or eight instruments every day, besides the organ, and on festivals by a great band.

——. "Passau"

In the cathedral, which is a very beautiful modern building, of the Corinthian order, there is a very magnificent organ. . . . On each side of the choir, in this church, there is likewise a small organ.

Burney, Account of performances in Westminster Abbey, 1785

The orchestra was built at the opposite extremity [of the Abbey], ascending regularly from the height of seven feet from the floor, to upwards of forty, from the base of the pillars; and extending from the centre to the top of the side aisle. . . .

At the top of the Orchestra was placed the occasional organ, in a Gothic frame, mounting to, and mingling with, the saints and martyrs represented in the painted glass on the west window. On each side of the organ, close to the window, were placed the kettle-drums. . . . The choral bands were principally placed in view of Mr. Bates, on steps, seemingly ascending into the clouds, in each of the side aisles, as their termination was invisible to the audience. The principal singers were ranged in the front of the Orchestra, as at Oratorios, accompanied by the choirs of St. Paul, the Abbey, Windsor, and the Chapel-Royal.

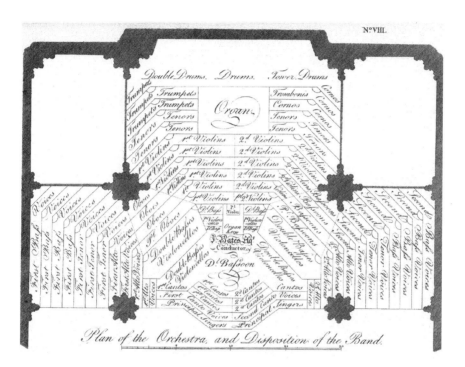

Plan of the Orchestra, and Disposition of the Band.

Berwald, description of Haydn *The Creation* performance March 19, 1799

When we entered, we saw that the stage proper was set up in the form of an amphitheatre. Down below at the fortepiano sat *Kapellmeister* Weigl, surrounded by the vocal soloists, the chorus, a violoncello, and a double bass. At one level higher stood Haydn himself with his conductor's baton. Still a level higher on one side were the first violins, led by Paul Wranitzky, and on the other side the second violins, led by his brother Anton Wranitsky. In the centre: violas and double basses. In the wings, more double basses; on higher levels the wind instruments, and at the very top: trumpets, kettledrums, and trombones.

Spohr, musical diary (1860–1861), "1802"

During Lent, when no public performances are allowed, the [St. Petersburg] Court Theater gave two big concerts a week. . . . The orchestra, at the first concert, consisted of thirty-six violins and twenty basses and doubled winds. In addition to this, and as reinforcement for the chorus, were forty hornists of the Imperial Band. . . . They served as an organ, and gave strength and security to the singing of the chorus, whose parts they doubled. . . .

Very popular was a performance of Haydn's *The Seasons*, given for the benefit of the Widow's Fund. . . . The orchestra was the largest I had ever heard. It consisted of seventy violins and thirty basses and doubled winds.

——. "Rome, 1816"

Rome has two private musical institutions. One is a kind of choral society that has its sessions every Thursday in the home of its founder, the voice and piano teacher Sirletti. . . . The second private institution meets every Monday at the home of Signor Ruffini. . . . Operas are given in concert form . . . for an audience of from two hundred to two hundred and fifty. The singers stand on an elevated platform. The orchestra, consisting of four violins, viola, cello, bass, two clarinets, two horns, and a bassoon, surrounds them on the floor level.

Parke, musical memoirs (1830)

1784. This year there was a grand commemoration of Handel that took place by command of their Majesties in Westminster Abbey. . . . The Abbey was arranged for the accommodation of the public, after the plan Mr. Wyatt, the King's architect, in a superb and very convenient manner. The orchestra, which contained upwards of five hundred performers, was formed in a rising manner in tiers, beginning about eight feet from the floor, and increasing gradually till it reached the center of the large painted window at the west entrance, the performers looking eastward.

1787. There were four grand performances of sacred music, by command of their Majesties, in Westminster Abbey this year. . . .

They commenced on Monday the 29th of May. The band of vocal and instrumental performers amounted to eight hundred and six, exclusive of the principal singers, consisting of twenty-two.

1791. Salomon gave twelve subscription-concerts in Hanover Square, which began on the 12th of March. These concerts had the powerful aid of the celebrated composer Haydn, who was engaged by Salomon to come to London and compose twelve new symphonies, one for each night, and to preside at the pianoforte during the performance of them.

1795. His Royal Highness the Duke of York presented a grand concert of instrumental music, March 2nd, at York House, Piccadilly, at which their Majesties and the Princesses were present. Salomon led the band, amongst whom was Haydn, who presided at the pianoforte. . . . The following week I attended a grand instrumental concert given by the Prince of Wales at Carlton House to their Majesties and the whole of the royal family. Haydn presided at the pianoforte, and Salomon led the band.

CONDUCTING

The physical coordination of ensembles was usually the responsibility of the principal violinist, called a leader, who, through the movement of his violin, gave indication of tempo. Under certain circumstances, however—such as in an ensemble with no violins or in an opera orchestra—coordination was the responsibility of the principal keyboard player. Sometimes, with large ensembles that were spread out over a considerable area of space, the coordination responsibilities were shared, often simultaneously, by the principal violinist and keyboardist. By the early decades of the eighteenth century, especially in France, a designated person beat time, generally by making noise on the floor with a role of paper or a stick. It was not until the second decade of the eighteenth century that a conductor became stationed in front of an ensemble, usually an orchestra, with baton in hand. Note the quotations by Spohr and Parke.

Quantz, flute treatise (1752), Chapter 17 "Of the Duties of Those Who Accompany or Execute the Accompanying or Ripieno Parts Associated with a Concertante Part"
Section I "Of the Qualities of a Leader of an Orchestra"

It would be desirable, in order to gradually further the cause of music in general, to have at each place where an orchestra has been established at least one able and experienced musician who has not only insight into clear execution, but also some understanding of both composition and harmony, so that he can hit correctly upon the style in which each composition must be executed. . . .

Whether a leader plays this instrument or that may be of no importance. Since, however, the violin is absolutely indispensable in the accompanying body, and is also more penetrating than any of the other instruments most used for accompanying, it is better if he does play the violin. . . .

The leader must frequently direct his eyes and ears both to the performer of the principal part and to the accompanists, in case it is necessary to accommodate the one and keep the others in order. . .

A good leader must try, in addition, to develop and maintain a good and uniform execution in the orchestra.

C. P. E. Bach, clavier treatise (1753), Introduction to Part I

The keyboard, entrusted by our fathers with full command, is in the best position to assist not only the other bass instruments, but the entire ensemble in maintaining a uniform pace. . . . The tone of the keyboard, which, if correctly placed, stands in the center of the ensemble and can be heard clearly by all. And I know that even diffuse, elaborate compositions, played by impromptu, average performers, can be held together simply by its tone. If the first violinist is positioned near the keyboard, as he should, disorder cannot be easily spread. . . . Should someone hasten or drag, he can most readily be corrected by the keyboardist. . . . Especially those parts that employ the tempo rubato will find herein a welcome, emphatic beat. . . . In a concerto or other heavily scored piece, when the bass and ripieno parts hold a tone while the principal part continues with its own motion, even varying it at times with syncopations, it is wise for the accompanist to maintain the beat and guide the other performers by playing a chord with the right hand on the divisions of the bar even though the harmony does not change.

Billings, *The New-England Psalm-Singer* (1770), Chapter 6 "Of Time in its various Moods, and how to Beat it in each of them"

There are several Sorts of Moods for Time . . . commonly us'd in Psalmody:

The First of these Moods is called Adagio, which is a very slow Movement. . . . You may Beat it two several Ways, either with your Hand once down, and once up in every Bar, which is called Minim [half note] Beating, or twice down and twice up, which is called Crotchet [quarter note] Beating. Where the Tune chiefly consists of Minims, I would recommend the first, but where the Musick consists of lesser Notes, I would recommend the latter to be the easiest and plainest way. . . .

The second Mood or Mark is called the Largo Mood, being half as quick again as the former. . . .

The third Mood or Mark is called the Allegro Mood, being as quick again as the first, so that Minims in this Mood are Sung to the Time of Seconds. . . .

There is another Mood sometimes used in Psalmody, mark'd as above, and is called two from four, each Bar containing two Crotchets, one to be beaten down, and the other up. . . .

Tripla Time is measur'd by odd Numbers, as 3, 6, 9, &c. each bar including either three Semibreves [whole notes], three Minims, three Crotchets, or three Quavers [eighth notes], two of which must be sung or play'd with the Hand down, and one up, so that you are just as long again down as up. . . .

The second Sort of Tripla Time is called Three from Four: Each Bar including three Crotchets, or one pointed [dotted] Minim. A Crotchet in this Mood is to be performed in the same Time as a Crotchet in Largo, two Beats down, and one up, mark'd thus 3/4.

The third Sort of Tripla Time is called Three from Eight, each Bar including three Quavers or one pointed Crotchet, two beats down and one up, each Bar being performed as quick again as Three from Four, mark'd thus 3/8.

Chapter One

Reichardt, letters (1774)

During the first few measures, Pisendel would, while playing the violin, indicate the beat by movements of the neck and head of the violin. If the beat were four, he would move the violin down once, up once, then to the side, and up again. For a three beat, he would move it down once, to the side, and up again. When he wanted to slow down the orchestra in the middle of a piece, he would bow only the first note of each measure—in order to make these notes more conspicuous and emphatic.

Burney, account of music in Germany, the Netherlands, and United Provinces (1775), "Brussels"

The theatre in this city is one of the most elegant I ever saw . . . . The orchestra of this theatre is celebrated all over Europe. It is, at present, under the direction of M. Fitzthumb, a very active and intelligent *maestro di capella*, who beats the time, and is indefatigable in preserving good discipline.

W. A. Mozart, letter to his father (1778), "Paris 3 July"

My symphony [K. 297] was performed to general applause on Corpus Christi, and the "Courrier de l'Europe," so I hear, has printed a notice on it, which makes it an exceptional success. I was very upset at the rehearsal, for I had not heard such miserable playing in all my days. . . . I would have liked to rehearse it once more, but as they always rehearse so many things, there was no time for it; and so I went to bed with a heavy heart and in a dissatisfied and angry frame of mind. The next day I resolved not to attend the concert, but with the weather turning fine in the evening, I finally decided to go—determined, however, that if things went as badly as they had at the rehearsal, I would certainly go up to the stage, snatch the violin from Mr. La Houssaye (the leader of the orchestra), and conduct myself.

Rousseau, dictionary (1779), "To Beat Time"

TO BEAT TIME is to specify the variety of time by motions of the hand or foot, which denote its duration, and by which all similar measures are rendered exactly equal in their chronical powers or time in the execution. There are measures which are struck by one time only, others by two, three, or four, which is the greatest number of times specified that can be contained within a measure. A four-tim'd measure also can always be divided into two measures of two times each. In all their different measures, the beaten time is always on the note which immediately follows the bar: the raised time is always that which precedes, unless it happens that the measure contains but one time, and even in that case we must always suppose a weaker time, since we cannot beat without having raised. . . .

The French musicians beat time differently from the Italians. The one, in a four-timed measure, strikes the two first successively and raises the others. They strike also the two first in a three-tim'd measure and raise the third. The French strike the first time only and specify the others by different motions of the hand on the right and left. However, the French music would be in want of a well-marked measure, much more than the Italian, for it does not convey its cadence within itself; its movements have no natural precision: the measure is extended or diminished at the option of the singer. How greatly are our ears disgusted at the French opera with the disagreeable and continual noise, which is made by the strokes of him who beats the time, and who has been ingeniously compared to a wood-cutter felling a tree! But 'tis an inevitable evil. Without that noise the measure could not be felt.

Busby, musical dictionary (c.1801)

BEATING TIME is that motion of the hand or foot used by the performers themselves, or some person presiding over the concert.

CONDUCTOR. A term applied to the person who arranges, orders, and directs the necessary preparation for a concert; and also superintends and conducts the performance. . . .

LEADER. A performer who in a concert takes the principal violin, receives the time and style of the several movements from the conductor, and communicates them to the rest of the band. . . .

MANU-DUCTOR. The name given by ancients to the officiate whose province it was to beat the time with his hand at public performances.

Chapter One

Kullak, Beethoven's piano playing (1901),
"General Remarks on Beethoven's Piano-Playing Down to 1809"

When Neefe [Christian Gottlob Neefe, Beethoven's music teacher] left Bonn temporarily, on June 20, 1782, Ludwig, now nearly twelve years old, was able to take his place on the organ-bench. Next year he was still further advanced; Beethoven became cembalist in the orchestra, having to lead the operatic performances at the piano.

Busby, musical grammar (1818),
"Examples of Beating and Counting Time"

Common Time of Four Crotchets [quarter notes] in a bar; in which the hand, or foot, falls at the first crotchet, and rises at the third; the voice counting two while it is down, and two while it is up.

Common Time of Two Crotchets in a bar; in which the hand, or foot, falls at the first crotchet, and rises at the second; the voice counting one while it is down, and one while it is up.

Triple Time of Three Crotchets in a bar; in which the hand, or foot, falls at the first crotchet, and rises at the third; the voice counting two while it is down, and one while it is up.

Compound Common Time of Six Quavers [eighth notes] in a bar; in which the hand, or foot, falls at the first quaver, and rises at the fourth; the voice counting three while it is down, and three while it is up.

Compound Triple Time of Nine Quavers in a bar; in which the hand, or foot, falls at the first quaver, and rises at the seventh; the voice counting six while it is down, and three while it is up.

Double Compound Common Time of Twelve Quavers in a bar; in which the hand, or foot, falls at the first quaver, and rises at the seventh; the voice counting six while it is down, and six while it is up.

The hand, or foot, acting as a chronometer, forms an unerring director for the division of each bar into equal portions of its time.

Spohr, musical diary (1860–1861), Chapter 8 "Journey to London, 1819–1820"

The time was now at hand for me to conduct my first Philharmonic concert, and I occasioned hardly less excitement than with my first appearance as soloist. It was still the custom in London that, in the playing of overtures and symphonies, the pianist sat at the piano with the score before him. He did not conduct, but rather read along and joined in when it suited him, which made a very bad effect. The actual conductor was the first violinist, who gave the tempo and, when things went wrong, beat time with his bow. An orchestra as large as the Philharmonic, with the musicians standing so far apart, could not achieve real precision under such a system. Despite the excellence of the individual musicians, the ensemble was much worse than that to which one was accustomed in Germany. I had decided, accordingly, that when it came my turn to conduct, I would attempt to improve matters.

Fortunately, when the time came, Ries was at the piano and gladly agreed to turn the score over to me and remove himself from the proceedings. I took my place, with the score before me, at a desk especially set up in front of the orchestra, drew my baton from my pocket and gave the signal to begin. Shocked at such an innovation, some of the directors wished to protest. However, when I asked them at least to give it a try, they consented. I had conducted the symphonies and overtures on the program many times in Germany and was abundantly familiar with them. Then I could not only set the tempos with authority, but also signal the entrances to the woodwinds and brass, giving them a degree of security they had never previously enjoyed. I also took the liberty of interrupting when things were not satisfactory, and politely but firmly making my wishes known, with Ries acting as interpreter. By this means the orchestra was prompted to extraordinary attentiveness. The visible outline of the beat contributed to security, and they all played with a fire and precision never achieved by them before.

Surprised and delighted by this success, the orchestra expressed its approval immediately after the first movement of the symphony, and there was no further opposition from the directors. Even in the choral pieces, the direction of which I entrusted to Ries, this method of giving the beat with a baton proved itself, particularly in the recitatives, and the singers expressed their satisfaction with the precision with which the orchestra accompanied them.

The success of the concert itself was even greater than I had hoped. The listeners were, to be sure, disturbed at first by the novelty, and there was a good deal of whispered comment. But when the music began, and the orchestra attacked the familiar symphony with such unwonted force and precision, prolonged applause after the first movement confirmed the favorable verdict. The victory of the baton was complete and never again was a pianist to be seen during the playing of overtures and symphonies.

——. "Journey to Paris, 1820"

We have visited the Italian Opera several times. . . . Yesterday, at long last, we saw *Don Giovanni*, which had been absent from the repertoire for some time. . . . The orchestra, rated by Parisians the best in the world, had some bad moments. The winds failed conspicuously on two occasions, and several times things got so out of hand that the director had to resort to beating time. I am more convinced than ever that a theater orchestra, be it ever so good, can only be directed by continuous time-beating, if only because the outer extremities of the orchestra are too far apart. Certainly it is not sufficient to attempt to mark time as [concertmaster Jean-Jacques] Grasset did, by movements of his body and his violin.

———. "Paris, 1821"

[Jean François] Lesueur and [Luigi] Cherubini, the two musical directors of the Court Chapel, alternate every three months in the directorship. . . . The directors do not themselves conduct the music, but rather preside in court dress at the head of the choir, without actually taking part in the performance. The actual musical director is [Charles Henri] Plantade. Kreutzer is leader of the first violins. . . . There are one or two rehearsals for each mass, and under Plantade's secure and spirited direction, all goes well.

Schindler, biography of Beethoven (1840), Third Period, Section 2 "1822"

Beethoven had stipulated that he should conduct at the ceremonial opening of the [Josephstadt Theater in Vienna]. Accordingly he took his place at the piano in a position in which he was facing most of the orchestra and where his left ear, which was still of some service to him, was turned toward the stage. The Kapellmeister Franz Gläser (now Court Kapellmeister in Copenhagen) placed himself on Beethoven's right where he could oversee the whole performance, while I led the orchestra from my place at the head of the first violins.

Parke, musical memoirs (1830)

1784. When the time of performance [a grand commemoration of Handel in Westminster Abbey] had arrived, and Mr. Cramer, the leader, had just tapped his bow, (the signal for being ready) and looked round to catch the eyes of the performers, he saw, to his astonishment, a tall gigantic figure, with an immense powdered toupee, full dressed, with a bag and sword, and a huge roll of parchment in his hand. "Who is that gentleman?" said Mr. Cramer. "Dr. Hayes," was the reply. "What is he going to do?" "To beat time." "Be so kind," said Mr. Cramer, "to tell the gentleman that when he has sat down I will begin." The Doctor, who never anticipated such a *set down* as this, took his seat, and Mr. Cramer did begin, and his Majesty and all present bore witness to his masterly style of leading the band.

1785. Their Majesties honored the oratorios at Drury Lane Theatre with their presence on the six Fridays in Lent. The first was on the 11th of February, when *Messiah* was performed. . . . The leader was Mr. Richards, and the conductor at the organ Mr. Stanley, who, though blind, performed with the utmost accuracy.

1795. A grand selection of sacred music, from the works of Handel, was performed in St. Margaret's church, Westminster, on the 25th of May. . . . Cramer led the band, and Dr. Arnold conducted at the organ.

1818. The Vocal concert, which was last year discontinued, was this season revived, and commenced at Hanover Square on the 6th of March. Mr. Weichsell led the band, and Mr. Greatorex was the conductor.

Chapter 2
TEMPO

Present-day views about tempo during the Classical era usually coincide with and are based upon opinions regarding basic philosophies of the era—philosophies expressed in terms such as "refinement" and "restraint" that are synonymous with the term classicism. These views are also normally in contrast with labels such as "emotionalism" and "subjectivity" that are often associated with and that routinely characterize the Romantic era. As a consequence, tempo during the Classical era is thought to be relatively restrained in scope, restricted in flexibility, and unassociated with expressive characteristics, especially those aligned with extra-musical considerations. While it is most certainly true that tempos in the Classical era were less varied and extreme than those during the Romantic era, this is only true in terms of comparison. Tempo, governed by the same factors in both eras, was neither restrained nor restricted in the Classical era, and it was not only associated with expressive characteristics, it was motivated by them.

As related in numerous primary sources, there was considerable attention to minute gradations of tempo (note the extensive definitions of terms in the violin treatise by Leopold Mozart and the keyboard primer by J. C. Bach and F. P. Ricci), to tempo fluctuation (described as recommendations for accelerations and retards and as a unique pliability of textures in tempo rubato), and to tempo being motivated and colored by expressive properties (summarized by Johann Philipp Kirnberger's statement that "the composer must never forget that every melody is supposed to be a natural and faithful illustration or portrayal of a mood or sentiment").

In terms of the means composers took to convey tempo to performers, it is important to understand the role of meter, which was an indicator and conveyor of tempo in metrically organized compositions (see Kirnberger's thorough discussion immediately following Example E below), but which was a mere convention, one not to be adhered to in recitative (note in particular Joseph Haydn's recommendations).

METER INFLUENCING TEMPO

Meter signatures conveyed more information to Classical-era musicians than they do to musicians of today. Whereas meter signatures in modern times convey information only about the organization and division of notational values into and within measures (e.g., 3/4 indicates that there are three beats per measure and that the quarter note is the unit of pulse), meter signatures in the Classical era conveyed this metric information as well as information about tempo, expression, relative patterns of stress or emphasis (called metric accentuation), and differing durational values of notes and rhythms (called quantitas intrinseca). It is important to know and understand the multiple meanings of meter signatures since Classical-era composers chose meters discriminately and expected performers to understand ramifications of their total and various meanings—ramifications that had considerable impact on performance.

Regarding tempo, meter signatures with low-numbered denominators of the metric fraction convey slow tempos while meter signatures with higher numbers as the denominator of the metric fraction convey fast tempos. Consequently, meters such as 4/2 and 3/2 indicate a relatively slow tempo while meters such as 4/8 and 3/8 indicate a relatively fast tempo. Since the quarter note was the standard unit of pulse during the Classical era, meter signatures such as 4/4 and 3/4 indicate a medium tempo. The numerator of the metric fraction also plays a part in communicating tempo, but only in duple meters. A small number as the numerator, generally 2, indicates a faster tempo than a larger number, generally 4. Thus, 2/4 indicates a faster tempo than 4/4.

The entire range of meters and their corresponding expressive characteristics are presented and described by Kirnberger in his composition treatise of 1771 (relevant portions of which appear at the beginning of the section of quotations below). However, Classical-era composers did not generally avail themselves of such diversity. Instead, composers most often restricted themselves to a narrow range of meters (usually 3/4, 4/4, 2/4, C, ¢, 6/8, 9/8, and 12/8), relying on Italian terms to indicate relative tempo and to convey special qualities of expression. When less-common meters were used, however, their intent was clearly to communicate the tempo and expressive characteristics described by Kirnberger. For instance, metric fractions with low-numbered denominators such as 3/2, 4/2, and 6/4 were used for sacred music of a somber, serious, or weighty nature. Example A below is illustrative: the text is the second verse of Psalm 51, one of the so-called Penetential Psalms, which translates as "Wash me yet more from my iniquity, and cleanse me from my sin." The beginning of this Psalm (Example B, the text of which translates as "Have mercy upon me, O God, according to your loving kindness") is notated in the most common usage of 4/2, indicated by ¢; the actual 4/2 metric fraction was almost never used in the Classical era. The meter of four half notes to the measure, however, like 3/2, was used for sacred music and indicates a slower-moving tempo than 4/4. The 6/4 meter (Example C) is used to convey a slower tempo than 6/8, even with the addition of a relatively fast Italian tempo term; the Allegretto relates the character and relative speed of a quarter-note pulse, not of a dotted-half-note pulse.

The alla breve, or ¢ meter, was used quite extensively by Classical-era composers, although very seldom scored with four half notes per measure as in Example B. Kirnberger's seemingly contradictory comments about the tempo considerations of alla breve (stating first that it, like 3/2 and 6/4, has a weightier and slower tempo than 2/4, and then stating that it has the same tempo as 2/4) reveal a significant difference between this meter and the others. Alla breve represents a disparity between its implications of character (weighty, emphatic, solemn, serious) and tempo (somewhat fast). The other meters have a consistency of character and tempo. Perhaps because of the special circumstances of alla breve, it received considerable commentary in Classical-era sources (reflected in all the quotations following Kirnberger's), and composers in particular were concerned about its interpretation. Note, for example, C. P. E. Bach's concerns expressed in the letter written to his publisher, Johann Breitkopf. In general, most commentary specifies directly that ¢ indicates a tempo twice as fast as C; some of the commentary, however, merely specifies that ¢ indicates a fast tempo. All of the commentary indicates that alla breve has a direct influence on tempo.

The tempos of ¢ meters reflect movement of half-note, not quarter-note pulses, and Italian tempo terms that may be used in conjunction with the meters also apply to the half note. Therefore, the tempos of the Andante in the "Tuba mirum" from Mozart's *Requiem* (Example D) and the Adagio in Mozart's *Ave verum corpus* (Example E) should be gauged to represent the speed of an andante or adagio half note, with resulting tempos faster than those normally taken during present times.

Example A
W. A. Mozart, *Miserere* K85, second verse, measures 1–9

Example B
W. A. Mozart, *Miserere* K85, first verse, measures 1–4

Example C
Joseph Haydn, *Missa Sancti Nicolai*, Kyrie, measures 1–10

Example D
W. A. Mozart, *Requiem* K626, Tuba mirum, measures 1–11

Example E
W. A. Mozart, *Ave verum corpus*, measures 1–10

**Kirnberger, composition treatise (1771), Volume 2, Part 1, Chapter 4
"Tempo, Meter, and Rhythm"**

Those meters having larger values, such as *alla breve*, 3/2, and 6/4, have a weightier and slower tempo than those having smaller values, such as 2/4, 3/4, and 6/8, and these in turn are less animated than 3/8 or 6/16 meter. Thus, for example, a *loure* in 3/2 meter has a slower tempo than a *minuet* in 3/4 meter, and the latter is in turn slower than a *passepied* in 3/8 meter. . . .

2/2 meter, or rather *alla breve*, which is always designated by ¢ or 2, is most frequently used in church pieces, fugues, and elaborate choruses. It should be noted about this meter that it is very serious and emphatic, yet it is to be performed twice as fast as its note values indicate, unless a slower tempo is indicated by the adjectives *grave, adagio*, etc. . . .

2/4 meter has the same tempo as *alla breve* but is performed much more lightly. The distinction in performance between the two meters is too obvious for anyone to think that it makes no difference whether a piece is written in ¢ or 2/4. Consider, for instance, the following melodic phrase in both meters.

If this phrase above is performed as it should be, everyone will notice that it is much more serious and emphatic in *alla breve* (A) than in 2/4 (B), where it seems to be somewhat playful. . . .

2/4 meter as well as 6/8 derived from it are mostly used in chamber and theater pieces. In their natural tempos, sixteenth notes and a few thirty-second notes together are their shortest note values. . . .

2/8 meter is appropriate for only short humorous dance pieces because of its rapid tempo and its extreme lightness of execution. . . . It differs from 6/8 in this hurried nature of its tempo and lightness of execution. . . .

4/2 meter, or O, like 2/1 time, is no longer in use. . . . They are mentioned here only because now and then one sees ancient pieces in these meters. Instead of these, it is better to use 4/4 and 12/8 with the adjective *grave* to indicate the heavy tempo and emphatic character inherent in the former meters. If youthful composers should come across church pieces in *alla breve* time with four half notes between the bar lines, they must not be misled and conclude that the meter is 4/2. The fewer bar lines are used only as a convenience. . . .

4/4 meter, which is indicated by C, is of two types: used with the adjective *grave* in place of 4/2 just mentioned, in which case it is referred to as large 4/4 time, or simply as common meter, in which case it is referred to as small 4/4 time.

Large 4/4 time indicates extremely heavy execution and slow tempo, and, because of this, it is best used for church pieces, other choruses, and fugues. . . . To distinguish it from small 4/4 time, it should be written as 4/4 instead of C. The two meters have nothing in common except for their meter signatures.

Small 4/4 time has a livelier tempo and much lighter execution. . . .

4/8 is the lightest of quadruple meters in execution and tempo. . . .

3/2 meter is used frequently, especially in church pieces, to indicate ponderous and slow performance. . . .

The 9/4 meter that is derived from 3/2 is used much more rarely than the frequently seen 9/8. It is easily comprehended that the two meters are quite different with respect to tempo. In the church style, where a ponderous and emphatic execution is often combined with a subdued and slow tempo, 9/4 is much preferred to 9/8 time since a melody that is meant to convey a serious expression in the former meter can easily seem to be playful in the latter.

Because of its lighter execution, 3/4 meter is not as common as 3/2 in the church style. It is, however, used often in chamber and theatrical styles. . . .

3/8 meter has the lively tempo of a *passepied*, performed in a light but not entirely playful manner, and also often used in chamber and theatrical styles. . . .

[In summary,] it is to be noted that among meters with the same number of beats, the one having the longer or larger beats is naturally a bit more serious than the one having shorter beats. Thus 4/4 is less lively than 4/8, 3/2 more ponderous than 3/4, and this not as lively as 3/8.

For music that is solemn and filled with pathos, such as motets and other solemn church pieces, *alla breve* is especially appropriate. Large 4/4 time is suited for the emphatic and serious motion of stately choruses, fugues in church pieces, and to pieces where pomp and gravity are required. 3/2 is emphatic and serious as long as there are not too many short notes used. 4/4 is best used for lively and exhilarating expression that is still somewhat emphatic. 2/4 is also lively but, because of its lightness, can be used to express playfulness. 4/8 is altogether fleeting and because of this conveys no emphasis of 4/4. The character of 3/4 expresses gentleness and nobility, particularly when it consists only, or at least mostly, of quarter notes. 3/8 has a liveliness that is somewhat frolicsome.

Quantz, flute treatise (1752), Chapter 5
"Of Notes, their Values, Meter, Rests, and Other Musical Signs"

In four-four time it is important to note that if a stroke goes through the C as illustrated below, the notes receive a different value, so to speak, and must be played twice as fast as when the C has no stroke through it.

This meter is called *alla breve,* or *alla cappella.* Since many people through ignorance commit errors with respect to the meter just mentioned, it is advisable to make yourself thoroughly acquainted with this difference. It is a meter that is more common in the *galant* style of the present day than it was in former times. . . .

In the alla breve meter the half notes receive as much time as the quarter notes in common time, and the quarter notes take as much time as the eighth notes in common time; hence only the half notes are marked with the foot [as a time keeping measure].

Marpurg, clavier treatise (1755), Chapter 5 "Concerning Meter"

The 2/2 meter. This meter consists of two divisions, each of which contains a half note. It is called the Lesser Alla breve Meter and is indicated by a large 2 or a large C slashed through, although one also finds the plain, large C mistakenly given. Perhaps it would be altogether better indicated by 2/2. It is nothing other than a 4/2 meter divided in half. When one finds after the signature for this meter the words *alla cappella* or *alla breve,* this means that the beats ought to pass very quickly.

Holden, musical essay (1770), Part 1, Chapter 4
"Of time, and the Characters relating thereto"

If we conceive the entire measure to be continually bisected, which is the easiest and most natural sub-division, such a partition constitutes the species of our time, called double or common time; which we mark, in written music, when slow, by a large C after the cliff [sic]; when quicker, by the same C, with a bar drawn down through it.

Binns (Hoyle), dictionary (1770), "Time"

Common or duple Time is of two species. 1st, When every Bar or Measure is equal to a Semibreve [whole note], or its value in any combination of notes of a lesser quantity. 2nd, When every Bar is equal to a Minim [half note], or its value, in lesser notes. The movements of this kind of measure are various, but there are three common distinctions; the first slow, signified by this mark C; the second brisk, signified by ₵, the third very quick, signified by ₵.

C. P. E. Bach, letter to Johann Gottlob Immanuel Breitkopf (1779)

If the middle section of my *Heilig* . . . has already been printed, then the following Nota, or footnote, can be printed at the very end of the piece: Since the interpretation of Adagio is not the same everywhere, the middle section, in spite of the designated Alla breve meter, must be performed rather too slowly than too swiftly. . . . If the printing of this middle section has not yet been started, then set the usual four-quarter meter ᶜ instead of the Alla breve meter ₵.

Hook, keyboard treatise (c.1785), "The Time"

Formerly the Character C shewed a Movement was to be played Slow, ₵ a little faster, etc. In triple Time 3/2 marked a Slow Movement, 3/4 a little quicker etc. but Words now are commonly used to express with what slowness or quickness a Movement is to be played.

Aitken, Litanies (1787), Chapter 3
"Of Time in its various moods and how to beat them"

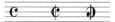

The First Mood, or Mark [above], is the Adagio Mood, which denotes a very slow Movement: The second Sort is the Largo Mood, half as quick again; The third Mood, is the Allegro Mood, or Retarted Mood, being as quick again as the Second.

J. C. Bach and F. P. Ricci, pianoforte treatise (c.1788), Part 5

ALLA BREVE, A CAPELLA, A measure in duple time, in fairly quick tempo in which the time unit is the whole note, or half note.

Türk, clavier treatise (1789), Chapter 1, Part 5
"Concerning the Tempo and Character of a Musical Composition"

Compositions in alla breve, or in what is called the tempo maggiore, are played once again as fast [as compositions in common time], so that an entire measure (of four quarters) in an allegro assai must not last any longer than a pulse beat.

Anonymous, *New Instructions for Playing the Harpsichord, Piano-forte, or Spinnet* (c.1790), "Of Time"

Common Time is of two Species; the first is when every Bar contains a Semibreve [whole note], or its value in lesser Notes, and is known by any of these Moods: C for slow movements, and ₵ or sometimes 𝄵 for brisker airs. Another Species of Common Time is where every Bar or Measure is equal to a Minum [half note], or its value in Lesser Notes, and is marked thus 2/4.

Triple Time is known by any one of these Characters, 3/2, 3/4, or 3/8. When marked thus 3/2 the Time is slow, when 3/4 brisk, and 3/8 quick.

Tromlitz, flute treatise (1791), Chapter 5
"Time signatures, and how the notes are divided and counted in them"

We have two kinds of meter: *duple* and *triple*; these are either *simple* or *compound*. *Duple* time is when the bar can be divided into two equal parts, and *triple* is when it cannot. *Simple duple* time is either four quarter notes or two quarter notes. Four-four time is indicated by a Latin C at the beginning of the system of staves after the clef; see (x); it is also called *common time* probably just as frequently as *simple time*. There is another time signature which indicates four quarter notes, it is denoted by a ₵ with a line through it, see (y). This time is called *alla Breve* or *alla Capella*, and goes as fast again as the normal quarter note beat, and is divided in two as in the two-four time. It is used for fugues or fugue-like movements, but is not very suitable to the *Galant* style of composition. Through the ignorance of copyists, however, mistakes are often encountered, since they draw a line through the C where there should be none, or draw a line through every C. To prevent this mistake, I think the best thing for the composer to do is to use the sign at (z) instead of the C with a line through it. This is called two-two time, and at the same time it determines the tempo more definitely, since it has just the same movement as two-four and is always divided in two equal parts. Two-four time is prefixed by two quarter notes; see (a). *Compound duple* time is either six quarter notes, six eighth notes, or twelve eighth notes; see (b). The first two kinds are divided in *two*, and the last in four equal parts; each part comprises *three* elements. These elements are quarter notes in the first, and eighth notes in the others.

Callcott, musical grammar (1806)

The barred Semicircle is used to denote a quicker Movement, and is called *Alla Breve*.

**Czerny, pianoforte treatise (1839), Volume 4, Chapter 2
"On the Proper Performance of all Beethoven's Works for the Piano Solo"**

Sonata op. 14, no. 2, 2nd movement
As the meter is *alla breve*, the time should be a tolerably lively *Allegretto*.

Sonata op. 27, no. 1, 1st movement

The *alla breve* measure being indicated, the whole must be played in moderate *Andante* time.

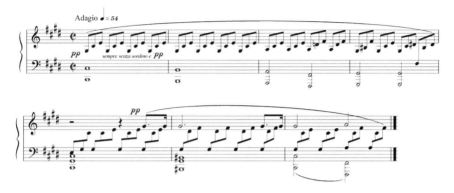

Sonata op. 29, no. 1, 3rd movement

As the *Allegretto* is in *alla breve* measure, the whole must be played a remarkably quick *Allegro molto*.

Sonata op. 30, no. 3, 2nd movement

As the time is *alla breve*, this *Adagio* must be performed as a moderate *Andante*, but with all that feeling of expression to which so noble and beautiful a melody must inevitably inspire every good player.

Chapter Two

CATEGORIES AND RATES OF TEMPO

There was a growing desire throughout the Classical era to be able to determine tempos with a reliable degree of specificity. Composers sought means to relate desired tempos to performers and performers felt obliged to understand tempos desired by composers and inherent in their compositions. Consequently, there were attempts, before the invention of the metronome in 1815 by Johann Nepomuk Maezel, to find a means by which a fixed rate of speed could be established and by which various speeds or degrees of fast and slow could then be related to one another. As a main result of these efforts, categories of tempo were established and explained, categories that were general and basic, as the authors admit, but nevertheless, categories that would affix terminology with recommended or idealized rates of tempo. In the following quotations, it is interesting to compare Türk (1789) with Quantz (1752) since Türk mentions and basis his recommendations on those of Quantz.

Quantz, flute treatise (1752), Chapter 17 "Of the Duties of Those Who Accompany or Execute the Accompanying or Ripieno Parts Associated with a Concertante Part" Section 7 "Of the Duties that all Accompanying Instrumentalists in General Must Observe"

It is certainly not one of the easiest matters in music to determine tempo. Therefore, it is all the more useful to establish the most definite rules possible. There is no doubt about this for those who understand the importance of the correct tempo for each piece of music and what great errors can be made. If definite rules exist and were followed, many pieces that are frequently garbled because of incorrect tempos would be correctly executed and would, therefore, bring more credit to composers than is often the case. With such rules, a composer, in absentia, could communicate his ideas in writing to another person who is to perform his composition. . . .

The means I consider to be the most useful as a guide for tempo is *the pulse at the hand of a healthy person.* I will attempt to give instructions as to how each of the various distinct tempos can be determined without much difficulty by use of the pulse beat. Indeed, I cannot boast of being the first to think of this means. However, it is certain that no one else has yet gone to the trouble of describing its methodology clearly and in detail, or of relating it to contemporary music. . . .

I do not pretend that an entire piece should be measured off in accordance with the pulse beat; this would be folly and impossible. My goal is simply to demonstrate how in at least two, four, six, or eight pulse beats, you can establish categories of tempo by yourself. After some practice, the nature of any tempo will so impress itself upon your mind, you will no longer find it necessary to consult the pulse beat.

Before I go further, I must discuss these various categories of tempo a bit more closely. There are so many in music, it would be impossible to note them all. However, there are main categories from which others can be derived. I will put forth four classes of these tempos as they occur in concerto, trio, and solo music, and will use these classes for further tempos. They are based on common or 4/4 time, as follows: 1) the *Allegro assai*, 2) the *Allegretto*, 3) the *Adagio cantabile*, 4) the *Adagio assai*. . . .

The *Allegro assai* is the fastest of the four main classes of tempo. The *Allegretto* is twice as slow. The *Adagio cantabile* is twice as slow as the *Allegretto*, and the *Adagio assai* twice as slow as the *Adagio cantabile*. . . .

In consideration of the term indicating tempo and the fastest notes used in passagework, and since no more than eight very fast notes can be executed in the time of a pulse beat, it follows that there is

In common time:
In an Allegro assai, the time of a pulse beat for each half note;
In an Allegretto, a pulse beat for each quarter note;
In an Adagio cantabile, a pulse beat for each eighth note;
And in an Adagio assai, two pulse beats for each eighth note.

In alla breve time there is:
In an Allegro, a pulse beat for each whole note;
In an Allegretto, a pulse beat for each half note;
In an Adagio cantabile, a pulse beat for each quarter note;
And in an Adagio assai, two pulse beats for each quarter note. . . .

If you strive to attain by arduous work the method just described, you not only can learn to give each note of each piece its proper time, but can in most instances discover the tempo intended by the composer.

I must, however, anticipate some objections that may be raised to this manner of determining tempos. One might object that the pulse beat is neither constant at each hour of the day, nor the same in every person, as would be required to accurately fix musical tempos with it. It will be said that the pulse beats more slowly in the morning before meal-time than in the afternoon after meal-time, and still faster at night than in the afternoon; likewise, that it is slower in a person inclined to melancholy than in an impetuous and jovial person. There may be some truth to these objections. Nevertheless, some definite standard can be set up to meet these circumstances. If you take the pulse beat as it is found from the midday meal until evening, and as it is found in a jovial and high-spirited and yet rather fiery and volatile person, or, if you will permit the expression, in a person of choleric-sanguine temperament, as your basis, you will have hit upon the correct pulse beat. A low-spirited, or melancholy, or cold and sluggish person could set the tempo in each piece a little faster than his pulse indicates. In case this is not sufficient, I will be still more explicit. Fix approximately eighty pulse beats to a minute as the standard. Eighty pulse beats in the fastest tempo of common time constitutes forty bars. A few pulse beats more or less make no difference in this regard.

Holden, musical essay (1770), Part 1, Chapter 4
"Of Time, and the Characters relating thereto"

For acquiring a proper idea of the natural sub-divisions of the measure in common time, the following observations will be found of great use to a learner. Upon applying a watch to our ear, and listening to its beats or pulses, we always find them proceeding by pairs, *i.e.* by two and two together; which is owing to the pulses being alternately a little stronger and weaker, even in the very best of watches; and they are often much more so, in the common sort. These pulses we can most easily count, 1,2,1,2,1,2, and so on; and in this way of counting, each single pulse may properly enough represent the time of a semiquaver [sixteenth note].

Türk, clavier treatise (1789), Chapter 1, Part 5
"Concerning the Tempo and Character of a Musical Composition"

Some teachers put all . . . degrees of tempo into four main categories. In the first belong all the fastest types, namely presto, allegro assai, etc.; in the second are the moderately fast, for example, allegro moderato, allegretto, etc.; in the third, the moderately slow, such as un poco adagio, larghetto, etc.; and in the fourth, the very slow, for example, largo, adagio molto, etc.

Others recognize only three main categories. . . . Still others make divisions into six categories. . . . In addition, some divide all compositions, in terms of tempo, into only two main categories. They only differentiate between those in fast tempos and those in slow tempos.

If one only knows, for example, that an allegro must be played faster than a largo, then one has a very uncertain concept of tempo. The question is, therefore: how fast is the tempo of an allegro assai and of relative tempos in other compositions? This question cannot be answered with assurance because other secondary factors cause modifications. For example, an allegro containing some thirty-second notes should not be played as fast as when the fastest passages consist of only eighth notes. An allegro for the church or in sacred cantatas, or in a trio or quartet in strict style, must be taken in a much more moderate tempo than an allegro for the theater or for the so-called chamber styles such as sinfonias, divertissements and so forth. An allegro with lofty, grave, and solemn ideas requires a slower and more emphatic pace than an allegro with the character of joviality.

These and other secondary considerations aside, Quantz teaches in his flute treatise that the duration of a pulse beat should be given to every half measure of an allegro assai in common or 4/4 time (he bases this on the pulse beat of a healthy and somewhat fiery person), a pulse beat to every quarter note in an allegretto, a pulse beat for every eighth note in an adagio cantabile (larghetto), and two pulse beats for every eighth in an adagio assai. . . .

Even though many objections can be raised against this standard, as Quantz himself remarks, and furthermore, even when the difference between an allegro assai and an adagio molto is thought to be greater than it should be, I am nevertheless very inclined to recommend his rule to beginners, for they will at least learn that an allegro assai must be played approximately once again as fast as an allegretto, etc. Through these rules they also learn to know how fast the tempo of various compositions should be.

Another resource, similar to that recommended by Quantz, is probably the pocket watch, which has a moderately fast tick, or which has approximately 260 to 270 ticks in a minute, and which can be used to determine a tempo. In this case, two ticks must be allowed for every quarter note in an allegro assai and four ticks for an allegretto, etc., and as a consequence, there are eight ticks for a common time 4/4 measure in an allegro assai. The other species of notes and measures can therefore be measured according to these.

Corri, singing treatise (1810), Lesson 10 "Tempo Andante"

The nearest measure we know of [in an andante tempo] is to make a Quaver [eighth note] the length of the pulse of a Watch; then a Crotchet [quarter note] will be equal to two pulses, a Minum [half note] to four, etc., etc., and therefore the criterion of Andante is at the rate of two pulses for one Crotchet [quarter note].

TEMPO TERMS

Valuable information about relative rates of tempo comes from source material that lists common Italian terms in groupings of speed and in sequential order from either fast to slow or slow to fast. In addition, definitions of terms from dictionaries and alphabetical listings from various sources confirm the widespread understanding of tempo during the Classical era.

The sequential listings, such as those presented by Leopold Mozart and Isaac Nathan, indicate gradations of tempo between terms of relatively similar speed. A performer is, therefore, able to differentiate between, for instance, Adagio and Largo (Largo being slower than Adagio). The definitions and annotations reveal tempo in terminology directly related to speed (such as fast, slow, etc.) and also in terminology related to expressive characteristics of the music (such as playful or mournful). The combined terminology allows the performer to attach a mood or emotional feeling to music and thus discern a rate of tempo likely to be in keeping with a composer's intentions.

It is interesting to discover that some of the terms are treated differently today than during the Classical era. Vivace, for instance, is typically interpreted as faster than allegro today, while during the Classical era it was comparable to allegro or slower. Note John Holden's comment that Vivace is "near the same, but not so brisk a movement as Allegro," and Daniel Gottlob Türk's observation that "compositions which are marked Vivace are usually played too fast." The understanding of a Classical-era Vivace has considerable impact on compositions containing both allegro and vivace in close proximity. For example, the Gloria from Haydn's *Mass in C* of 1796 ("Paukenmesse") is in three sections—fast, slow, fast—with the first fast section marked Vivace and the last section marked Allegro. Similarly, the three portions of the Credo from Haydn's *Mass in B-flat* of 1801 ("Schöpfungsmesse") are marked Vivace, Adagio, Allegro. If the Vivace sections are taken as they might be today, faster than the Allegro sections, the movements seem out of balance. This is because the harmonic motion (i.e., the speed or rate of harmonic change) in the Vivace sections is faster than in the Allegro sections; the Vivace sections are rather dense harmonically, with rapid changes of harmony, while the Allegro sections are sparser, with slower changes of harmony. If, then, the Vivace sections with faster harmonic motion are taken at a faster tempo than the Allegro sections with slower harmonic motion, either the Vivace sections seem too cluttered and frenetic or the Allegro sections seem too leisurely and lifeless. The balance between the sections seems upset or awkward. However, if the Vivace sections are taken at a slower tempo (while, nevertheless, with a vivacious articulation) than the Allegro sections, the two sections seem balanced in relation to each other, and the movement as a whole has a logical pacing.

Marpurg, clavier treatise (1755), Chapter 5 "Concerning Meter"

One must know how to determine the length or brevity of time in which, for example, a whole note, a half note, etc., should be played, and, consequently, the degree of rapidity or slowness with which this whole note or half note should be rendered. This means that one must know the movement, or the tempo, of the measure. The movement is usually indicated by certain Italian terms; of these, we shall give the most common pertaining to the three main degrees of fast and slow movement:

Very fast or very rapid	Fast or rapid	Not so or less fast, moderately rapid
Presto, It. Prestissimo	Allegro	Allegretto
Allegro assai	Veloce	Poco Allegro
Allegro di molto	Vivace	Poco Vivace
Velocissimo	Poco presto, etc.	Poco Veloce
Vivacissimo, etc.		Moderato
		Allegro ma non troppo
		(non tanto, non presto), etc.

Very slow	Slow	Not so or less slow
Adagio assai	Adagio	Andante
Adagio di molto	Largo	Andantino
Largo assai or di molto	Lento, etc.	Larghetto
Lento assai or di molto, etc.		Poco Adagio
		Poco Largo
		Poco Lento, etc.

L. Mozart, violin treatise (1756), Chapter 1, Section 3
"Of the Duration or Value of the Notes, Rests, and Dots, together with an Explanation of all Musical Signs and Technical Words"

Prestissimo indicates the quickest tempo, and *Presto Assai* is almost the same.

Presto means quick, and *Allegro Assai* is but little different.

Molto Allegro is slightly less than *Allegro Assai*, but is quicker than

Allegro, which, however, indicates a cheerful, though not too hurried tempo, especially when moderated by adjectives and adverbs, such as:

Allegro, ma non tanto, or *non troppo,* or *moderato,* which is to say that one is not to exaggerate the speed. For this a lighter and livelier, but at the same time somewhat more serious, and rather broader bowing is demanded than in a quicker tempo.

Allegretto is rather slower than *Allegro,* usually having something pleasant, charming, neat, and playful, and much in common with *Andante.* It must therefore be performed in a pleasing, amusing, and playful manner. . . .

Vivace means lively, and *Spiritoso* is to say that one has to play with understanding and spirit, and *Animoso* has nearly the same meaning. All three kinds are the mean between quick and slow, and a musical composition before which these words are placed must show us the same in various respects.

Moderato, moderately, temperately; neither too fast nor too slow. This is indicated by the piece itself, during the course of which we cannot but perceive its leisurely character.

Tempo Commodo and *Tempo Giusto,* again throw us back on the piece itself, and tell us that we must play neither too fast nor too slowly, but in a proper, convenient, and natural tempo.

Sostenuto means drawn out, or rather held back, and the melody not exaggerated. We must therefore in such cases use a serious, long, and sustained bowing, and keep the melody flowing smoothly.

Maestoso: with majesty; deliberately, not hurried. . . .

Andante: walking. The very words tell us that the piece must be allowed to take its own natural course; especially if *Un poco allegretto* be added.

Lento or *Lentemente*: quite leisurely.

Adagio: slow.

Adagio Pesante: a mournful *Adagio*, must be played somewhat more slowly, and with great tranquility.

Largo: a still slower tempo, to be performed with long strokes and much tranquility.

Grave: sadly and seriously, and therefore very slowly. One must, indeed, indicate the meaning of the word *Grave* by means of long, rather heavy and solemn bowing and by means of consistent prolonging and maintaining of the various notes.

Billings, *The New-England Psalm-Singer* (1770), Chapter 6 "Of Time in its various Moods"

There are several Sorts of Moods for Time. . . . The First of these is called Adagio, which is a very slow Movement. A Semibreve [whole note] in this Mood is precisely the Time of four Seconds. . . . The second Mood or Mark is called the Largo Mood, being half as quick again as the former, so that three Minims [half notes] in the Mood are to be perform'd in the same Time that two Minims are in the Adagio mood. . . . The Third Mood or Mark is called the Allegro Mood, being as quick again as the first, so that Minims in this Mood are Sung to the Time of Seconds.

Holden, musical essay (1770), Part 1, Chapter 5 "Miscellaneous Explanations"

To give a better idea of the comparative degrees of movement, denoted by those words which chiefly relate to the time, the following list may be of some service; where the slowest movement is placed uppermost, and the others are gradually quicker, to the bottom.

Adagio, Adagio, very slow.
Adagio.
Largo, or *Lento.*
Larghetto.
Andante.

Andantino.
Allegretto, or *Poco Allegro,* or *Vivace.* [*]
Allegro.
Presto.
Prestissimo, very quick.

[*] A lively and spirited manner; near the same, but not quite so brisk a movement, as *Allegro.*

Binns (Hoyle), dictionary (1770)

ADAGIO, or by way of abbreviation ADAG or AD, is the slowest movement in Musick, especially if the word be repeated twice over, as *Adagio, Adagio.*

ALLEGRO, or by way of abbreviation ALL, signifies that it is to be played in a sprightly, gay, brisk, and lively manner; yet it must be played without hurry or precipitation, or the performer will find that the notes will not be heard clear and distinct as they ought to be. Piu Allegro is when the piece is to be performed still quicker than it was before the word Piu was added to it. But when the word Poco is added to it, it signifies that it must be played a degree slower than the word Allegro alone does require.

ALLEGRETTO, is a degree faster [sic] than Allegro, but seldom used, as Piu Allegro is the same.

ANDANTE, this word has respect chiefly to the Thorough Bass, and signifies that in playing, the Time must be kept very just and exact, and every note made very equal and distinct the one from the other; sometimes you will find the word Largo jointed with it as

ANDANTE LARGO, or LARGO ANDANTE, which is as much to say, that though the Musick must be performed slow, yet the Time must be observed very exactly, and the sound of each note made very distinct, and separated one from another.

ANIMATO, is to give life to, to quicken, to enliven, or to inspire with the power of harmony, and must be played a degree faster than Largo, but slower than Allegro.

GRAVE, or GRAVEMENT, denotes a very slow motion, somewhat faster than Adagio, but slower than Largo.

LARGETTO, or LARGHETTO, denotes a movement a degree quicker than Largo.

LENTO, or LENTEMENTE, both denote a slow movement; as Tres Lentemente is very slow, and signifies a movement between Largo and

Grave, the same as when the word Largo is twice repeated: but Lentemente alone is much the same as Largo.

MODERATO, is to sing or play with moderation, judgment, care, and discretion.

PRESTO, intimates to perform very quick or fast; Prestissimo is excessive quick; or Men Presto, not too quick; and Poco Presto not very quick.

VIVACE, or VIVACISSIMO, is as much as to say, with life and spirit. By this word is commonly understood, a degree of movement between Largo and Allegro, but more inclined to the latter than the former.

Rousseau, dictionary (1779), "Movement"

MOVEMENT, A degree of quickness or slowness, which the character of the piece we execute gives to the measure. Every kind of measure has a movement peculiar to itself, and which is designated in Italian by these words, Tempo giusto. But besides this, there are five principal modifications of movement, which, in the order from slow to quick, are expressed by the words largo, adagio, andante, allegro, presto; and these words in English are rendered, by slow, moderate, pleasing, gay, quick. We must, however, take notice, that, the movement always having much less precision in the French music, the words that express it have a sense much more vague than in the Italian.

Each of these degrees is sub-divided and modified into others also, in which we must distinguish those which express the degree only of quickness or slowness, as larghetto, andantino, allegretto, prestissimo, and those, moreover, which mark the character and expression of the air, as agitato, vivace, gustoso, combrio, &c. The first may be rendered by all the musicians, but there are only those which have sentiment and taste, who feel and render the others.

Hook, keyboard treatise (c.1785), "A DICTIONARY Explaining such Greek, Latin, Italian & French Words as are used in Music"

Adagio	Slow Time.
Allegro	Brisk.
Andante	Signifies that the Notes are to be played distinctly.
Grave	Very Slow.
Larghetto	Slow.

Largo	Slow. Slower than Larghetto, but not as slow as Grave.
Moderato	Moderately quick.
Presto	Fast or quick.
Tempo Giusto	In Just or equal Time.
Vivace	With Life or Spirit.

J. C. Bach and F. P. Ricci, pianoforte treatise (c.1788), Part 5

The DEGREE OF FAST OR SLOW speed that befits a particular kind of measure, depends, in the first place, on the value of the time unit. One may agree that a measure containing a whole note is articulated with greater firmness and sustaining power than the one consisting of quarter notes. Secondly, it is the character of the melody—provided it is well composed—from which one derives the true speed of the movement; this is the case, in particular, where there is no tempo indication at the head of the tune, or where the words, *Tempo Giusto*, mark the movement.

Otherwise, there are five principal modifiers for movements; in the order from slow to fast, they are called: LARGO, ADAGIO, ANDANTE, ALLEGRO, PRESTO; their equivalent terms in French are: LENT, POSEMENT, MODERE, GAI, VÎTE. . . .

At this point I should explain the most commonly used Italian terms for tempo modifications, because one should understand them when playing music; the composer put them there for good reason. They are in alphabetical order as follows.

ADAGIO. Found at the head of a tune, this Italian term means at ease, poised, indicating the manner in which the movement of the melody should be conceived.

AFFANNOSO expresses languor, weariness, sadness, and discouragement; it also depicts despair or bewilderment of contrasting passions. One has to imagine and feel vividly the character and carry it with proper degree of expression into the performance.

AFFETTUOSO, CON AFFETTO (in Fr. *Affectueusement*). A movement between *Andante* and *Adagio* in the character of an affectionate, tender, and sweet song.

AGITATO. Strong agitated movement.

ALLA BREVE, A CAPELLA, (in Fr. *Gros-Fa*). A measure in duple time, in fairly quick tempo in which the time unit is the whole note, or half note.

ALLA ZOPPA. A movement in duple time with syncopated, affected rhythms, unequal note values, like a limping march.

ALLEGRETTO (in Fr. *un peu Gaiment*). A tempo marking which is less gay, more moderate and less fast than *Allegro*.

ALLEGRO, (in Fr. *Gai*) is the fourth among the five principal degrees of movement. It indicates gay.

AMOROSO (in Fr. *Tendrement*). Slow, sweet movement filled with feeling and tender expression.

ANDANTE (in Fr. *Modéré*) is the third in the five categories of movements from slow to fast. It is in marked tempo without, however, becoming gay, best expressed with the term moderate.

ANDANTINO (in Fr. *Gracieusement*) is less gay than Andante.

ARIOSO. The movement of a sustained, broadly developed, and affected Aria.

A TEMPO, A BATTUTA (in Fr. *Mesuré*). These words mark the return to measured tempo.

BALLABILE (in Fr. *Dansant*) means dance-like.

BRILLANTE (in Fr. *Brilliant*). A very fast movement with gaiety reaching the limit.

CANTABILE (in Fr. *Chantable*), in singing style.

COMMODO (in Fr. *Commodement*) indicates a pleasant easy movement.

CON ANIMA (in Fr. *Passioné*). With touching, tender expression.

CON BIZARRIA or BIZARRO (in Fr. *Bisarrement*). The intensification of gaiety in the movement, playing at times in a strong, straightforward manner, other times sweetly, but always in accordance with the diverse expressions of the piece.

CON BRIO (in Fr. *Légèrement*). Movement between *Allegro* and *Presto*.

CON MOTO. Faster and more animated tempo.

CON PORTAMENTO (in Fr. *Pompeux*). Stately without becoming slow.

EXPRESSIVO (in Fr. *Expressif*), signifies that the ideas are to be expressed lively with energy.

FLEBILE, is best expressed with the French term *Lent*, and *Plaintif*, or *Lamentable*.

GAJO. Gay without becoming fast.

GRAVE (in Fr. *Pathétique*), marks a slow movement to be played with solemnity and weightiness of expression.

GRAZIOSO, like *Amoroso* but less slow.

GUSTOSO alludes to the moving, agreeable character of a melody that requires a certain animated accent in the expression.

LARGHETTO. A movement somewhat less slow than *Largo*, slower than *Andante*, approaching *Andantino*.

LARGO (in Fr. *Lent*) is the slowest movement indication.

LEGGIARDO corresponds with the French terms, *Gaillardement, Gaiment*.

LENTO. A movement between *poised* and *moderate*; but not the one which is marked in French *Lent*, for that term signifies *Largo* with different meaning of time and measure.

MAESTOSO. Majestic and gay movement combining sweetness with majesty.

MODERATO signifies that the measure and movement has to stay in a happy medium between slow and fast, without exaggeration; herein lies its difference of character.

PONATO (in Fr. *Pointé*) indicates that emphasis should be given to the point, that is, to the unequal proportions between alternating long and short notes.

PRESTISSIMO (in Fr. *Très-vîte*). A movement that is faster and more pressed than *Presto*.

PRESTO (in Fr. *Vîte*). The most animated among the five principal movements of music.

PRESTO QUANTO SI PUO, CON FURIA (in Fr. *Impétueux*). Passionate, fiery kind of movement.

RALLENTATO, RALLENTANDO (in Fr. *Languissant*) means the control of the song and its measure by gradually holding back the speed established in the course of the piece.

RISOLUTO. Fast and resolute character.

RISUEGLIATO (in Fr. *Réveillé*). This term indicates that after having played languidly, like in a dream, the expression has to be revived, revitalized through quicker and gayer playing.

SCHERZANDO (in Fr. *Sautillant*). A gay and playful air.

SCIOLTO (in Fr. *Delié*) means prompt and detached movement.

SOSTENUTO (in Fr. *Soutenu*) intends to say: in pompous emphatic manner of playing and with a certain gravity, but, at the same time, with presence of, and well articulated expression.

SPICCATO (in Fr. *Coupé*). A movement approaching *Allegro* but played with the clear separation or detachment of notes.

SPIRITUOSO (in Fr. *Saillant*) improperly CON SPIRITO, means more animated than *Allegro*, but less than *Presto*.

STACCATO, TRONCO (in Fr. *Détaché*). A tempo between *Adagio* and *Andante* played with dry and well-separated articulation of notes.

STENTATO, STENDANDO (in Fr. *Peiné*). In forced manner.

TEMPO DI PRIMA, calls for returning to the first tempo from which the movement deviated in the course of the piece.

VELOCE (in Fr. *Vif*) A movement between *Allegro* and *Presto*.

VIVACE (in Fr. *Hardiment*). Bold, daring performance with ample fire.

Türk, clavier treatise (1789), Chapter 1, Part 5
"Concerning the Tempo and Character of a Musical Composition"

Because faster and slower tempos especially contribute much toward the expression of the various passions and feelings in all their ramifications, there are generally accepted gradations of the former, and to define them various words, to a large degree Italian, have been chosen.

The most important of these are as follows:
Presto, rapidly; *allegro*, swiftly, that is, not quite as quickly as *presto*; *veloce*, quick; *vivace*, vivaciously; *commodo, (comodo)*, easy-going, leisurely, not fast; *moderato*, moderately; *tempo giusto*, at the proper tempo; *maestoso*, majestically, lofty, and as far as tempo is concerned, slower rather than faster; *andante*, essentially walking or walking in step, and in music, a moderate tempo, which is neither slow nor fast; *grave*, seriously, and consequently more or less slow; *adagio*, slow; *lento*, somewhat similar to *adagio*, but not quite as slow; *largo*, with breadth, spacious, expansive, and consequently slow (almost slower and usually more serious than *adagio*). To these terms which indicate tempo, one can also add *alla breve*, or every note once again as fast as usual.

Other terms are derived from these main ones 1) in order to show a very high degree of speed or slowness (in other words, superlatives), for example: *Prestissimo*, very, extremely rapid, the fastest of all; *allegrissimo*, very, extremely swift, as swiftly as possible; and in the same fashion: *velocissimo*, *vivacissimo*, *adagissimo*, etc.; 2) in order to indicate a smaller degree (as a diminutive), for example: *allegretto*, somewhat fast; *commodetto*, somewhat leisurely; *larghetto*, somewhat slowly; *andantino*, somewhat, and therefore not too much, of a walking tempo, that is somewhat slower than *andante*. . . .

I have especially noted that compositions which are marked Vivace are usually played too fast. Presumably this term, which particularly specifies the kind of execution, is incorrectly applied only to the tempo.

Anonymous, *New Instructions for Playing the Harpsichord, Piano-forte, or Spinnet* **(c.1790), "A Dictionary of Foreign Words commonly used in Music"**

Adagio, very slow.

Andante, exact, distinct, and moderately slow.

Andantino, more slow and distinct than Andante.

Allegro, brisk, lively.

Grave, very slow and solemn.

Largo, or *Lento*, slow.

Moderato, moderately quick.

Presto, fast or quick.

Tempo Giusto, in just or equal Time.

Vivace, with life and spirit.

Tromlitz, flute treatise (1791), Chapter 5 "Time Signatures"

How fast or slow a movement is supposed to be can be determined by the superscription written at the beginning of the piece, such as *Presto, Prestissimo, Allegro assai, Allegro di molto*; these indicate a very rapid tempo. *Allegro, Poco presto, Vivace* are used for fast tempos. *Allegretto, poco Allegro, poco Vivace, Moderato, Allegro ma non troppo, non Presto* are found on less quick pieces. To the above-named movements belong everything that is joyful, fanciful, bold, haughty, etc. A very slow tempo is indicated by *Adagio assai, Adagio di molto, Largo di molto*, and suchlike. To slow tempos belong *Adagio, Largo, Lento*, and finally to moderately slow ones *Andante, Andantino, Larghetto, poco Adagio, poco Largo, poco Lento*. Among these belong everything mournful, melancholy, plaintive, modest, etc. To these tempo indications should be added words describing the emotional state and inner character of the piece, such as *affettuoso, amoroso, arioso, cantabile, grazioso, maestoso, mesto, scherzando*, and others.

Altenburg, trumpet and kettledrum treatise (1795), Chapter 11 "On Clarino Playing and the Style of Execution Required Thereby. Some Rules"

There are certain technical terms which indicate the tempo or the motion of a piece, others which indicate its proper character, as to whether it is happy or sad, &c.; and [from these terms one] always [chooses] the required style of execution.

The tempo is indicated by the following technical terms:

(1) *Adagio assai* or *di molto*, that is, very slow.
(2) *Largo, adagio, lento,* slow.
(3) *Larghetto, andante, poco andante, andantino,* rather slow.
(4) *Moderato, allegretto, poco allegro, poco vivace, allegro ma non troppo, allegro non molto* or *allegro moderato,* moderate or not too fast.
(5) *Allegro,* brisk; *poco presto,* rather fast; *veloce,* fast; *vivace,* lively.
(6) *Presto,* fast; *prestissimo, presto assai, allegro assai, allegro di molto,* very fast.

The character and [style of] execution are indicated by the following technical terms:

Affetuoso or *con affetto,* moving, with emotion; *amabile, amarevole,* pleasant, lovely.
Brillante, lively, cheerful, shimmering; *brioso, con brio,* lively, boisterous.
Cantabile, singing.
Dolce, gentle, pleasant.
Expressivo, con espressione, expressive.
Furioso, furious; *con fuoco,* with fire.
Grave, serious; *grazioso,* agreeable, charming; *gustoso, con gusto,* with taste.
Innocentemente, innocently.
Lagrimoso, lamentoso, lamenting; *legato,* tied; *lugubre,* sad; *lusingando,* flattering.
Maestoso, stately; *mesto,* sad.
Pastorale, pastoral; *piacévole,* agreeable; *pomposo,* splendid.
Risoluto, resolute, bold.
Scherzando, jesting; *sostenuto,* sustained; *spiritoso, con spirito,* spirited fiery; *staccato,* tongued separately.
Tenero, con tenerezza, tenderly; *tempo giusto,* in the proper tempo; *tranquillamente,* contentedly, calmly.
Vivo, vivace, lively;
    . . . and so on.

Chapter Two

Clementi, pianoforte treatise (1801), "Explanation of Various Terms"

The *degree* of velocity in every composition is ascertained by some *Italian* word or words prefixed to it: as *Adagio, Poco Allegro*, etc. We shall annex a list of the terms mostly in use; beginning by the *slowest* degree, which is *Adagio*, and gradually proceeding to the *quickest*, which is *Prestissimo*.

1. Adagio	6. Andantino	11. Maestoso	16. Spiritoso
2. Grave	7. Andante	12. Con commodo	17. Con Brio
3. Largo	8. Allegretto	13. Allegro	18. Con Fuoco
4. Lento	9. Moderato	14. Vivace	19. Presto
5. Larghetto	10. Tempo Giusto	15. Con spirito	20. Prestissimo

**Corri, singing treatise (1810),
"A Dictionary explaining such Italian Words as occur in Vocal Music"**

Allegro	Gay, lively, quick.
Allegretto	No so quick
Andante	[See above]
Grave	The slowest time.
Largo or Lento	A degree less slow than grave.
Larghetto	Not so slow as largo.
Moderato	Between slow and quick.
Presto	Fast.
Prestissimo	Very fast.
Vivace	Lively Quickly.

Busby, musical manual (1828)

Adagio	Slow, but less so than Largo.
Alla Breve	A species of common time; a measure of two breves, formerly called Tempo di Cappella, and in general use; but now seldom employed.
Allegretto	The diminutive of allegro: less quick than Allegro.
Allegro	Quick, even to rapidity. An adjective applied both to lively and to impetuous movements; and often joined with other words expressive of the feeling meant to be excited; as Allegro Vivace, quick and lively.
Andante	A word denoting that the movement to which it applies is to be performed in a gentle, delicate, and tender style. It is sometimes used adjectively, as, when we say an Andante movement.

Andantino	Somewhat less slow than Largo.
Grave	Slow and solemn.
Larghetto	Somewhat less slow than Largo.
Largo	Slow.
Lento	Slow.
Presto	Quick.
Vivace	A word implying a brisk and cheerful style of performance.

Nathan, singing treatise (1836), Chapter 12 "On Time"

Terms to denote the various Degrees of Time, etc.

Grave	The slowest time.
Largo, or Lento	A degree slower than grave.
Larghetto	Not so slow as Largo.
Poco Largo	Rather slow.
Poco Piu Lento	A little slower.
Largo di Molto	Very slow.
Molto Adagio	Very slow.
Adagio	Slow with grace and embellishments.
Adagio Assai	More slow.
Lamentevole	Slow and mournful.
Lentemente	Somewhat slower.
Lentando	The notes are to be sung with increasing slowness.
Andante	Rather slow, distinct, tender and soothing.
Andantino	Somewhat slower than Andante.
Allegro	Quick.
Allegretto	Moderately quick.
Poco piu Allegro	A little quicker.
Allegro de Molto	Very quick.
Allegro Assai	More quick.
Un poco meno Allegro	A little less gaily.
Allegro non tanto	Not too quick.
Non troppo Allegro	Not very quick.
Moderato	Between slow and quick.
Tempo Ordinario	In the usual time.
Presto	Gaily, quick.
Piu Presto	Very quick and gay.

Prestissimo	Extremely quick, with fury.
Veloce	In rapid time.
Marcato	With marked time.
Tempo Primo	Resume the former time.
Tempo Giusto	In exact time.

Schindler, biography of Beethoven (1840), Musical Section, Part Two

Regarding the history of the Maelzel metronome, we must recall that there were two separate and quite different machines. The first [1815] was a pyramid about twelve inches high with a pendulum . . . rod that had only the numbers 50 to 160. . . . As early as the 1820s Maelzel had his brother manufacture a smaller machine, about eight inches high; its pendulum had numbers from 40 to 208. The differences between the two types soon gave rise to complaints that any given tempo mark was ambiguous unless it specifically stated which of the two machines was implied.

We should add that Beethoven's metronome marks are according to the first machine. The score of the A major symphony that was published in the 1820s by Steiner & Co. has metronome marks, assigned by the composer, that are quite different. They are for the smaller machine, and indicate a slower tempo throughout. This proves not only that the same number on the pendulum rod of both does not produce the same tempo, but also that the smaller machine gives in general a much quicker beat.

Does not this circumstance answer the question so often asked: Why did Beethoven neglect to use the metronome? Actually, he himself assigned metronome marks to only two of his works: the great sonata opus 106 . . . and the ninth symphony. In connection with the latter, there occurred an event that illustrates the master's low opinion of the metronome. He asked me to make a copy for London of the metronome notations he had a few days before made for Mainz, but the list had been mislaid and we could not find it. London was waiting and there was no time to lose, so the master had to undertake the unpleasant task all over again. But lo, no sooner had he finished than I found the first version. A comparison between the two showed a difference in all the movements. Then the master, losing patience, exclaimed, "No more metronome! Anyone who can feel the music right does not need it, and for anyone who cannot, nothing is of any use."

RHYTHMIC DENSITY INFLUENCING TEMPO

Classical-era composers generally wrote note values compatible with meter signatures. For example, in 4/4 or 3/4 the rhythmic values of the composition normally consisted of eighth, quarter, and half notes—with only occasional use of sixteenth notes. In 2/8, 3/8, or 9/8 the rhythmic values normally consisted of sixteenth, eighth, and dotted eighth notes—with occasional use of thirty-second notes. The basic texture of the rhythms, therefore, would center around the note unit indicated by the denominator of the metric fraction (i.e., 4/4 = quarter notes, while 3/8 = eighth notes).

With a basic compatibility of meter and rhythm, tempo was standard and determined by the meter signature and any Italian term that may be affixed; rhythmic texture was not a factor. If, however, the rhythmic values and meter signature of a composition were not compatible (i.e., if the general note values of a composition were either shorter or longer than the note value represented by the denominator of the metric fraction), the rhythmic values became a factor in determining tempo: very short note values indicated a slower than normal tempo, while very long note values indicated the reverse, expressive considerations discussed below notwithstanding. Consequently, a composition with a meter signature of 4/4 or 3/4 containing a profusion of short-note values (eighth, sixteenth, and occasional thirty-second notes) would require a slower tempo than a composition with a meter of 4/4 or 3/4 and eighth, quarter, and half-note values (regardless of any Italian tempo term).

The following two Agnus Dei movements illustrate. The first Agnus Dei (Example A) requires a tempo considerably slower than the second Agnus Dei (Example B).

Example A
W. A. Mozart, *Missa Brevis in C* K259 (Organ Solo Mass), Agnus Dei,
measures 1–6

Example B
Joseph Haydn, *Missa Brevis in B-flat* (Little Organ Mass), Agnus Dei,
measures 1–10

In addition to metric and rhythmic compatibility influencing the basic character of tempo, density of rhythmic values affected tempo related to performance concerns of technical facility and musical intelligibility. Short notes performed at too fast a tempo could sound technically messy or musically jumbled. Long notes performed too slowly could sound boring or musically disconnected. Consequently, performers were admonished to not perform a general texture of short rhythmic values too rapidly or a general texture of long rhythmic values too slowly. As stated by Kirnberger, "*tempo giusto* [the correct tempo] is determined by the meter and by the longer and shorter note values of a composition."

Quantz, flute treatise (1752), Chapter 12 "Of the Manner of Playing the Allegro"

No attempt ought to be made to play the Allegro more quickly than the passage-work can be played with uniform quickness, lest you be forced to play some passages, perhaps more difficult than others, more slowly, which causes a disagreeable alteration of the tempo. The tempo must be set in accordance with the most difficult passage-work. . . .

Just as the Allegro in duple time has two principal categories of tempo, namely a fast and a moderate one, the same is also true of triple meters, such as three-four, three-eight, six-eight, twelve-eight, etc. For example, if in three-four time only eighth notes occur, in three-eight only sixteenths, or in six-eight or twelve-eight only eighths, the piece is in the fastest tempo. If, however, there are sixteenth or eighth triplets in three-four time, thirty-second or sixteenth-note triplets in three-eight time, or sixteenth notes in six-eight and twelve-eight time, they are in the more moderate tempo, which must be played twice as slow as the former. To get to the main point, namely how each of the types of meter cited can be put into its proper tempo by using the pulse beat, it must be noted that it is most important to consider both the word indicating the tempo at the beginning of the piece and the fastest notes used in the passage-work.

C. P. E. Bach, clavier treatise (1753), Part 1, Chapter 3 "Performance"

The pace of a composition, which is usually indicated by several well-known Italian expressions, is based on its general content as well as on the fastest notes and passages contained in it. Due consideration of these factors will prevent an allegro from being rushed and an adagio from being dragged.

Marpurg, clavier treatise (1755), Chapter 5 "Concerning Meter"

With regard to the [meter] signature, an error often arises whereby the plain, large "C" is confused with the " ₵ " In such a case one must judge the nature of the piece from the most rapid notes and from the caesuras, sections, and cadences occurring therein, in order to know whether it belongs to the meter of two or of four divisions.

Kirnberger, composition treatise (1771), Volume 2, Part 1, Chapter 4 "Tempo, Meter, and Rhythm"

Regarding note values, dance pieces involving sixteenth and thirty-second notes have a slower tempo than those that tolerate only eighth and at most sixteenth notes as the fastest note values in the same meter. Thus, for example, a sarabande in 3/4 meter has a slower tempo than a minuet, even though both are written in the same meter.

Thus the *tempo giusto* is determined by the meter and by the longer and shorter note values of a composition. Once the young composer has a feeling for this, he will soon understand to what degree the adjectives *largo, adagio, andante, allegro, presto,* and their modifications *larghetto, andantino, allegretto,* and *prestissimo* add to or take away from the fast or slow motion of the natural tempo. He will soon be able not only to write in every type of tempo, but also in such a way that this tempo is captured quickly and correctly by the performers.

Türk, clavier treatise (1789), Chapter 1, Part 5 "Concerning the Tempo and Character of a Musical Composition"

The best way presently available [to achieve proper tempo in performance] is for the composer, on his part, to indicate the tempo as exactly as possible; on the other hand, the player does have need of his own feeling, power of judgment, and long practice in order to choose the correct tempos, especially in compositions he does not know, for all the possible rules which could be given concerning this, in all likelihood, would not be completely sufficient. Nevertheless, the already somewhat skilled player, after a short but much to be recommended survey of the composition, can with some certainty find the right tempo from the note values, figures, passages, and the like.

EXPRESSIVE FACTORS INFLUENCING TEMPO

As can be gleaned from the reading of primary source material about virtually every aspect of performance practice, including meter influencing tempo and tempo terms, music of the Classical era was not devoid of expressive characteristics. Indeed, feeling and emotion were essential components of performance, and extra-musical aspects of expression were important to both composers and performers—with character, mood, and purpose of a composition playing a significant role in the determination of tempo. Music to be performed in church, for instance, was to be treated differently, regarding tempo, than music intended for the theater, and all tempo terms were colored by an understanding of a composition's expressive content or meaning. Tempo governed by expression was especially significant in compositions with text, the emotional conveyance of which was important to composers and performers (see Chapter 7). But expression was important in purely instrumental compositions as well. Composers sought to capture a mood or character in their compositions, and performers were expected to detect this mood or character and manifest it in performance.

Quantz, flute treatise (1752), Chapter 12 "Of the Manner of Playing the Allegro"

Epithets [tempo terms] are often used by composers more out of habit than to accurately characterize the matter itself, so to make tempo clear by the performer, cases may occur in which the terms are not binding and the intention of the composer discovered instead from the content of a composition.

The principal character of an Allegro is one of gaiety and liveliness, just as that of the Adagio, on the contrary, is one of tenderness and melancholy. . . .

Principle ideas must be clearly distinguished from those interspersed with them; they are, indeed, the best guide to the expression. If there are more gay than majestic or flattering ideas in an Allegro, it must be played happily and quickly for the most part. But if majesty is the character of the principal ideas, in general the piece must be played more seriously. If the principal sentiment is flattery, greater composure must prevail.

Avison, essay on musical expression (1753), Part 3, Section 1 "On the expressive performance of music in general"

The different Species of Music for the *Church*, the *Theatre,* or the *Chamber*, are, or should be, distinguished by their peculiar Expression. It may easily be perceived that it is not the *Time* or *Measure*, so much as *Manner* and *Expression*, which stamps the real Character of the Piece. A well wrought *Allegro*, or any other quick Movement for the Church, cannot, with Propriety, be adapted to theatrical Purposes; nor can the *Adagio* of this latter Kind, strictly speaking, be introduced into the former: I have known several Experiments of this Nature attempted, but never with Success. For, the same Pieces which may justly enough be thought very solemn in the Theatre, to an experienced Ear, will be found too light and trivial when they are performed in the Church, and this, I may venture to assert, would be the Case, though we had never heard them but in some Anthem, or other divine Performance, and were, therefore, not subject to the Prejudice, which their being heard in an Opera might occasion.

It is also by this Efficacy of musical Expression, that a good Ear doth ascertain the various Terms which are generally made use of to direct the Performer. For Instance, the Words *Andante, Presto, Allegro*, etc. are differently apply'd in the different kinds of Music above-mentioned. For, the same Terms which denote *Lively* and *Gay,* in the Opera, or Concert Style, may be understood in the Practice of Church-Music, as, *Cheerful* and *Serene*, or, if the Reader pleases, less lively and gay. Wherefore, the *Allegro*, etc. in this kind of Composition, should always be performed somewhat slower than is usual in Concertos or Operas.

Holden, musical essay (1770), Part 1, Chapter 4 "Of Time, and the Characters relating thereto"

It matters not though the real length of the measure ought to be made something more, in Church music; and often much less, in Opera music. The learner, who by practice in counting the pulses of a watch, after this manner, has rendered this sort of sub-division familiar to his mind, will find no difficulty in applying it to any measure, whether longer or shorter.

**Kirnberger, composition treatise (1771), Volume 2, Part 1, Chapter 4
"Tempo, Meter, and Rhythm"**

The composer must never forget that every melody is supposed to be a natural and faithful illustration or portrayal of a mood or sentiment, insofar as it can be represented by a succession of notes. The term *Gemüthsbewegung,* which we Germans give to passions or affections, already indicates their analogy to tempo. In fact, every passion and every sentiment—in its intrinsic effect as well as in the words by which it is expressed—has its faster or slower, more violent or more passive tempo. This tempo must be correctly captured by the composer to conform with the type of sentiment he has to express.

Thus I must admonish the aspiring composer above all that he study diligently the nature of every passion and sentiment with regard to tempo, so that he does not make the terrible mistake of giving the melody a slow tempo where it should be fast, or a fast tempo where it should be slow. However, this is a field that is not limited to music, and that the composer has in common with the orator and poet.

Tromlitz, flute treatise (1791), Chapter 5 "Time Signatures"

A generally applicable set tempo for each [Italian superscription written at the beginning of a piece] cannot be established, chiefly since there are so many gradations in between them, and no composer can be bound by a fixed tempo like this, but is guided by the feelings arising out of his own temperament and taste; and since almost every composition is different, the meaning of the superscription cannot be the same for each temperament; so it follows that no generally meaningful and exact movement in respect of tempo can be possible; e.g. *Allegro* means joyful, happy, but certainly not in the same degree for different temperaments; and so a piece with this superscription will always be played slower or faster by persons of different temperaments, according to what one's temperament dictates. The method suggested by Quantz of setting the tempo according to a pulse-beat would indeed seem suitable here to some extent, since one would think that the rapidity of the pulse would at all times be dictated by the disposition of the temperament, but that is not my experience. Every observation I have made has always led me to believe that a person of a particular temperament does not have the same pulse-beat from one day to the next, not even in fact from one hour to the next, and that each age (for temperaments do change with the years) has a different pulse rate, to say nothing of the fact that this rate can be altered very much by internal as well as external influences, such as unforeseen circumstances, weather, food and drink, and suchlike, without considering other difficulties. Therefore, I doubt that this method could be used profitably. Nonetheless, anyone who wants can give it a try, for it at least gives a tempo; but in the end one must allow feeling to decide if one is to keep to the right path. . . .

However, if one is to find out the correct tempo for a movement by feeling, one must first of all be familiar with the content of the piece. To be governed solely by the superscription is in my opinion a mistake, or at best a very vague expedient. Often a composer superscribes a movement *Allegro*, but not merely with the meaning *fast*. Rather, he has attempted thereby to convey a particular degree of joy and happiness. Now if the performer is guided by the bare meaning *fast*, as very often happens, then he will certainly, or at least most of the time, mistake the composer's intention, for he will not be in accordance with the content, the substance, on which his aim should be quite set, and on which everything depends.

Spohr, musical diary (1860–1861), commenting on a performance of a Mass by Charles Henri Plantade, musical director of the Court Chapel, "Paris, 1820"

Altogether I was prepared to hear music stylistically quite different from what we call churchly, I was still astonished by the brilliant theatrical style of a mass by Plantade which we heard during our first visit to the Chapel. . . . The final allegro, presumably to the words *"Dona nobis pacem"* (I cannot be sure, since the French pronounce Latin in a manner wholly unintelligible to the German ear) was so entirely in the style of an opera finale (including a tempo three or four times too fast) that when it was over, I quite forgot where I was and awaited the fall of the curtain and a burst of applause.

Carl Maria von Weber, comments about tempo published in the *Berliner Musik-Zeitung* (1827)

The beat, the tempo, must not be a controlling tyrant nor a mechanical, driving hammer; it should be to a piece of music what the pulse beat is to the life of man. There is no slow movement without places that demand a quicker motion in order to avoid a sense of dragging. In the same way, there is no Presto that does not require a contrasting, more tranquil execution of many passages, for otherwise, the expressiveness would be lost in excessive speed. . . . A quickening of the tempo or a holding back . . . occurs in periods or phrases (in the musical and poetic sense of the words) as the emotional content of the performance demands. . . . In music we have no way of indicating all this. It resides only in the feelings of the human heart, and if the feelings are not there, nothing is of any avail, neither the metronome, which serves only to prevent the grossest misunderstandings, nor the expression marks, which are so unsatisfactory but which I might be tempted to use in great abundance if the warning of repeated experience did not remind me that such indications are superfluous, useless, and generally misinterpreted.

Schindler, biography of Beethoven (1840), Musical Section, Part Two

[Beethoven's] playing was free of all constraint in respect to the beat, for the spirit of his music required freedom.

TEMPO FLUCTUATION

The presumed proper tempo of a composition was not merely a fixed or steady rate of speed, it was motion that was pliable. Tempo fluctuations, in the form of accelerations and retardations, were commonplace and were yet additional aspects of performance during the Classical era that attempted to convey the expressive content of music. The quotations immediately below deal with the simultaneous acceleration and retardation of the entire texture of a composition—all voices and instruments, including in orchestral works, moving together; tempo rubato was different and is discussed in its own section.

Quantz, flute treatise (1752), Chapter 17 "Of the Duties of Those Who Accompany or Execute the Accompanying or Ripieno Parts Associated with a Concertante Part" Section 7 "Of the Duties that all Accompanying Instrumentalists in General Must Observe"

I do not pretend that a whole piece should be measured off in accordance with the pulse beat; this would be absurd and impossible.

C. P. E. Bach, clavier treatise (1753), Part 1, Chapter 3 "Performance"

In general, retards fit slow or more moderate tempos better than very fast ones. For instance, in the opening allegro and the following adagio of [my] B Minor Sonata, No. 6 [Württenberg Sonatas], especially in the adagio where a melody in octaves is transposed three times against rapid notes in the left hand, each transposition can be effectively performed by gradually and gently accelerating and immediately thereafter retarding. In affetuoso playing, the performer must avoid frequent and excessive retards, which tend to make the tempo drag. The affect itself readily leads to this fault. Hence every effort must be made despite the beauty of detail to keep the tempo at the end of a piece exactly the same as at the beginning, an extremely difficult assignment. There are many excellent musicians, but only a few of whom it can be said truthfully that in the narrowest sense they end a piece as they began it. Passages in a piece in the major mode which are repeated in the minor may be broadened somewhat on their repetition in order to heighten the effect. On entering a *fermata* expressive of languidness, tenderness, or sadness, it is customary to broaden slightly.

Burney, account of music in France and Italy (1770), September "Arrived at Rome"

SUNDAY 30. Went this morning to S. Peters to hear Mass where I staid 2 hours and had a delightful contemplative lounge—from hence to Signor Santarelli, with whom I spent 2 hours more very profitably. . . . With regard to the famous *Miserere* of Allegri, he says its beauty and effect arise more from the manner in which it is performed than from the composition—there are many stanzas to the same music—and the singers have by tradition certain customs and expressions and graces of convention, which produce great effects—such as swelling and diminishing the notes altogether, accelerating or retarding the measure, singing some stanzas quicker than others con certe expressioni e gruppi etc.

Rousseau, dictionary (1779), "Chronometre"

There is not, perhaps, in an air two measures which are exactly of the same duration: two things contributing thro' necessity, to slacken the one and hasten the other, taste and harmony in pieces of many parts, taste and a presentiment of the harmony in the solo. A musician who understands his art, has not played four measures of an air but he enters into the character of it, and is intirely [sic] wrapt up in it: The pleasure of the harmony only suspends him. He wishes the concords to be struck *here* and *there*, that they should be omitted, that is to say, that he should sing or play more or less slowly, from one measure to another, and even from a time [beat] or quarter time, to him who follows.

Junker, handbook for church music directors (1782), "Of tempo"

Even if it is possible for the composer to indicate various tempo gradations within basic lively or slow tempos, how many modifications lie between the two that he cannot indicate because as yet he has no notation for them. For the conductor . . . an allegro cannot be tied to a single all-embracing fast tempo, just as an adagio cannot be tied to a slow one. The precise determination of tempo rests on good taste—on its internal sense of rightness—which can only be fixed through previous study of the score.

Must every piece be performed through to the very end at a stated tempo, never even approaching greater speed or slowness? Or might a tempo, even in the middle of a piece, be slightly modified, accelerated, or held back? To answer the first of the two questions positively and without qualification would mean to deprive the art of music of one of its most powerful means of expression and emotion, and would remove from it all possibility of different gradations and modifications of expressive movement. To answer the second question positively and without qualification would have the river overflow its banks; it would cause a thousand cases of disorder and would deprive music of its truth. But as soon as the last sentence is qualified and limited, it can be answered in the positive.

Furthermore, as little as I support the use of unqualified tempo fluctuation (because it is so often misused), I nonetheless insist that a good orchestra will perform tasteful tempo variations where appropriate and where, under certain circumstances, they can produce a good effect.

Just as slight expressive nuances can never be applicable to the same degree in allegro tempos as they might be in adagio ones, so too, tempo fluctuation is less applicable and true in an allegro than in an adagio. There is no passion whose movement would be so circumscribed as to be absolutely regular; movement constantly ranges through various modifications of tempo.

Chapter Two

Türk, clavier treatise (1789), Chapter 6, Part 5
"Concerning the Need for Personal and Genuine Feeling
for All the Emotions and Passions which can be Expressed in Music"

Even when the composer has indicated the proper manner of expression as well as he can—in general and for specific parts, there still remains special cases for which the expression can be heightened by *extraordinary* means. Among these, I particularly include the following: 1) playing without keeping steady time; 2) quickening and hesitating; 3) the so-called tempo rubato. These three resources *when used sparingly and at the right time* can be of great affect. . . .

It is difficult to specify all of the places where quickening and hesitating can take place; nevertheless, I will seek to make at least some of them known. I am assuming, however, that the means that I am about to describe will be only used when one is playing alone or with a very attentive accompanist. . . .

In compositions whose character is vehemence, anger, rage, fury, and the like, the most forceful passages can be played with a somewhat hastened (*accelerando*) motion. Also, certain thoughts that are repeated in a more intensified manner (generally higher) require that the speed be increased to some extent. Sometimes, when gentle feelings are interrupted by a lively passage, the latter can be played somewhat more rapidly. A hastening of the tempo may also take place in a passage where a vehement affect is unexpectedly to be aroused.

For extraordinarily tender, longing, or melancholy passages, in which the emotion, as it were, is concentrated in one point, the effect can be very much intensified by an increasing hesitation (*Anhalten, tardando*). The tempo is also taken gradually slower for tones before certain fermatas as if their powers were gradually being exhausted. The passages toward the end of a composition (or part of a composition) which are marked diminuendo, diluendo, smorzando, and the like, can also be played in a somewhat more lingering manner.

A tenderly moving passage between two lively and fiery thoughts can be executed in a somewhat hesitating manner; but in this case, the tempo is not taken gradually slower, but *immediately* a little slower (however, only a *little*). Compositions in which two characters of opposite types are represented, especially provide a suitable opportunity for a gradual slowing of the tempo.

Corri, singing treatise (1810), "Dialogue, Introductory Requisites for Vocal Music"

—QUICKENING OR RETARDING OF TIME—

Another improvement, by deviation from strict time, is to be made by the singer delivering some phrases or passages in quicker or slower time than he began with, in order to give emphasis, energy, or pathos, to particular words; and I cannot illustrate what I would inculate on this head more forcibly, than by reciting an instance of the effect produced by this kind of expression, by my much esteemed friend, Mr. Braham, in my song of "Victory," in the Opera of the Travellers. When I composed this song, in arranging the music to the first Stanza -

"He was fam'd for deeds of Arms; She was a maid of envied charms." &c. &c.

I could not imagine the same melody would be suitable to the words of the second verse

"Battle now with fury glows, "Hostile blood in torrents flows." &c. &c.

and accordingly varied the music. - At the first rehearsal, the melody of the first verse having produced some effect, Mr. Braham advised me not to change it, but repeat the same melody to the second verse, to which I reluctantly agreed, fearing to be criticized by the connoisseurs on two points: first, for having expressed two passions so contrary to each other with the same melody; and, secondly, as that melody had not any change of modulation, consequently might seem monotonous; - however, Mr. Braham thought that accelerating the time at the second verse, and adding a fuller accompaniment, would produce the change in point of sense and expression, the effect fully justified his advice and opinion.

TEMPO RUBATO

The present-day understanding of tempo fluctuation as tempo rubato was not the understanding during the Classical era. Tempo fluctuation refers to and is characterized by the simultaneous flexible movement of the entire texture of a composition (i.e., all the voices of a choir or all the instruments of an orchestra accelerating or retarding together), whereas tempo rubato refers to a stratum of the musical texture of a composition, usually a melodic line, that moves freely or apart from the otherwise steady tempo of its accompaniment. An example of this would be the free motion of a solo vocal or instrumental line over a steady keyboard or orchestral accompaniment. Another example would be the flexible tempo of the melodic line (usually played by the right hand) of a keyboard composition performed with a steady accompanimental pattern (usually played by the left hand).

C. P. E. Bach clavier treatise (1753), Part 1, Chapter 3 "Performance"

Tempo rubato is simply the presence of more or fewer notes than are contained in the normal division of the bar. A whole bar, part of one, or several bars may be, so to speak, distorted in this manner. The most difficult but most important task is to give all notes of the same value exactly the same duration. When the execution is such that one hand seems to play against the bar and the other strictly with it, it may be said that the performer is doing everything that can be required of him. It is only rarely that all parts are struck simultaneously. . . . Slow notes and caressing or sad melodies are the best, and dissonant chords are better than consonant ones. Proper execution of this tempo demands great critical faculties and a high order of sensibility. He who possesses these will not find it difficult to fashion a performance whose complete freedom will show no trace of coercion, and he will be able to manipulate any kind of passage. However, practice alone will be of no help here, for without a fitting sensitivity, no amount of pains will succeed in contriving a correct rubato. As soon as the upper part begins slavishly to follow the bar, the essence of the rubato is lost, for all the other parts must be played in time. Other instrumentalists and singers when they are accompanied, can introduce the tempo much more easily than the solo keyboardist. The reason for this is the one just stated. If necessary, the solo keyboardist may alter the bass, but not the harmony. Most keyboard pieces contain rubato passages. The division and indication of these is about as satisfactory as can be expected. He who has mastered the tempo rubato need not be fettered by the numerals which divide notes into groups of 5, 7, 11, etc. According to his disposition but always with appropriate freedom, he may add or omit notes.

Mancini, singing treatise (1774), Article 2 "Of the different schools, and the worthy men and women, who have flourished in the art of singing at the end of the century just passed, and still flourish today"

This excellent lady [Francesca Cuzzoni] lacked nothing which seems important to us, for she possessed sufficient agility; the art of leading the voice, of sustaining it, clarifying it, and drawing it back, all with such attention to perfection that she has been given the valued name of "Mistress." If she sang a cantabile aria, she did not fail in fitting places to vitalize the singing with rubato.

W. A. Mozart, letter to his father (1777)

The fact that I always maintain the beat accurately amazes everyone. They simply cannot understand the idea that the left hand goes on as usual during the tempo rubato in an Adagio. They imagine that the left hand always follows along.

**Türk, clavier treatise (1789), Chapter 6, Part 5
"Concerning the Need for Personal and Genuine Feeling
for All the Emotions and Passions which can be Expressed in Music"**

The so-called *tempo rubato* or *robato* (actually *stolen* time) . . . should be left to the sensitivity and insight of the player. This term . . . commonly is understood as a kind of shortening or lengthening of notes, or the displacement (dislocation) of these. There is something taken away (stolen) from the duration of a note and for this, another note is given that much more, as in the following examples (b) and (c).

At (a) are the basic notes, at (b) tempo rubato is put to use by means of the *anticipation*, and at (c) by means of the *retardation*. From this it can be seen that through this kind of execution, the tempo, or even more, the meter as a whole is not displaced.

Chapter Two

Corri, singing treatise (1810), "Dialogue, Introductory"

—RHYTHM OF TIME—

Master: Time is indispensably necessary in music where many parts are combined, and consequently to be executed by many performers: -We are, therefore, under great obligation to this invention; but to meliorate the rigour of its laws in melody, eminent singers have assumed a license, of deviating from, the strict time, by introducing the Tempo Rubato.

Scholar: What is this Italian Term?

—TEMPO RUBATO—

Master: Is a detraction of part of the time from one note, and restoring it by increasing the length of another, or vice versa; so that, whilst a singer is, in some measure, singing ad libitum, the orchestra, which accompanies him, keeps the time firmly and regularly. Composers seem to have arranged their works in such a manner as to admit of this liberty, without offending the laws of harmony: one caution, however, becomes highly necessary; namely, that this grace, or license, is to be used with moderation and discretion, in order to avoid confusion; for too frequent a use of Tempo Rubato may produce *Tempo indiavolato*.

This Italian license of Tempo Rubato, may be used in any species of music where there is a leading or predominant melody, and the management of it must be left to the skill and prudence of the performer, on account of the various characters and meaning peculiar to different compositions, which the performer must carefully discriminate in order to know where this alteration will produce happy effect.

Nathan, singing treatise (1836), Chapter 12 "On Time"

There is a license allowed to those who are perfectly familiarized with the different branches of time, for the purpose of enforcing any particular passion; namely, that of borrowing from, or adding to a note, a little detraction of sound, and making up the time by contracting, or detracting from the sound of another in the same bar; or, in other words, accelerating the time of one part of a bar, and retarding the other part, and *vice versa*. This is called by the Italians *tempo rubato*, but it should only be used by those whose knowledge dictates to them how to steal discreetly.

Schindler, biography of Beethoven (1840)

Everything I have ever heard Beethoven perform was, with very few exceptions, entirely free from constraint in the matter of tempo; it was "Tempo rubato" in the truest meaning of the word, induced by the content and context of the music, and it never had the least resemblance to a caricature. It was the most lucid and the most intelligible declamation, which could be studied to such a degree perhaps only in his compositions.

Garcia, singing treatise (1840–1847), Part 2, Chapter 2, Section 3 "Time"

Tempo Rubato

The momentary prolongation of value which one gives to one or to several tones to the detriment of others is called *tempo rubato*.

This distribution of the values by lengthening and shortening certain notes, at the same time as it serves to break the monotony of equal movements, is favorable to outbursts of passion. Examples:

Donizetti, *Anna Bolena*, from Act 1 Cavatina "Non v'ha sguardo cui sia data"

Mozart, *Le Nozze di Figaro*, from Act 3 aria "Dove sono"

Rossini, *La gazza ladra,* from Act 1 Cavatina "Di piacer mi balza il cor"

Zingarelli, Romeo

In order to make the effect of the tempo rubato perceptible in singing, it is necessary to sustain the tempo of the accompaniment with precision. The singer, free on this condition to increase and decrease alternately the partial values, will be able to set off certain phrases in a new way. The accelerando and the rallentando require that the accompaniment and the voice move together and slow down or speed up the movement as a whole. The tempo rubato, on the contrary, accords this liberty only to the voice. One thus commits a grave fault, when, in order to render warmly the very animated cadences of the duet from the *Barber,* one suddenly uses the ritardando in place of the tempo rubato in the next-to-the-last measure, as for example at (A) below:

Rossini, *Il Barbiere di Siviglia* from Act 1 duet "All' idea di quel metalo"

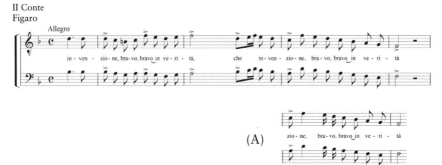

By the first means, while looking for enthusiasm, one falls into awkwardness and sluggishness.

One gives this prolongation to appoggiaturas, to notes that carry the long syllable, to notes *naturally important to the harmony*, or to those which one wants to make stand out. In all these cases, one makes up the lost time by accelerating the other notes. It is one of the best means of giving color to melodies. Examples:

Donizetti, *Lucia*, Cavatina

Donizetti, *Anna Bolena*, from Act 1 Cavatina "Non v'ha squardo cui sia data"

Two artists of a very different kind, Garcia (my father), and Paganini, excelled in the use of the tempo rubato applied *by phrase*. While the orchestra maintained the tempo regularly, they, on their part, abandoned themselves to their inspiration to rejoin with the bass only at the moment the harmony would change, or else at the very end of the phrase. But this means requires before everything an exquisite feeling of the *rhythm* and an imperturbable poise. One can scarcely use such a procedure except in passages where the harmony is stable, or slightly varied. Outside of these exceptions it would appear conspicuously harsh to the ear and would present great difficulties to the performer.

RECITATIVE

Recitative during the Classical era was as it had been during the Baroque: flexible in terms of tempo and free of metric and rhythmic constraints. The tempo of recitative was governed by a desire to convey text in a natural flow of time, and the mood or character of text and the nature of its dramatic intent determined both overall rates and fluctuations of speed. The meter signatures of recitative merely provided composers of the time a means for aligning strong and weak syllables of spoken declamation (or imaginary declamation in some purely instrumental passages such as in the final movement of Beethoven's *Symphony #9*) with strong and weak beats of each measure (see Chapter 4). There was no intent that the strong and weak syllables/beats should be performed in evenly or regularly spaced time. Regularity of metric performance was in direct opposition to the natural oratorical or speech-like delivery that recitative was meant to portray. Meter in recitative was, therefore, only a compositional requisite.

The notated rhythms of recitative were a general guide as to the temporal shape of text, and as with meters, the rhythms were not to be adhered to rigidly. The spacing of rhythmic values was in many instances determined more by a need to put strong declamatory syllables on strong beats than by any desire for specific expression. Consequently, the relative duration of both strong and weak beats was determined by natural speech-like delivery of text.

In the following recitative (Example A), the primary accents of text are, as was the standard practice, aligned with primary metrical accents (i.e., beats one and three of common time measures). These are marked with an asterisk. However, some very weak syllables of text, those marked with a circle, are aligned with secondary metrical accents. If one were to perform the recitative adhering to the specified printed rhythms, the aforementioned weak syllables would receive undue and unintentional stress. This is true whether the performance would be sung in German or in English. On the other hand, performance in a rhythmically free manner, one delivered according to natural speech patterns, would alleviate text accent problems.

Example A
Joseph Haydn, *Die Schöpfung* (The Creation), Und die himmlischen Heerscharen
(And the heavenly host), measures 1–4

A rhythmically free manner of delivery would also alleviate other problems associated with translations, especially in regards to *Die Schöpfung* (The Creation). Haydn set the music to a German text, but this was a translation of an original English libretto that was then applied (with adjustments) to Haydn's music with his approval. The first published edition of the score had both German and English texts, and many of the earliest performances were sung in English. Nevertheless, the English text is occasionally troublesome in the recitatives. In Example B, the first appearance of the word "firmament" has logical metrical placement in German (which, when spoken, has a stress on the final syllable). This is not the case in English (which, when spoken, has a stress on the first syllable). A rhythmically free performance sung in English could avoid this problem.

The accompaniment of this recitative would also have to be metrically free to avoid problems with performances in English. In order not to have a stress on the final unaccented syllable of "firmament," the E minor chord on the downbeat of the second measure should not be performed until after the completion of the word. This delayed chord practice was a common aspect of performance in recitatives, especially at final cadences. Although there are frequent instances of chords printed simultaneously with final syllables of text, the general expectation during the Classical era was that the vocal part would finish a statement of text before a chord would be sounded (see Haydn's instructions below from the preface to his cantata *Applausus*).

Example B
Joseph Haydn, *Die Schöpfung* (The Creation), Und Gott machte das Firmament
(And God made the firmament), measures 1–6

In the continuation of the recitative shown in Example B, the orchestra depicts a feature of nature (storms, winds, lightning, thunder, rain, hail, and snow) followed by the vocalist commenting on that depiction. In the first two of the depictions (storms and winds), the vocal part finishes before the orchestra begins. But in the next two depictions (lightning and thunder), the vocal part finishes simultaneously with the beginning of the orchestra. As seen in Example C, there is conflict between the finish of the vocal part commenting on the depiction of thunder and the beginning of the orchestra depicting rain. The delay of the orchestral entrance in these two locations would alleviate this conflict between the singer and orchestra. It is particularly interesting that Haydn specifically did not intend simultaneous performance even though he wrote it that way.

Example D is illustrative of the most common situation involving printed simultaneity with the expectation that performance would be otherwise. The penultimate chord of the recitative and the final note of the vocal part are both printed on beat four of the measure. However, the general performance practice of this combination of vocal and instrumental parts was to delay the chord until after the singer had finished the final note. The last two chords would then have been struck in quick succession (see Haydn's quote below that specifically addresses this very example). Although most cadences were performed in the manner described above, some internal cadences in lengthy recitatives of a theatrical nature requiring rapid delivery of text were performed in a "telescoped" manner: the final note of the vocal part and the penultimate chord of the instrumental part were performed simultaneously.

Example C
Joseph Haydn, *Die Schöpfung* (The Creation), Und Gott machte das Firmament (And God made the firmament), measures 21–30

Example D
Joseph Haydn, *Applausus*, Theologia's final statement in Recitativo XV

Other elements of the accompaniment in recitatives were also treated in a free manner. This is especially so in secco recitatives, the scores of which usually appear as in Example E (illustrated with English text only for clarity): a vocal line and an accompaniment comprised of a bass line doubled at the octave, and a treble part of chords. The doubling of the bass line and all the chords are recommendations of an editor; they are not original. The original recitative appeared as in Example F: a vocal line and a single basso continuo line with figured bass numbers. Playing from this basso continuo line would have been a string player (usually a cellist) and one or more keyboardists (playing a harpsichord, pianoforte, and/or organ).

Example E
Joseph Haydn, *The Creation*, And God said: Let the earth bring forth grass

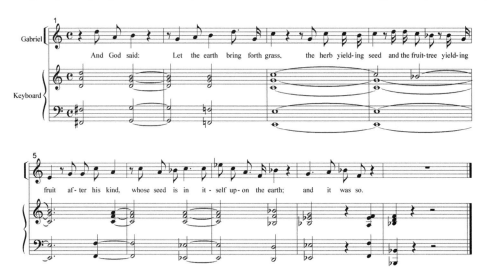

Example F
Joseph Haydn, *The Creation*, And God said: Let the earth bring forth grass

The basso continuo notes were not necessarily to be sustained for the entirety of their printed values, and the chords indicated by numbers did not imply mandatory performance. The basso continuo performers, who had text printed in their instrumental parts, played freely to reinforce the expression of the text and to follow the singer. The basso continuo players could, therefore, decide not to play a certain chord or, on the other hand, to reiterate a chord. Generally, however, the string player (cellist) played each indicated note with no deletions or reiterations, while the keyboard player improvised at will. The most common manner of performance was for both players to strike each chord and release it immediately (see Example G), thus allowing the voice to be heard with clarity and to move with freedom. Having struck and released a note/chord, the keyboardist and string player were then poised to strike successive chords as the singer approached them. This flexible nature of performance allowed the accompanying forces to vary the length of the chords, from fully held to very shortly struck, according to the relative speed of the singer, the dramatic implications of expression, and the harmonic structure of the chord progressions. Example H illustrates how this might be done.

Example G
Joseph Haydn, *The Creation*, And God said: Let the earth bring forth grass

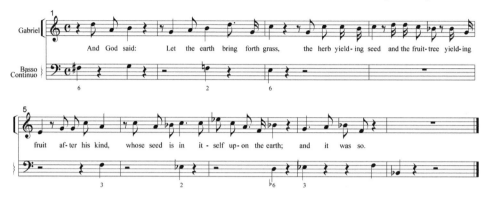

Example H
Joseph Haydn, *The Creation*, And God said: Let the earth bring forth grass

Yet another aspect of free performance is illustrated in Example I. The accompanimental chords, in this instance played by the orchestra, would be played as expressive punctuations to the vocal line. The singer would recite the vocal line freely, not following a conductor; the conductor would follow the singer, indicating the chords to the orchestra out of metric context.

Example I
Joseph Haydn, *The Creation*, And God said: Let the waters bring forth abundantly

The following quotations speak variously to the three attributes of rhythmic/metric flexibility discussed above: 1) text delivered in a natural speech rhythm; 2) accompanying chords held shorter than their printed durational value; and 3) final cadence chords struck after the delivery of the final vocal note.

Quantz, flute treatise (1752), Chapter 17 "Of the Duties of Those Who Accompany or Execute the Accompanying or Ripieno Parts Associated with a Concertante Part" Section 7 "Of the Duties that all Accompanying Instrumentalists in General Must Observe"

In an Italian *recitative* the singer does not always adhere to the tempo, and has the freedom to express what he is to execute quickly or slowly, as he considers best and as the words require. If, then, the accompanying parts have sustained notes to execute, they must accompany the singer rather by ear, using their discretion, than by the beat. If the accompaniment is in notes that must be performed in tempo, however, the singer is obliged to regulate himself by the accompanying parts.

Sometimes the accompaniment is interrupted to give the singer freedom to recite at will, and the accompanying parts enter only from time to time, namely at the caesuras when the singer has completed a phrase. Here the accompanists must not wait till the singer has uttered the final syllable, but must enter at the penultimate or preceding note, in order to maintain constant animation. If, however, the violins have a short rest instead of a note on the downbeat, and the bass precedes them by a note, the latter must enter with certainty and power, especially in cadences, where the bass is most important. In general, the bass in all cadences of theatrical recitatives, whether accompanied with violins or plain, must begin its two notes, usually forming a descending leap of a fifth, during the last syllable; these notes must be performed in a lively manner and must not be too slow. The keyboard player executes them with an accompaniment in full chords, the cellist and double bass player with a short accent with the lowest part of the bow; they repeat the stroke and take both notes with down-strokes. If in a lively recitative the accompanying parts at the caesuras have quick notes which must be played precipitately following a rest on the downbeat (see Fig. 11), the accompanists again must not wait until the singer has fully articulated the last syllable, but must begin during the penultimate note, so that the fire of expression is constantly maintained. They will start together more precisely, particularly in a large orchestra, if they use the penultimate syllable of the singer as their guide.

Fig. 11

C. P. E. Bach, clavier treatise (1753), Part 1, Chapter 3 "Performance"

In accompanied recitatives, tempo and meter must be frequently changed in order to rouse and still the rapidly alternating affects. Hence, the metric signature is in many cases more a convention of notation than a binding factor in performance.

——. Chapter 6, Section 1 "Recitative"

Some recitatives, in which the bass and perhaps other instruments express a definite theme or a continuous motion that does not participate in the singer's pauses, must be performed strictly in time for the sake of good order. Others are declaimed now slowly, now rapidly, according to the content, regardless of the meter, even though their notation is measured. . . .

When the declamation is rapid, the chords must be ready instantly, especially at pauses in the principal part where the chord precedes a following entrance. At the termination of a chord, its successor must be struck with dispatch. Thus the singer will not be hampered in his affects or their requisite fast execution, for he will always know in good time the course and construction of the harmony. Were it necessary to choose between two evils, it would be preferable to hasten rather than to delay. Indeed, the latter is always better. . . . These fiery recitatives often occur in operas where the orchestra has a wide range with the basses playing *divisi*, while the singer declaims upstage, far removed from his accompaniment. Such being the case, the first harpsichordist, when there are two, does not wait for the termination of the singer's cadences, but strikes on the final syllable the chord that should rightly be played later. This is done so that the remaining basses or other instruments will be prepared to enter on time.

The pace with which a chord is arpeggiated depends on the tempo and content of a recitative. The slower and more affetuoso the latter is, the slower the arpeggiation. Recitatives with sustained accompanying instruments are well adapted to arpeggiation. But as soon as the accompaniment shifts from sustained to short, detached notes, the accompanist must play detached, resolute chords, unarpeggiated, and fully grasped by both hands. Even if the score expresses tied white notes, the sharply detached execution is retained. . . .

In recitatives with sustained accompanying instruments, the organ holds only the bass, the chords being quitted soon after they are struck. Organs are seldom purely tuned, with the result that held chords, which are often chromatic in such recitatives, would sound ugly and disagree with the other accompanying instruments. It is often difficult in such a case to make an orchestra—which need not be wretched—sound in pitch.

Rousseau, letter on French music (1753)

I call recitative a harmonious declamation, that is, a declamation of which all the inflections are formed by harmonious intervals. It therefore follows that as each language has its own particular declamation, each language ought also to have its own particular recitative. . . . It is evident . . . that the best recitative, in any language whatever, if this language fulfills the necessary conditions, is that which comes the nearest to speaking; if there were one which came so near to it as to deceive the ear or the mind while still preserving the required harmony, one might boldly pronounce that it had attained to the highest perfection of which any recitative is capable.

Agricola, singing treatise (1757), Chapter 5 "Concerning the Recitative"

1. There are three different kinds of recitatives, and in three different kinds of recitatives must the teacher instruct his students.

2. The first kind is the *church recitative*, and [is first] for good reason. It is performed in a manner suitable to the sanctity of the place. It does not permit the lightheartedness of a free composition style but rather requires here and there a long sustaining of a note [messa di voce], many appoggiaturas, and a noble seriousness that is constantly maintained. The art of expressing it cannot be learned in any other way than out of a conviction of this truth: that one is speaking to *God*.

3. The second kind is the *theatrical recitative*. Because it is connected with the action of the singer, this recitative requires the teacher to instruct the student in a certain imitation that is true to nature and that cannot be beautiful unless it is performed with the stately decorum with which princes and those who consort with them speak.

4. The third kind, called the *chamber recitative*, is, according to the judgment of knowledgeable men, more capable than the others of touching the natural emotions of the human heart. This almost always requires a special artistry with regard to the words, which, since they are largely devoted to the expression of the strongest feelings of the heart, oblige the teacher to teach his students that lively art of participation that can convince [the listener] that the singer truly feels that which he is performing. . . .

5. The *church recitative* allows the singers more freedom than the others and releases them from an exact observation of the time, especially in the final cadences. The singers should, however, make use of this freedom as singers, not as violinists. A certain amount of sustaining (which is filled in) in places rich in Affect is permitted at times for

the purpose of improvised ornamentation. This ornamentation, however, is not allowed to be as extensive or extravagant as that which is permitted in arias. . . .

6. Since it might impede the natural art of the narrative, no improvised ornamentation is permitted in the *theatrical recitative*, with the exception of certain sentences in many a soliloquy that are set in the manner of the chamber style.

All three types of recitative share in common that which I have specified above for the church recitative: that it is not sung in strict time. One must be guided more by the length and shortness of syllables in common speech than by the written value of the notes in the recitative. To be sure, these notes must be adapted by the composer to the duration of the syllables, but there are instances in which one holds the notes for a longer or shorter time than their prescribed value requires. . . . To be sure, the short phrases that the instruments play between [the sung phrases of] the accompanied recitatives must be performed in strict time. However, the singer is not bound to this, but he must wait out the short phrases if he is not supposed to enter as they are playing, just as the instrumentalists, on the other hand, must always wait for him. When, however, as often happens, ariosos or other phrases that can and should be performed in strict time and that the composer generally indicates with the words *a tempo* or *in measured rhythm*, occur in the recitative, the singer is obliged to follow this direction, whether he be singing from memory or with the music.

It is customary to change some notes in all three kinds of recitatives and to add a small supplement [ornament] to others. This practice, however, is more common in the church and chamber recitatives than in the theatrical ones.

The recitative cadences are usually written out in the following manner: (a) the penultimate note is sung a fourth higher and thus repeats the preceding note (b). Some composers prefer to write them as they are to be sung. If the cadence ends with a single long syllable, one simply changes the fourth before the last note to an appoggiatura (c).

When several notes are repeated on one pitch, a mordent proper may be sometimes introduced between the strong notes and the passing notes of the same. Here are some examples of this:

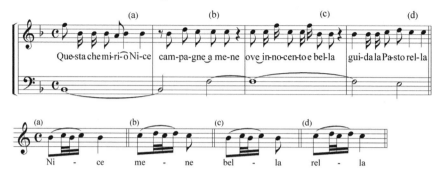

But since too many ornaments of the same type become offensive, these should not be used all the time.

Diderot, Rameau's nephew dialogue (c.1760)

What is the model for the musician or the song? Declamation, if the model is living and thinking; sound, if the model is inanimate. You must think of declamation as a line, and song another line that snakes its way above the first. The more this declamation, a type of song, is strong and realistic, the more beautiful the song that conforms to it. . . . Consider then how difficult and how important it is to know how to write recitative well. There is no beautiful air from which one cannot make a beautiful recitative, and no recitative from which in turn a clever man cannot draw out a beautiful air.

Grimm, encyclopedia (1763), "Poème lyrique"

There are two quite distinct moments of the lyric drama, the quiet moment and the passionate moment; the primary concern of the composer must be to find two sorts of declamation that are essentially different and specific, the one to convey quiet discourse, the other to express the language of passion in all its force, variety, and disorder. This latter type of declamation bears the name of air or aria; the former has been called recitative. . . . Recitative functions without the help of the orchestra, and differs from ordinary declamation only in that it marks the inflections of speech with intervals that are more perceptible and suited to notation.

Haydn, preface to *Applausus* (1768)

In the accompanied Recitatives notice that the accompaniment should not enter until after the singer has finished singing the text completely, even though the score often shows the contrary. For example, in the beginning, each time the word *metamorphosis* appears, the voice has an appoggiatura [*Anschlag*] on *-phosis*. There one must be careful to allow the last syllable of the Recitative to be heard completely and then the accompaniment must come in promptly on the downbeat. For it would be ludicrous if one were to fiddle the word away from the mouth of the singer so that nothing but *quae metamo* was intelligible. But I leave this up to the cembalist because everyone else must follow him.

Binns (Hoyle), dictionary (1770)

RECITATIVO, or RECITATIVE, the Adagio or Grave parts in Cantatas, Motets, Operas, etc. have generally this word fixed thereto, by which is meant a kind of singing that differs very little from ordinary pronunciation, such as that in which the actors at the opera or theatre deliver their speeches when they are to express some sort of action or passion, or relate some event or design. Notwithstanding this sort of composition is noted in true time, the performer is at liberty to alter the Bars, or Measure, according as his subject requires; hence the Thorough Bass is to observe and follow the singer, and not the person that beats time.

Chapter Two

Holden, musical essay (1770), Part 1, Chapter 5 "Miscellaneous Explanations"

Vocal music is distinguished into *Recitative* and *Air*. The word *Recitative* comes from *recitare* to recite or to rehearse; and expresses a particular style of music, nearly related to the manner of speaking, which may be called a kind of musical declamation.

The chief difference between recitative and declamation lies in the difference between a musical tone and natural speech. . . . This sort of music is wrote [sic] with as much regularity of time and measure as any other; but yet the singer is more at liberty to transgress the strict rules of time, for the sake of expression. In general, the sentiment ought to engage our attention, more than the music, in *Recitatives*; and the music, more than the sentiment, in *Airs*.

Schröter, figured bass treatise (1772)

There are three kinds of recitatives. The first kind may be recognized by the fact that above the bass notes with their figures a vocal part is written, without the remark *Accompagnement*, or *col stromenti*. Although the bass in such cases is written mostly in half and whole notes, nevertheless the organist must play all such long notes, together with the harmonies prescribed, detached and almost like 8th-notes.

Mancini, singing treatise (1774), Article 14 "Of recitative and action"

I say in advance that there are two kinds of recitative; one is called simple, the other instrumental. We call that one simple which is accompanied only by the bass. . . .

The other recitative is called instrumental because it requires the accompaniment of the orchestra. Its cantilena is not at all different from that of the simple. . . .

Now the cantilena of one and the other of these recitatives, however intoned, should always be loosened in such a manner that it resembles a perfect and simple spoken declamation. Thus it would be a defect if the actor, instead of speaking the recitative with a free voice, should wish to sing it tying the voice continuously, and not thinking of ever distinguishing the periods and the diverse sense of the words by holding back, reinforcing, detaching, and sweetening the voice, as a gifted man will do when he speaks or reads. . . .

I know that among our professors the opinion was at one time prevalent that the recitatives for the chamber should be spoken differently from those for the theater, as well as those for the concert hall or the church. As much as I have reflected on this, I have found no certain reason why there should be this difference. I think that the recitatives for the church, the chamber, the theater, ought all to be given in the same manner, I mean to say, in a natural and clear voice, which gives the just and complete strength to every word; which distinguishes the commas and the periods; in a manner which enables the listener to understand the sense of poetry. I conclude, then, that if there is any difference among these recitatives given above, it is a difference relative to their location; this can consist only in the quantity of voice which the singer, understanding his own strength, ought always to adapt to the place in which he sings.

Manfredini, harmony treatise (1775), Part 3, Chapter 4, Section 2

Recitative consists a little more in speaking than in singing; but nonetheless, as though one spoke musically, and in a music which is sometimes more affecting and efficacious than that of certain weak and insignificant arias; give very great attention to the manner of singing recitative, and above all else observe that you do not sing it too much.

Burney, account of music in Germany, the Netherlands, and United Provinces (1775)

Vienna: The symphonies to the songs in [Gluck's] opera *Alceste* are few and short; there are no divisions in the voice parts; no formal closes at the end; scarce any but accompanied recitatives, and not one *da capo* is to be found throughout the piece; which, say those who have seen it represented, was so truly theatrical and interesting, that they could not keep their eyes a moment off the stage . . . so that the music only gave energy or softness to the declamation, as the different situations of the several characters required. The syllables were indeed lengthened, and the tones of speech ascertained, but speech it still was.

Chapter Two

Rousseau, dictionary (1779), "Recitative"

RECITATIVE. A discourse recited in a musical and harmonious tone. A method of singing which approaches nearly to speech, a declamation in music, in which the musician should imitate, as much as possible, the inflexions of the declaiming voice. . . .

The perfection of the recitative depends much on the character of the language; the more the language is accented and melodious, the more the recitative is natural, and draws near to real discourse. . . . The best recitative is that wherein we sing the least. . . .

The recitative is not measured singing. This measure, which characterizes the airs, would spoil the reciting declamation. It is the accent, whether grammatical or oratorical, which ought alone to direct the slowness or rapidity of the sounds; in the same manner also their elevation or lowering. The composer, in making the recitative on some determined measure, has nothing in view but to fix the correspondence of the thorough bass and music, and to denote, nearly, how the quantity of the syllables should be mark'd, cadenc'd, and the verses scann'd.

RECITATIVE ACCOMPANIED. Is that to which, besides the thorough bass, is added an accompaniment of violins. This accompaniment, which cannot by any means be syllabic, together with the rapidity of the utterance, is generally formed of long notes sustained on entire measures; and we write, for this purpose, on all the parts of the symphony, the word *sostenuto*, chiefly in the bass, which, without that, would strike only flat and detached strokes at each change of the note, as in the ordinary recitative. . . .

RECITATIVE MEASUR'D. These two words are contradictory. Every recitative, wherein we find any other measure than that of the verses, is no longer recitative. But an ordinary recitative is often changed suddenly in music, and takes from measure and melody whatever is marked in writing on the parts *a tempo*, or *a battula*. . . .

The recitative is also measured when the accompaniment with which it is charged, being tuneful and measured itself, obliges the recitant to conform his voice to it. It is less than a measured recitative, than, as I have said before, a recitative accompanying the accompaniment.

Türk, organ in worship treatise (1787), Chapter 3 "Accompaniment"

Recitatives in general, especially those unaccompanied by other instruments, require close attention. . . .

One of the most important rules for the organist consists of the following: for prescribed long or tied notes that are often several measures long, he should not hold out the tone but lift the finger (foot) immediately after striking the key, and continue to pause until a new fundamental note or another harmony is indicated over the bass, for example:

Here in the first measure, the C chord is struck and each finger (also in the bass) is then lifted immediately; in the second measure one rests completely; in the third, the major seventh chord is struck or arpeggiated; etc. . . .

If the harmony remains unchanged for a long time, or if the declamation is very slow, the organist can, perhaps at a break in the phrase, play the same chord again in another register, in order to help the singer and to fill up the void to some extent. Moreover, the accompanist must absolutely refrain from all additions [ornaments] that are contrary to the content, that bother the singer, etc., for here is not his place to extemporize or play the leading voice, but merely to accompany. . . .

The chords should not always be struck in only one way. For the sake of expression and variety, the notes of the chords should sometimes be played all together (at the same time) and sometimes one after the other (broken). For vigorous, fiery, daring, defiant effects, when the singer declaims more rapidly, a strong, firm attack is better than an arpeggiated one, which, on the other hand, may be employed for more gentle sentiments.

In general, the arpeggio should not be used too frequently on the organ and not always in the same manner. Sometimes one begins with the lower notes, at other times with the higher ones; now the intervals will be sounded rapidly one after the other, now only moderately fast; sometimes one arpeggiates the chord so that each note is played only once, at other times the notes are played more often, etc.

Expression also demands various modifications, even in the recitative without instrumental accompaniment, with respect to loud and soft, high and low, fast and slow, etc. . . .

The fact that recitatives should never be sung with a strict beat unless *a tempo* is indicated, or the instruments accompany a certain passage in a prescribed tempo, is another reason why the organist should have the vocal part written over the bass part if he is not playing from the full score. Otherwise, how can he follow the singer note for note when the singer requires complete freedom to declaim now slowly, now more rapidly, according to the content of the text?

Many leaders and cantors have the extremely silly habit of beating the measure during a recitative that is only narrative and without instrumental accompaniment. . . . To divide each measure into beats by movements of the arm and hand is completely contrary to musical expression and reveals great ignorance on the part of the conductor.

Türk, clavier treatise (1789), Chapter 6, Part 5
"Concerning the Need for Personal and Genuine Feeling for all the Emotions and Passions which can be Expressed in Music"

In addition to free fantasies, cadenzas, *fermatas*, and the like, those passages marked *recitativo* must be played more according to feeling rather than meter. Some passages of this sort are found now and then in sonatas, concertos, and the like, for example in the Andante of the first sonata by C. P. E. Bach dedicated to the King of Prussia. Such passages would have a poor effect if they were played strictly according to the specified values of the notes (measured). The more important notes must therefore be played slower and louder, and the less important notes more quickly and softer, approximately the way a sensitive singer would sing these notes or a good orator would declaim the words thereto.

Koch, composition treatise, Volume 3 (1793), Section 4, Chapter 4, Part 1
"Recitative"

Recitative differs from real song through the following characteristics. First, it is bound to no definite movement within the measure. Only those syllables that also stand out in declamation are somewhat extended. The remainder are just treated curtly; they may be notated with quarter, eighth, or sixteenth notes. The fitting of recitative in the measure therefore occurs mainly so that both the larger and smaller resting points through which the poetry is comprehensible and also those syllables that should have more emphasis than others can be presented according to the correct expression. Secondly, recitative has neither a definite meter nor a definite relationship between the lengths of its sections. Its larger and smaller resting points are subject to no other rules than those which ordinary declamation also follows.

Kollmann, composition essay (1799), Chapter 10, Part 2, Section A "Of Recitatives"

There are two sorts of Recitatives hitherto in use, viz: those with an accompaniment for a mere *Bass* or *Thorough-Bass*, and those with an accompaniment for *divers instruments*. . . .

The above *first* sort of recitatives, or those with a mere *Thorough-Bass* accompaniment, are recitatives in the strictest sense of the word. They are generally written in two staves of five lines each, the lower containing the bass accompaniment, and the higher the vocal part; and this method of setting the vocal part over the accompaniment, has been adapted for the purpose of enabling the player to accompany the singer more precisely than what it would be in his power to do otherwise.

The particulars which must be considered in this sort of Recitatives are their *Time* and *Rhythm*, their *Modulation*, and their *Declamation*.

In regard to *Time*, the Recitatives in question are not confined to any fixed Movement or Measure, though they are generally written in common or 4/4 time, to assist the vocal and instrumental performer in hitting together. According to this measure, every word and syllable is placed so as to obtain its proper accent, which the Singer must strictly attend to; but the different *lengths of notes* the Singer need not closely adhere to, nor to any fixed *movement*, as that would take away the required ease of the recitative. The harmonies by which the vocal part is supported, must therefore be laid under it in such a manner, that the Player has time to attend and follow the Singer, or even to assist him in not missing a difficult interval; but not in so crowded a succession that the Singer be confined, by keeping time with the accompaniment. How quick or how slow therefore a recitative shall be performed, or where it shall increase or decrease in quickness, is generally left to the discretion of the Singer, which renders the just performance of a recitative one of the most difficult tasks for a Singer. . . .

Respecting the manner in which the Recitatives in question should be *accompanied*: it needs no demonstration, that according to the usual manner of writing them, their proper accompaniment is one of the greatest tasks for a Thorough Bass Player. For, the holding Bass notes . . . should in general not be held to their full length; the Chords should sometimes be struck like Chords, and sometimes as Harpeggios [sic]; the Harmony should in some cases be taken in four or more, and in others but in three or two parts; the Singer should be assisted in difficult intervals; and wherever the Singer deviates from the strict length of the notes, the Player should precisely follow him.

The *second* sort of recitatives mentioned [above] are those with accompaniments for *divers instruments*, commonly called *Recitatives accompanied*, or *Accompaniments*. They are similar to the former in all respects but one, viz: that the accompaniments must be set so, as to be fully at ease to attend to the liberties which the Singer takes in respect to time; and that in those places where the accompaniments require it, the Singer must more closely adhere to the prescribed measure and a certain movement, than in the above first sort of Recitatives.

Corri, singing treatise (1810), "Recitative"

The Recitative is well known to be a Style of Music peculiar to the Italians—the true and correct expression of which like the Idiom of a language is best learnt from oral communication, indeed it is almost impossible to convey in writing any idea of its peculiar character.

Revo [Recitative] resembles speaking in Musical notes—but mere description cannot fix the exact measure of that inflection of tone necessary to be used, which should be a medium of sound between speaking and singing; the only certain way by which a Scholar can obtain any accurate knowledge of this Style, is from opportunities of hearing it executed by skillful Performers; besides the peculiar delivery belonging to this Style, the manner in which it is written is not always sufficient to direct its performance, nor will the various changes to which it is subject, admit of those general rules that might apply on every occasion; therefore the ear must be the first Instructor, and judgment, taste, and experience, the subsequent guides.

No particular degree of time is marked to Recitative, but it is left to the Singer to prolong or shorten notes, which he ought to do agreeable to the passion and accent of the words.

Busby, musical grammar (1818), "Recitative"

Recitative is speech delivered through the medium of musical intonation. There are two kinds of *Recitative*; the accompanied, and the unaccompanied. . . .

Unaccompanied Recitative—[which] seems to approach the nearest to the recitation of the ancient rhapsodists—is so denominated, not because it is delivered without any instrumental accompaniment whatever; but for the reason, that it is only accompanied by a bass part and chords, which bass part is always figured, in order to designate the harmonies on which the vocal phrases are founded, and to guide the hand of the thorough-bass accompanist. The accompanist here alluded to, is the piano-forte, or organ performer; who merely gives the bass note, struck together with the combinations indicated by the thorough-bass signatures.

Accompanied Recitatives, in which the band [orchestra] merely preserves a sustained harmony, without aiming at a melodial effect, are not delivered according to any stated time, or measure; but the instrumental performers attend to, and follow the progression of the singer; to facilitate which, the *parts* they play from, contain, in addition to their own notes, and in a distinct stave, the recitative itself.

Busby, musical manual (1828), "Recitative"

Recitative. Musical declamation. A species of vocal expression more rhetorical than melodial; and which, for its effect, trusts rather to the inflection and emphasis of natural speech, than to the artificial floridity of song. When *Recitative* has only an appended bass, it is said to be *unaccompanied*; and then the execution is not confined to the observance of time or measure; but when the composition includes parts for a band [orchestra], or for any instruments except the bass, time is necessarily regarded, since, without its guidance, there could be no concinnity of performance.

Czerny, composition treatise (1834), Part 3, Chapter 9 "On the Component Parts of Opera"

The simple recitative . . . supplies the place of dialogue in the Italian, French, and even in many German operas, and is used to unfold the more *tranquil* parts of the action, while the more remarkable and striking situations are represented by the actual vocal pieces. Hence, all that, in ordinary life, would be spoken or related in a tranquil tone of voice, without particular emotion, belongs to this simple species of recitative.

It is invariably written in common time of four crotchets [quarter notes], though the performance is, for the most part, wholly without measure, and dependent on the will of the singer. . . .

The accompaniment either consists entirely of violoncellos and basses, which sustain the lowest note of each chord, which must then be figured, (and in this case the recitative requires only two staves); or it is written for all the stringed instruments, which sustain each chord until the following occurs. . . .

The accompaniment must continue to hold each chord, until the singer arrives at that syllable which forms the commencement of the next chord following; for the singer has not only perfect freedom in regard to the time, but may also, if agreeable to him, introduce embellishments and cadences, whose duration the orchestra must wait for.

The obbligato recitative distinguishes itself from the preceding, in that we are at liberty to give the accompaniment to the full orchestra, which performs short passages between the recitation of the words, and thereby depicts and characterizes that which has already been said, or what is about to be spoken.

Here also the singer recites *ad libitum*, but the intermediate orchestral passages have their precise degree of movement and species of time determined by the composer. This kind of recitative can be rendered very interesting, as it forms a sort of melodrama and can be used in each species of opera. . . .

Lastly, no phrase must be so interrupted by an orchestral ritornel, as to destroy or render indistinct the meaning of the words.

Garcia, singing treatise (1840–1847), Part 2, Chapter 5, Section 1 "Recitatives"

Sometimes music rigorously follows the beat and sometimes it frees itself from it. The first kind includes the measured pieces, to which are commonly given the name of *song*. To the second kind belong the non-measured pieces which are called *recitatives*, from the Italian word *recitare*, which means to *declaim*.

The recitative is then a free musical declamation. One can distinguish two kinds of them: the spoken recitative [secco] and the sung recitative [accompanied]. In both cases, it has for its base the grammatic prosody, the laws of which it rigorously follows. Thus, it subordinates the values of the notes, those of the rests, the rate of the delivery and the accents to the prosodic length or brevity of the syllables, to the punctuation, in short, to the movement of the discourse. The application of this precept is absolute, and assumes the singer has a perfect understanding of the prosody of the language in which he is singing, and the knowledge of what he is saying. Only this knowledge can prevent him from displacing the accents, and from misrepresenting the meaning of the words by false inflections, or by badly placed pauses.

To the rules relative to prosody we will add the following observations. The values of the notes and those of the rests often being determined only by the need to regularly divide the measure, they are only, to tell the truth, an indication of the movement which the thought should have. The true movement will arise from the meaning of the lines and from that of the musical phrases.

Chapter 3

ARTICULATION AND PHRASING

There was considerable commentary during the Classical era about the relative volume and duration of single notes (articulation), but there was little commentary about the grouping of notes (phrasing), and at that, the commentary about grouping was mostly in reference to slurs that bind together a small number of notes. Discussion of phrasing and use of the slur to indicate a combination of notes into a longer musical thought did not occur until the second quarter of the eighteenth century. The Classical-era musician was much more focused on details of how one note related to another or how small groups of notes were connected or separated than on details regarding the interplay or relationship of phrasing as the term is generally understood today. Nuances of articulation were the result of this interest in short spans of time, with many levels of volume characterizing the attack of notes and many degrees of length characterizing the duration of notes. Included in this consideration of volume and duration are nuances of special effects, such as wedges and dots signifying different qualities of staccato, silences of articulation that affect certain rhythmic patterns, the fashionable crescendos and decrescendos of messa di voce, and the myriad ramifications of metric accentuation. Articulation during the Classical era was complex and intricate.

The volume level of the attack of notes was in keeping with general ideals of elegance. A preference for sweetness of tone (see Chapter 1) coupled with a distaste for harshness and all things unrefined resulted in an articulation characterized by softness.

L. Mozart, violin treatise (1756), Chapter 5
"How, by skillful control of the Bow, one should seek to produce a good tone on a Violin and bring it forth in the proper manner"

Every tone, even the strongest attack, has a small, even if barely audible, softness at the beginning of the stroke; for it would otherwise not be a tone but only an unpleasant and unintelligible noise. This same softness must be heard also at the end of each stroke. Hence one must know how to divide the bow into weakness and strength, and therefore how by means of pressure and relaxation, to produce the notes beautifully and touchingly.

The first division can be this: Begin the down stroke or up stroke with a pleasant softness; increase the tone by means of an imperceptible increase of pressure; let the greatest volume of tone occur in the middle of the bow; after which, moderate it by degrees by relaxing the pressure of the bow until at the end of the bow the tone dies completely away.

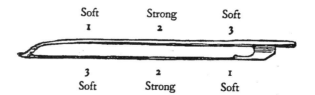

Tartini, violin treatise (1771), "Rules for bowing"

To draw a beautiful tone from the instrument, place the bow on the strings gently at first and then increase the pressure. If the full pressure is applied immediately, a harsh, scraping sound will result.

Türk, clavier treatise (1789), Chapter 6, Part 4 "Concerning the Appropriate Use of Ornaments and Certain Other Means that are Required for Good Execution, or that Take Part in it to Some Extent"

The achievement of a beautiful and singing tone must be a matter of the most extreme importance for the clavichord player. In this regard, I would particularly advise those who still do not have a good tone to play a number of notes of long duration often, striking the keys with only moderate strength and pressing them down only as long as is necessary for the tone to reach its maximum strength, but not beyond the point at which (by exerting even greater pressure) the pitch of the tone would become higher. One accustoms oneself through this practice to a very supple stroke, which is even required for maximum strength.

MESSA DI VOCE

The crescendo-decrescendo effect advocated and described above by Leopold Mozart was perhaps the most distinguishing and pervasive characteristic of articulation throughout the Classical era. Called messa di voce, it was discussed, recommended, praised, and universally appreciated as an ingredient of all musical expression by singers and instrumentalists alike—even by keyboardists, whose accomplishment of crescendos and decrescendos was unfortunately hindered by the mechanical restrictions of the instruments. Although often referred to as an ornament, the widespread application of messa di voce caused it to be an overall characteristic of articulation and one of the most recognizable and significant characteristics of performance practice during the Classical era.

Most commentary about messa di voce is in reference to solo performers, although there are quotations (by Charles Avison, Charles Burney, and Louis Spohr) that refer to messa di voce in ensemble performances and in accompanying. Notwithstanding the frequency of reference to solo performers, a convention of performance so much a part of the technique of singers and instrumentalists was surely an attribute of virtually all their music making—solo or ensemble.

Caution should be exercised when reading from the primary sources that the range of volume of the messa di voce went from pianissimo to fortissimo. The Classical-era fortissimo was much softer than the fortissimo of today and, furthermore, Classical-era levels of loudness were in the context of sweet tone production and light articulation (see Chapter 1).

The following quotations are addressed to flutists, violinists, keyboardists, trumpeters, singers, composers, and oboists, with definitions of messa di voce from dictionaries and primers, and with sources from Italy, Germany, England, and America. The absence of France reflects the lack of French primary sources during the Classical era, not the absence of the practice of messa di voce in France.

Geminiani, violin treatise (1751), "Example 1 B"

One of the principal Beauties of the Violin is the swelling or encreasing [sic] and softening the Sound; which is done by pressing the Bow upon the Strings with the Fore-finger more or less. In playing all long Notes the Sound should be begun soft, and gradually swelled till the Middle, and from thence gradually softened till the End.

———. "Of Swelling and Softening the Sound"

These two Elements may be used after each other; they produce great Beauty and Variety . . . and employ'd alternately, they are proper for any Expression or Measure.

**Quantz, flute treatise (1752), Chapter 14
"Of the Manner of Playing the Adagio"**

If you must hold a long note for either a whole or a half bar, which the Italians call *messa di voce*, you must first tip [the flute] gently with the tongue, scarcely exhaling; then you begin pianissimo, allow the strength of the tone to swell to the middle of the note, and from there begin to diminish it to the end of the note in the same fashion, making a vibrato with the finger on the nearest open hole.

Each note, whether it is a quarter note, eighth note, or sixteenth note, must have its own Piano and Forte, to the extent that time permits. If, however, several long notes are found in succession where, in strengthening the tone, the time does not permit you to swell each note individually, you can still swell and diminish the tone during notes like this so that some sound louder and others softer.

———. Chapter 12 "Of the Manner of Playing the Allegro"

Long notes must be sustained . . . by swelling and diminishing the strength of the tone, but the succeeding quick notes must be set off from them by a jovial execution.

——. Chapter 17, Section 5 "Of the Double Bass Player in Particular"

If in the Adagio a singer or solo player allows the tone of a long note to swell and diminish, and the movement of the bass beneath it is in different values, it is good for the accompanist likewise to strike each note more strongly and again more softly, in accordance with the example of the principal [solo] part.

——. Chapter 17, Section 7
"Of the Duties that All Accompanying Instrumentalists
in General Must Observe"

If in an Adagio the soloist alternately swells and moderates his sound, and thus plays more expressively by introducing light and shadow, the most beautiful effect is achieved if the accompanists assist him in the same manner, swelling and moderating their tone together with him. . . . This is particularly important in dissonances and in notes that prepare for a foreign tonality or cause a halt in quick motion. If in such cases you play everything with the same color or volume, the listeners will remain completely unmoved. If, on the contrary, you express the Forte and Piano by turns, in accordance with the nature of the ideas, you will achieve the goal you seek, namely, to maintain the constant attention of the listener, and guide him from one passion into another.

C. P. E. Bach, clavier treatise (1753), Part 2, Chapter 6 "Accompaniment"

When the principal [solo] part has a long held note which, according to the rules of good performance, should commence pianissimo, grow by degrees to fortissimo, and return similarly to pianissimo, the accompanist must follow with the greatest exactness. Every means available to him must be employed to attain a forte and piano. His increase and decrease must coincide with that of the principal part; nothing more, nothing less.

Avison, essay on musical expression (1753), Part 3, Section 2
"On the expressive performance of music in parts"

Sounds continued, or succeeding each other without Interruption, must be gently swelled and decreased, and this without drawling or Languor. All cut Sounds should be moderately struck, yet clear and distinct, that every shrill and sudden jerk with the Bow may be entirely avoided.

**Agricola, singing treatise (1757), Chapter 1
"Observations for the Use of the Singing Teacher"**

Practicing the crescendo and decrescendo when sustaining longer
notes generally extends the benefits to singing. A basic rule of good taste
is that every note regardless of its length should be given a crescendo and
decrescendo. . . . From the very beginning, then, an aspiring singer becomes
conditioned when sustaining all appropriate notes to make the crescendo
and decrescendo, with the result that it becomes fluent and all the easier.

——. Chapter 4 "Concerning Divisions"

Any note of considerable length must begin softly, then gradually
strengthened, or made to swell, and then ended piano. The only notes that
are excepted from this are those requiring a vigorous expression, or an
exclamation, or those on which a staccato is indicated—all of which one
must immediately articulate loudly, of course. . . .

It is not possible to express in mechanical rules how to increase and
decrease the loudness of a note. Much depends upon the discretion or the
sensitivity of the performer, and especially upon the main Affects [passions]
that dominate the entire piece.

For the sake of those who are unable to form an adequate idea of abstract
rules without having examples before their eyes, *Quantz* has performed the
laudable task, in his flute treatise, of prescribing most explicitly the loudness
and softness of almost every note of many individual phrases and even for
an entire adagio. Although all of this is actually meant for the flute, an
aspiring singer may find these examples very useful as he goes through them
and tries to put into practice that which is possible for his voice, according
to the rules.

Tartini, letter to Signora Maddalena Lombardini (1770)

You should make yourself a perfect mistress in every situation and part
of the bow—in the middle as well as at the extremities—and in moving it
up as well as in drawing it down. To unite all these laborious particulars
into one lesson, my advice is that you first exercise yourself in a swell upon
an open string, that you begin *pianissimo*, and increase the tone by slow
degrees to its *fortissimo*; and this study should be equally made, with the
motion of the bow up, and down, in which exercise you should spend at
least an hour every day, although at different times, a little in the morning,

and a little in the evening; having constantly in mind, that this practice is, of all others, the most difficult, and the most essential to playing well on the violin. When you are a perfect mistress of this part of a good performer, a swell will be very easy for you—beginning with the most minute softness, increasing the tone to its loudest degree, and diminishing it to the same point of softness with which you began, and all this in the same stroke of the bow.

Binns (Hoyle) dictionary (1770)

SOFTENING, in opposition to swelling, when you have been swelling a note, and then towards the end begin to soften, it is made more agreeable than it would be if it was all the time swelled without softening.

SWELLING, of a note, is to swell out the note by degrees stronger and stronger, and produces great beauty and variety in the Melody.

Burney, account of music in France and Italy (1770), "September. Arrived at Rome"

SUNDAY 30. Went this morning to S. Peters to hear Mass where I staid [sic] 2 hours and had a delightful contemplative lounge—from hence to Signor Santarelli, with whom I spent 2 hours more very profitably. He had looked out several curious things to show me, among which 2 MS [manuscript] volumes of extracts from curious authors and anecdotes concerning the lives of musicians by himself. . . . With regard to the famous *Miserere* of Allegri, he says its beauty and effect arise more from the manner in which it is performed than from the composition—there are many stanzas to the same music—and the singers have by tradition certain customs and expressions and graces of convention, which produce great effects—such as swelling and diminishing the notes altogether; accelerating or retarding the measure, singing some stanzas quicker than others *con certe expressioni e gruppi* etc.

Mancini, singing treatise (1774), Article 9 "Of the Messa di Voce"

Messa di voce describes that action which . . . gives to each long note a gradation, putting in it at the first a little voice, and then with proportion reinforcing it to the very strongest, finally taking it back with the same gradation as used in swelling.

Ordinarily this messa di voce should be used at the beginning of an aria, and on notes with hold signs [fermatas]; and similarly it is necessary at the beginning of a cadenza: but a true and worthy professor [teacher] will use it on every long note, which are found scattered through every musical cantilena.

It is certain that the messa di voce lends great excellence to singing, as it renders it more pleasing to the ear, and if it be executed with perfection, and with the union of a trill, is enough to make a cadenza perfect. . . .

The scholar [student] should not presume to be able to execute the messa di voce if he has not first acquired the art of conserving, reinforcing, and taking back the breath: since on this alone depends the gift of the just and necessary gradation of the voice. Finding himself then in a state of sustaining long notes, the scholar should exercise himself in giving each note the gradation and the proportionate value which he can without great effort, that is to say, from the beginning he gives a little voice, and proportionately reinforces it to that certain set grade from which he can diminish it with the same gradation which he adopted in swelling.

Do not doubt that in the beginning the scholar will find no little difficulty in the execution of the swell and diminish with equal gradation. But this difficulty will be in part reduced, if in doing the exercises he will fix the mouth well, as he should understand. The mouth should be scarcely open when starting the note, which helps the voice very much in coming forth sweetly, and then gradually it should be reinforced by opening the mouth until it reaches the limits prescribed by art. The scholar is advised to undertake the exercise of the messa di voce with moderation, because otherwise he will run the risk of tiring the chest, hence it will be best if at the beginning of this study, which should be daily without fail, he takes an occasional rest and relaxation.

I have gone far beyond the call of duty, reasoning so much on the messa di voce, but I tell you, studious youths, that it is so close to my heart that I could speak of it forever.

Bremner, *Six Quartettos for Two Violins, a Tenor, and Violoncello* (1777), Preface "Some Thoughts on the Performance of Concert-Music"

The practice of the swell . . . is of utmost consequence to those who wish to send a melodious Adagio, or any air home to the heart; but such slow movements as are composed more for the effects of harmony than melody, like those in the trios of Corelli, and many modern compositions, claim, in most instances, a steady equal pressure of bow. A daily practice of this manner of bowing is of equal importance with that of the swell, if not more so, to those who wish to be useful in concert; as it accustoms the student to have at all times length of bow to spare, of which every good performer makes a point. These two, namely the swell, and *sostenuto*, or sustained bow, may be said to be the roots from whence all the other powers of the bow spring.

W. A. Mozart, letter to his father (1777)

The leading soprano [at the German National Theater of Munich] is named Mlle. Kaiser. . . . She has a beautiful voice, not powerful, but by no means weak, very pure, and her intonation is good. . . . When she sustains her voice for a few bars, I have been astonished at the beauty of her *crescendo* and *decrescendo*. . . . People here are delighted with her—and I am delighted with them.

Tenducci, singing treatise (1782), "Instructions"

[The sixth rule in singing is] to sing the Scale, or Gamut frequently, allowing each sound one double half note or two whole notes, which must be sung in the same Breath; and this must be done, in both, a MEZZA DI VOCE, that is, by swelling the Voice, beginning Pianissimo, and increasing gradually to Forte, in the first part of the Time, and so diminishing gradually to the end of each Note. . . .

[The fifteenth rule in singing is] that a good MEZZA DI VOCE or swell of the Voice must always precede the AD LIBITUM Pause [fermata] and Cadenza.

Türk, clavier treatise (1789), "Introduction"

In spite of all [its] advantages, the clavichord is in many ways quite imperfect, as no unbiased person would begin to deny. For example, the short duration of the tone is unquestionably one of the imperfections to which the organ is an exception. A clavichord will seldom be found in which a tone in a moderate tempo will continue to sound at the same level of intensity for as long as the value of three to four quarter notes. However, one can hold a tone on a number of other instruments for several measures quite comfortably, with increasing and decreasing intensity. Alas, we must forego the crescendo and decrescendo of tone on the clavichord, by which we are often moved by singers and instrumentalists.

Tromlitz, flute treatise (1791), Chapter 10 "The Ornaments"

I count the *crescendo* and *decrescendo* among the discretionary ornaments. They are indicated with Italian words or the first with the sign ◁ and the other like this ▷. They can be used as well on a single note, especially a long one.

Wragg, oboe treatise (1792)

A swell ◁ or ◁◿ is executed by touching the Note, over which it is placed, at the first gently, and by degrees increasing the tone till it arrives at its full pitch; then diminishing it almost imperceptibly, till it falls off to its first softness. This I cannot recommend too much, having one of the finest effects on the ear which the instrument is capable of producing.

Law, *Harmonic Companion* (1807)

The swell is . . . applicable to all music. There is something of it on every note.

**Corri, singing treatise (1810),
"Dialogue. Introductory. Requisites for Vocal Music"**

Scholar. What are the requisites, or gifts, necessary for a good singer.
Master. First, a singer ought to have a good ear, which is a most important and indispensable requisite—a gift, without which no perfection can be obtained. . . .

Secondly, the voice. . . . It is not the extent or compass, nor the body of voice, which alone will constitute a good singer, but its proper and skillful management; good quality, or sweetness of voice, however, is a very desirable possession.

Thirdly, the swelling and dying of the voice [the crescendo and diminuendo]; without this important requisite no other can avail.

Scholar. I have always understood that the voice was the principal requisite for a singer.

Master. I allow that a good voice is one of the principal requisites, for voice alone will, in general, impose a great effect; yet a correct ear, a gradual swelling and dying of the voice, distinct articulation (which creates expression) along with a moderate compass of voice will certainly produce *more real effect* on the *heart* than the voice alone . . . can do.

———. "Hints to Parents"

Scholar. My ambition is to sing well, in whatever style you may think I am most likely to succeed.

Master. I will then first direct my attention, to determine which will be most suitable to your natural endowments, the cantabile, bravura, characteristic, comic; and thereby be better enabled to render you service: but I must repeat, whatever style we may fix on, in order to sing with meaning and expression, the following important requisites are indispensable.

First, Intonation.

Secondly, Crescendo and Diminuendo.

Thirdly, Articulation.

Fourthly, giving the proper character to the words and the different styles of music, leaving extravaganzas and stage tricks to professors.

———. "Progressive rules for daily practice"

The intention of this Exercise is to acquire the art of taking breath and how to retain it, by which is effected the swelling and dying of the voice, the most important qualification in the vocal art.

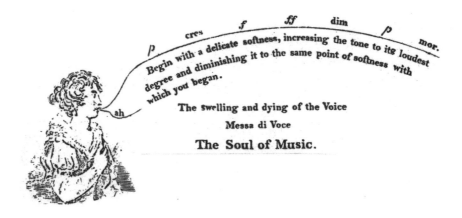

p cres f ff dim p mor.

Begin with a delicate softness, increasing the tone to its loudest degree and diminishing it to the same point of softness with which you began.

ah

The swelling and dying of the Voice

Messa di Voce

The Soul of Music.

Spohr, musical diary, "Switzerland and Italy, 1816"

Last Sunday, Prince Friedrich of Gotha took me to the Sistine Chapel, where I heard the famous choir. . . . Several times we heard crescendos achieved by the gradual addition of voices, and diminuendos achieved by the same process in reverse, the device which is said to produce such a stunning effect in the Good Friday performances of the famous *Miserere*! It was not ineffective, but one can hear it from any well-trained choir.

Jenks, *Harmony of Zion* (1818)

Swell should be applied by striking the note soft and gradually increasing the sound to the centre, then diminishing in the same proportion.

Busby, musical manual (1828)

Messa di Voce. A swell of the voice upon a continued or holding note.

Nathan, singing treatise (1836), Chapter 6 "Of the Human Voice, and its General Qualities, On the Swelling and Dying of the Voice"

This swelling and dying of the voice is the most important to practice, and one of the easiest requisites to acquire, if judiciously treated; on it depends the principal art of singing, for it sweetens, enriches, and gives that delicious roundness and fullness to the tone so desirable for every branch of vocal science.

It is this swell and dying of the voice, which makes music respond to the various passions, and passes the feeling of one mind to another. . . .

Monotonous tones, that are produced with an equal degree of loudness, without any preparation by the *crescendo* and *diminuendo*, by their uniformity tire the ear, as a country, whose sterility admits of no varying scene, wearies the mind; but, as a prospect rich in hill and glade, whereon the eye gazes with delight, the swelling and dying of the voice, by the pleasing versatility of light and shade fascinate the imagination. . . .

The swell should be commenced in the *feigned voice*, gradually stealing and increasing on the ear in magnitude of tone, and melting again by the same ratio into its original softness. [Nathan makes similar statements about messa di voce five other times in his treatise].

Czerny, pianoforte treatise (1839), Volume 4, Op. 500, Chapter 3 "On the Proper Performance of all Beethoven's Works for the Pianoforte," *Quintett for Pianoforte, Hautboy, Clarinet, Horn and Bassoon*, Op. 16, movement 2

Here, in order to vie with the wind instruments in the performance of the beautiful melody, the pianist must employ all of his art of delicate *cantabile* touch and expression. Without degenerating into a drawl, he must impart to the theme, by a suitable swelling and by a very gentle *diminuendo* (particularly in the 7th bar), that utterance of feeling, which in general characterizes all the melodies by Beethoven.

Garcia, singing treatise (1840–1847), "The Messa Di Voce, Etc."

Besides being equally sustained in any degree of power, sounds may be swelled and diminished. . . . Swelled sounds (*messa di voce*) begin pianissimo and by degrees acquire increasing force till they arrive at their loudest, which should happen at half their length; then the process should be reversed. . . . A free note under a pause [fermata] is generally swelled and diminished; when long enough, though measured, it receives the same treatment.

Meyerbeer, *Roberto*

"Undulated sounds" are each slightly swelled and diminished with a dying prolongation.

Meyerbeer, *Crociato*

INSTRUMENTAL ARTICULATION

As with most elements of performance practice during the Classical era, the articulation of instrumental music depended upon its mood or character. Two general categories of tempo governed the character of most music—fast and slow. A composition to be performed in a fast tempo, called the allegro style, had an incisiveness of attack and a degree of separation between notes. A composition to be performed in a slow tempo, referred to as cantabile in style, had a soft smoothness of attack and no separation between notes except that perceived by the effect of messa di voce or by intentional breaks for phrasing. Regarding the effect of messa di voce, the softness of volume created by one note ending a decrescendo and the next note beginning a crescendo caused an apparent separation between the notes even though there may not have been an actual stoppage of sound. Consequently, the legato style of articulation in the Classical era was quite different from that which became common later in the Romantic era. The Classical-era legato was characterized by undulations of volume whereas the Romantic-era legato, with notes beginning and ending at relatively the same volume, was characterized by a sustained quality.

Whether actual (the allegro style) or implied (the cantabile style), separation of articulation was an aspect of performance that was idealized and that portrayed a lightness of texture supportive of and corresponding to other aspects of Classical-era elegance. Separation, or silence, was also understood as an integral element of the durational value of notation. This is to say, as described by Bédos de Celles below, the length of a note was not measured only in sound, it was measured in sound and silence.

Bédos de Celles, organ treatise (1766), Part 4, Chapter 4, Section 2

All the notes in execution, whether ornamented or not, are partly in *hold* and partly in *silence*; which means that they all have a certain length of *sound* and a certain length of *silence*, which united makes the whole value of the note.

These *silences* at the end of each note fix its articulation and are as necessary as the holds themselves, without which they could not be detached from one another; and a piece of music, however beautiful, would be no more agreeable without these *silences d'articulation* than these country songs of *Poitou*, performed upon insipid bagpipes which only give a noisy and inarticulate sound.

To be convinced of the necessity of these *silences* at the end of each note, let one play upon an organ, harpsichord, or any other keyboard instrument, a piece of music, no matter which, and in the playing of it pay more attention to the execution than to the way it is written; it will be noticed that a finger which has just finished a note is often lifted long before it is placed on the next note, and this interval is necessarily a *silence*, and if one takes care, it will be seen that between all the notes there are intervals more or less long, without which the execution would be bad: even the notes of the most rapid shakes are separated by very small intervals. Those intervals, more or less long, I call *silences d'articulation* in music, from which no note is exempt, like the articulated pronunciation of consonants in speech, without which the syllables would have no other distinction than the inarticulate sounds of the vowels.

The understanding of durational value incorporating silence was also an integral aspect of metric accentuation. As presented in Chapter 4, patterns of emphasized and de-emphasized notes were a significant facet of performance practice during the Classical era, especially in regard to quantitas intrinseca—the intrinsic quantity or length of notes. With notes on weak beats of measures and on weak parts of beats having intrinsically shortened values, the texture of the music in performance was filled with many silences caused by separations between notes. However, not all notes were separated. Notes on strong beats were long and fully, or almost fully, occupied by sound, messa di voce notwithstanding. Only notes on weak beats were shortened. In Example A, the notes on beats one and four of each measure of the bass part, being on strong beats, have an intrinsic full value and therefore would not be noticeably separated from the notes following them. All other notes, being on weak beats of the measure and therefore intrinsically short, would be separated from each other. Similarly in Example B, the note on beat one of measure two would not be noticeably separated from the note on beat two. The other notes would be separated. The two notes in measure one would be separated only by the softness of messa di voce crescendos and decrescendos.

Example A
Joseph Haydn, *Missa Sancti Nicolai,* Kyrie, measures 1–3

Example B
W. A. Mozart, *Requiem* K626, Tuba mirum, measures 1–2

The term "silences of articulation" was generally used to refer to a particular type of quantitas intrinseca, one in which the dots of dotted rhythms were silent. Seen in the examples below, the notated rhythms on the left would be performed as illustrated on the right.

Notated   Performed

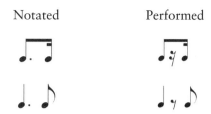

The practice of silences of articulation was pervasive in the early years of the Classical era, especially in the allegro style. In the later years, articulation of dotted rhythms, as with articulation of all music, depended upon a variety of expressive characteristics.

Along with tempo, messa di voce, the quantitas intrinseca aspect of metric accentuation, and silences of articulation, varying degrees of separation between notes in instrumental music were determined by the instrument being used for performance. Keyboard touch, string bowings, and wind and brass tonguings each created slightly different degrees and qualities of separation. Recommendations regarding articulation in treatises devoted to specific instruments, therefore, are also slightly different from one another, although the resulting qualities of articulation are relatively similar. For instance, there was no need to recommend separation between notes in the cantabile style to string players, because the bow in use (see the Leopold Mozart drawing at the beginning of this chapter) was concave and could produce little pressure (and, therefore, little volume) at its outward ends. As a result of this, sounds made at the beginning and end of the bow were soft, creating a messa di voce by the mere physical properties of the bow. With the invention of a convex bow by François Tourte at the end of the eighteenth century, consistent pressure could be applied throughout the bow stroke and, consequently, consistent volume could be achieved. The Tourte bow did not come into general use, however, until the very late years of the Classical era. Bow direction also contributed to the differing qualities of articulation. The pressure of the up bow was noticeably less than the pressure of the down bow, causing notes played by the up bow to seem softer, or weaker, than notes played by the down bow.

The players of wind and brass instruments pronounced syllables such as "ti" and "di" to create differing qualities of articulation. The sharper consonant ("ti") caused a sharper attack, while "di" caused a correspondingly duller attack. Furthermore, the relative energy produced by the articulated consonant overshadowed the vowel, which was soft in comparison and also generally short. Additional recommendations for silence or separation were not needed; slurs, which are discussed below, were used to indicate that notes under their arch were to be played legato.

Keyboard instruments required the greatest degrees of separation in order to create desirable qualities of articulation. Fingers had to be lifted from one note before the next note was sounded, the degree of separation being anywhere from approximately a quarter to half the value of the printed note. This was referred to as "ordinary touch."

Articulation that was to differ from the basic separation of the allegro or cantabile styles was conveyed to the performer through slur, wedge, or dot markings. Regardless of the instrument being played, a slur indicated a connection of the notes under its arch, with no noticeable break. The slur also conveyed a decrescendo. That is, each note under the slur was to become progressively softer. The slur sign thus obviated the pattern of metric accentuation. As a bow was drawn across a string or a breath was gradually exhaled, a natural dissipation of volume occurred. Additionally, it was understood that slurs would be clearly separated from one another, not connected in the fluid fashion that became the norm in more modern times.

Wedges or dots, both signifying a staccato articulation, were used to express extreme shortness or separation. Wedges indicated a weightier and therefore somewhat longer staccato than dots, which indicated a light and short staccato. Wedges and dots were not, however, always clearly indicated in manuscripts; this resulted in printed scores with either all wedges changed to dots, or a confusion of the two. Composers were also occasionally careless. Nevertheless, an important differentiation of articulation of staccatos was part of Classical-era performance.

All the qualities and degrees of separation discussed so far would not have created particularly disjunct or seemingly disconnected melodic lines in the relatively reverberant acoustics of churches, halls, and other venues used for performance during the Classical era. Articulative separations, on the other hand, would have enabled the music to maintain important qualities of lightness, clarity, and elegance. A question, then, might be asked about modern-day performances in non-reverberant acoustics. Should separations between notes exist? The answer to this question can be yes if degrees of separation produce results similar to those during the Classical era. The qualities of messa di voce, quantitas intrinseca, silences of articulation, and expressive staccatos and slurs can, with artful manipulation, be as much an appreciated aspect of modern-day performance as they were during the Classical era.

During the early years of the era, articulation was rather rule-oriented and regular: straightforward rhythmic patterns allowed for pervasive application of messa di voce; strong and weak beats were designed for a regularity of metric accentuation; there was infrequent indication of staccato markings; and moods or characteristics governing tempo were simple and direct. By the latter years of the era, articulation was more varied and complex: expressive markings such as sforzandos were used to displace regular stresses of metric accentuation; slur markings combined notes into unusual and irregular groupings; a more legato style of execution was becoming the desirable norm; and mood was becoming multi-faceted and more and more the governing agent of articulation. By the end of the era, there were many degrees of separation, and separation itself was not always expected.

Quantz, flute treatise (1752), Chapter 6
"Of the Use of the Tongue in Blowing upon the Flute"

The tongue is the means by which we give animation to the execution of the notes upon the flute. It is indispensable for musical articulation, and serves the same purpose as the bow-stroke upon the violin. . . .

To make the tone of the flute speak properly with the aid of the tongue, you must, as you blow, pronounce certain syllables, in accordance with the nature of the notes to be played. These syllables are of three kinds. The first is *ti* or *di*, the second *tiri*, and the third *did'll*. The last is usually called the *double tongue*. The manner in which each is to be learned and applied will be treated in separate sections.

——. Section 1 "Of the Use of the Tongue with the Syllable ti or di"

Since some notes must be tipped firmly and others gently, it is important to remember that *ti* is used for short, equal, lively, and quick notes. *Di*, on the contrary, must be used when the melody is slow, and even when it is gay, provided that it is still pleasing and sustained. In the Adagio *di* is always used, except in dotted notes, which require *ti*. Those accustomed to the Upper Saxon dialect must take particular care not to confuse the *t* with the *d*. . . .

All notes do not have to be tipped: if an arc [slur] stands above two or more, they must be connected. Thus you must remember that only the note on which the slur begins needs to be tipped; the others found beneath the arc are slurred to it, and the tongue meanwhile has nothing to do. Ordinarily *di* rather than *ti* is used for slurred notes (see Fig. 5).

Fig. 5

di‿ di‿ di‿ di‿ di

If, however, a stroke [wedge] stands above the note preceding the slur, both the first and the following note receive *ti* (see Fig. 6). . . .

Fig. 6

ti‿ ti—— di—— ti ti

It is impossible to define fully in words either the difference between *ti* or *di*, upon which a considerable part of the expression of the passions depends, or all of the different kinds of tongue-strokes. Individual reflection will suffice to convince everyone that, just as there are various shades between black and white, there is more than one intermediate degree between a firm and a gentle tongue-stroke. Hence you can also express *ti* and *di* in diverse ways with the tongue. You simply must try to make the tongue supple enough to be able to tip the notes more firmly at one time, more gently at another, in accordance with their nature. This is accomplished both by the quicker or slower withdrawal of the tongue from the palate, and by the stronger or weaker exhalation of the wind.

——. Supplement "Several Remarks for the Use of the Oboe and Bassoon"

Except in matters of *fingering* and *embouchure,* the oboe and bassoon have much in common with the transverse flute. Hence those who apply themselves to one of these two instruments may profit not only from the instructions given for the use of the two kinds of tongue-strokes with *ti* and *tiri,* but, in general, from the entire method for the flute, in so far as it does not have to do with fingering and embouchure.

——. Chapter 11 "Of Good Execution in General in Singing and Playing"

You must avoid slurring notes that ought to be articulated, and articulating those that ought to be slurred. The notes must not seem stuck together. The tonguing on wind instruments, and the bowing on bowed instruments, must always be in conformity with the aims of the composer, in accordance with his indications of slurs and strokes; this puts life into the notes. [Articulation of this sort] distinguishes these instruments from the bagpipe, which is played without tonguing. The fingers, no matter how smoothly or animatedly they move, cannot convey musical articulation by themselves, if the tongue or the bow does not contribute its greater share, by proper movements suitable to the piece to be performed. Musical ideas that belong together must not be separated; on the other hand, you must separate those ideas in which one musical thought ends and a new idea begins, even if there is no rest or caesura. This is especially true when the final note of the preceding phrase and opening note of the following one are on the same pitch. . . .

Sustained and flattering notes must be slurred to one another, but gay and leaping notes must be detached and separated from one another.

——. Chapter 17, Section 2 "Of the Ripieno Violinists in Particular"

In Fig. 10 the second and third notes are taken with an up-stroke in the Allegro, but the stroke is stopped or detached a little at the dot; the following two G's, however, must each receive down-strokes. . . .

Fig. 10

In slurring notes in the Adagio, you must be careful not to make them seem detached, unless there are dots beneath a slur that is above the notes (Fig. 20). Likewise, *pincemens* [pizzicatos] must not be introduced, especially if they are not indicated, lest the sentiment that the slurred notes are to express be in any way impeded. But if strokes are used instead of dots, as in the last two notes of this example, the notes must be attacked sharply, in a single stroke of the bow. For just as a distinction is to be made between strokes and dots without slurs above them, that is, the notes with strokes must be played with completely detached strokes, and those with dots simply with short strokes and in a sustained manner, so a similar distinction is required when there are slurs above the notes. Strokes, however, appear more often in the Allegro than in the Adagio.

Fig. 20

C. P. E. Bach, clavier treatise (1753), Part 1, Chapter 3 "Performance"

Attack and touch are one and the same thing. Everything depends on their force and duration. When notes are to be detached from each other strokes or dots are placed above them, as illustrated [below].

Notes are detached with relation to: 1) their notated length, that is, a half, quarter, an eighth of a bar; 2) the tempo, fast or slow; and 3) volume, forte or piano. Such notes are always held for a little less than half of their notated length. In general, detached notes appear mostly in leaping passages and rapid tempos.

Notes which are to be played legato must be held for their full length. A slur is placed above [or below] them in the manner [shown here].

The slur applies to all of the notes included under its trace. . . .

Tones which are neither detached, connected, nor fully held are sounded for half their value, unless the abbreviation *Ten.* [*tenuto*] is written over them, in which case they must be held fully. Quarters and eighths in moderate and slow tempos are usually performed in this semidetached manner. . . .

Short notes which follow dotted ones are always shorter in execution than their notated length. Hence it is superfluous to place strokes or dots over them. . . . Dots after long notes or after short ones in slow tempos, and isolated dots, are all held. However, in rapid tempos prolonged successions of dots are performed as rests, the apparent opposite demand of the notation notwithstanding. A more accurate notation would remove such a discrepancy. Lacking this, however, the content of a piece will shed light on the details of its performance. . . .

In general, the briskness of allegros is expressed by detached notes and the tenderness of adagios by broad, slurred notes. The performer must keep in mind that these characteristic features of allegros and adagios are to be given consideration even when a composition is not so marked, as well as when the performer has not yet gained an adequate understanding of the affect of a work. I use the expression, "in general," advisedly, for I am well aware that all kinds of execution may appear in any tempo.

Marpurg, clavier treatise (1755), Chapter 7
"Concerning Various Musical Symbols"

An arc drawn from one note to another note not on the same pitch means that these two notes are to be slurred. "To slur" means not to raise the finger from the foregoing note before one touches the following note. . . . In direct contrast to slurring is detachment, which consists of sustaining a note not for its value, but for only approximately half of it. This is indicated by dots placed over or under the notes intended to be detached. One often uses a small straight stroke for the same purpose. . . . Both slurring and detaching are contrary to ordinary progression, which consists of very swiftly raising the finger from the preceding key just shortly before touching the following note. This ordinary method of progressing is never indicated since it is always presumed.

**L. Mozart, violin treatise (1756), Chapter 1, Section 3
"Of the Duration or Value of the Notes, Rests, and Dots,
together with an Explanation of all Musical Signs and Technical Words"**

In quick pieces the bow is lifted at each dot: therefore each note is separated from the other and performed in a springing style. For example:

——. Chapter 7, Section 1 "Of the varieties of Bowing in even notes"

If in a musical composition two, three, four, and even more notes are bound together by the half circle [slur], so that one recognizes by this that the composer wishes the notes not to be separated but played singingly in one slur, the first of such united notes must be somewhat more strongly stressed, but the remainder slurred on to it quite smoothly and more and more quietly.

Tartini, violin treatise (1771), "Rules for bowing"

In performance it is important to distinguish between cantabile and allegro music. In cantabile passages, the transition from one note to the next must be made so perfectly that no interval of silence is perceptible between them; in allegro passages, on the other hand, the notes should be somewhat detached.

**Türk, clavier treatise (1789), Chapter 6, Part 2
"Concerning the Clarity of Execution"**

Mechanical clarity requires that even for the most rapid passage as well as for the essential and extemporaneous ornaments, every tone must be played with its proper intensity, plainly and clearly separated from the others. Those who play with lack of clarity either leave some of the tones out completely (the tones are "choked out" or "skipped over"), or at least they are not fully and clearly separated from one another. Similarly, when the keys are struck too hard or soft, the execution can become unclear. This is also true if the keys are played in a too detached manner, or if the fingers are allowed to remain on the keys too long.

———. Chapter 6, Part 3
"Concerning the Expression of the Prevailing Character"

The detaching or separating of tones is indicated as we know by a stroke (a) or a dot (b) above (or below) the notes. If an entire piece or a major part of it, or often only a single musical idea, is to be played in a detached manner, then this is shown at the beginning of the piece, or above the passage to be so detached, by the word staccato (c).

The signs at (a) and (b) have the same meaning, although some would like to indicate by the stroke (a) a shorter staccato than that indicated by the dot (b). If it is desired to introduce some melodic ideas in which the tones are to be slurred, into a composition with the superscription *staccato*, then these are indicated by a curved line unless the composer has presumed that the player would introduce this variation in touch himself. Afterward, the staccato again holds good.

In playing detached tones one lifts the finger from the key when half the value of the note is past and pauses for the remaining period. . . . Mistakes are often made with respect to detaching tones, for a number of people are accustomed to striking keys as quickly as possible without regard for the values of the given notes, even though in most cases the finger should remain on the key long enough to take up at least half the note's duration. In general, in performance of detached notes, one must particularly observe the prevailing character of the composition, the tempo, the required loudness or softness, etc. If the character of a composition is serious, tender, sad, etc., then the detached tones must not be as short as they would be in pieces of lively, humorous, and the like, nature. Occasional detached tones in a songful Adagio are not to be as short as they would be in an Allegro. For forte one can play detached notes a little shorter than for piano. . . . The playing of notes which are to be slurred and yet detached is signified either as shown in (a) or by the word *appoggiato*. The dot indicates the pressure which every key must receive, and by the curved line the player is reminded to hold the tone out until the duration of the given note has been completed.

The slurring (binding) of tones is commonly shown by a curved line as in the following examples. If all tones of a composition or most of its parts are to be slurred, then this manner of treatment is indicated at the beginning by the word *legato*. Often curved lines are written only over the first measures and serve to indicate to the player that he should continue to use this form of execution, until the contrary is designated by strokes or rests.

For tones which are to be slurred, the finger should be allowed to remain on the key until the duration of the given note is completely past, so that not the slightest separation (rest) results. By the length of the curved line, the composer indicates how many tones are to be slurred together. For example:

At (a) all eight tones are slurred and in (b) each group of four tones is slurred. It should be observed, in addition, that the note on which the curved line begins should be very gently (and almost imperceptibly) accented. In example (g) this gentle emphasis falls (contrary to the rule which is otherwise to be followed) on the weak notes marked with + and in (h) on f#, d, b, etc. The sign at (k) signifies that all the notes are to be slurred; nevertheless, the first, third, fifth, and seventh tones are to be softly marked. . . .

For tones which are to be played in customary fashion (that is, neither detached nor slurred) the finger is lifted a little earlier from the key than is required by the duration of the note. Consequently, the notes in (a) are played approximately as in (b) or (c), depending on the circumstances. If there are some notes intermingled which should be held out for their full value, then *ten.* or *tenuto* is written over them (d).

Bach says on p. 112 [of his clavier treatise]: "The notes which are neither detached nor slurred nor to be sustained are held down as long as one half of their value." But taken in general, this kind of playing does not seem to me to be the best. For 1) the character of a composition necessitates a variety of restrictions in this respect; 2) the distinction between the tone which is actually detached and that which is to be played in the customary manner is practically abolished; and 3) the execution would probably become too short (choppy) if every note not slurred was held for only half of its value, and consequently the second half would be a rest, as shown above in (e). [Türk then provides detailed descriptions of the various shadings of detachment or connection related to different tempo markings and expressive characteristics.]

Tromlitz, flute treatise (1791)

If the composer wants to have notes articulated as a unit, he must put a slur over them. This connecting of notes is usually called slurring, and in my opinion is not suitable, for it implies that the first note is articulated and the second slurred to the first. It is unclear, for it does not say which note must be stressed. It is true that the first note, because of its intrinsic importance, must be articulated with more emphasis than the second, which because of its position is appropriately shorter; but it should nevertheless be articulated clearly. The expression of slurring is responsible for the fact that the second note is often very unclear and at times inaudible. . . .

Upon close examination, you will notice that the tongue forms a kind of syllable through its movement to produce tone, the syllables put together form words, and a kind of language or articulation is put together, one that can be used in all instances according to the proper affect. Quantz has already dealt with this matter in his instructions on playing the flute, but his instructions in how to use the tongue are applicable only to very specific passages, and not to the subject of articulation as a whole. . . .

Quantz says that single notes, when they are to be articulated separately, should get the syllable *ti* or *di*. I think, however, that the vowel *i* does not give the best effect in producing a sound on the flute, because with this articulation the inner cavity of the mouth and the muscles tighten up and make the tone shrill. . . .

This has motivated me to choose another vowel which makes the tone fuller, rounder and bigger, and in my opinion none is more appropriate than *a*. Try to pronounce the *a* as much like an *a* as possible, and you will discover that with the expansion of the throat and other inner cavities the tone becomes fuller. Instead of *ti* or *di* you form the syllable *ta, da,* or *ra,* the use and proper application of which will be explained in the following paragraphs. [Tromlitz then lists a profusion of rules for the use of the syllables, expanding upon, but not contradicting Quantz's recommendations.]

Altenburg, trumpet and kettledrum treatise (1795), Chapter 10
"On the heroic fieldpieces, principle playing, and playing at table,
as well as on so-called tonguing and huffing"

[The] tongue stroke is of different kinds, for both in single and double tonguing one does not pronounce the syllables in one manner only. . . . In single tonguing one uses the four syllables *ritiriton* or *kitikiton*, and in double tonguing one prefaces the syllable *ti*, for example, *tiritiriton* or *tikitikiton*. These syllables or tonguings are used only in the low register, and appear in musical notation as follows:

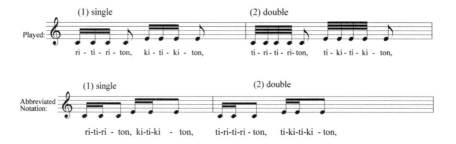

It can be seen that in the performance of these two tonguings there are certainly just as many syllables as there are notes. However, in the interest of brevity, this notation is not necessary. These syllables are sometimes exchanged, depending on the circumstances and the music, so that the last syllable *ton* is expressed first and the others thereafter. An example will make the matter clearer:

Notated:

Played: ton   ri-ti-ri,   ton - ki-ti-ki,   ton -ti-ri-ti-ri,   ton-ti- ki-ti-ki,

It thus depends mainly on the eighth note, whether it comes first or at the end.

——. Chapter 11, "On Clarino Playing and the Style of Execution Required Thereby"

Seek to express well the singing character of the slow movements, and to execute properly the ornaments which occur. Long notes must be sustained with moderation and be skillfully joined to one another. It is well known that the human voice is supposed to serve as the model for all instruments; thus should the clarino player try to imitate it as much as possible, and should seek to bring forth the so-called *cantabile* on his instrument.

Clementi, pianoforte treatise (1801), "Style, Graces, and marks of Expression, etc."

The best general rule is to keep down the keys of the instrument the *full length* of every note; for when the contrary is required, the notes are marked either thus:

called in *Italian*, *staccato*; denoting *distinctness*, and *shortness* of sound; which is produced by lifting the finger up, as soon as it has struck the key: or they are marked thus:

which, when composers are *exact* in their writing, means *less* staccato than the preceding mark; the finger, therefore, is kept down somewhat longer: or thus

which means *still less* staccato: The nice degrees of *more* and *less*, however, depend on the *character,* and *passion* of the piece; the *style* of which must be *well observed* by the performer. The notes marked thus:

called *legato* in Italian, must be played in a *smooth* and *close* manner; which is done by keeping down the first key, 'till the next is struck; by which means, the strings *vibrate sweetly* into one another.

N.B. When the composer leaves the legato and *staccato* to the performer's taste, the best rule is to adhere chiefly to the *legato,* reserving the *staccato* to give *spirit* occasionally to certain passages and to set off the *higher beauties* of the *legato.*

Czerny, pianoforte treatise (1839)

[The earlier manner of articulation was] a clear . . . style more inclined to *staccato* than to *legato;* . . . the pedal hardly ever used and never necessary.

Czerny, letters on playing the pianoforte (c.1837–1841)

Beethoven. . . . insisted on legato technique, which was one of the unforgettable features of his playing; at that time [early nineteenth century] all other pianists considered that kind of legato unattainable, since the *hammered*, detached staccato technique of Mozart's time was still *fashionable.*

Thayer, biography of Beethoven (1866–1879), Volume 2

Beethoven told Czerny that he had heard Mozart play; his execution was delicate, but choppy, without *legato*, a style of which the first admirable master was B[eethoven], who treated the piano like an organ. . . .

Beethoven, who had heard Mozart play, said afterwards that his playing was neat and clear, but rather empty, weak, and old fashioned. The *legato* and *cantabile* on the piano were unknown at that time, and B[eethoven] was the first to discover [these] new and grand effects on that instrument. . . .

In teaching, Beethoven insisted on a correct position of the fingers according to Em. Bach's method. . . . He used the pedal a great deal, far more than is indicated in his scores. His interpretation of Handel's and Gluck's scores, and of Seb. Bach's fugues, was unique; the first-named [Handel] he reproduced with a fullness of harmony and a spirit which transformed these compositions.

Extraordinary as was his playing in improvisation, it was often less satisfying in the execution of his already engraved compositions; for, as he never had patience or time to practice anything, his success in interpretation depended chiefly on chance and mood; besides, his playing, as well as his compositions, being in advance of his period, his titanic execution was too much for the pianofortes then made, which (up to 1810) were very weak and incomplete. Hence it came that Hummel's pearly and brilliant style, so well adapted to the times, was, of course, much more intelligible and attractive to the general public. But, Beethoven's playing of the Adagio and Legato . . . has never, so far as I know, been surpassed by anyone.

VOCAL ARTICULATION

A smooth connection of notes was the idealized manner of vocal articulation throughout the Classical era. This so-called "singing" or "cantabile" style was even idealized by instrumentalists, who frequently expressed that all instrumental playing should be modeled after singing (see Chapter 1). Counter to this expression, however, was an equally frequent commentary about separations of articulation in the allegro style. Moreover, and much more important, the smooth connection of notes in the Classical era was not the same as that in more recent times, and one should not think of the Classical-era cantabile as equivalent to the Romantic-era legato. A number of significant differences distinguish the two.

The pervasive crescendos and decrescendos of messa di voce caused the Classical-era cantabile to have a quality of softness between notes that portrayed articulative separation or silence. Actual separations of sound between notes may not have existed, but the undulating variation in volume produced this effect. The impression of the vocal line was rather like a string of pearls—round-shaped objects connected by a thread.

In addition, the strong and weak rendering of textual syllables associated with the practice of metric accentuation (see Chapter 4) caused variations in volume and duration. Weak syllables or words sung softer and shorter than strong syllables or words gave the music a sense of contrast that mitigated a smoothness of connection.

Furthermore, staccato and slur markings caused separations to the general smooth connection of notes. Both markings were treated as in instrumental music, where they were utilized extensively. Staccatos in vocal music, seen in Examples A and B, were often indicated by wedges, which were longer and weightier staccatos than those indicated by dots.

Example A
W. A. Mozart, *Mass in C Minor* K139, Kyrie,
measures 48–55

Example B
W. A. Mozart, *Mass in C* K66 (Dominicus-Messe), Credo,
measures 260–263

Slurs in vocal music were used mainly for syllabification purposes (i.e., to bind together all notes sung to a single syllable of text). However, as seen in Examples C and D, slurs were also occasionally used to indicate articulation. The appearance of these articulative slurs indicated not only the smooth connection of notes under the arch of the slur mark, but also, and significantly, a break between the final note of one slur and the beginning note of the succeeding slur.

Example C
W. A. Mozart, *Vesperae solennes de Confessore* K339, "Laudate pueri," measures 1–8

Example D
Joseph Haydn, *Missa in Angustiis* (Nelson Mass), Credo, measures 233–239

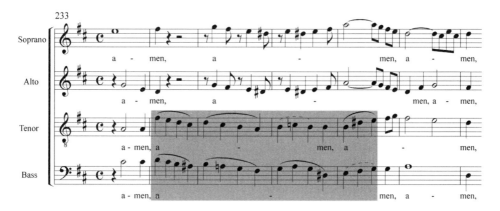

The applications of messa di voce (crescendos and decrescendos), metric accentuation (strong and weak emphases of notes), quantitas intrinseca (long and short durations of notes), and expressive variations of staccatos and slurs were universal in the Classical era; they were discussed in a wide variety of treatises, instrumental and vocal, and were, therefore, an integral part of all performance. Other performance practices, such as silences of articulation (the practice of silencing dots in dotted rhythms), were discussed only in treatises for specific instruments. However, because of the importance or extensiveness of these practices, they were also an integral part of all performance, instrumental and vocal. Silences of articulation, in particular, was universal for several reasons: 1) it was a logical extension of the general state of articulation; silences between many notes was common; 2) it reinforced metric accentuation by creating rhythmic activity at the inception of beats; and 3) it was a necessary ingredient to the accomplishment of clear, elegant musical textures in the commonplace reverberant acoustical environments. A melodic line such as seen in Example E (a fugal subject occurring many times in a dense vocal and instrumental texture) is illustrative. The dotted quarter notes would have been shortened by the duration of the dot by both vocalists and instrumentalists, and the music would have had requisite separations between notes to maintain clarity.

Example E
W. A. Mozart, *Requiem* K626, measures 1–3

The melodic line would not have sounded disconnected in a reverberant church or concert hall. The echo of reverberation would have provided an aural connection between notes. Does this mean that present-day performances should forego silences of articulation and, for that matter, messa di voce and metric accentuation? The answer to this question, as discussed in regards to instrumental articulation above, should be no. The separations that were a part of Classical-era performance should continue. However, the degrees of the separations should be adjusted to provide the effect or outcome of articulation heard during the Classical era. Actual and long silences should be a part of vocal production in very reverberant churches, whereas implied or short silences should occur in non-reverberant settings.

The main features of vocal articulation were determined by text—by the physical circumstances of producing consonants. Consequently, the majority of commentary in the Classical era about vocal articulation is in reference to clarity and distinctness of enunciation. Furthermore, the communication of the spirit of the words being sung by a singer or the mood that the composer may have intended in his composition was equally important.

Quantz, flute treatise (1752), Chapter 11
"Of Good Execution in General in Singing and Playing"

Excepted from the [Metric Accentuation] rule is all quick passage-work which must be executed by the human voice, unless it is supposed to be slurred. Since every note of passage-work of this [unslurred] kind for the voice must be performed distinctly and stressed by a gentle breath of air from the chest, there can be no inequality [of rhythm].

Agricola, singing treatise (1757), Chapter 4 "Concerning Divisions"

It is obvious how concerned and careful a singer must be with correct pronunciation, not only of the vowels but also of the consonants. If a singer is remiss in clear enunciation of one or the other, a lack of clarity results, made more obvious by singing than by speech because of the constantly changing pitches, because the syllables are held longer, and because of the variety of different pitches that can appear above the same syllable, etc.—all of which are responsible for the unintelligibility.

In large buildings or in the open air . . . consonants must be pronounced more crisply—in fact, almost excessively so—than in common speech, but with close attention to their individual hardness or softness. Close at hand, such crisp enunciation would not be especially pleasant to hear and would sound somewhat affected; but it is greatly effective at a distance, delivering all words clearly to the ear and simultaneously losing all unpleasantness. A singer accustomed to precise pronunciation of consonants will always be better understood at a distance, if he does not sing too loudly, than one who yells with all his might but does not enunciate the consonants crisply and clearly enough.

When several consecutive notes on the same pitch occur in moderate tempo, above which there is a slur sign and under the slur sign there are dots, one must neither separate nor detach the notes, but execute each note instead with a slight pressure from the chest.

Manfredini, harmony treatise (1775)

How is it possible to give perfect pleasure to listeners, and to oneself, if one does not pronounce clearly, and if that which is said is not well understood, even though sung?

Tenducci, singing treatise (1782), "Instructions"

[The fifth rule of singing is] to articulate perfectly each Syllable. . . .

[The 16th rule is] that in pronouncing the Words care must be taken to accord with the sentiment that was intended by the Poet.

Callcott, musical grammar (1806)

When the Slur is placed only over two Notes, the second is generally made shorter than its proper length. Formerly, the effect was produced by exact [beamed] Notation.

**Corri, singing treatise (1810),
"Dialogue. Introductory. Requisites for Vocal Music"**

Scholar. What are the requisites, or gifts, necessary for a good singer. . . .

Master. Distinct articulation of words and sounds; by which only, meaning and sentiment can be expressed.

─────. "On Expression"

[One should strive] to separate words which when conjoined might lose their true and precise meaning.

Example

The following Song, "Angels ever bright" &c. of Handel, if the first sentence is sung without any separation of the words as written, thus,

the effect would be the same to the Ear as if these two words "bright and" were joined together thus "brightand" whereas, if the word "and" was separated from "bright" by a break as in the following Example, it would preserve the true accent of the words, thus,

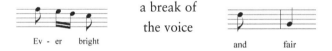

a break of the voice

Nathan, singing treatise (1836), Chapter 7 "Articulation"

The first and most essential point in articulation is distinctness, as without strict attention to a clear and elegant pronunciation, the effect of the most beautiful song must be destroyed. How often do ladies, in particular, warble languishingly through an air, of which, when concluded, the listener has been puzzled to determine whether the words were English, French, or Italian!

Articulation refers equally to *words* and *notes*, and includes that distinctness and accuracy of expression, which gives every syllable and sound with truth and perspicuity, and forms the very foundation of pathos and grace. . . .

Singing and articulation are more nearly allied than is generally imagined. What can be more elegant in a vocal performer than an articulation at once distinct, unaffected, and true to the sense of the poetry. . .

After acquiring purity, fullness, roundness, softness, mellowness, and accuracy of tone, articulation should be strictly attended to before ornaments of any kind are attempted; for the singer who cannot please by his enunciation in the performance of plain notes, will, if he attempts to add the gaudiness of bad execution, resemble a person, who, to hide a slovenly under-garment, should put on a fine transparent dress, which only exposes in ridiculous contrast all that it is intended to conceal.

——. Chapter 8 "Emphasis and Accents"

Group is a term in music used to signify a cluster of notes tied together

thus  or

In common time, for instance, we have four or eight quavers [eighth notes] or semi-quavers [sixteenth notes] grouped—but in triple time we play only three or six in a group. When a note, therefore, is unexpectedly separated from the accustomed manner of grouping it with others—as for example

thus

the note so parted must be sung in a short abrupt style, as if it were staccato. It is usual for singers on such occasions to catch their breath instantaneously, after the separated note, as if in haste to begin another sentence; for whenever one note is so severed from the rest, it is considered a kind of close or finish to the preceding passage: consequently the first note of the succeeding group becomes the commencement of a new sentence, and must be accented or emphasized accordingly.

In the last bar of the preceding example, it will be observed, that I have accentuated the third note which is separated from the group—this is according to law, for when the last note instead of the first of a group is parted from the rest, the sentence is supposed finished before it, and the note so parted becomes accentuated, as beginning a new sentence.

Garcia, singing treatise (1840–1847)

Where notes are united in groups, the last note of the group must be quitted as soon as intonated.

PHRASING

Phrasing, understood as the connection and separation of musical material beyond short rhythmic patterns, was not a focus of performance practice during the Classical era and thus was not a topic of much discussion in the primary sources of the time. Attention was given instead to the articulation of single notes and small groupings of musical material, with focus on messa di voce, staccato markings, and slurs that connected a small number of notes. Phrasing marks (i.e., expanded slurs covering notes usually longer than a measure) were not used until the second quarter of the nineteenth century. This is not to say that phrasing was not practiced during the Classical era or that performers had no concern for how small units were arranged and executed into larger patterns. Commentary about the comparison of music-making to oratory testifies to an awareness and concern for defined and well-executed phrasing. In addition, widespread interest in and discussion of expressive characteristics (see Chapter 7) also reinforce the idea that phrasing was important during the Classical era. Nevertheless, a concern for the performance of small units of musical material seemed to eclipse concern for the grouping of notes and rhythms into larger units of phrases. Furthermore, commentary about phrasing during the Classical era is generally limited to basic matters of performance practice such as the physical connection and separation of musical ideas.

The following quotations all describe aspects of phrasing considered at the time to be common sense.

Quantz, flute treatise (1752), Chapter 7
"Of Taking Breath, in the Practice of the Flute"

You must strive to learn to see clearly and grasp what constitutes good musical sense, and what must therefore hang together. You must be just as careful to avoid separating ideas that belong together as you must be attentive not to link passages that contain more than one idea, and hence must be divided; a great part of true expression in performance depends on this. Those singers and wind players (of whom there are a large number) who are not able to discern the intention of the composer are always in danger of committing errors in this respect, and betraying their weaknesses. String players seem to have an advantage in this, provided that they strive for the required insight mentioned above and do not allow themselves to be misled by the bad example of those who join everything together without any distinctness, in the fashion of a hurdy-gurdy.

L. Mozart, violin treatise (1756), Chapter 5
"How, by adroit control of the Bow, one should seek to produce a good tone on a Violin and bring it forth in the proper manner"

Not a little is added to evenness and purity of tone if you know how to fit much into one stroke. Indeed, it goes against nature if you are constantly interrupting and changing. A singer who during every short phrase stopped, took a breath, and especially stressed first this note, then that note, would unfailingly move everyone to laughter. The human voice glides quite easily from one note to another; a sensible singer will never make a break unless some kind of expression, or the divisions or rests of the phrase demand one. And who is not aware that singing is at all times the aim of every instrumentalist, because one must always approximate to nature as nearly as possible. You must therefore take pains where the Cantilena of the piece demands no break, not only to leave the bow on the violin when changing the stroke, in order to connect one stroke with another, but also to play many notes in one stroke, and in such fashion that the notes which belong together connect with each other and are only differentiated by means of *forte* and *piano*.

Koch, composition treatise, Vol. 2 (1787), Part 2, Section 3
"The Nature of Melodic Sections"

If we consider the various sections in musical works that comprise their periods, then two main characteristics are found through which they distinguish themselves as divisions of the whole. The first is the type of their endings, or that which characterizes the resting points in the material aspect of the art. The second is the length of these sections, together with a certain proportion or relation between them. . . . Generally speaking, only feeling can determine both the places where resting points occur in the melody and also the nature of these resting points, if they are more or less noticeable, that is, if they indicate whether the sections of the whole thus ended may be considered complete or not . . . when we sing or play.

Türk, clavier treatise (1789), Chapter 6,
Part 2 "Concerning the Clarity of Execution"

Just as the words: "He lost his life not only his fortune" can have an entirely different meaning according to the way they are punctuated (He lost his life, not only his fortune, or, He lost his life not, only his fortune), in the same way the execution of a musical thought can be made unclear or even wrong through incorrect punctuation.

Thus, if a keyboard player, other than at the end of a musical period, does not join the tones together well, and consequently divides a thought where it should not be divided, then he makes the same mistake that an orator would if the latter would pause in the middle of a word and take a breath. I have indicated this incorrect kind of division in the following examples by rests.

If a musician would play through a point of rest in the music without breaking the continuity—in one breath as it were—this would be as faulty and contrary to purpose as if, while reading, one would read beyond the point where a phrase or a sentence ends without interruption. Consequently, the following execution in (a) would be completely in opposition to musical sense.

Since I do not remember having ever read anything about musical punctuation and its relation to execution in an instructional work on keyboard playing, I will go into more detail concerning this very important subject for the musical practitioner, for I am convinced that the following remarks could have some influence on correct (logical) execution.

Answering the two following questions is of particular importance in the explanation of this subject: 1) How can one execute a musical thought with suitable continuity and separate two periods from one another, without doing injury to the progress of the meter? 2) How does one recognize existing places of rest in a composition?

The requisite means for executing a musical idea with continuity and for separating two periods from one another by means of execution are the following:

1. A musical thought which has not been completed may never be divided by lifting the fingers from the keys at the wrong time (or by rests). Therefore, the first examples shown [above] must be executed as follows:

Periods must not be separated even in the bass, therefore the fingering in the following example (a) and the execution which would result from it would not be good. The fingering in (b) and (c) is very much better. For moving the fifth finger from one key to another causes a short pause which after the *g* is incorrect; on the contrary, the first *c* of the second measure may appropriately be separated from the following *c*. As subtle as this observation may seem to many, it is all the more necessary to make, since the mistake is so common. In general, the left hand is also usually far more neglected, in this regard, than the right.

2. The end of a period is made more perceptible, if on its last note, the finger is gently lifted from the key and the first note of the following period is played somewhat more strongly. Consequently, through this raising of the finger there results a short rest which must always be counted in the duration of the last note of the period, as in (b).

If the composer has himself included a rest after the last note of the period, as below in (c) then the above observation is unnecessary because the finger will be lifted from the key anyway. Of course, even in this case, the last note is given a somewhat shorter duration than its actual value requires. Therefore the execution in (d) is even more common than that example in (c).

For a very refined execution, with regard to the lifting up of the finger, one must take into consideration whether the periods are larger or smaller and more or less joined to each other. The finger is lifted sooner from the key at the end of a full cadence, or such a conclusive note is played with a shorter duration than when only a phrase member of the composition has been completed.

**Tromlitz, flute treatise (1791), Chapter 13
"The taking of breaths in flute playing"**

The taking of breath . . . is a refinement that . . . does not apply only to flute players, but every wind player and singer must possess this skill as well. I have often witnessed singers and wind players committing the fault of breaking up the sense of the music by separating connected ideas by means of unsuitable breathing, especially in cadenzas. . . .

One should take a breath before the note that begins a phrase so that the phrase will not be broken up. Such a phrase is either designated by rests or is not; if there are no rests, but simply notes, one must know how to find the end of such a phrase and always take a breath again after it. It is one of the principal features of a good instrumentalist to be able to understand the composer's meaning. . . . I will indicate just a few cases from which you will be able to see how you should proceed:

In these four little examples the strokes on top of the staff show the places where breath can be taken in a suitable way and without spoiling the piece.

Corri, singing treatise (1810)

A phrase in Music is like a sentence in Language, with this difference, that one word will not form a sentence, but one Note can form a Phrase in Music.

| Thus a Phrase | Thus is not a Phrase | Thus a Phrase | Thus is not a Phrase |

| Thus a Phrase | Thus is not a Phrase | Thus a Phrase | Thus is not a Phrase |

and so on of any number of Notes that form a passage, wherever the Voice falls by a diminuendo.

Some sentences containing many words may be uttered in one breath; indeed a sentence is seldom or ever broke in the midst by taking breath; whereas, in a musical Phrase you are frequently compelled to do so, from the length of some Notes, and the slow movement of the Music but when the Singer finds it necessary to take breath, he should always contrive to do so by a dying or diminuendo of the Voice, because the break will then be less perceived.

Spohr, musical diary, "Journey to Paris 1821"

The accentuation of the last note of a phrase by increased pressure and a rapid upward sweep of the bow is common, more or less, to all French violinists. . . . I cannot imagine how such a practice could have been generally adopted, for the effect is as if a speaker were to continually accent the short last syllables. If they [the violinists] had modeled the phrasing of their cantabiles on human song (which I believe every instrumentalist should do), they would never have strayed into such byways.

**Garcia, singing treatise (1840–1847), Part 2, Chapter 2
"The Art of Phrasing"**

1. The Formation of the Phrase

In order to measure with precision a melody or the parts that compose it, we have recourse to a series of regularly spaced percussions marking what are called the *beats* of the measure. But this series of successive beats, if they were constantly the same, would produce, after some moments, only a vague and monotonous impression. In order to escape this uniformity, one gives to certain beats of the succession, symmetrically spaced, a stress, a more characterized accent. The beats accented in that fashion, which are called *strong beats*, in opposition to the unaccented beats, which are called *weak beats*, serve to group the beats by two or three, and to form the two elementary measures which are the basis of all the others (the *binary* measure, formed of a strong beat and a weak beat, and the *ternary* measure, formed of a strong beat and two weak ones). With the aid of these accents, the ear easily distinguishes the groups that are attached to them and counts as many measures as there are first beats perceived by it.

Let us notice that the beats whose function is simply to determine the movement can be complete only when a second stroke is heard, so that each beat is always enclosed between two strokes. Likewise, the measure, which has for its objective the grouping of the beats by two or by three is complete only after the stroke of the initial beat of the following measure. Only then does the ear recognize the kind of measure that governs the piece.

The length of a measure confined between two down-beats constitutes a *member of the phrase*.

The measure, in its turn, plays with regard to the melody the role of marking the simple time. Here again the ear, in order to grasp a large number of details in one stroke, joins these measures themselves by twos or by threes, and there is thus formed a new binary or ternary measure of a higher order. The slightest attention suffices to cause one to be struck by the analogy that exists between the joining of several beats constituting a measure, and the aggregation of several measures constituting a musical thought. In order to understand well a musical thought, we need to be struck at equal intervals by more vigorous accents, which, by grouping themselves, offer to our ear new points of reference. These accents, of a nature still more characteristic than those of the measure, are formed by the cooperation of the harmony and the resting places, and serve to group the measures by two or by three, one strong and one weak, or else one strong and two weak. It is this last extent of two or three measures enclosed between three or four first beats that is usually called the *musical phrase*, and that we have called the *melodic line*. Examples:

Chapter 4
METRIC ACCENTUATION

Metric accentuation refers to the practice of stressing or emphasizing certain notes and de-emphasizing others as determined by the placement of the notes in regular metric schemes. As such, meter signatures during the Classical era not only indicated the number of beats within a measure, meter signatures indicated that the notes on and between these beats had varying degrees of emphasis or accentuation in performance. Notes on the emphasized beats were generally referred to as "strong" or "good" notes, while notes on the de-emphasized beats were called "weak" or "bad" notes.

The practice of metric accentuation developed during the middle years of the Baroque era from a significant number of performance factors related to the common notational usage of bar lines. Important among these factors are: conducting patterns and bow strokes, which produced inevitable weight on downward motions as compared to upward motions; organization of text, with stressed syllables on downbeats and unstressed syllables on upbeats; and short motivic patterns and functional harmony that aligned important elements of melody, rhythm, and harmony with important structural beats of measures.

By the latter years of the Baroque and throughout the Classical era, metric accentuation was highly systematized and idealized as an important trait of performance. The practice was mentioned in virtually every treatise discussing meter; it was acknowledged by theorists, teachers, composers, performers, and observers; definitions of it and descriptions for its application were given to vocalists and players of all major instruments of the time (keyboards, violin, flute, oboe, trumpet, and timpani); and it was discussed in sources from a wide variety of countries. Metric accentuation was such an integral and pervasive aspect of making music, there is not a major performance practice source of the Classical era in which it is not discussed.

As with material dealing with other subjects, the quotations presented here about metric accentuation cover the entire duration of the Classical era. However, in order to show that the practice was in full force at the end of the era and even beyond, there are quotes included from the Romantic era. The quote from Wagner's conducting treatise is especially noteworthy in this respect. It shows that metric accentuation was an ingrained element of performance practice until the 1860s. The quote from Isaac Nathan's singing treatise of 1836 is also significant in that it advises singers to make corrections to scores that are faulty (i.e., singers were advised to alter the placement of notes in compositions that do not fully align strong and weak syllables with strong and weak metrical beats).

Metric accentuation was accomplished in two ways simultaneously: one was through volume (emphasized notes were louder than de-emphasized notes), while the other was through rhythmic duration (emphasized notes were held longer than de-emphasized notes). The volume aspect of metric accentuation was only slight, given the soft ideals of the era and the limited range of amplitudes capable by many of the instruments (see Chapter 1); stressed notes were not much louder than unstressed notes. The rhythmic aspect of metric accentuation was more significant; emphasized notes being extended beyond their notational value or held their full value were in obvious contrast to de-emphasized notes, which were always shorter than their printed value. This rhythmic durational aspect of metric accentuation is referred to as quantitas intrinseca (intrinsic quantity or length) and is discussed under a separate subheading below.

Within the system of metric accentuation, the notes to be emphasized are determined by the duple or triple arrangement of beats within each measure and the duple or triple arrangement of notes within each beat. At the most basic level, duple meters (all those with numerators of the metric fraction divisible by two, such as 2/2, 2/4, 4/4, 2/8, 4/8, 6/8, and 12/8) indicate that, beginning with the downbeat, notes on alternate beats are to receive an emphasis greater than notes on the other beats. Notes within beats are to receive even less emphasis. In the following rhythmic patterns, therefore, notes marked with the poetic sign – would be emphasized, notes marked ⌣ would be de-emphasized somewhat, and notes marked with ◡ would be completely de-emphasized.

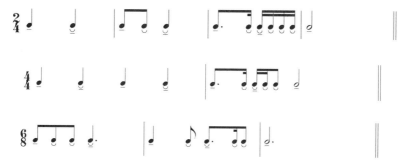

Triple meters (all those with numerators of the metric fraction divisible only by three, such as 3/2, 3/4, 3/8, and 9/8) indicate that notes on the downbeat are to receive an emphasis greater than notes on the other beats. Notes within the beats, as with duple meters, are to be de-emphasized. The following rhythmic patterns illustrate.

Not all emphasized notes are to receive equal stress, however. Variations or degrees of emphasis are determined by factors of melodic structure, harmonic function, and text declamation—the greater the importance of each factor and the greater the congruence of the factors, the greater the emphasis. De-emphasized notes are treated similarly: the weaker the point of melody, harmony, and text declamation, the weaker the stress (or greater the de-emphasis).

The composition and performance of metric accentuation was considered akin to oratory, in both vocal and instrumental music. In their choice of melodies, harmonies, and placement of text, composers sought to match the natural oratory of the texts they set or the imaginary oratory of their instrumental compositions (see Chapter 7). Performers, then, sought to capture the composer's intent and manifest all the gradations of syllabic stress—real or imaginary—that they would in speech. Gradations of metric accentuation were, therefore, numerous.

In Example A below, the downbeats (highlighted by the shaded screenings) are strong and the other beats not so strong because the melodic patterns, harmonic functions, and syllabic stresses lead from downbeat to downbeat. In addition, the downbeats of measures three and five are, for the same reasons, stronger than the other downbeats. The third beats of each measure are considerably weak since they are aligned with harmonic passing tones and their textual syllables are insignificant within the scheme of the oratorical phrase.

Example A

W. A. Mozart, *Missa Solemnis in C* K337, Gloria, measures 1–5

In Example B, the third beats are somewhat equal to the downbeats because the text and their accompanying motivic patterns, each of which is a half measure in length, repeat; the design of the musical phrases matches the natural design of the oratorical phrases, with the result that similar accentuation emphases occur on beats one and three of each measure.

Example B
Joseph Haydn, *Missa Sancti Nicolai*, Benedictus, measures 10–12

In Example C, the third beats are stronger than the downbeats, which are quite weak, since all three factors of melodic pattern, harmonic function, and syllabic stress lead to the third beats. The repeated construction of the two identical short phrases suggests that the syllables "mo" and "il" are equally stressed.

Example C
W. A. Mozart, *Requiem* K626, Lacrimosa, measures 3 and 4

Examples D and E illustrate a relatively common notational occurrence: a strong beat occupied by a rest. In this instance, it is inevitable that a primary emphasis will follow on the first strong metric beat. In Example D, the emphases are on the third beats of measures one and two, and are almost identical; the third beat of measure two is somewhat stronger because of the sequential nature of the melodic patterns. In Example E, the emphases are also on the third beats of the measures. However, because of the unfolding harmonies and oratorical phrase, each emphasis increases slightly. In addition, because the textual phrase and harmony pull forward, there is a variance in the degrees of de-emphasis of the weak beats. Beat four of measure 44 has considerably more strength than the fourth beats of measures 45 and 46.

Example D
W. A. Mozart, *Regina coeli* K276, measures 1 and 2

Example E
W. A. Mozart, *Requiem* K626, Offertorium, measures 44–46

It should be noted that melodic structure, harmonic function, and text declamation do not always operate together to indicate metric emphasis. Harmonic function and text declamation, for instance, may be in direct conflict with one another—the harmonic function indicating emphasis and the text declamation indicating de-emphasis. This conflicting situation occurs frequently at cadence points, where the strength of harmonic function takes precedence over the importance of text declamation. Although composers of the Classical era were text sensitive, putting strong speech syllables in metrically emphasized locations, the text was not always the governing factor of musical emphasis. Harmonic function was sometimes more important.

In Examples F and G, the final notes would be considered very strong and would, therefore, receive an emphasis regardless of the weak textual syllable.

Example F
W. A. Mozart, *Requiem* K626, Introitus, measures 15–19

Example G
Joseph Haydn, *Missa In Tempore Belli* (Paukenmesse), Kyrie, measures 17–20

Triple meters did not have a variability of strong beat emphasis because the uneven and, therefore, non-alternating arrangement of beats allowed for only one strong beat per measure. Consequently, as can be seen in Examples H through K, the downbeats would be emphasized, while second and third beats would be de-emphasized. It can also be seen in these musical examples (as in Example A) that there is a variability of emphasis among the downbeats. This is to say that all downbeats, while strong, are not equally emphasized. Variability of emphasis is determined by the previously mentioned factors of melodic structure, harmonic function, and text declamation. Text declamation affects variability of downbeat emphasis because of the interplay of multiple stressed syllables of words within phrases of text. In Example H, for instance, the declamation of the beginning phrases of text, "Et resurrexit tertia d<u>ie</u>, secundum scripturas, et ascendit in c<u>oe</u>lum," has emphasis on the two underlined syllables even though there are multiple word stresses within each of these phrases. The same is true of Example I, with the beginning text "Hostias et preces tibi <u>Do</u>mine, tibi Domine laudes of<u>fe</u>rimus." Because of these phrase declamations as well as supporting harmonic functions and melodic structures, the downbeats of measures 58 and 62 in Example H and measures 6 and 10 in Example I would receive an emphasis greater than the other downbeats.

Example H
Joseph Haydn, *Missa Sancti Nicolai*, Credo, measures 55–62

Example I
W. A. Mozart, *Requiem* K626, Hostias, measures 1–10

In example J, the downbeats of measures 2 and 4 would receive an emphasis greater than the downbeats of measures 1 and 3 because of the melodic structure (supported by harmonic function and phrase declamation). The downbeat of measure 8, because of its cadence, would receive an emphasis greater than the other downbeats.

Example J
W. A. Mozart, *Missa Solemnis in* C K337, Credo, measures 1–8

All parts (soprano, alto, tenor, bass, violin, flute, etc.) in the musical examples above are aligned homophonically to produce unified emphases. However, this is not always the case in repertoire from the era; patterns of emphasis occasionally differ in each part or in combinations of parts. In example K, for instance, the vocal parts, as a result of varying text placements, have different patterns of emphasis (see the screened areas).

Example K

Joseph Haydn, *Missa In Tempore Belli* (Paukenmesse), Gloria, measures 70–87

All of the examples above illustrate degrees of emphasis on what were termed "strong" or "good" beats. The examples also illustrate corresponding degrees of de-emphasis on the "weak" or "bad" beats, namely beats two and four in the 4/4 measures and beats two and three in the 3/4 measures. In general, beat two of both 3/4 and 4/4 meters is the weakest beat of the measure. Only a rest on beat one could cause a stress on beat two, unless, as often happened in the latter part of the Classical era, an accent mark was put on beat two (thus altering its expected de-emphasis). Beat four of a 4/4 measure and beat three of a 3/4 measure might not be as de-emphasized as beat two depending on the functional relationship of the beat to its ensuing downbeat. If the final beat of a measure has a significant harmonic pull to the downbeat, this final beat would not be as de-emphasized as a preceding weak beat (beat two) in that measure. If, on the other hand, the final beat of a measure has a conclusive quality with no harmonic pull to the following downbeat, this final beat would be as de-emphasized or, perhaps, more de-emphasized than preceding weak beats. In Example A above, the fourth beats of each measure would not be as de-emphasized as the second beats because the harmonies on the fourth beats clearly lead to the following downbeats. Contrary to this, Examples C and D illustrate a conclusive quality of the fourth beats, which would, consequently, be weak; with no melodic, harmonic, or textual reinforcement, the beats would have no reason for emphasis. In Example F, beat four of the first measure (15) would be the weakest beat of the measure, while beat two would be the weakest beat of the following measure; beat four of this second measure would not be too weak due to its pull to the downbeat of the third measure.

In Example H and I, all the second beats would be weaker than the third beats. Only the third beats in Example I of measures 6 and 10 would be weaker than the second beats. In Example K, beats two and three of measures 76 and 77 change de-emphasis patterns: beat two is the weakest beat of measure 76, while beat three is the weakest beat of measure 77. This alternating pattern continues in measures 78–81, but in measures 82–87 the growth of musical intensity almost prohibits any quality of de-emphasis; all beats are pulled to the cadence.

The circumstances of melodic structure, harmonic function, and text/ phrase declamation heretofore described and discussed explain why some of the primary sources of the Classical era prescribe greater stress to the downbeats of each measure while other primary sources prescribe equal stress to beats one and three in common time and also a degree of emphasis to beat three in triple time. The sources, often rudimentary in nature and therefore not intended to provide subtle details of practice, are not in conflict with each other. In presenting general rules, they do not discuss exceptions or variations that may be the result of special musical circumstances.

Tessitura or intervallic relationships have no effect on accentuation beyond the physical fact of relative loudness or agogic duration. Pitches on weak beats that are high in range or pitches on strong beats that are low in range do not alter the rules of metric accentuation. Similarly, intervallic leaps, either high or low, create no cause for emphasis or de-emphasis. Beat two of measure two in Example L would, therefore, be de-emphasized regardless of the intervallic leap of the melodic line or the wedge articulation marking in the accompaniment. Staccato markings also do not negate patterns of emphasis and de-emphasis; successive notes with staccato markings, while of equal short duration and therefore not affected by *quantitas intrinseca* (see below), are subject to and are characterized by differing stresses.

Example L
W. A. Mozart, *Requiem* K626, Osanna, measures 1–6

In addition to the factors of consideration discussed above, the typical manner of conducting triple meters during the Classical era aided the de-emphasis of second beats. In a 3/4 measure, the conductor's arm would lower on the downbeat, remain stationary for beat two, and rise on beat three. There would be no motion on beat two to cause an emphasis. The modern-day practice of making a lateral motion on beat two causes a degree of emphasis the musicians of the Classical era would not have experienced.

Exceptions to patterns of metric accentuation are indicated by slur signs, the presence of rests (as discussed earlier), and expressive markings. In the case of slurs, the first note under the sign is to receive an emphasis, while all succeeding notes are to be de-emphasized. This is the case as long as the slur begins on a strong beat and ends on a weak one. If irregular slurring patterns occur, regular patterns of metric accentuation prevail. Slurs are used in instrumental much more than in vocal music, although vocal slurs for articulation purposes are not unheard of (see Chapter 3). The slur markings in Example M are consistent in two appearances of an identical melodic pattern (Alto and Bass) and indicate that there should be somewhat of an emphasis on the downbeat of the third measure (Alto measure 24 and Bass measure 32), but no emphasis on the downbeat of the second measure (Alto measure 23 and Bass measure 31).

Example M
W. A. Mozart, *Requiem* K626, Osanna,
Alto part measures 21–25 and Bass part measures 29–33

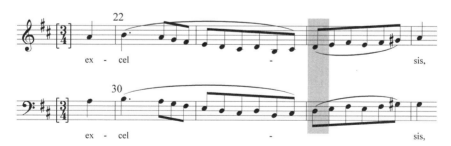

Expressive markings such as *sf*, *fz*, *sfz*, and *fp* were utilized to indicate an emphasis where one ordinarily would not be applied, a greater emphasis than what might ordinarily be indicated, or a quality of emphasis apart from the usual manner of articulation. These expressive markings are rarely seen in repertoire from the early part of the Classical era when regular patterns of accentuation were the norm. They are seen more in repertoire composed at the end of the era when diversity and irregularity became desirable. The utilization of expressive markings was especially commonplace on weak beats, providing a means by which performers would know to emphasize a note normally to be de-emphasized (Example P). No information from the Classical era describes any difference between the various expressive signs used, although it seems logical to assume that *fp* (forte piano) indicates emphasis followed by de-emphasis.

Example P
W. A. Mozart, *Missa Brevis in D Minor* K65, Credo, measures 58–62

QUANTITAS INTRINSECA

Emphasis and de-emphasis were made audible in terms of volume and rhythmic duration, both aspects of performance occurring simultaneously. An emphasized ("strong" or "good") note would therefore be louder and longer than a de-emphasized ("weak" or "bad") note. In terms of rhythmic duration, Classical-era musicians equated the intrinsic length or durational quantity of a note to its relative level of emphasis. Therefore, the notes of the rhythmic pattern in Example A could not only be termed "strong-weak-weak, strong-weak-weak" but also "long-short-short, long-short-short."

Example A

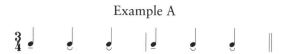

The reference to "short" does not mean that the note values were reduced or that they were not held for their so-called full value. Notes that were short, as a result of their placement on weak beats of measures, were intrinsically short, or inherently not completely filled with sound. The quotation by Bédos de Celles at the beginning of the Instrumental Articulation subheading in Chapter 3 explains this phenomena: "All the notes in execution . . . are partly in *hold* and partly in *silence*, which united makes the whole value of the note." In other words, notes could have silence as a part of their durational value, or put yet another way, the total durational value of a note was seen as a combination of sound and silence.

Called "quantitas intrinseca" (intrinsic quantity), this rhythmic durational aspect of metric accentuation was discussed often until the very end of the eighteenth century. Perhaps by then, as general articulation became more connected (see Chapter 3) and factors of expression in performance were more varied and made more explicit by specific markings from composers, metric accentuation became more a factor of weight, stress, and volume than of length.

Sources are not in agreement as to the exact degree of lengthening or shortening that was a result of metric accentuation. Quantz recommends that certain emphasized notes be performed longer than their printed value—"almost dotted." Leopold Mozart recommends a similar treatment by saying that an emphasized note should be "held slightly longer" than printed, while a following de-emphasized note should be executed "slightly late." It is difficult for present-day musicians to comprehend, yet alone commit to, a performance practice so rhythmically flexible. Sustaining notes beyond their printed value seems contrary to established perceptions of musical execution. When viewed, however, in the context of the notes inégales practice of the Baroque era—which transformed patterns of two equal eighth notes into patterns of unequal duration, and which was a practice that lasted well into the middle of the eighteenth century and was an attribute of performance well beyond France and French repertoire—perhaps rhythmic extension is understandable. We know, for instance, that Handel rather frequently used the term "Andante" to specifically request that rhythms not be altered—that performers not transform patterns of equal eighth notes. In Example B, for instance, the use of "Andante" is not intended to modify the "allegro" and suggest a slower tempo. The "Andante" instructs performers to leave the bass "walking" as it is and not to change it to dotted rhythms.

Example B
Handel, *Messiah*, For unto us a child is born, measures 1–3

Because Handel utilized a term advising performers not to exercise rhythmic alteration, we must assume that the practice of notes inégales was rather prevalent during the latter years of the Baroque era. Commentary by Quantz (1752) and Leopold Mozart (1756) that may have affected the music of their time is, therefore, understandable. Later commentary by Türk (1789), which is more detailed, gives a greater sense of reality to the practice of quantitas intrinseca. His statement, "Because it is recognized by everyone, I do not have to provide evidence for the possibility of lingering somewhat longer on a very important note than one less important," gives support to the belief that rhythmic extension was indeed practiced, but not on all emphasized notes. His subsequent statements give yet a clearer picture as to the limited nature of the practice: "As far as how long a note should be held is concerned, I would like to establish the rule that it should at the most not be lengthened more than half its value. Usually the holding of a note should be only scarcely perceptible." In all probability, rhythmic extension was applied to notes of special consequence by solo performers, but not applied pervasively in all areas of performance. In this regard, rhythmic extension would be closely related to tempo rubato—an aspect of expression used for purposes beyond the ordinary (see Chapter 2).

The practice of lengthening and shortening was not so much the lengthening of strong notes beyond their printed value and thus the delaying of the attack of the weak note that followed. The practice of lengthening and shortening most frequently extended strong notes beyond their normal articulated value, which was generally shorter than printed (see Chapter 3), and, conversely, abbreviated the duration of weak notes. Strong notes would then receive their full durational value as printed and weak notes would receive less. Rhythmic examples such as seen in Example C might then be performed as seen in Example D.

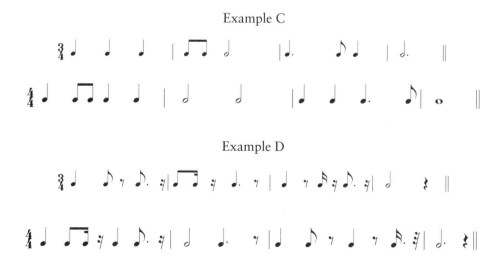

Example C

Example D

By sustaining strong notes for their full printed durational value, their intrinsic quantity would be long. Vice versa, by abbreviating sound on weak notes, their intrinsic quantity would be short. This proportional lengthening and shortening practice seems most logical and most helpful to the accomplishment of musical rhetoric discussed so often during the Classical era.

In making determinations of emphasis and de-emphasis for performance, the present-day performer should consider general factors of volume and articulation (discussed in Chapters 1 and 3, respectively). Levels of volume have become so much louder than those in the eighteenth century, and standards of articulation have become so much more evenly regulated, applying any emphasis to the music of the Classical era would impart a weight inappropriate to the texture or fabric of the music. It may be better to concentrate on the de-emphasis factor of metric accentuation, making sounds less loud and forceful in order to bring about the patterns integral to the music. There is little doubt that the degrees of emphasis were subtle, keeping with the entire nature of lightness and elegance deemed ideal by the people of the time.

As to decisions regarding degrees of emphasis within a subtly confined scope of volume, it is helpful for the performer to think of music as speech, with intricate gradations of stress. Much commentary of the Classical era relates the practice of metric accentuation to the practice of spoken oratory, with musical notes receiving varying degrees of stress just as spoken words receive varying degrees of stress. Moreover, as speech is characterized by degrees of inflection associated with the delivery of phrases and sentences, music is characterized by degrees of inflection associated with the design of harmonic motifs, phrases, and larger structural units. And, as speech can be varied from person to person with equal degrees of effectiveness, so music can likewise be varied. Within general guidelines of expression, one delivery can be as appropriate as another.

The numerous quotations that follow are meant to underscore the significance and general agreement of the practice of metric accentuation (including quantitas intrinseca). The quotations are also meant to point out the extensiveness of the practice throughout different countries and throughout the era. Furthermore, quotations dated from the Romantic era testify to the scope of implementation.

To fully appreciate the quotations that follow, the reader is encouraged, as already mentioned, to keep in mind all factors of Classical-era performance, especially those concerning volume and articulation, and also to consider the intended nature of the commentary, whether it be directed to composers or performers, whether it be advice or observation, or whether it be rudimentary or advanced.

Quantz, flute treatise (1752), Chapter 11
"Of Good Execution in General in Singing and Playing"

Here I must make a necessary observation concerning the length of time each note must be held. You must know how to make a distinction in execution between the *principal notes*, ordinarily called *accented* or in the Italian manner, *good* notes, and those that *pass*, which some foreigners call *bad* notes. Where it is possible, the principal notes must always be emphasized more than the passing. In consequence of this rule, the quickest notes in every piece of *moderate tempo*, or even in the *Adagio*, though they seem to have the same value, must be played a little unequally, so that the stressed notes of each figure, namely the first, third, fifth, and seventh, are held slightly longer than the passing, namely the second, fourth, sixth, and eighth, although this lengthening must not be as much as if the notes were dotted. Among these quickest notes I include the quarter note in three-two time, the eighth note in three-four time and the sixteenth note in three-eight time, the eighth note in alla breve, and the sixteenth or thirty-second note in two-four or common duple time; but these are included only as long as no figures of still more rapid notes, or doubly quick ones, are intermingled in each meter, for then the latter must be executed in the manner described above. For example, if the eight sixteenth notes [seen in Examples] (k), (m), and (n) are played slowly with the same value, they will not sound as pleasing as if the first and third of four are heard a little longer, and with a stronger tone than the second and fourth.

Fig. 1

Excepted from the rule, however, is first, quick passage-work in a very fast tempo in which the time does not permit unequal execution, and in which length and strength must therefore be applied only to the first of every four notes. Also excepted is all quick passage-work which must be executed by the human voice, unless it is supposed to be slurred. Since every note of passage-work of this kind for the voice must be performed distinctly and stressed by a gentle breath of air from the chest, there can be no inequality in them. Further excepted are the notes above which strokes or dots are found. The same exception must be made when several notes follow one another upon the same pitch; or when there is a slur above more than two notes, that is, above four, six, or eight; and finally with regard to eighth notes in gigues. All of these notes must be executed equally, that is, one as long as the other.

——. Chapter 12 "Of the Manner of Playing the Allegro"

Hurrying of passage-work may occur, particularly in ascending notes, if the fingers are raised too quickly. To avoid this, the first note of quick figures must be stressed and held slightly, especially since the principal notes should always be heard a little longer than the passing ones. To this end, the principal notes which form the fundamental melody may also be stressed from time to time through chest action.

——. Chapter 17 "Of the Duties of Those Who Accompany or Execute the Accompanying or Ripieno Parts Associated with a Concertante Part" Section 2 "Of Ripieno Violinists in Particular"

If sixteenth notes of the kind seen in Fig. 21 are to be elegantly performed in a slow tempo, the first of each two must always be heavier than the following one, both in duration and volume; and here the *b* in the third beat must be played *almost* as though it were dotted.

Fig. 21

——. Chapter 17, Section 6 "Of the Keyboard Player in Particular"

The accompanist will often encounter notes that require more emphasis than the others, and thus he must know how to strike them with greater liveliness and force, and how to distinguish them clearly from the other notes that do not require emphasis. The former include the long notes intermingled among quicker ones, also the notes with which a principal subject enters, and above all the dissonances. A long note, which may be struck with its lower octave, interrupts the liveliness of the melody. The *thema* always requires an increase in the strength of the tone to make its entry clearer; and the dissonances serve as the means to vary the expression of the different passions.

C. P. E. Bach, clavier treatise (1753), Part 1, Chapter 3 "Performance"

Patterns of two and four slurred notes are played with a slight scarcely noticeable increase of pressure on the first and third tones. The same applies to the first tones of groups of three notes. In other cases only the first of the slurred notes is played in this manner. It is a convenient custom to indicate by appropriate marks [slur or staccato] only the first few of prolonged successions of detached or legato notes, it being self-evident that all the tones are to be played similarly until another kind of mark intervenes. . . .

The notes of Figure 170 are played in such a manner that the first of each slur is slightly accented. Figure 171 is played similarly except that the last note of each slur is detached.

Marpurg, clavier treatise (1755), Chapter 5 "Concerning Meter"

There are in every type of meter "good" and "bad" beats. That which is termed "good" is longer intrinsically and is a beat capable of concluding a caesura or section or cadence in the music. A beat which is termed "bad" is shorter intrinsically and is not capable of concluding a caesura in the usual manner. . . .

The good beats of the [4/2 and 4/4] measure occur on the first parts of each down and up stroke. The bad beats are contained in the last parts of the down and up stroke. There are, then, in both of these duple meters of four beats two good and two bad beats.

If, in the first species of meter [4/2], one divides the half-note beats into quarter- note pulses, then, among the eight resulting quarter notes the first, third, fifth, and seventh are good pulses; the second, fourth, sixth, and eighth are bad pulses. The good notes are also termed "long" and the bad ones "short" in reference to their intrinsic quality. One can make the same application to the 4/4 meter.

[The 2/2 and 2/4] meters each have only one good beat, which falls on the down stroke. The bad beat falls on the up stroke. If one divides the two beats into pulses, then, in the 2/2 meter, the first and third among the quarter notes are good pulses, the second and fourth are bad pulses. In the 2/4 meter, if one divides both beats into four eighth notes, the good pulses fall on the first and third eighth notes, and the bad pulses on the second and fourth eighth notes.

The good beats [of 3/2, 3/4, and 3/8 measures] fall on the first division and the other two divisions constitute bad beats. If one divides the three beats into six pulses, the good pulses are the first, third, and fifth; the bad pulses are the second, fourth, and sixth.

The first and third [beats of 12/4 and 12/8 meters] are good, and the second and fourth are bad. The nature of the three pulses into which each beat is divided is the same as that of the triple meters. The first pulse is always good and the other two pulses are always bad. Accordingly, among the twelve pulses, the good are the first, fourth, seventh, and tenth; the bad are all the rest.

The good [beats of 6/4 and 6/8 meters] fall on the down stroke, and the bad fall on the up stroke. Among the six pulses, the first and fourth are good, the rest are bad.

The first [beat of 9/4 and 9/8 measures] is good, and the second and third are bad. Of the three pulses, every first is good, and the remaining two are bad. Consequently, the good pulses are the first, fourth, and seventh; the rest are bad.

How does it happen that [some] music which is set to words in verse, in spite of possessing good melody and beautiful harmony, nevertheless revolts the ear? It is because the intrinsic quantity of the beats is not observed, because there is no relationship between the quality of the beats and that of the syllables, and because the short syllables fall on good beats while the long syllables fall on bad beats.

L. Mozart, violin treatise (1756), Chapter 12
"Of Reading Music correctly, and in particular, of Good Execution"

Generally, the accent . . . of the expression or the stress of tone falls on the ruling or strong beat, which the Italians call Nota Buona. These strong beats, however, differ perceptibly from each other. The especially strong beats are as follows: In every bar, the first note of the first quarter note, the first note of the half-bar or third quarter note in 4/4 time; the first note of the first and fourth quarter notes in 6/4 and 6/8 time; and the first note of the first, fourth, seventh, and tenth quarter notes in 12/8 time. These may be called the strong beats on which the chief stress of the tone always falls if the composer has indicated no other expression. . . .

The other good notes are those which, it is true, are at all times distinguished from the remainder by a small accent, but on which the stress must be applied with considerable moderation. They are, namely, quarter and eighth notes in alla breve time, and quarter notes in the so-called half-note triplet; further, there are eighth and sixteenth notes in common and also in 2/4 and 3/4 time; and finally, sixteenths in 3/8 and 6/8 time, and so on. Now if several notes of this kind follow each other, over which, two by two, a slur is placed, then the accent falls on the first of the two, and it is not only played somewhat louder, but it is also sustained rather longer, while the second is slurred on to it quite smoothly and quietly, and somewhat late. . . . But often three, four, and even more notes are bound together by such a slur and half-circle. In such case the first thereof must be somewhat more strongly accented and sustained longer; the others, on the contrary, being slurred on to it in the same stroke with a diminishing of the tone, even more and more quietly and without the slightest accent.

There are in the present time certain passages in which the expression of a skillful composer is indicated in a quite unusual and unexpected manner, and which not everyone would discern, were it not indicated. For example:

For here the expression and accent falls on the last quarter note of the bar, and the first quarter of the following bar is slurred on to it quite quietly and without accent. These two notes, therefore, are on no account to be differentiated by an after pressure of the bow, but are to be played as if they were merely a half note.

—. **Chapter 7, Section 1 "Of the varieties of Bowing in even notes"**

If notes are slurred in pairs with the down stroke and up stroke, we have at once another variation. For example:

The first of two notes coming together in one stroke is accented more strongly and held slightly longer, while the second is slurred on to it quite quietly and rather late. This style of performance promotes good taste in the playing of the melody and prevents hurrying by means of the afore-mentioned sustaining of the first note.

In a very quick tempo one can even play a whole bar in one stroke. But here also, as in the previous style, the first notes of each quarter note must be marked by emphasis. For example:

Now if you wish to accustom yourself to a really long stroke of the bow—that is, if you wish to learn to play many notes in one bow, with expression, clarity, and evenness, and therefore make yourself really master of your bow—you can play well the following passage first in an up stroke, then in a down stroke. But do not forget to apply on the first note of each quarter the emphasis which must distinguish one quarter clearly from the other.

If indeed three notes are slurred together but not the usual three, and of each triplet the second and third notes are slurred to the first of the following triplet or to another figure following it, special care must be taken with regard to the evenness of the triplet, and the stress or accent must not be applied at the beginning but at the end of the bow; otherwise this accent falls in the wrong place, namely, on the second note [of the triplet], while it should fall on the first. The example will make this clearer:

Agricola, singing treatise (1757), Chapter 2 "Concerning the Appoggiatura"

Among the types of *duple meter*, 4/4 and the true *alla breve* [4/2] (which properly has one double whole note or four half-note beats) have two actual and indeed equal parts per measure, the first beginning with the first [quarter or half note] and the second part with the third quarter or half note. Each quarter note, or, in the *alla breve* meter each half note, constitutes a *beat*, of which the first and the third (which coincide with the beginning of each pulse of the measure) may be designated *strong*, and the second and fourth may be called *passing*. Among the even smaller note values into which the beat may be further subdivided, the odd-numbered notes are called *strong* or *good*; those of even number, *passing* or *bad* notes. For example, the first, third, fifth, or seventh quarter note, eighth note, or sixteenth note is *strong*. The second, fourth, sixth, and eighth of these smaller note values are *passing*. In 2/4 time and in the *divided alla breve meter* [2/2], consisting of two half-note beats, for each measure there is only one pulse, but two beats. Here every measure consists of only one part. The *true triple time* signatures [3/4, 3/8] have only one pulse per bar, but three beats, the first of which in this case is *strong* and the other two *passing*. *Compound triple time*, such as 6/8 and 12/8, has two pulses, and 12/8 time has four beats, each of which consists of three eighth notes. Smaller notes in uneven time have the same relationship with regard to strong or passing as those in even time.

Antoniotto, composition treatise (1760), Book 3, Chapter 2 "Of the Accent"

The measures which may be divided in two equal parts have their first part accented and the second part unaccented; when the same measures are divided in four parts, by four equal notes, the first and third notes are accented and the second and fourth not accented, as it is illustrated in Example 7. However, when the second note, which is unaccented, is comprised of two notes, the first of the two notes becomes accented and the second unaccented; also, when the first part of the measure is divided into four equal notes, the first and the third notes are accented, the second and fourth notes not accented, as is seen in Example 8, where every note is marked with its particular sign long, or short, expressed thus (– long, N short).

The general rule is this, that all notes of whatsoever but like value are joined together, the first is accented and the second unaccented, likewise the following notes, so far as they continue composed by the same value. The principal accents are always two, the first on the first note of the measure, which may be considered as the very first principal, and the second accent, which also may be considered as the second principal, is on the first note of the second part of the same measure. In triple time the accent falls somewhat different into the notes of their relative measures. . . . The first accent, when the measure is divided by three equal notes, is on the first note, and the second accent is on the last; the middle note is consequently unaccented, as is seen in Example 9.

Holden, musical essay (1770), Chapter 4 "Of Time, and the Characters relating thereto"

In the performance of music, there is a certain emphasis, or accent laid on the beginning of every measure, which plainly distinguishes one species of time from another; so that a hearer is naturally led to distribute a tune into its proper measure, though he should take no notice of the manner of beating time; nay, though he should know nothing at all of the rules relating to the time of music. . . . The emphasis always falls upon the number 1, in the methods of counting a watch, or clock; and accompanies the putting down of the hand, or toe, in beating time.

There is no occasion to make the beginning, or emphatic part, of the measure, always stronger, or louder than the rest, though it is sometimes best to do so; for, it is not so much the superior loudness of the sound, as the superior regard which a hearer is led to bestow upon it, that distinguishes one part of the measure from another. This is a truth of great importance, as will hereafter appear, and deserves to be well fixed in mind, before we proceed. For illustration of this, it may be observed, in the method of counting a watch [see Chapter 2] that although the alternate stronger pulses . . . be undoubtedly all equal, yet when we count one, and pass over the next, and count the next, and pass over the next, and so on; we imagine the pulses which we count, to be really stronger than the intermediate ones, which we pass over. The superior regard which we bestow on the counted pulses is, here, the sole cause of these imaginary accents.

If we extend these observations still further, we shall find, that in all the methods of counting a watch, the pulse which answers to 1, that is, the pulse which begins the measure, seems stronger than any of the others; especially after we have continued the same method of counting, for several times over. We shall find, also, that the pulse which answers to the number 3, in common time, will seem stronger than either of those which answer to 2, or 4; and even in triple time, the same number 3, is more emphatical than 2.

The case is just the same with the successive sounds of music, because we naturally conceive these sounds, as possessing such and such parts of the established measure of the piece. The regard, paid to the beginning of every measure, renders the note, which possesses that part, more remarkable, and therefore, more emphatical, than any of those which occupy the other parts of the measure; the beginning of the third division of the measure, is also accented, in a smaller degree, both in common and triple time; and the beginning of every primary division of the measure is more emphatical than that of any of the secondary sub-divisions. All these remarks are direct consequences from the foregoing observations.

Binns (Hoyle), dictionary (1770)

ACCENT, is a certain modulation or warbling of the sounds, either by the voice or instruments, to express a passion. Every bar or measure is divided into accented and unaccented parts; the accented are the principal, being those chiefly intended to move and affect the hearer. . . .

CATTIVO, or CATTIVO TEMPO, properly signifies what is called the unaccented part of a Bar, and is the second or last Note in Common Time, and the middle one of every three in Triple Time; or it is a certain part of Measure wherein it is not proper to perform certain things, as to end a Cadence or place a long syllable.

Tartini, violin treatise (1771), "Rules for bowing"

Where one beat of the bar is divided between two or more notes, the note falling *on* the beat should be accented.

Sulzer, general theory of music (1771–1774)

All of the beat types . . . share the same character in that each one of the beats is only of one foot, which consists of parts that differ from one another in internal length and brevity (shortness). Each straight [duple] beat has really two main parts, the first of which is long and the second short. For example:

HERR, MEIN GOTT

If, however, the notes are divided into smaller types, for instance into quarters in the *Alla breve*, then the first note of the second beat part receives a greater weight and the quarters relate to one another (among themselves) as do the beat parts. Example:

EN - GEL PREI - SEN DICH

If the beat consists of still smaller parts, such as eighths, then even these are by their internal quantity clearly distinguishable. Example:

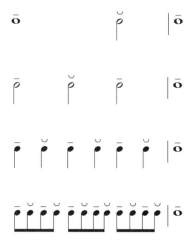

ER, DER AL - LES ORB-NET UND ER - DIT

The following illustration shows the difference in the internal quantity of the beat parts in the uneven [triple] meter type:

The application of the treatment of these beat parts with respect to their different weights and the accents to be placed upon them is easily done. When speaking of the triple beat, however, it must be noted that the second beat can also be long, but only in the case when the caesura (rest) falls on the first beat, as here:

MUR- RE NICHT, LIE - BER CHRIST

But if the tempo is fast or if the beat consists of tripled divisions, as 12/8 and 6/4, then the triple always has the first quantity, that is to say, $\cup - -$, and the other meters behave in relation to one another depending on whether they are even or uneven, for example:

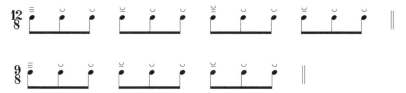

After what has been demonstrated about the internal quantity of the beat parts, it is hardly necessary to prove that the 6/4 differs immensely from the 3/2, or the 6/8 from the 3/4 through the different weight of the beat, even though both beats contain the same number of one type of note. The following illustration shows this clearly:

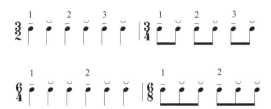

All we need to show yet is: 1) how two beats can be compounded to become one, 2) of which necessity the compounded beat types are, and 3) how they are different from one another. To get a clear conception, one has but to try to put notes of appropriate length and shortness with consideration of the accents and of the beat weight above the words: *Ewig in der Herrlichkeit.* Because they are all spondees, a meter of two beats, the 2/4 meter for instance, seems most appropriate; consequently, the notes would be:

This would consider the long and the short syllables of the poetic feet; the final note would fall on the first beat note and the rhythm would be completely correct. But one must notice that the word *in* and the last syllable of *Herrlichkeit*, which are of no importance when spoken, now receive the greatest weight because they fall on the first note of the measure. To avoid this, no other possibility exists than to compound two of these beats to make only one, thusly:

Ew - ig in der Herr - lich - keit:

By doing this, the two syllables are brought to the middle of the beat, that is to say on the weak or short beat thereof, where they still maintain an accent, but one that is not so long and heavy as the first and necessary with the latter as final syllable. An opposite example will clarify this more. If one puts this sentence:

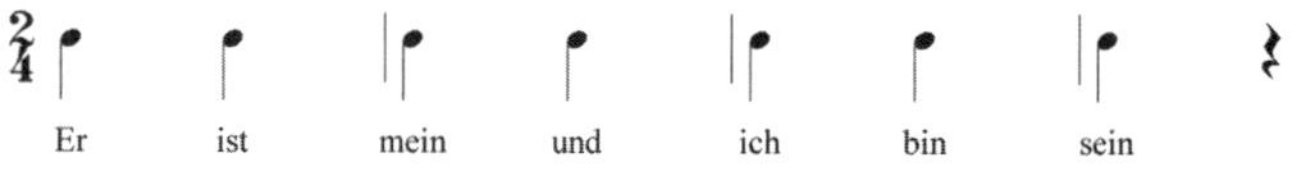
Er ist mein und ich bin sein

into the compound even beat [4/4 meter], then the words *mein* and *sein* lose all emphasis because they do not receive enough beat weight. Just as one can place the noun at the beginning, in the middle, or at the end in two verses, which by the way consist of the same feet, so can two melodic sentences which consist of the same type of notes, the same measure of beat and tempo, have their accent in different places. While this circumstance does not alter the type of verse in poetry, it does so in music; in music the beat is determined by the place of the accent and its weight, which then remain constant so long as the piece continues in the same meter.

Kirnberger, composition treatise (1771), Vol. 2, Part I, Chapter 4 "Tempo, Meter, and Rhythm"

A succession of notes that mean nothing by themselves and are differentiated from one another only by pitch can be transformed into a real melody—one that has a definite character and depicts a passion or a particular sentiment—by means of tempo, meter, and rhythm, which give the melody its character and expression. It is immediately apparent to everyone that the most moving melody would be completely stripped of all its power and expression if one note after another were performed without precise regulation of speed, without accents, and without rest points, even if performed with the strictest observance of pitch. Even common speech would become partly incomprehensible and completely disagreeable if a proper measure of speed were not observed in the delivery, if the words were not separated from one another by the accents associated with the length and brevity of the syllables, and finally if the phrases and sentences were not differentiated by rest points. Such a lifeless delivery would make the most beautiful speech sound no better than the letter-by-letter reading of children.

Thus tempo, meter, and rhythm give melody its life and power. *Tempo* defines the rate of speed, which by itself is already important since it designates a lively or quiet character. *Meter* determines the accents in addition to the length and brevity of the notes and the lighter or more emphatic delivery; and it shapes the notes into words, so to speak. But *rhythm* establishes for the ear the individual phrases formed by the words and the periods composed of several phrases. Melody is transformed into a comprehensible and stimulating speech by the proper combination of these three things.

But it must be kept in mind that none of these elements is sufficient by itself to give the melody a precise character; the true expression of the melody is determined only by their synthesis and their interaction. Two compositions may have the same rate of allegro or largo, yet still have an entirely different effect; according to the type of meter, the motion is more hurried or emphatic, lighter or heavier, even while the speed remains the same [see Chapter 2]. From this it is clear that tempo and meter must combine their forces. The same is also true of rhythm: the components from which a melody is formed can assume an entirely different expression depending on meter and tempo. . . .

Meter actually consists of the precise uniformity of accents that are given to a few notes and of the completely regular distribution of long and short syllables. That is, when these heavier or lighter accents recur at regular intervals, the melody acquires a meter or a measure. If these accents were not distributed regularly, so that no precise periodic recurrence occurred, the melody would be similar only to common prosaic speech; but with this periodic return it is comparable to poetic speech, which has its precise meter. . . .

If one hears a succession of equal pulses that are repeated at the same time interval, as in example 4.2, experience teaches us that we immediately divide them metrically in our minds by arranging them in groups containing an equal number of pulses; and we do this in such a way that we put an accent on the first pulse of each group or imagine hearing it stronger than the others. This division can occur in three ways, as shown in example 4.3.

Example 4.2

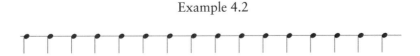

Example 4.3

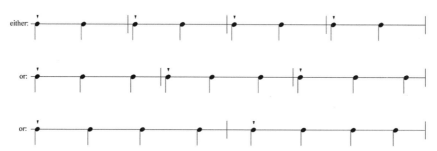

That is, we divide the pulses into groups of two, three, or four. We do not arrive at any other division in a natural way. No one can repeat groups of five and even less of seven equal pulses in succession without wearisome strain. It can be done more easily with six, especially when the pulses go rather quickly; however, one will notice that groups of six or more pulses are not easily comprehended without thinking of a subdivision, in which case they once again resemble the above-mentioned groups of two, three, and four.

Example 4.4

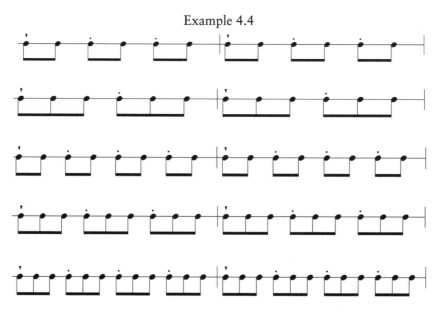

Here many kinds of pulses are used in one group. The dots indicate the main pulses to which the others are subordinate, since they are not felt as strongly as the former; thus these groups become similar again to those mentioned above, or rather they are the same. With fast pulses, even many more can be subsumed under one principal pulse, but the arrangement of the groups is always the same.

It is easy to apply this. Instead of the word "pulse," one uses *beat*, and *measure* instead of "group"; in this way one gets an idea of what the measure is and of its many varieties. The measure consists of two, three, or four equal beats; besides these, there is no other natural type of measure.

In quadruple meter, the first and third beats are accented, but the second and fourth unaccented. The former are also called strong and the latter weak beats. Of the accented beats, the first is in turn stressed more than the third, as can be seen from example 4.12, where – means accented and N unaccented. . . .

Example 4.12

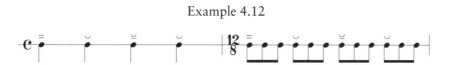

Triple meters have the common element that, in each, three beats are felt per measure, the first of which is always accented, the third unaccented. The second can be accented or unaccented, depending on the nature of the piece. That is, it is usually accented in ponderous meters and in serious pieces, as in chaconnes and many sarabandes; but in light meters this second beat is weak. This two-fold treatment of the second beat in triple meter is clarified by example 4.20.

Example 4.20

In the first example, a nonessential dissonance, which can only appear on a strong beat, falls on the second quarter. In the second, the cadence falls on the same beat; consequently it is also accented here. But in the third example it is weak. . . .

In duple as well as in triple meter, there are melodies in which it is obvious that whole measures are alternately strong and weak, so that a whole measure is heard as only one beat. If the melody is of such nature that the entire measure is felt as only one beat, two measures must be grouped together to form just one, whose first part is accented and the other unaccented. If this contraction were not to occur, the result would be a melody consisting only of accented beats, because of the necessary weight of the downbeat. This would be as unpleasant as a sentence in speech consisting of entirely one-syllable words, each of which had an accent.

Hiller, singing treatise (1774)

I cannot put off the following remark any longer as a preparation to singing metrically organized music. Between two notes, side by side, of the same kind and value, and in a duple or equal division of the beat, one will always be long and the other short, according to their inner quantity. (The outward or apparent quantity deals with the change in the kind and value of notes, such as whole and half notes, quarters, eighths, etc.) This fact has its basis in the natural feelings of man, which is also found in speech. Two syllables cannot be spoken together without it appearing that one is shorter than the other, prosody may take exception to this if it desires. The division of the measure determines which of the two is long and short. This is made apparent on paper by means of a bar line (what is included between two bar lines, whether one, two, three, or twenty notes is called a measure), and in the performance by up and down beats of the hand.

The downstroke of the hand is called *thesis* and the up stroke, or as is sometimes said, the upbeat, is called *arsis*. These two words are found in several books used for the parts of the measure, others translate this to "good part" and "bad part" of the measure, after the Italian words *nota buona, nota cattiva*. I would rather not have [these terms], as I disagree with them. I would say "longer part" instead of "good part" and "shorter part" instead of "bad part."

Rousseau, dictionary (1779), "Time"

In the different time[s] [beats] of a measure, there are some more sensible, more marked than the rest, tho' of equal powers. The time which marks most, is called strong time; that which is marked less, is called weak. The strong times are, the first in the measure of two times and the first and third in the measures of three and four. In regard to the second time, it is always weak in all the measures, and it is the same thing with the fourth in the four time measure.

If we sub-divide each time into two other equal parts, we shall have besides a strong time, for the first half, a weak time for the second, and there is no part of a time which may not be sub-divided in the same manner.

J. C. Bach and F. P. Ricci, pianoforte treatise (c.1788), Part 4
"The Measure and its diverse species"

Each measure or time unit is made up of notes which pass over more or less quickly, depending on their proportion and number; they are marked with diverse symbols to indicate their different duration. A perpendicular line drawn across the five stave lines, called the bar line, separates the measures; strong is the time unit that follows the bar line, and weak is the one that precedes it. . . .

The strong beat is the first beat in a 2/4 or 3/4 measure, and the first and third beat in a 4/4. The second beat is always weak in all measures and the same is true of the fourth beat in a 4/4 measure. A note which begins on the weak beat and ends on the strong one is called syncopation, because it acts against the rule of stress and upsets, in some ways, the measure.

Koch, composition treatise, Volume 2 (1787), Part 2, Section 3, Chapter 1
"The Punctuation Signs of Phrases and their Incises,
or the Ending Formulas of Melodic Sections"

At the moment of the invention of a melody certain tones that have inner value or emphasis distinguish themselves. These determine the separation of measures in the presentation of the melody, provided that other musicians can understand and perform them just as the composer imagined them. Let us suppose the composer invented the following sequence of notes in Example 59, allowing that the relative duration of tones has already been determined.

Example 59

In inventing this beginning melodic section, the composer may let the emphasis of the division fall either on the tones marked * or on the tones marked with the sign o. If he conceived this melody so that the emphasis falls on the tones marked *, then, as soon as he wishes to represent it through notes, he must write the melody according to this conception. That is, he must bring those tones which are emphasized in his conception into that of the measure which is stressed according to the nature of the meter. Thus, in this case, this beginning melodic section must appear in the metrical division as in Example 60. On the other hand, if the emphasis falls on the tones marked with o, then he must divide the phrase into measures as in Example 61.

Example 60

Example 61

From this it is apparent that simultaneously with the genesis of an idea, those stressed tones which necessitate this or that metrical division are already determined.

——. Vol. 3 (1793), Section 4, Chapter 1 "Meter or Metrical Stress"

It is well known that the technical term *meter* is borrowed from poetry, where it defines the flow and length of the line by help of feet.

These feet are of either two or three syllables.

Disyllabic are:

1. the *trochee*, which consists of a long and a short syllable (– ◡); for example, the words *Künste, schöne* are articulated in this way;

2. the *iamb*, whose first syllable is short, but the second long (◡ –); for example, *Figur, Entzückt;*

3. the *spondee*, a succession of two long syllables (– –); for example, Nennest du, würdigest du *etwas* Seligkeit dann;

4. the *pyrrhic*, a succession of two short syllables (◡ ◡); for example, *In umw*ölkender Nacht rufet des Strahls Gefährt.

Trisyllabic feet, on the other hand, are:

1. the *dactyl*, a series of one long and two short syllables (– ◡ ◡) ; for example, Empfangt mich *heilige* Schatten, ihr;

2. the *anapaest*, a reverse dactyl, or a succession of two short and one long syllable (◡ ◡ –); for example, *Das Gestad* hallet, es donnert das Meer;

3. the *tribrach*, a series of three short syllables (◡ ◡ ◡); for example, *In der Entzückung*;

4. the *molossus*, a succession of three long syllables (– – –); for example, *Herr! Herr! Gott! Gerechter*;

5. the *ampibrach*, which has a short, long, and short syllable (◡ – ◡); for example, Sie sah *die junge* berbende Streiterin;

6. the *bacchius*, a series of one short and two long syllables (◡ – –) ; for example, *In Wettlauf*;

7. the *antibacchius*, a series of two long and one short syllables (◡ ◡ –); for example, Zweykämpfe! Verflucht *ist der Bruder*mord;

8. the *cretic* or *amphimacer*, a succession of long, short, long syllables (– ◡ –); for example, *Edle That*!

The extraordinary similarity of these feet to the different movements of parts of the measure is easily perceived, for already in the simplest divisions of the measure these feet are very noticeable. Thus, for example, the division of the measure in Examples 193 and 194 is trochaic, in Examples 195 and 196, on the other hand, iambic. In Examples 197 and 198 the phrase begins with a spondee, in Example 199, however, with a pyrrhic.

Example 193

Example 194

Example 195

Example 196

Example 197

Example 198

Example 199

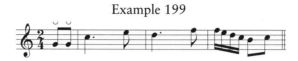

Different divisions of the measure are just as similar to the trisyllabic feet. The phrase in Examples 200 and 201 consists of dactyllic feet, that in Example 202 of anapaestic feet. In Example 203 the phrase begins with a tribrach, in Example 204 with a molossus, and in Example 205 with an ampibrach. Movement of the bacchius, the antibacchius, and the amphimacer is found in the first measures of the phrases in Examples 206, 207, and 208.

Example 200

Example 201

Example 202

Example 203

Example 204

Example 205

Example 206

Example 207

Example 208

Türk, clavier treatise (1789), Chapter 1, Part 4 "Concerning Meter"

When in a succession of several tones of apparently the same duration, some of these are given more emphasis than others in a certain maintained (uniform) order, there then arises through these accents the sensation we call meter, for example:

But since in most compositions there are many notes of various values, then, besides the above-mentioned accents, longer or shorter note values and rests must each receive their specific durations. When this happens, one is playing according to the meter. Meter, insofar as practice is concerned, is most generally understood as the correct arrangement of a certain number of notes, etc., which are to be played within a certain period of time. . . .

Each meter has strong and weak beats, although according to their external value or duration, they are equal to each other as shown by the following examples. However, more emphasis (internal value) is given to one than to the other. For everyone feels that in (*a*) of each group of two notes, and in (*b*) of each group of three notes, the first note is the most important.

For this reason, strong beats are also said to be internally long, or are called struck or accented beats. In beating time, they occur as the downbeat (*thesis*).

Weak beats are also called internally short, passing, or unaccented beats, etc. They are executed by a lifting of the hand, which in technical terminology is called *arsis*.

In every two-part meter, only one is a strong beat, namely, the first; the four-part meters have two strong beats, namely, the first and third, of which the first gets the greater emphasis. In three-part meters, the first one is really the strong beat, nevertheless, in some cases, the third is given emphasis, just as in a few cases the second is internally long and thereby the third is short. Beat divisions are also not regarded as having the same internal value, for in duple figures the first, third, fifth, and seventh, and in triple figures the first, fourth, seventh, and tenth members are strong or accented, the others weak or transitory. The same is true for smaller note values.

——. **Chapter 6, Part 2 "Concerning the Clarity of Execution"**

Whoever would read a poem or a similar text in such a way that it becomes comprehensible to the listener must place a marked emphasis on certain words or syllables. The very same resource is also at the disposal of the practicing musician. The question which then arises is: What tones are to receive a special emphasis (accent)? It would be difficult to specify every one, but those which are especially to be so treated are: 1) those tones which fall on a strong beat or on an important part of the measure and 2) the beginning tones of sections of a composition and phrase members. Besides these, there are 3) various tones to be stressed in performance which will be discussed in more detail. . . .

For a fine performance, aside from the first and most important note in a measure, the second strong beat is also played with emphasis, although not as noticeably as the first beat which is always more important. Consequently, the following notes are to be played approximately at the indicated degrees of strength, without regard for their longer or shorter values.

If the composer does not wish this kind of realization in certain places, then he must expressly specify the opposite. For example:

In general, the above rule is only valid for as long as no indication of forte and piano, etc., appears, or until an exception becomes necessary for other reasons.

The beginning tone of every period and the like must be given an even more marked emphasis than an *ordinary* strong beat. Strictly speaking, these beginning tones are themselves stressed to a greater degree or lesser degree according to whether they begin a larger or smaller part of the whole, that is, after a full cadence, the beginning tone [of the following section] must be more strongly marked than after a half cadence, or merely after a phrase division, etc. Here is an example which serves to illustrate these points in concise fashion.

As necessary as it is to place emphasis on the first tone of a section or phrase member, it is also important to keep the following limitation in mind: only the first tone that falls on a strong beat must be so stressed. The [pitch] *a* marked [in the example above] with an *o* in the sixth measure should therefore not be struck as loudly as the following *b*, although that section as a whole should be played more strongly than the preceding one. Violations of this are often committed, for a first tone which is only transitory in its importance and marked forte is often played as loudly as the following note on a strong beat.

There are still a variety of single tones which must be played with emphasis. To these, other than appoggiaturas, belong especially those intervals which are dissonant with the bass (a), or through which (by means of a tie) dissonant intervals may be prepared (b), further, syncopated notes (c), intervals which do not belong to the diatonic scale of that key, by means of which one has modulated (d), those tones which are distinguished by their length, highness, and lowness (e), etc. The notes I have marked with a ^ must be played with somewhat greater strength.

Another means of accent, which is to be used much less often and with great care, is lingering on certain tones. The orator not only lays more emphasis on important syllables and the like, but he also lingers upon them a little. But this kind of lingering, when it occurs in music, cannot, of course, always be of the same duration, for it appears to me to depend primarily on 1) the greater or lesser importance of the note, 2) its length and relationship to other notes, and 3) the harmony which is basic to them.

Because it is recognized by everyone, I do not have to provide evidence for the possibility of lingering somewhat longer on a very important note than on one of less importance. Therefore, the question is simply: what are the more important notes and how long can they be held out? I have sought [above] to make known the many notes which can be accented and these are mainly the ones which, depending on the circumstances, can be lengthened. The other tones on which a brief hesitation may take place must be felt by the player himself, for who is able to demonstrate every possible case? As far as how long a note should be held is concerned, I would like to establish the rule that it should at the most not be lengthened more than half its value. Usually the holding of a note should be only scarcely perceptible, for example, when a note becoming important enough to receive an accidental is already marked by the height of its pitch, or by an expected change of harmony, etc. That the following note loses as much of its value as has been given to the accentuated note goes without saying.

Holding a note for a longer or shorter time depends also on the length of the note and its relationship to the others, for it should be easy enough to understand that one can linger longer on a quarter note than on a sixteenth. If shorter note values follow an accented note then a hold may be dispensed with, because in this case the longer note accents itself without assistance.

When I said that a hold also depends on the basic harmony, I meant that the hold should be very short or there should be none at all, if through the hold a mistake in the harmony comes about in the bass or in another voice. By means of some presupposed knowledge of thoroughbass, it is easy to recognize those cases where a hold should or should not take place. I will only include a few contrasting examples here. At (a) a hold can be made without disadvantage to the harmony, at (b), however, not.

In Example (b) fifths would result if one were to lengthen the *b* by a dot as in Example (c), but even a very short hold would not be pleasant here.

**Burney, history of music (1789), Book 2, Chapter 3
"On the Formation of the Time-table"**

Time is of such importance in music, that it can give meaning and energy to the repetition of the same sound; whereas, without it, a variety of tones, with respect to gravity and acuteness, has no effect. . . .

In repetitions of the same sound, in notes of equal duration, Time is made sensible to the hearer by accents; without which he would have no means of discovering the different portions into which it is divided. If, therefore, we have a succession of notes of equal length and intonation, the ear may be impressed with an idea of some certain rhythm or measure, by marking the first of every two or three notes thus:

In the first example the accents being on the first and third sounds, imply Common Time of four equal members or portions; and in the second, the repetitions of the same sound having an accent on the first of every three sounds, an idea is impressed of Triple Time. By this means the mind is employed in a kind of perpetual calculation, and a uniformity of sensation is impressed on the ear.

Albrechtsberger, composition treatise (1790)

Time-units are usually denoted by the upper figure of the signature; for example, 2/4 has two time-units. The downbeat or the first quarter note is called the good time-unit; the upbeat or second quarter note is called the bad time-unit. . . .

3/4 time has one good time-unit and two bad ones; the downbeat or the first quarter note is called the good time-unit; the second and third beats or the second and third quarter notes are called the bad time-units. The same applies to 3/2 time. . . .

Common or so-called 4/4 time, though it has four time-units, is actually double 2/4 time; the downbeat or the first quarter note is the good time-unit; the second beat or quarter note is the first bad time-unit; the third beat or quarter note is the second good time-unit, and the fourth beat or the fourth quarter note the second bad time-unit.

In times with nine time-units [9/8], the first note . . . is the good time-unit; the second and third are bad time-units; the fourth note is the second good time-unit; the fifth and sixth are bad; the seventh note is again a good time-unit; the eighth and ninth are bad time-units. In times with twelve time-units [12/8], the first, fourth, seventh, and tenth notes are good time-units and the remaining notes . . . are bad time-units.

Anonymous, *New Instructions for Playing the Harpsichord, Piano-forte or Spinnet* (c.1790), "Of Discords"

The Accented part of the Bar is the first Note, and the Unaccented part the 2nd of two Notes in a Bar of Common Time. In Triple Time the Accent lays on the 1st Note, with a weaker one on either the 2nd or 3rd part.

Tromlitz, flute treatise (1791), Chapter 5 "Time signatures"

In 2/4 time the first quarter note is inherently long and the second inherently short. In 3/4 and 3/8 the first beat is long and the second and third short. In four-four time (C) the first and third are long and the second and fourth short.

——. Chapter 8 "On Proper Articulation"

When two notes of equal duration, the first of which is a good note and the second a bad note, follow each other on different degrees of the scale, they are articulated clearly; the first one gets *ta* and the second *a*, so that you pronounce the word *taa*

When four notes of equal duration are grouped together, they are articulated with the word *taaraa*; the first note receives *ta*, the second *a*, the third *ra*, and the fourth *a*.

When more than four notes of equal duration, or whole passages consisting of identical figures, follow one another, *ta* is replaced by *da*, in order to keep the resemblance with *ra*.

ta - a,   ra - a,   da - a,   ra - a,   da,   ta - a, ra - a, da- a, ra- a, da- a, ra- da, da

Just as vowels and syllables are joined together, the notes must also be connected and you should not be able to hear any break or space between them. The air must continue to flow and the tongue to articulate without stopping the wind. Interrupting the air flow should be indicated by the composer by means of either a rest or the end of a phrase. . . .

With two notes of equal duration, the first, by virtue of its intrinsic value, is longer than the second: it is called a long note, because the weight or stress, or as we say, the accent, falls on this note. The second note is shorter. The long notes always get *ta*, *da*, or *ra*, according to the circumstance, for *ta* occurs by itself, whereas *da* and *ra* are grouped together, as I have already shown.

If I have four notes of equal duration, the first is long, the second short, the third long, and the fourth short. The first gets *ta* (here *ta* is grouped with the others, but is only used in the beginning), the second *a*, the third *ra*, and the fourth *a* again. Whether the notes are halves, quarters, eighths or sixteenths, they get the same treatment. In these groupings the short note always gets *a*; however, if a short note stands alone, it gets *ta*, whether it occurs in the beginning or in the middle of a phrase, and the following good note gets *ra*.

s.   l.   s.   l.   s.   l.   s.   s.   l. s.   s.   l. s.   s.   s.   l.   s.
ta   ra - a   da - a   ra   ta   ta   ra - a   ta   ra - a   ta   ta   ra - a

Altenberg, trumpet and kettledrum treatise (1795), Chapter 11
"On Clarino Playing and the Style of Execution Required Thereby"

Make a distinction between principal and passing notes, so that the former are played somewhat louder than the others. In simple meter, the principal notes to which I am referring are ordinarily the first, third, fifth, etc., and the passing notes generally the second, fourth, sixth, etc., which can be played with somewhat less stress, comparatively speaking.

f p f p f p f p   f p f p f p

Milchmeyer, pianoforte treatise (1797)

With two connected [slurred] notes the first is played strongest, the second the weakest; and with three connected notes (if it is not a triplet), the first is the strongest, the second somewhat weaker, and the third the weakest; with four we find this same shading from strongness to weakness from the first to the fourth instead.

Kollmann, composition essay (1799)

Of duple meters,
In all these, the first part of the bar is *accented* and the second part *unaccented*.
Of triple meters,
In all these, the first note is the *accented*, and the other two the *unaccented* ones. If any one of them is divided, the first note of every division is also accented a little.
Of quadruple meters,
All these measures of four equal times in a bar are accented on the first note of the bar only, being the first of every four times, and thereby become materially different from the measures of two times, in which the first half of every bar is accented.

Spohr, musical diary (1860–1861), "1802"

On October 20 we continued on to Koenigsberg, where we remained until November 18. . . . The Pixis family arrived on their journey from St. Petersburg [and] we met at a musicale given by Count Calnheim. It began with the younger [Pixis] brother playing some variations on the piano, which he did with brilliance and taste. Then the older played a quartet by [Franz] Krommer. Neither the composition nor its performance met with my approval. . . . After him came [Franz] Eck, also with a quartet by Krommer. But, heavens, what a difference! The contrasts between strong and weak in his playing, the clarity of the passages, the tasteful embellishments . . . lent to his playing an irresistible charm.

Callcott, musical grammar (1806), "Of the Accent of Notes"

The Bars of Music are not only useful for dividing the Movement into equal Measures, but also for shewing the Notes upon which the *Accent* is to be laid.

The Measures of Common time are divided into four parts; of these, the first and third are accented; the second and fourth unaccented. In the course of this work, the accented will be termed *strong* parts, and the unaccented, *weak* parts of the Measure.

The Measures of Triple Time consist of three parts; the first *strong*, the two others *weak*; although the last part is rather *strong*, in comparison of the middle part.

In *slow Common Time* [C] the Accents are more frequent; but they are found in the same proportion on the first, third, fifth, and seventh Quavers [eighth notes]; which are the *strong* parts, while the second, fourth, sixth, and eighth, are the *weak* parts.

In *three Crotchet* [quarter] *Time* [3/4], when divided into Quavers, the first, third, and fifth Quavers are *strong*; the second, fourth, and sixth, *weak*.

In six *Quaver Time* [6/8], the first and fourth Quavers are strong; the others *weak*.

In the further division of simple Measure, the Accents are known by the Groups, which are regulated by the *Times* of the Measure, as before noticed; thus,

In Triple measure, the same arrangement of Groups is in general use; thus,

These inferior Accents, which belong to the *Times* of the Measure, do not, by any means, destroy that great and predominant Accent that belongs to the first Note which follows the Bar, and which is accompanied by the *THESIS*, or depression of the hand in beating Time. The *ARSIS*, or elevation of the hand, always follows on the weak part of the measure.

In compound Time, the difference between six Crotchet [6/4] and three Minum [3/2] Measure, or between six Quaver [6/8] and three Crotchet [3/4] Measure, (both of which contain an equal portion of Time between the Bars), is only known by the Accent. The Groups, indeed, regulate the Accent to the eye, and shew the compound Time of six Quaver [6/8] Measure by their equal division.

Thus, in the Example before mentioned, the simple Measure contains the Quavers [eighths] grouped by Sixes, which have one strong Accent on the first, and two inferior ones on the third and fifth Notes; thus,

In compound Time, the Accents are as under,

The compound Triples of nine Crotchets, or nine Quavers [9/8], take their Accents from the simple Measures.

Corri, singing treatise (1810), "Musical Accent"

To this study the Performer should particularly apply, for without Accent there can be no expression, it is this knowledge that directs the Singer to moderate the Voice to that exquisite degree of tone adapted to the spirit and meaning of every Note.

The accented Note or Notes of a Bar, are those on which the Emphasis falls; in Even time there are two Accents in the Bar, in Triple Time, there is only one Accent in a Bar.

Singers ought rigorously to adhere to the meaning of the subject, and this, if guided by common sense, they may easily do, by first reading the words with attention and marking the most important in each sentence, which word will be always found to correspond with the accented Note of the Music; the Voice can then be regulated in the manner that will best enable the Singer to give to the passage the degree of Energy or Pathos its subject demands, and without such appropriate execution no effect can ever be produced.

Burney, in Rees' encyclopedia (1819)

Accent, in music. In the mechanism of melody, or measured musical tones, musicians have long agreed to regard the *first* and *third* notes of a bar, in common time, whether vocal or instrumental, as accented, and the *second* and *fourth* notes as unaccented. In triple time, divided into three portions, the *first* note and *last* are accented, the *second* unaccented. But these accents are variously modified; often to produce some comic effect, as wantonly limping, to ridicule lameness. If the *third* note in triple time is accented in serious music, it is always less forcibly marked than the first.

Hastings, dissertation on musical taste (1822), Chapter 2, Section 5 "Of Accent and Emphasis"

Accent and emphasis . . . give variety, interest, dignity and significancy, both to poetry and to prose. Without these requisites, the ear would suffer from the most tedious monotony; the subject would fail to animate our feelings, and the very meaning of an author would be ambiguous and unintelligible.

Accent, in its more limited sense, has been termed the essence of words. Let the words *desert, object, conjure,* for instance, be uttered without any accentual distinction of syllables, and their meaning will be entirely ambiguous: but place an accent on one of the syllables of each of these words, and its significancy will be readily acknowledged. If, again, the accent be removed to the other syllable, the meaning will then be totally changed, though it will be equally as obvious as before. . . .

Nor are accent and emphasis by any means unnecessary to the melody of song: and hence it is, that an occasional stress of voice is to be found among every class of performers, illiterate as well as learned. . . . Modern compositions, especially, are so distinguished for their rhythmical effects, that a disregard of this single rule would deprive them of all character and interest. Even in the slowest movements, where the rhythm is less important, the succession of chords (as every theorist knows) requires the observance of this rule.

Busby, musical manual (1828)

Accented. Accented notes are those which are naturally given with emphasis; either on account of their situation in the bar, or because they carry with them some strong meaning.

Unaccented. Those measures [notes] of a bar on which the emphasis, or expression, does not naturally fall, are called *Unaccented* measures [notes]. In common time of four crotchets [quarter notes], these consist of the second and fourth crotchet: in triple-time, are the second and third measure [note].

Hummel, pianoforte treatise (1829)

1) Four-quarter time (4/4), usually called common time and marked by a C, is divisible by the number 2 into twice 2 parts, of which the former is always accented and the second unaccented; consequently each bar of four quarter time contains 2 accented and 2 unaccented parts as:

a = accented
u = unaccented

2) The less Alla breve, or 2 half-note time (2/2), generally indicated by ¢, contains two parts or beats, each of which is a half note.

3) Two-quarter time (2/4) differs from the less Alla breve only in this, that in the latter the parts of the bar are half notes, in this quarter notes.

II. Triple times are those of which the bars may be divided into 3 equal parts, of which the first is accented and the other two unaccented.

To triple times belong:

1) three-half-note time (3/2) the bar of which consists of 3 half notes:

2) three-quarter time (3/4) as well as three-eighth-note time (3/8), differing from the foregoing only by the alteration in the kind of notes:

6/4 is a doubled 3/4; 6/8 is a doubled 3/8; 9/4 is a tripled 3/4; 9/8 is a tripled 3/8; 12/8 is a quadrupled 3/8.

Although these compound meters may be divided into three parts, yet on account of their multitude nature they always admit of being divided by the numbers 2, 3, or 4 into 2, 3, or 4 principal divisions or aggregates of parts, and thereby, with regard to their accent, possess a certain resemblance to the simple common and triple time.

Glover, psalmody treatise (1835), Part 1 "Rhythm"

Rhythm chiefly consists in the due arrangement of *time* and *accent*. The points of division of time are chiefly marked by bars and commas. A bar (|) represents a loud beat, a comma (,) a soft beat; the former should be struck on something more sonorous than the latter, and they should be repeated at regular intervals with the exactness of the clicking of a clock. A beat, when performed, accompanies the commencement of the note which immediately follows it on paper.

Every tune is divided into a certain number of feet; which feet form the *measure*. A simple foot consists of one loud beat and of one or two soft beats. A compound foot consists of two loud and of two soft beats, or of two loud and of four soft beats, or of three loud and of three soft beats; the predominant accent is expressed by a bar, an inferior accent by a semicolon.

——. Part 2 "Directions for Instructing a School," Section 6

Beating time in different measures may be taught in the following manner. Strike the palms together to express a loud beat, bend the hands into fists and strike them together for a soft beat. Let the Teacher count | 1,2, | 1,2, | 1,2, | 1,2, etc. striking palms and fists alternately, the children imitating the action of her hands. Then count | 1,2,3,4, | 1,2,3,4, etc. striking palms, viz. loud beats to 1; and fists, viz. soft beats to 2,3,4. Change the measure afterwards to 1,2,3, striking palms to 1, fists to 2,3. The beating of the time of rests may be taught by striking the fore-fingers downwards at the accented, and sideways at the unaccented part of the measures.

Nathan, singing treatise (1836), Chapter 8 "Emphasis and Accents"

Accent in singing, as in reading, is a certain modulation of the voice—an extra-force of sound intended particularly to be impressed upon the hearer, or to express a passion.

As in all languages there are, in words of different syllables, certain letters accented, so in music is each bar or measure divided into accented and unaccented parts.

In common time of four crotchets [quarter notes] in each bar, the first and third are accented, the second and fourth unaccented. In triple time of three crotchets or quavers [eighth notes] in a bar, the first only is accented, the second and third unaccented.

"In common time remember well by art,
The first and third is the accented part;
And if your music triple time should be,
Your accent is the first of every three."

There are, however, instances where the accents are differently placed, according to the fancy of the composer, to express particular passions or ideas; in which case the expression of such a license is understood by the following significations. When, for example, the regular note for accentuation at the commencement of a bar is immediately succeeded by a note of greater value, with respect to duration,

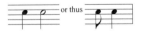

the second note then becomes accented instead of the first.

Accented words will always fall on the accented parts of the bar, if the composition be good. When an instance to the contrary occurs (for errors will creep in, even from the pens of the first masters), the singer will be at liberty to correct such an over-sight. Free pardon will be granted to those who take upon themselves to alter the following passages, which are as inelegant to read thus emphasized, as repugnant to the laws of composition to be so adapted to music.

The Law of Jara - Bishop

Don John - Bishop

Henri *Quatre*

Twelfth Night - Bishop

Mason, vocal manual (1839), Chapter 3
"Singing in Connection with Beating Time and Accent"

The teacher says, if you attend closely, you will find that, it is natural to sing one part of the measure louder than the rest; certain parts of the measure require thus to be sung. The loud parts are said to be ACCENTED, and the soft parts of a measure are said to be UNACCENTED.

The *double* measure [2/4] has one accented and one unaccented part. The first or downward beat is *accented*, and the second or upward beat is *unaccented*.

The pupils are now required to beat the time, and sing one *la* to each part of the measure, with particular reference to accent. Sing also such words as ho-ly, glo-ry, &c.

In triple measure [3/4], the *first* part is *accented*, the *second* and *third* parts unaccented.

Exercise as before.

Words of three syllables accented on the first, may now be substituted for *la*; as glo-ri-ous, joy-ful-ly, &c.

In *quadruple* measure [4/4], the *first* part of the measure is *accented*, the second *unaccented*, the third *slightly accented*, and the fourth the *softest*. Thus quadruple measure has two loud and two soft parts, yet the louds are not equally loud, and the softs are not equally soft.

Exercise as before. Such words as mo-men-ta-ry, plan-e-ta-ry, &c. may be substituted for *la*, or similar words to those used in double measure, the scholars being reminded that *two double* measures are equivalent to *one quadruple* measure.

In *sextuple* measure [6/4], the *first* and *fourth* parts are *accented*, and the others *unaccented*. Thus sextuple measure, is like two triple measures, only the last half is softer than the first.

Questions.

Exercise as before.

Spir-i-tu-al-it-y, im-pos-si-bi-li-ty, or words of six syllables may be substituted.

The teacher now sings at one time this, at another that kind of measure *without beating the time,* and lets the scholars determine by the accentuation, what kind of measure he has sung.

Garcia, singing treatise (1840–1847)

To bring time into bold relief in compositions of decided rhythm the strong beat, especially the first of the bar, must be accented. Warlike songs, and all other outbursts of enthusiasm, require a very marked and regular beat.

Sound an a-larm,   sound an a-larm, your sil - ver trum-pets sound

Non più andrai far-fal-lo-nea-mo-ro-so   not-tee   gior no d'in-tor-no gi-ran-do

Wagner, conducting treatise (1869)

Has not every German heard the overture to "Der Freischütz" over and over again? I have been told of sundry persons who were surprised to find how frequently they had listened to this wonderful musical poem, without having been shocked when it was rendered in the most trivial manner; these persons were among the audience of a concert given at Vienna in 1864, when I was invited to conduct the overture. At the rehearsal it came to pass that the orchestra of the imperial opera (certainly one of the finest orchestras in existence), were surprised at my demands regarding the execution of this piece. . . .

I arranged with the excellent musicians that they were to play this theme:

legato, and with an equable *piano*, i.e., without the customary commonplace accentuation and *not* as follows:

The good result was at once apparent.

Porges, commentary on Wagner rehearsing The Ring in 1876 (1881), Chapter 1
Das Rheingold, Scene 2

The rendering of the Valhalla theme should convey a feeling of sublime calm. The tempo throughout should be a broad adagio, which does not mean that the span of the phrasing should be wide: on the contrary, accents should demarcate the two-bar sections of the longer periods. These accents, together with a proper grading of the different dynamic levels, bring out the inner dramatic development of this monumental tonal image which we must regard as the principal musical theme of the whole *Ring*. . . .

Singers should not be tempted to lapse into a weak or perhaps even casual style; on the contrary they should try all the harder to bring out the flexible melodic and thematic contours as concisely as possible, by means of clear-cut phrasing and precise metric and rhythmic accents.

There must be no frivolous, shallow characterization [of Loge in *Das Rheingold*] and this will be prevented only if the rhythmic and metrical accents are made with utmost precision.

——. *Die Walküre*, **Act 2, Prelude and Scene 1**

Wagner insisted that the metrical accents, i.e. those at the beginning of each bar, should have their full weight.

Chapter 5

RHYTHMIC ALTERATION

Rhythms in the Classical era were not thought of as mathematical divisions of time to be performed strictly, but rather as outlines or contours to be realized according to physical circumstances or musical characteristics. As a consequence, the practice of altering rhythms— performing them differently from their notated appearance—was commonplace, with many rhythmic patterns considered to be flexible and often transformed in performance according to conventions of the time. A number of these conventions have been discussed in previous chapters, including the displacement of notes in tempo rubato and the conforming of rhythms to natural speech patterns in recitative (Chapter 2), the interpolation of rests as a result of silences of articulation (Chapter 3), and the elongation or shortening of notes as an element of quantitas intrinseca (Chapter 4). Other conventions will be discussed in forthcoming chapters, including the variable lengths of appoggiaturas (Chapter 6). However, there are two conventions— overdotting and triplet conformity—that relate to no broader category or subject and thus are treated here.

The reasons for the various conventions of rhythmic alteration are as varied as the conventions themselves. Some alterations are circumstantial in nature: the dots of dotted notes, for instance, are treated as silences so as to achieve clarity in reverberant performance venues. Some alterations are necessitated by practical considerations: rhythmic representations of natural speech in recitative are simply too complex to notate with precision, and therefore, the rhythms serve only as general guidelines. Some conventions are the result of notational limitations of the time: double dotted notes, for example, were either not yet known by composers and performers or were just being introduced and used. Most of the alterations of rhythm, however, are caused or motivated by expressive concerns: notes are lengthened or shortened in order to capture and express a composition's fundamental mood or sentiment. As components of the expressive palette, then, rhythms could be lightened or shaded, adjusted, or altered for subtle and nuanced meaning. Classical-era composers, who were motivated by expressive principles, counted on the intuitive understanding of performers to comprehend the character of the rhythms of their compositions and to make those rhythms pliable in performance.

OVERDOTTING

Overdotting is the practice of extending the value of dotted notes and reducing the value of corresponding short notes in rhythmic patterns such as seen in Example A (patterns that are contained within a single metric beat). Dotted notes that extend beyond one metric beat, such as seen in Example B, are generally not overdotted unless there would be a need to conform the short note following the dotted note to a prevailing rhythmic texture (see Example I).

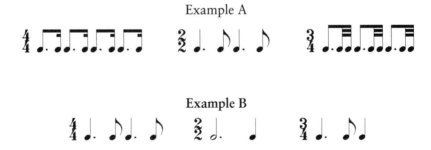

Example A

Example B

The length of extension to the dotted note is variable. Likewise, the consequent shortness of the note that follows is also variable. Duration can be extended a little, a lot, or not at all, depending upon the mood or character of the music, its indicated or desired articulation, the tempo of the performance, or, as mentioned above, the need to conform to a prevailing rhythmic texture. Common alterations of one rhythmic pattern are shown in Example C. The first illustration of alteration, with triplets, might be used to express a gentle, perhaps pastoral mood. It might also be used if the general prevailing rhythmic texture of a piece has triplets. The second illustration of alteration might be used in fast tempos to express a lively, animated character. The third illustration might be used in a slower tempo to express majesty or grandeur. Of course, other permutations are possible, including those in between the three illustrations and including rhythms too mathematically complex to notate.

Example C

Written

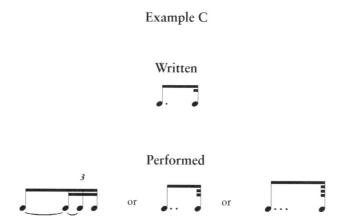

Performed

Because of the variability of extension, the term "overdotting" is more appropriate than the term "double dotting," which is sometimes used. Whereas the extension of a dotted note may in fact be double dotted, and whereas some primary sources recommend that composers use double dots, extension is not limited to that ratio or proportion. Even the term "overdotting" is somewhat of a misnomer since the principle of the practice or the rationale for its employment comes not from desiring a longer dotted note, but from desiring a shorter short note.

In light of this, the practice of overdotting does not apply only to dotted notes that precede short notes. The practice also applies, as seen in Example D, to dotted notes that follow shorter notes. In these instances, the duration of the dotted note would be extended to accommodate the desired shortness of the short note.

Example D

The principle of rhythmic alteration applies to rests as well, and here the rationale for shortness rather than length is clearly apparent, for extending or overdotting the rest, as seen in Example E, merely accommodates the desired shortness of the following note.

Example E

Written

Performed

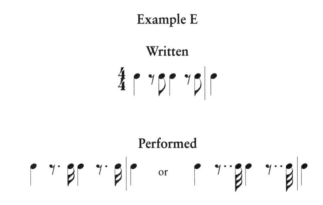

In consideration of general articulation principles of silences of articulation, it should be noted that the extension of dotted notes does not usually result in continuous sound. Degrees of silence customarily occupy the duration of the dot—the degrees being modified with more or less silence depending upon the acoustical properties of the performance venue or the rhythmic or articulative character of the music. To wit, if the acoustical reverberation is slight, as in many modern-day concert halls, it may be desirable to fill most of the dotted note with sound, leaving only a slight amount of space before or after the short note or notes. On the other hand, more space or silence might be desirable in reverberant venues. Also, more silence might be appropriate for performances that are majestic in character or sharp in articulation; performances that are lyrical or legato might warrant less silence.

It is musical circumstance—character of portrayal, quality of articulation, and tempo—that determines both rhythmic length/shortness and amounts or degrees of silence. Character of portrayal is the foremost determinant, since it suggests the quality of articulation and the tempo. The desired qualities of articulation and tempo then suggest degrees of alteration.

In Example F, the dotted-eighth/sixteenth-note rhythms in measures 10–13 and the dotted-eighth-rest/sixteenth note in measure 14 might be altered to characterize the majesty and splendor of the sunrise that Haydn portrays in the music. Given that the alla breve meter signature implies a faster tempo than common time (see Chapter 2) and that the Andante term refers to movement of the half note, the overdotting of rhythms would likely result in double dots.

Example F
Joseph Haydn, Die Schöpfung (The Creation),
Im vollem Glanze (In splendor bright),
measures 1–15

In Example G, the dotted-eighth/sixteenth-note rhythms in the vocal parts of measures 6–11 might be altered to characterize the text (King of tremendous majesty) and also to conform to the prevailing dotted-sixteenth/thirty-second-note rhythms of the orchestral texture and to the alto and tenor parts of beat four in measure 10. The "sal" of "salvandos" could or could not be altered, depending upon the view of the conductor.

Example G
W. A. Mozart, *Requiem* K626, Rex tremendae, measures 1–12

In Example H, the trombones in measures 10–16 should conform to the vocal parts they are doubling (colla parte).

Example H
W. A. Mozart, *Requiem* K626, Confutatis, measures 10–17

In Example I, the soprano and bass parts of measure 9, the alto and tenor parts of measure 10, and the tenor and bass parts of measure 11 should conform to the bass part of the orchestral accompaniment. In addition, beat four of the soprano part in measure 12 might be altered to a dotted eighth/sixteenth note, with beat four of the next measure being altered by the soprano, tenor, and vocal and orchestral bass parts.

Example I
W. A. Mozart, *Missa Solemnis in* C K337, Credo, measures 9–15

In Example J, the rhythms in the orchestral part on beats three and one of measures 10–11 and 12–13 might be altered to have shorter short notes. In addition, the dotted-quarter/eighth-note rhythms of the vocal parts in measures 9 and 13 might be altered to reflect the pattern introduced in measure 5.

Example J
W. A. Mozart, *Vesperae solennes de confessore* K339, Dixit, measures
1–14

In Example K, the soprano, tenor, and bass parts of measure 30 might be
altered to conform to the alto part and to similar rhythms established prior
to measure 30.

Example K
W. A. Mozart, *Missa in C Minor* K427, Credo, measures 24–31

The following quotations, drawn from primary sources that extend from 1752 to 1810 and that represent both instrumental and vocal performance, speak to the general and prevalent practice of overdotting. The authors of the quotations make it clear that this practice was the rule rather than the exception, and that most dotted rhythms, as defined and illustrated at the beginning of this chapter, are to be considered for alteration. In addition, the authors emphasize that mood, character, or sentiment of music determine whether or not a note should be overdotted and the degree of the overdotting. Further rationale for expressive considerations can be found in Chapter 7.

Quantz, flute treatise (1752), Chapter 5
"Of Notes, their Values, Meter, Rests, and other Musical Signs"

The dotted half note (see Fig. 7 (a)) receives six beats, and the following quarter note receives two beats. The dotted quarter (see (b)) receives three beats, and the following eighth only one beat.

Figure 7

(a)   (b)

In dotted eighths, sixteenths, and thirty-seconds (see (c), (d), and (e)) you depart from the general rule because of the animation that these notes must express. It is particularly important to observe that the notes after the dots in (c) and (d) must be played just as short as those in (e), whether the tempo is slow or fast.

(c)   (d)   (e)

As a result, the dotted notes in (c) receive almost the time of a full quarter note and those in (d) the time of an eighth, since the time of the short notes after the dots cannot actually be fixed with complete exactness. To grasp this more clearly, play the lower notes in (f) and (g) slowly, yet in accordance with their proper duration in each example, that is, those in (g) twice as fast as those in (f), those in (h) twice as fast as those in (g), and imagine that the upper notes are dotted. Then turn this around, play the upper notes, and hold each dotted note until the time of the lower dotted note has passed. Make the note after the dot just as short as the sixty-fourth note below it. In this manner you will see that the upper dotted notes in (f) receive the time of the three sixteenths and a dotted thirty-second, those in (g) the time of a sixteenth and a dotted thirty-second, and those in (h) only the time of a thirty-second with a dot and a half, since double dots are found in the lower notes. . . .

With regard to the length of the dot and the shortness of the first note, the notes in Fig. 8, in which the dot stands after every second note, are similar to the dotted notes mentioned above. Their order is simply reversed. The notes D and C in (a) must be just as short as those in (c), whether the tempo is slow or quick.

Figure 8

The two quick notes in (b) and (d) are treated in the same manner, two quick notes here receiving no more time than one in the examples above.

In (e) and (f) the notes after the dots are played just as quickly as those before the dotted notes in (b) and (d).

The shorter you make the first notes in (a), (b), (c), and (d), the livelier and bolder the expression. The longer the dots in (e) and (f) are held, on the other hand, the more flattering and pleasing notes of this kind sound.

——. Chapter 12 "Of the Manner of Playing the Allegro"

Care must be taken not to begin prematurely the notes following short rests that occur in the place of the principal notes on the downbeat. For example, if there is a rest in the place of the first of four sixteenth notes, you must wait half as long again as the rest appears to last, since the following note must be shorter than the first one. The proportion is the same in thirty-second notes.

——. Chapter 17, Section 2 "Of the Ripieno Violinists in Particular"

To make your bow-strokes uniform, and to make yourself equally familiar with the up and down movement, practice a Gigue or Canarie in six-eight time which proceeds in eighth notes and in which the first of each three of these eighths is dotted. Give each note its separate stroke, so that, without repeating strokes, the first and third notes of each figure first receive downstrokes, then upstrokes; and always play the note after the dot very short and sharply. . . .

If in slow alla breve or common time a sixteenth note rest appears on the downbeat, and dotted notes follow (see Figs. 30 and 31), the rest must be regarded as if it were dotted, or as if it were followed by another rest of half the value, and the following note as if it were of half the value.

Figure 30   Figure 31

C. P. E. Bach, clavier treatise (1753), "Introduction to Part 1"

I know from experience that rapid syncopations and, above all, short rests cause great ado among the most rhythmically sure and accomplished of other instrumentalists. All enter too late, even though other parts that enter just ahead of them provide the same assistance as the keyboardist has in his hands. To the latter, these things are easy even when he omits the left hand or accompanies with other instruments. Provided that he is certain of the tempo, his entrance will always be exactly right. Quantz in his Flute Method, page 113, even advocates a delayed entrance (which goes to prove that a correct entrance is nearly impossible) and thus takes the lesser of two evils.

——. **Part 1, Chapter 3 "Performance"**

Short notes that follow dotted ones are always shorter in execution than their notated length. Hence it is superfluous to place strokes [wedges] or dots over them. Figure 172 [second score] illustrates their execution: the division [of the bottom part] must occasionally agree with the notated values [of the top part]. . . . Short notes, when they precede dotted ones, are also played more rapidly than their notation indicates. All of the short notes of Example (c) [Figure 173], even the sixteenths, when the tempo is not too slow, follow this rule. It would be a better practice to add a beam to all the notes. It is only generally true that the short notes described here should be played rapidly, for there are exceptions. The melodies in which they appear should be carefully examined. Should ornaments of length, such as the trill or turn, appear over them, their performance must be broader than that of undecorated short notes. Likewise, in sad or expressive passages and in slow tempos the exception is less accelerated than in other cases.

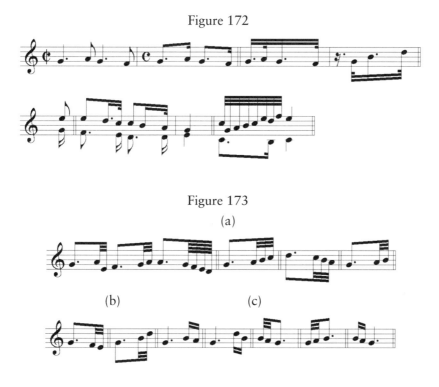

Figure 172

Figure 173

(a)

(b)   (c)

——. Part 2, Chapter 6 "Accompaniment"

Because proper exactness is often lacking in the notation of dotted notes, a general rule of performance has been established which, however, has many exceptions. According to this rule, the notes that follow the dots are to be played in the most rapid manner, and often they should be. But sometimes notes in other parts, with which these must enter, are so divided that a modification of the rule is required. Again, a suave affect, which will not survive the essentially defiant character of the dotted notes, obliges the performer to shorten the dotted note slightly. Hence, if only one kind of execution is adopted as the basic principle of performance, the other kinds will be lost. . . .

In slow or moderate tempos, caesuras are usually extended beyond their normal length, especially when the rests and notes in the bass are the same as those in the other parts, or in the principal part in the case of a solo. Great pains must be taken to achieve a uniform performance and prevent someone from coming in before or after the others. This applies to fermatas, cadences, etc., as well as caesuras. It is customary to drag a bit and depart somewhat from a strict observance of the bar, for the note before the rest, as well as the rest itself, is extended beyond its notated length. Aside from the uniformity which this manner of execution achieves, the passage acquires an impressiveness which places it in relief (Figure 433).

Figure 433

L. Mozart, violin treatise (1756), Chapter 1, Section 3
"Of the Duration or Value of the Notes, Rests, and Dots,
together with an Explanation of all Musical Signs and Technical Words"

There are certain passages in slow pieces in which the dot must be held rather longer than the [notation suggests] if the performance is not to sound too sleepy. For example, if here

the dot were held its usual length, it would sound languid and sleepy. In such cases dotted notes must be held somewhat longer, but the time taken up by extended value must be, so to speak, stolen from the note standing after the dot.

In the above example, therefore, the note E with its dot is sustained longer, but the note F is taken with a short stroke of the bow and so late that the first of the four G notes comes punctually at the right time. The dot should in fact be held at all times somewhat longer than its value. Not only is the performance thereby enlivened, but hurrying—that almost universal fault—is thereby checked; for otherwise, owing to the shortening of the dot, the music easily tends to increase in speed. It would be a good thing if this long retention of the dot were insisted on, and set down as a rule. I, at least, have often done so, and I have made clear my opinion of the right manner of performance by setting down two dots followed by a shortened note:

It is true that at first this looks strange to the eye. But what does this matter? The point has its reason and musical taste is thereby promoted.

——. Chapter 7, Section 2
"Of variations of Bowing in Figures which are composed of varied and unequal notes"

It is only too easy to err in tempo, and nothing is easier than to hurry dotted notes if the value of the dot is not held out. It is therefore always better if the note following the dot is played somewhat late. . . . The dot must rather be held too long than too briefly. In this manner, hurrying is avoided and good taste promoted, for that which is added to the dot will be subtracted imperceptibly from the following notes. That is, the latter are played more rapidly.

Agricola, singing treatise (1757), Chapter 4 "Concerning Divisions"

Short notes in slow or fast tempos—specially sixteenth or thirty-second notes or eighths in the *alla breve*—that occur after a dot are always executed very short, whether there may be one or several of them; the note occurring before the dot, therefore, is held so much longer. For example, these notes

are executed as if they were written thus:

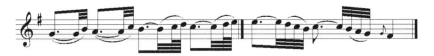

The note before the dot is stronger, the one after the dot, weaker.

If a short note precedes and the second note is dotted, the first note is executed as short as possible, and the remainder of the time [of the first note] is assigned to the dotted note. For example:

Execution:

In these figures, however, the first note is sung loudly and the one before the dot, which is always slurred to the previous note, is sung more quietly, and, if time permits, a crescendo is made.

**Türk, clavier treatise (1789), Chapter 1, Part 3
"Concerning the Durations of the Notes and of Dots and Rests"**

When two dots are placed directly after each other, the value of the first dot . . . is half the note preceding. The second dot is one half the value of the first dot. . . . Incidentally, in the chapter on performance, it will be shown that in many cases, one has to linger somewhat longer on the dots than their actual value suggests.

———. Chapter 6, Part 3
"Concerning the Expression of the Prevailing Character"

Dotted notes . . . require a varied treatment according to the context in which they occur. It is customary, generally, to dwell on dotted notes longer (and therefore to play the following shorter notes even more quickly) than the notation indicates. For example:

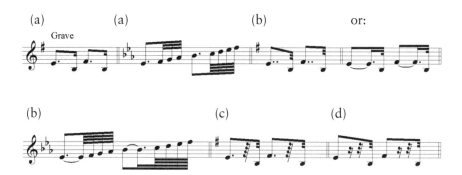

The realization of dotted notes as in (b) is generally chosen when the character of the composition is serious, solemn, exalted, etc., thus not only for an actual grave but also for overtures or compositions which are marked sostenuto and the like. The dotted notes are executed in this case with emphasis, and consequently they are prolonged. For the expression of livelier or more joyous sentiments, the playing must be somewhat lighter, approximately as in (c). The execution shown in (d) is particularly appropriate for compositions which are to be played in a vehement or defiant manner or those which are marked staccato. . . . For agreeable and lyric thoughts and the like, dotted notes are prolonged a little as shown below in (e). . . . Especially in such cases, the short notes after the dot are to be played softly and should be slurred. If a second voice occurs with the voice containing the dotted notes, as in (f), then prescribed values are to be retained.

Now and then when several voices are involved, the dotted notes are prolonged in only one voice and the short notes in both voices are played at the same time in order that the whole be more uniform [see (a) and (b) below].

(a)   in actuality: (b)   in actuality:

The short rests which take the place of dots are also often prolonged in compositions of a lively character, and the like, as here [below] in (b).

(a)   (b)

Allegro con spirito

Figures in which the first note is short and the second is dotted are slurred without exception and played for the most part in a caressing manner. The first (short) note, of course, is to be accented, but the emphasis should be only a very gentle one.

(a)   (a)   (b)

The first note should not be rushed, especially in a slow tempo, because the melody can easily degenerate into flippancy, or lose its essential roundness if the first tone is played too short, and moreover, if the dot is transformed into an incorrect rest, as in (b).

Rellstab, clavier treatise (1790)

Dotted notes as at (a) are played as at (b). In most cases, the dot is regarded as a rest and the last note taken shorter than its strict value. [In sostenuto passages] the dot is sustained conscientiously, although the last note is still played shorter than its strict value. Yet at other times, the short note must be kept at its strict value because of the speed or the synchronization. Again, a tender expression or longer note values make exceptions here; the following passage (c) is played with the notes fully sustained and with the shorter notes taken at their strict value.

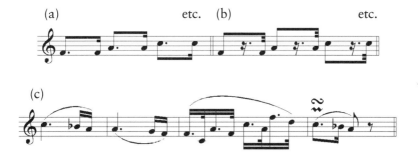

Tromlitz, flute treatise (1791), Chapter 8
"The articulation proper to this instrument, or the means of governing the wind suitably, as well in slow as in moderately quick movements; also called the single tongue"

Rule Seven:

When a short note comes after a dotted note, it gets 'ta,' but the long note after the short one gets 'ra'; this gives rise to the word: 'tara,' and is kept up as long as this kind of figure goes on, even when it makes leaps. See example (l).

Rule Eight:

If figures and passages such as the ones described in the above Rule Seven occur in a moderate tempo and in a tender and agreeable melody, or are marked by the composer with slurs, they are best executed with 'taaraa,' so that the first one with the dot is always held very long and the short one is made very short, and for the sake of evenness the 'ta' is subsequently changed to 'da,' as can be seen in (m):

Note: Although I would rather put this figure among the exceptions, where it is also to be found, I have still put it here as a rule because it is in widespread use. All these figures are played in fast and lively movements as though the dotted notes had two dots, so that the short one can be made really short; or else the first is held (if for instance these two notes make up a quarter note) almost as long as an entire quarter note, and in the moment when the second quarter note is supposed to begin, the short one is played according to the foregoing rule, and then the proper time belonging to both will be attained. The same should be done if there are several notes after the dot, except that these short notes after the dot are not attacked separately, but gently slurred to the note with the dot; see (n):

(n)

In slow movements, the first notes are held even longer and the short notes shorter, but they are not treated so severely as in fast movements, but more gently and tenderly. Since two notes, the second of which is dotted, cannot be separated, and therefore each of them cannot be tongued separately, they are best articulated with '*tăā*,' though the first should be so short that it seems as if one were only saying 'ta'; if there are several, one should say 'ra.' This applies also if there are several short notes before the dot; see (o):

(o)

Prudent intuition can easily decide in all such matters. Of course, it would be best and most reliable if gentlemen composers would put two dots in those places where they would have the short notes after the dot very short, in contrast to only one dot, and then the player would know where he was and would not have to be governed by such a vague rule as the one given above, whereby frequently many things are spoiled because an individual does not have the correct feeling, see (p):

Corri, singing treatise (1810), "On Expression"

The manner of executing the Scotch, Irish, and Welch [sic] Slow Airs partakes more of the familiar than the grand. . . .

In these styles any passage of the following description

Thus ♪ or ♪

the shortest of the two notes ought to be made still shorter and a smart accent given to the second note thus

♪ or ♪

TRIPLET CONFORMITY

Triplet conformity refers to the practice of aligning the short note of dotted rhythms to the short or final note of triplet rhythms. Example A illustrates. Composing music with such a rhythmic situation was not as in favor during the Classical era as it had been during the Baroque. Classical-era treatises that address the topic generally speak disparagingly of it, and Classical-era composers usually indicated compound meters such as 6/8, 9/8, or 12/8 when they wrote in a predominately triple texture.

Example A

written   performed

Nevertheless, the simultaneity of dotted rhythms against triplets appears occasionally in repertoire of the Classical era, with commentary in treatises about the performance practice of the notation divided as to whether to align the short note of the dotted rhythm with the final note of the triplet or to execute the short note after the final note of the triplet. Sources early in the era generally recommend conformity, while later sources recommend non-conformity, although the recommendations do not specify whether to perform the short note of the dotted rhythm as it is notated (1/4 the value of the rhythm) or shorter (perhaps 1/6 the value), as an alteration of the general practice of overdotting. It seems logical to assume that since the practice of overdotting was so pervasive and the concept of rhythmic duration so flexible, some manner of conformity would be appropriate. The short note of the dotted rhythm would either sound simultaneously with the final note of the triplet or after it as the final note of a sextuplet division. This latter recommendation would probably be the case with the dotted rhythms of the soprano part (both instances) in measure 14, the alto part in measure 13, the tenor part in measures 11 and 12, and the vocal bass part in measures 10, 11, and 14 of Example B.

Example B
Joseph Haydn, Missa Sancti Nicolai, Sanctus, measures 9–15

Instances of triple and duple simultaneity (such as two eighth notes against an eighth note triplet) also occurred occasionally during the Classical era. In these instances, as can be seen on beat three of the first measure of the vocal bass part and other similar locations in Example B, no conformity is recommended; the duple notes should be performed as written. Similar non-conformity is recommended in Example C, where the vocal bass part on beat three of measure 20 and beats three and four of measure 21 should remain in opposition to the triplet figurations of the orchestral accompaniment. However, the dotted rhythm on beat one of measure 21 might be conformed to the accompanimental triplets. Since these triplets are not the prevailing rhythmic texture of the music (they occur for the first time in measure 20) and since the music has had a consistent duple texture, beat one of measure 21 might stand as it is.

Example C
Michael Haydn, *Requiem in C Minor*, Offertorium, measures 20–22

Another form of conformity can be seen in Example D. The placement of the opening notes of each voice part can either be conformed to the final note of the triplet pattern of the accompaniment or executed after it, as 1/6 the value of the beat.

Example D
W. A. Mozart, *Vesperae solennes de confessore* K339, Magnificat,
measures 1 and 2

Once a decision is made about the anacrusis note, similar application of the ensuing dotted rhythms would be logical. If the soprano first note becomes 1/6 the value of the beat, then the second note of measure two should also be 1/6 the value of the beat. The following duple rhythms (beat three) should probably not be altered to conform to the accompanimental triplets, but should remain as two notes against three.

Conformity, whether aligning the final notes of beats or putting the final duple notes into a triple context, depends upon the prevailing rhythmic texture of the music. If this prevailing texture is as in Example D—a constant series of triplets—then conformity is certain. With a relatively fast tempo and a moderately energetic mood, the notes would be exactly aligned. With a relatively slow tempo and a markedly grandiose mood, however, the notes would be conformed (to 1/6 value), but not exactly aligned. Conformity is less certain with music having only an occasional triplet texture.

The following quotes, as mentioned earlier, generally speak to non-alignment. That is, they generally advise that the final notes of the beat (see Example A for reference) should not coincide. This does not imply non-conformity, however. The authors of the quotations do not specify the duration of the final duple note when recommending that it be after the final triple note. One assumes conformity by nature of so many other quotations regarding rhythmic flexibility and by such overwhelming support of overdotting.

**Quantz, flute treatise (1752), Chapter 5
"Of Notes, their Values, Meter, Rests, and Other Musical Signs"**

This rule . . . must be observed when there are triplets in one part and dotted notes against them in the other part.

Hence you must not strike the short note after the dot with the third note of the triplet, but after it. Otherwise it will sound like six-eight or twelve-eight time.

The two passages must be treated quite differently. . . . If you were to play all the dotted notes found beneath the triplets in accordance with their ordinary value, the expression would be very lame and insipid rather than brilliant and majestic.

C. P. E. Bach, clavier treatise (1753), Part 1, Chapter 3 "Performance"

With the advent of an increased use of triplets in common or 4/4 time, as well as in 2/4 and 3/4, many pieces have appeared which might be more conveniently written in 12/8, 9/8, or 6/8. The performance of these notes is shown in Figure 177.

Figure 177

Marpurg, clavier treatise (1755), Chapter 5 "Concerning Meter"

If . . . two notes of equal value come to stand against three others of equal time—for instance, two eighth notes against three other eighth notes, [or] two quarter notes against three other quarter notes—then the first two notes of the three equal notes are played against the first of the two. Thus, for example, the notes in Fig. 42 (a) are all played as in Fig. 43; even if the first of the two equal notes should be dotted once, as in Fig. 42 (b), they must nevertheless be performed as in Fig. 43.

Fig. 42 (a)   (b)   Fig. 43

Löhlein, clavier treatise (1765)

When triplets stand against dotted notes in a fast tempo, they are distributed as follows:

Example 47

Otherwise the sixteenth note must conform to its proper value, being played right after the triplet.

Agricola, general German reference (1769)

On page 70 [of the clavier treatise by Löhlein] it is learned that in dotted notes against triplets, the note after the dot would be played with the third note of the triplet. This is true only in the utmost speed. Except for such cases, the note standing after the dot must be played not with, but after the last note of the triplet. For otherwise, a differentiation between equal measure, wherein notes of such kind appear, and 3/8, 6/8, 9/8, and 12/8 measure is lost. Thus J. S. Bach taught it to his pupils; also Quantz taught it thus in his flute treatise. Against the manner of performance and the fine sensitivity of these men no one has the right to take exception.

Heck, harpsichord treatise (c.1770)

Example 50

Sulzer, general theory of music (1771–1774)

In some keyboard pieces of two or more voices one guards against setting two notes against a triplet as in (a), since the contrary movement is adverse and difficult to play. On the other hand, two notes can always be fitted to the triple notes and be played without the slightest difficulty as in (b).

Also, if one were to lengthen by a dot the first and third bass notes of the first example, and make the second and fourth into sixteenth notes, the sixteenth note is played not with the last note of the triplet, but just after it.

Türk, clavier treatise (1789), Chapter 1, Part 4 "Concerning Meter"

The playing of dotted notes against triplets presents difficulties and is not to be expected of beginners in the most exact fashion. In Example (a), the sixteenth note should be played only after the last note of the triplet and in such a fashion that between the triplets there should be no gap; generally, however, beginners play such a passage as in (b). For this reason, it would be better to take away some of the value of the dot and play the sixteenth note with the last note of the triplet, as in (c). This latter realization may have been what various composers had in mind in such cases.

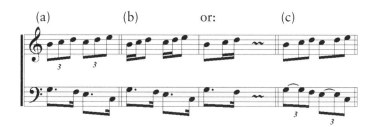

In compositions of a vehement character, in which there are many dotted notes, the latter realization would not correspond to the whole, but then, such pieces are not suitable for beginners. . . .

Note: Some composers make use of two – (a) or four-note figures (b) against three-note figures (c):

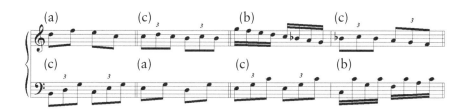

Whether this kind of setting is in general pleasant or repugnant to one's feelings and whether it promotes or destroys the unity of the composition, is something which I will leave for others to decide. . . . However, such passages are by no means for beginners, particularly when they occur in slow tempos, which as far as counting is concerned an otherwise secure player is not able to play in their true arrangement. Therefore, the beginner should not be tormented with such things, for at best what one would get from him would be one of the incorrect realizations as shown in the following examples.

If the student is to learn such passages correctly, one should first let him practice each part separately until he has gained mechanical security in each hand. He should then probably succeed when both parts are put together, particularly when a fast tempo is taken, for it is more difficult to play such passages slowly than fast. It would also be possible at first to allow the small notes in the next example to rest, and to simply play the quarters:

because I fear that the correct execution of similar passages is only possible when a greater facility has been reached.

Tromlitz, flute treatise (1791), Chapter 5 "Time Signatures"

Triplets can be used in any time signature. However, putting dotted notes under the triplets to be played at the same time, as in (o), is in my opinion

(o)

not a good idea, for it is quite contrary to correct and natural feelings; and this is the reason why people cannot agree on the performance of these and similar figures. One person wants the short note to come after the triplet and another insists that the short note should be played together with the last note of the triplet; according to this last method you would get three quarter notes out of the dotted figure. These two kinds of figure, then, are seldom—I might well say never—executed correctly, in such a way that the short note of the dotted figure comes just after the last note of the triplet; and even when it is done properly it makes such an unfavorable effect that I would gladly condemn such a style of composition as mistaken except that great masters have used it. Also, quite equal notes played two to a triplet have a miserable effect, especially in slow movements; see (p):

(p)

Here too, some people insist that the second eighth note should come together with the third note of the triplet; so if the first two notes of the triplet came on the first eighth note, it would be a 3/8 or 6/8 time, and it is not supposed to be.

The triplet, as a special ornament of the melody, consists of three equal notes. Although the second and third notes, because of their intrinsic value, are shorter than the first, you must try to make them as even as possible.

Callcott, musical grammar (1806)

521. The mixt Measures . . . take their Accents from their Measure-notes; and the Groups decide the alteration made in the Time marked at the Clef.

522. Thus, in the Air, "Whither, my Love" (La Rachellina of Paisiello), although the Melody is written in two Crotchets [quarter notes], the Accompaniment is in six Quavers [eighth notes], thus,

523. If, however, any variation in the subordinate parts of these mixed measures should be requisite, they must be changed to their relative Compounds; thus, 2/4 will become 6/8, 3/4 will become 9/8, and common Time will become 12/8.

Czerny, pianoforte treatise (1839)

In the 5th bar [of Beethoven's op. 27, no. 1, movement 1], the real melody commences, in the upper part, which must be delivered with rather more emphasis. The sixteenth note must be struck after the last note of the triplet; but, let it be well observed, the whole triplet accompaniment must proceed strictly legato and with perfect equality.

Chapter 6
ORNAMENTATION

CONVENTIONAL PRACTICES

It is generally assumed that ornamentation was not significant in the Classical era—that embellishments were limited to trills, appoggiaturas, turns, and mordents indicated by composers in their scores, with no additions by performers except, perhaps, for relatively short cadenzas. This assumption is not true. Extemporaneous ornamentation was a significant phenomenon in and throughout the entire duration of the Classical era. As Holden noted in 1770, "the occasional insertion of other notes besides those represented in the written music, when judiciously managed, adds greatly to the spirit of a performance," and as stated by Türk in 1789, "I regard any attempt to prove the necessity of ornamentation . . . superfluous, since the need is so evident that none can fail to recognize it. Especially in the light of present taste, ornaments have become a very necessary requirement. For one knows by experience that many excellent compositions lose much and perhaps have only half their effect when played without ornamentation; on the contrary, a very mediocre work can be extraordinarily improved by well-chosen ornaments."

While acknowledging the desirability of ornamentation added in performance, Holden, Türk, and many other authors state that embellishments should be applied with discernment and moderation. C. P. E. Bach writes that ornaments should be regarded "as spices, which may ruin the best dish, or baubles, which may deface the most perfect building[;] an excessive use of embellishments must be avoided." And numerous authors comment disparagingly about the seemingly common excesses of the time. Corri, for instance, says that "at present [1810], no one thinks of singing a song without flourishing on every note, as is now the general practice and manner," and Spohr, writing in 1816 about a performance he attended, notes that "[Manuel] Garcia, as Don Giovanni, provided rather too much of a good thing. At every conceivable opportunity he is ready with a lengthy embellishment. . . . He throws in ornaments all over the place, even slowing the tempo to make room for them." Spohr also writes about excessive ornamentation in orchestral ensembles: "Each [player] makes his own embellishments according to his own dictates, with the result that the sound resembles that of an orchestra tuning up rather than a coordinated performance. I forbade the playing of any note not in the score, but to no avail. Free ornamentation has become so much a habit with them, they cannot do without it."

For the idealized or appropriate quantity of ornamentation and also for the types of ornaments in use during the Classical era, it is helpful that authors such as Quantz (1752), Tromlitz (1791), and Corri (1810) not only describe them, but they also provide musical examples with recommended embellishments. In addition, it is illuminating to observe portions of Haydn's personal copy of his oratorio *The Creation*, which has numerous examples of embellished vocal passages that were evidently performed with his approval, but that do not appear in the published score.

With primary source musical examples and with numerous comments on the subject, the modern-day musician can realize that extemporaneous ornamentation was a significant performance practice during the Classical era and can also be guided in the choice and distribution of appropriate ornaments.

Quantz, flute treatise (1752), Introduction
"Of the Qualities Required of Those Who Would dedicate
themselves to music"

The student must be wary of a teacher who . . . does not know how to play a plain air intelligibly and who cannot introduce *appoggiaturas*, *pincemens*, *battemens*, *flattemens*, *doubles*, and *trills* at the proper places—who in an Adagio does not know how to add extemporaneous ornaments to a plain melody as this melody and the harmonies require.

——. Chapter 11 "Of good execution in general in singing and playing"

I have stated above that melodies must be enhanced and heightened by the addition of ornaments. Care must be taken, however, that a melody is not overburdened or crushed by them. The all too colorful performance, like the all too plain, may in the end become offensive to the ear. Therefore, both the extemporaneous embellishments and the essential ornaments must be used sparingly and not too extravagantly. Observance of this rule is particularly important in very quick passages, where the time does not permit many additions.

——. Chapter 8
"Of the appoggiaturas and the little essential graces related to them"

Embellishments should be used like seasonings in a meal; if the prevailing sentiment is taken as the guiding principle, propriety will be maintained and one mood will never be transformed into another.

——. Chapter 12 "Of the manner of playing the Allegro"

Few extemporaneous variations are allowed in the Allegro, since it is usually composed with melodies and passages of a kind that leave little room for improvement. But if you still want to make some variations, you must not do so before the repetition; this is most conveniently applicable in a solo where the Allegro consists of two reprises. Beautiful singing ideas, however, which are not likely to become tiresome, and brilliant passages which contain sufficiently agreeable melodies, must not be varied; only ideas of the kind that leave but a slight impression require variations.

——. Chapter 14 "Of the manner of playing the Adagio"

The Adagio may be viewed in two ways with respect to the manner in which it should be played and embellished, that is, it may be viewed in accordance with the French or the Italian style. The first requires a clean and sustained execution of the melody, and embellishment with the essential ornaments, such as *appoggiaturas, whole* and *half-trills, mordents, turns, battemens, flattemens,* &c., but not extensive passage-work or significant addition of extemporaneous embellishments. The example in Fig. 26, played slowly, may serve as a model for playing in this manner.

Figure 26

In the second manner, that is, the Italian, extensive artificial ornaments that accord with the harmony are introduced in the Adagio in addition to the little French embellishments. Here the example in Table 18, in which all of these extemporaneous embellishments are directly indicated with notes, may serve as a model.

Table 18

C. P. E. Bach, clavier treatise (1753), "Embellishments"

No one disputes the need for embellishments. This is evident from the great numbers of them everywhere to be found. They are, in fact, indispensable. Consider their many uses: they connect and enliven tones and impart emphasis and accent; they make music pleasing and awaken our close attention; expression is heightened by them—let a piece be sad, joyful, or otherwise, and they will lend a fitting assistance; embellishments provide opportunities for fine performance as well as much of its subject matter; they improve mediocre compositions; without them the best melody is empty and ineffective, the clearest content clouded. . . .

Above all things, an excessive use of embellishments must be avoided. Regard them as spices, which may ruin the best dish, or baubles, which may deface the most perfect building. Notes of no great importance and those sufficiently brilliant by themselves should remain free of them, for embellishments serve only to increase the weight and importance of notes and to differentiate them from others. Otherwise, I would commit the same error as orators who try to place an impressive accent on every word; everything would be alike and therefore unclear. . . .

All ornaments stand in proportioned relationship to the length of the principal note, tempo, and affect of a piece. In those cases where a variety of embellishments are used and the performer is not too restricted by the affect, the more tones contained in an ornament, the longer the principal note must be, regardless of whether the source of this length is the note itself or the tempo. The brilliance of an embellishment must not be dulled by excessive space following its execution. On the contrary, the performer must avoid a too hurried performance that blurs certain ornaments. . . .

Nevertheless, it is permissible for one to introduce an embellishment that does not completely fill the notated length of a note of long duration. However, the final tone of the embellishment must not be released until the following note begins, for the primary aim of all embellishments is to connect notes.

Therefore, embellishments are better suited to slow or moderate than to rapid tempos, and to long rather than short notes. Observe especially that embellishments are best applied to those places where a melody is taking shape, as it were, or where its partial, if not complete, meaning or sense has been revealed. As such, with regard to the latter case, they are found chiefly at half or full cadences, rests, and fermatas.

**Holden, musical essay (1770), Chapter 5
"Of Several Marks and Terms relating to particular Passages,
and to larger Sections"**

The occasional insertion of other notes besides those represented in the written music, when judiciously managed, adds greatly to the spirit of a performance; but then, such freedoms ought to be used with great discretion, and seldom with any other view than that of imitating the natural inflexions of the voice. If this be disregarded and a luxuriant fancy let loose, the true design of the composer is sure to be buried under a heap of extravagant flourishes and graces, which are neither consistent with the original design, nor with each other.

**Burney, account of music in France and Italy (1770),
"Siena, Wednesday 19 September"**

I visited Signor Guarducci at his new house, called here a palazzo. . . . He was so obliging as to sing to me a delightful song of Sacchini's composition . . . which . . . he sung [sic] divinely—such smoothness, taste and expression! and the few notes he put in, so select that I was truly charmed. He treated me with 2 long and learned cadences. He says the English love only a few notes in gracing, but they must be good.

Manfredini, harmony treatise (1775), Chapter 4, Paragraph 2 "Of the ornaments of melody"

The ornaments of melody consist of several notes that the singer or player adds to music at his own will. Otherwise, he will come upon them written in the music, but with smaller notes or other signs for demonstrating that they are extra to the harmony.

Türk, clavier treatise (1789), Part One "Concerning Ornaments in General"

Ornaments are used in many ways. They contribute markedly to the adornments of the melody; they animate it and make its tones more cohesive; they sustain attention; they give greater emphasis to those tones on which they are used so that a composition has a more telling effect; they strengthen the expression of the passions and feelings; and in addition to necessary variety, as it were, they bring light and shadow in a composition.

I regard any attempt to prove the necessity of ornamentation at greater length as superfluous, since the need is so evident that none can fail to recognize it. Especially in the light of present taste, ornaments have become a very necessary requirement. For one knows by experience that many excellent compositions lose much and perhaps have only half the effect when they are played without ornamentation (appoggiaturas are included). On the contrary, a very mediocre work can be extraordinarily improved by well-chosen ornaments. . . .

Although I have just recommended the suitable use of ornaments, I must also warn against their overloaded and indiscriminate use. A single example should be sufficient to convince those with any refinement that too many ornaments have a very distasteful effect. The following measures should first be played simply (a) and then with the prescribed ornaments (b).

How disgusting! But nevertheless, the most touching compositions are all too often played in this tasteless manner. Nothing more can be done for the person who does not feel that the example above would be more effective if played in a beautiful, singing manner, instead of as shown in (b). . . .

In general, one should not be extravagant in the use of ornaments, especially in compositions of sorrowful, painful, melancholy, serious, innocent, or naïve character, for often in such cases, an ornament which is used at the wrong time drastically weakens the desired effect. . . .

One should choose ornaments that are suitable to the character of a composition. In a *largo mesto* [slow and mournful], for example, many trills, mordents, inverted mordents and the like would not produce the best effect, whereas a dotted double appoggiatura would be far more appropriate to the affect.

One should be guided as much as possible by the character and the more or less animated tempo of a composition in determining whether ornaments are to be played faster or slower. In an *allegro* for example, trills must be played faster than in an *adagio*. Likewise, dotted slides, double appoggiaturas, and the like are given a faster or slower execution suitable to the character of a composition.

The use of the various ornaments should be alternated in order to avoid too much uniformity. Nevertheless, it must be understood even in this regard, that the choice made should correspond to the prevailing character of the composition. Often a larger or smaller ornament is chosen because of the longer or shorter duration of the note.

All ornaments indicated by small notes . . . receive their durations—as do the appoggiaturas—from their following notes. Therefore, these ornaments must never be played until the time when the main note itself would be played, as the realization at (b) shows below. Ornaments are, for the most part, also slurred to their principal notes.

Tromlitz, flute treatise (1791), Chapter 10 "The Ornaments"

Ornaments are adornments and embellishments of a melody; if they are used with care, they make it more pleasing, varied, and flowing. These ornaments are indispensable and can never be left out. If the composer has himself provided his melody with an abundance of them, then the performer must be very sparing and careful with his supplementary ones if he does not wish to spoil more than he improves. Ornaments are either *essential* or *discretionary*. The essential ornaments are represented by small notes before or between the notes themselves, or by certain signs over them, or even written out with ordinary notes and included in the beat in various ways. If the composer has not expressed them, then it is left to the judgment of the performer to put them in. This requires a knowledge that can only be attained by long experience and in which feeling is always a deciding factor. Since everyone feels differently, everyone must make ornaments according to his own feeling. . . . Rather too little than too much.

———. Chapter 14 "The discretionary ornaments, or how to vary a simple melody according to the rules of harmony, and to use these variations in a good and suitable way appropriate to the material"

Since the discretionary ornaments are an element of good and varied playing and make up a part of it, it is important to deal with them specifically. If they were to be left out, it would unfortunately be likely that the inclination and craving for variation that seems to be innate to everybody would, without proper direction, do more harm than good. . . .

I will therefore *first* [see (a)] set a melody with its essential ornaments, and not quite empty of discretionary ornaments, so that it can be played as it stands; *afterwards* [see the staff under (a)] I will indicate the main notes of each measure; and *finally* [see (1), (2), and (3)] I will give a few variations arising from this and their suitable usage [nine measures of which are shown here]. This kind of lesson will get the beginner used to studying, in the way indicated, every piece he wants to perform.

(a)

Altenburg, trumpet and kettledrum treatise (1795), Chapter 13 "On Trumpet Ornaments"

Composers differ from one another with regard to the use of ornaments. In order to convince oneself of this, one need only ask different composers to determine the ornaments for one and the same piece. . . . In general, the French [composers] are accustomed to writing down very many ornaments, while the Italians, on the other hand, add them sparingly, perhaps entrusting too much to the discretion of the player. Thus, musicians of cultivated taste are required to perform Italian pieces of music so that neither too many nor too few ornaments will be introduced.

Haydn, personal conducting score of *The Creation* (1798–1802), #19 "Most beautiful appear," measures 60–77, and #27 "In rosy mantle appears," measures 33–50:

Corri, singing treatise (1810), "Dialogue Introductory, Requisites for Vocal Music"

Ornaments should always be in subordination to the character and design of the composition, and introduced only on words which will admit of decoration, without destroying the sentiment; nor, indeed, should they be introduced but by singers capable of executing them with precision and effect; when used properly, and with moderation, they are no doubt brilliant concomitants to the vocal art; but, at present, no one thinks of singing a song without flourishing on every note, as is now the general practice and manner of our first performers, whereas, would they content themselves with singing according to their ability, observing the character and meaning of the composition, to give to each its true expression, though their performance be not ornamented, they may be entitled to as much admiration as sometimes is excited by a display of superfluous decoration. . . .

A deficiency of ornament displeases as much as the too great abundance of them; that a singer makes one languid and dull with too little, and cloys one with too much; but of the two, he will dislike the former most, though it gives less offense, the latter being easier to be amended.

———. Volume 2 "Songs, Duets, etc., Embellished with Cadenzas, Graces, and other Ornaments" [21 measures shown here]

Spohr, musical diary (1860–1861), "Journey to Switzerland and Italy, Milan, September 16, 1816"

This afternoon we attended a concert by the Societa del Giardino. Soloists were the Signore Marcolini and Fabré. They sang duets and arias by Rossini, Paccini, Bonfichi, and Poer. Everything was done in the same manner, and adorned with the same familiar ornaments, regardless of whether the music was comical or serious.

———. "Florence, November 5"

On the day of our arrival, and almost every evening since then, we have visited the theater in the Via della Pergola. In production is an opera by Rossini, *L'Italiana in Algeri*, as well as a large ballet. . . .

Among the singers, the prima donna, Signora Georgi, was outstanding. She has a full, strong voice with an extraordinary range of two and one-half octaves. Her part is for deep alto, and the upper part of her range is heard, therefore, only in the ornaments. Like most singers whom I have heard in Italy, she indulges in too much ornamentation, and, therefore, gets less out of her sumptuous voice than is to be had. I am told, moreover, that she contributes nothing of her own, but rather accepts what is drilled into her, with the result that her ornaments, which are precisely the same, note for note, every night, soon become tiresome.

———. "Florence, November 15"

[At] our concert last night . . . Signora Georgi sang the popular cavatina from *Tancredi* very beautifully. My only complaint was that at the recapitulation of the main theme she embellished it so outrageously that the tune itself was unrecognizable.

———. "Rome, December 19"

Since I was not permitted to give a public concert during Advent, I was obliged to arrange it privately, without public announcement. . . . The orchestra was drawn from the best musicians in Rome—and was the worst of any that has played for me in Italy. The ignorance, tastelessness, and impudent arrogance of these people were beyond description. Nuances of *piano* and *forte* are unknown to them. Even with this, however, one can make do. But each one makes his own embellishments according to his own dictates, with the result that the sound resembles that of an orchestra tuning up rather than a coordinated performance. I forbade the playing of any note not in the score, but to no avail. Free ornamentation has become so much a habit with them that they cannot do without it.

——. "Journey to Paris, December 31"

We have visited the Italian Opera several times and have had much artistic pleasure there. Yesterday, at long last, we saw *Don Giovanni*, which had been absent from the repertoire for some time. . . . [Manuel] Garcia, as Don Giovanni, provided rather too much of a good thing. At every conceivable opportunity he is ready with a lengthy embellishment. These were most disturbing in the Serenade, where the figurations of the mandolin accompaniment rule out even the simplest ornament. He pays no attention to them, but throws in ornaments all over the place, even slowing the tempo to make room for them.

Parke, musical memoirs (1830)

1801. In the course of this Lent season, Madame Mara, for the first time, sang the well known and admired air "Consider fond shepherd," in Handel's "Acis and Galatea," in which I had to respond to the different passages of the voice on the oboe. As it is not, perhaps, generally known, it may be observed, that the singer has the advantage of studying the embellishments she intends to introduce, while the instrumental performer, who has nothing but what is written by the composer before him, must, if his talent will carry him so far, follow the singer spontaneously through all the mazes of a luxuriant fancy. On the occasion alluded to, Mara was uncommonly florid and tasteful, and it was remarked by Dr. Arnold and all present, that in the responses I followed her through all her flights of genius to a note. The song was vehemently encored, and in the repetition of it, although Mara again drew largely on her prolific imagination, it was given with such effect as produced a burst of applause rarely witnessed.

Czerny, letters on playing the pianoforte (c.1837–1841), Letter 4 "On Expression, and Graces or Embellishments"

The *graces*, namely, the shake, the turn, the appoggiatura, &c. are the flowers of music; and the clear, correct, and delicate execution of them embellishes and exalts every melody and every passage. But, when they are played stiff, hard, or unintelligibly, they may rather be compared to blots of ink or spots of dirt.

APPOGGIATURAS IN GENERAL

Appoggiaturas were a frequent element of ornamentation and an important ingredient in the musical fabric of Classical-era compositions. They added grace and interest to the music and were applied liberally in performance, whether indicated by the composer in the score or not. Indeed, appoggiaturas were thought to be so essential and were understood so well by the musicians of the time, their notation in music was thought by many to be superfluous. However, they were explained and discussed, often at great length, and they were often the topic of much other commentary as well. Appoggiaturas were the main ornament of the Classical era and were also a part of many of the other ornaments. For example, many trills, especially those at cadences or on long notes, are merely decorated appoggiaturas.

The appoggiatura was indicated by a note that was smaller in size than the prevailing notation and it was usually written as an eighth note.

This small and short note should not be confused with what has come to be termed the grace note, indicated with a slash through the flag or tail of the note (♪). The grace note, which was to receive a short duration and which was to be performed before the time of the note it decorated, did not appear until the late years of the Classical era. The appoggiatura was generally to receive a long duration and to be performed during the time of the note it decorated.

Whether written as an eighth note or other short value, the rhythmic duration of the notated appoggiatura did not indicate the rhythmic duration to be applied in performance. Nor was the short value and small size of the appoggiatura's notation a reflection of its duration or emphasis. The eighth note was merely a convention. Most appoggiaturas were considerably long in duration (1/2 or 2/3 the value of the note before which they stood). This lengthy application is difficult for the present-day performer to grasp, especially given an almost universally short treatment in modern times. However, understood in terms of the appoggiatura's meaning—a leaning—and given the intended usage of the ornament—to heighten the expressive nature of a melody by means of a temporary dissonance—today's performers can comprehend the logic behind the appoggiatura's length of application. In addition to length, other treatments were also important in performance: all appoggiaturas were to be emphasized, with their resolving notes softer in amplitude; appoggiaturas were at all times to be slurred to their resolving notes; and, if tempos were slow enough and their notes to be ornamented long enough, appoggiaturas were to be shaped with the crescendo and decrescendo of a messa di voce (see Chapter 3).

Quantz, flute treatise (1752), Chapter 8 "Of the Appoggiaturas and the Little Essential Graces Related to them"

In performance, appoggiaturas (Italian, *appoggiature*, French, *ports de voix*) are both ornamental and essential. Without appoggiaturas a melody would often sound very meager and plain. . . .

To avoid confusion with ordinary notes, they [appoggiaturas] are marked with very small notes and they receive their value from the notes before which they stand. It is of little importance whether they have one or two crooks [flags on the stem of the notes]. Usually they have only one. . . .

It is not enough to be able to play the different types of appoggiaturas with their proper values when they are marked. You must also know how to add them at the appropriate places when they are not indicated. To learn this, make the following rule your guide: if a *long* note follows one or more *short* notes on the downbeat or upbeat and remains in a consonant harmony, an appoggiatura may be placed before the long note in order to maintain the agreeability of the melody. . . .

Appoggiaturas must be tipped gently with the tongue [while playing the flute], allowing them to swell in volume if time permits; the following notes are slurred a little more softly.

C. P. E. Bach, clavier treatise (1753), Part I, Chapter 2 "Embellishments"

Because the sign of the appoggiatura is universally known (like that of the trill), it is one of the few ornaments whose introduction is usually notated. Nevertheless, . . . one cannot always depend on this. . . .

With regard to execution, . . . appoggiaturas are louder than the following tone, including any additional embellishment, and they are joined to it in the absence as well as in the presence of a slur. Both of these considerations are in accord with the purpose of appoggiaturas, which is to connect notes. They must be held until released by the following tone so that both are smoothly joined.

Marpurg, clavier treatise (1755), Chapter 9 "Concerning Ornaments"

The rule for performance of the appoggiatura is as follows: the note which comprises the appoggiatura must always be brought out a bit stronger than the main, or substantive note, and must slide smoothly into the latter. . . . After playing a long appoggiatura, one sounds the main note very lightly and allows it to die away quickly.

L. Mozart, violin treatise (1756), Chapter 9 "Of Appoggiaturas and some related Embellishments"

Appoggiaturas are little notes that stand between ordinary notes but are not reckoned as part of the time of the measure. They are demanded by Nature herself to bind the notes together, thereby making a melody more song-like. I say by Nature herself, for it is undeniable that even a peasant closes his peasant-song with grace notes.

Nature herself forces him to do this. In the same way, the simplest peasant often uses figures of speech and metaphors without knowing it. The appoggiaturas are sometimes dissonances, sometimes a repetition of the previous note, sometimes an embellishing of a simple melody and an enlivening of a sleepy phrase, and finally they are that which binds the performance together.

Agricola, singing treatise (1757), Chapter 2 "Concerning the Appoggiatura"

Of all the ornaments of singing, none is easier for the master to teach or for the student to learn than the appoggiatura. In addition to its pleasing quality, it alone in art enjoys the privilege of being heard frequently without becoming tiresome to the listener, so long as it does not exceed the boundaries of good taste as prescribed by those who understand music. . . .

Appoggiaturas have become so familiar through regular practice that the student who has been taught them correctly, though just out of school, will laugh at composers who indicate them by notes because they either think the practice fashionable or want to give the impression that they know how to sing better than the singers themselves. . . .

The performer's purpose in adding appoggiaturas to some tones of a melody is to 1) make better connections in the melody, 2) fill in the movement of the melody when it seems somewhat empty, 3) enrich the harmony and make it even more diverse, or finally, 4) impart to the melody more liveliness and brilliance. At times only one of these reasons necessitates the appoggiatura and at times more apply. . . .

If the goal is to make better connections in the melody, the appoggiatura should be joined in a legato fashion to the following note so that no space remains between them. Thus all appoggiaturas must be slurred to their main note.

In a trill preceded by an appoggiatura, it is therefore incorrect to rearticulate the first note of the trill after singing the appoggiatura, since the appoggiatura is simply a lengthened first note of the trill. For example:

Incorrect execution   Correct execution

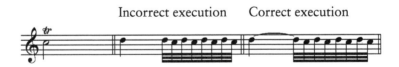

If a composer desires the opposite of this, he should notate the note "d" not as an appoggiatura, but as a main note.

So that the ornaments which have been added to the melody with the help of the appoggiatura are more apparent and more clearly perceived, each appoggiatura, whether long or short, variable or invariable, must always be more loudly performed than its main note which follows. The discretion of the performer dictates [the degree to which] the appoggiatura is louder than the main note, although the former must always be somewhat louder than the latter. If the appoggiaturas are long, they should start softer and become louder like all long notes of a melody, and thereafter diminish as they are slurred onto the main note [messa di voce].

Holden, musical essay (1770), Chapter 5
"Of Several Marks and Terms relating to particular Passages, and to larger Sections"

In written music, and especially in the vocal part, we often find notes of a smaller size inserted here and there which are not to be reckoned in the time, for the bars are complete without them. Such a small additional note is called an *appoggiatura*, which word is derived from the Italian verb *appoggiare*, to lean or rest upon, probably because the voice ought to touch and make some stay upon that sound, in its passage from the preceding to the following *principal* note. The *appoggiatura* should always be tied to one of the principal notes; and, tho' we are not strictly obliged to give it just the time which its figure would require, yet whatever length of time is bestowed upon it, must be as it were, borrowed from the principal note with which it is tied, so that the *appoggiatura* and the principal note, both taken together, may be no longer than the principal note would be of itself. See Ex. 32.

Ex. 32

These small notes may be looked upon as the finishing touches of the composer and the truest specimens of such occasional insertions as are suitable to the genuine spirit of the piece.

Türk, clavier treatise (1789), Chapter 3, Part 2
"Concerning Variable Appoggiaturas"

Many copyists and probably even some composers still have the bad habit of notating all appoggiaturas alike, without regard for the following longer or shorter note, for example, by notating them as eighths or sixteenths, even though these little notes should sometimes be notated as quarters or eighths. One should therefore not be mislead by the note shape into playing an appoggiatura before a half note with only the value of a sixteenth, even when it is written in this way.

Regarding the execution of all variable appoggiaturas, there are two rules to observe, as follows:

1. Every variable appoggiatura must be played with more emphasis than the following tone (indicated by means of a main note), approximately as follows:

Because the tone indicated by the main note is softly and unnoticeably released, this kind of execution is referred to as an *Abzug*. Even when the appoggiatura is written out, as in (a) and (b) above, one makes use only of the manner of playing just described.

2. Every appoggiatura must be slurred to the following tone, whether a slur sign is present (a) or not (b). The execution shown in (d) would be incorrect, whereas the two types of execution shown in (c) are correct, depending upon the circumstances.

Tromlitz, flute treatise (1791), Chapter 10 "The Ornaments"

According to custom, the emphasis always falls on the long appoggiatura; if you have the time, you begin the appoggiatura weakly and let it grow to the full strength of the note, and then play the following note very gently, almost as if it were to disappear [messa di voce]. . . .

Whether the appoggiatura is long or short, it must fall on the beat; even if there is another voice, the appoggiatura must be played simultaneously with the principal note of the second voice and then slurred to the note delayed by the appoggiatura.

Altenburg, trumpet and kettledrum treatise (1795)

Not only is every appoggiatura played louder than the principal note itself, but [it is] also slurred to [the principal note].

Clementi, pianoforte treatise (1801)

The Appoggiatura is a Grace prefixed to a note, which is always played legato and with more or less emphasis; being derived from the Italian verb *Appoggiare*, to lean upon, it is written as a small note.

Cramer, pianoforte treatise (1810)

The Appoggiatura is always played *Legato*, and (if long), with emphasis; it takes more or less of the duration of the principal note, according to the length of the passage.

Busby, musical grammar (1818)

The *Appogiature* [sic], or *Leaning Note*, is sometimes employed to soften and smooth the effect of certain distances. A chain of Appogiatures not only serves to supply the intermediate sounds between extensive intervals, but gives display to the voice or singer, and scope for intonation and passionate expression. The Appogiature is, however, more generally a transient repetition of a preceding note, employed for the purpose of a smoother and more gradual introduction of that to which it is applied. It is always written in a smaller character, and it borrows the time of its execution from its principal, to which it is attached by a Curve [slur].

Written thus:

Executed thus:

LONG APPOGGIATURAS

Appoggiaturas during the Classical era were classified into two categories: long and short. The long appoggiatura—called "superior," "accented," or "variable"—was much more prevalent in application and had a duration that took a considerable portion of the note before which it stood. The short appoggiatura—called "inferior," "passing," or "invariable—was applied much less often and its length was dictated by the speed of the prevailing short rhythms of a composition.

Determination of an appoggiatura as either long or short depends upon a number of factors, chief of which is the expressive nature of the music. Appoggiaturas are to be long if the music is of serious expression, whether fast or slow in tempo, or if the music does not fit certain specific criteria (generally a fast tempo with a light-hearted expression, and melodies with descending thirds). Consequently, appoggiaturas are only short under special circumstances (which are detailed in the quotations under the subheading Short Appoggiaturas).

The long appoggiatura, which always begins on the beat, generally takes half the value of the note following it if that note is divisible by two, or two-thirds the value of the note following it if that note is divisible by three.

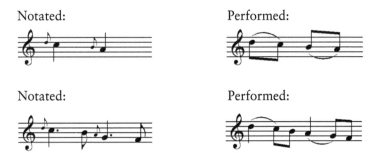

Notated: Performed:

Notated: Performed:

If the appoggiatura stands before a note that is tied to another note, the appoggiatura takes the value of the note at the beginning of the tie.

Notated: Performed:

If the appoggiatura stands before a note that is followed by a rest, the appoggiatura takes the value of the note, and the note itself takes a portion, or the entire value of, the rest.

Notated: Performed:

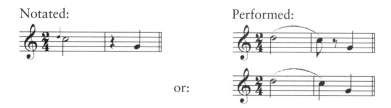

or:

In consideration of the above guidelines, long appoggiaturas may be applied to several melodic passages in the Benedictus of the Mozart *Requiem*. The first application is in measure 8 of the initial soprano melody. Example A illustrates this melody as notated in the score (Neue Mozart Ausgabe) and with an appoggiatura applied according to recommended conventions. Creating an appoggiatura here, which is on the first syllable of the word "Domini," adds interest to the phrase by reducing the number of repeated notes. The appoggiatura also provides a degree of musical stress to an important word in the phrase and, in addition, reflects similar appoggiaturas throughout the movement.

Example A
W. A. Mozart, *Requiem* K626, Benedictus, measures 6–10

Another appoggiatura may be added in measure 15 of the tenor part (Example B). This instance corresponds to a simultaneous appoggiatura in the soprano part and also conforms to the notated appoggiatura in the second violin part, which is *colla parte* to the tenor.

Example B
W. A. Mozart, *Requiem* K626, Benedictus, measure 15

Realizations of other appoggiaturas—those notated in scores and taking half the value of the note they precede—are illustrated in Examples C, D, and E.

Example C
W. A. Mozart, *Requiem* K626, Benedictus, measures 42 and 43

Example D
Joseph Haydn, *Missa Sancti Nicolai*, Credo, measures 29 and 30

Realized appoggiaturas

Example E
Joseph Haydn, *Missa in Tempore Belli* (Paukenmesse), Agnus Dei, measures 73–76

Realized appoggiaturas:

In Examples F, G, H, I, and J, the appoggiaturas highlighted in the screened areas should receive two-thirds of the value of the note before which they stand; only one third of the value should be given to the main note.

Example F
Joseph Haydn, *Missa Brevis St. Joannis de Deo*, Benedictus, measures 13–15

Example G
W. A. Mozart, *Ave verum corpus* K618, measures 18–21

Example H
W. A. Mozart, *Mass in C Minor* K427, Laudamus te, measures 27 and 28

Example I
W. A. Mozart, *Mass in C Minor* K427, Kyrie, measures 34–37

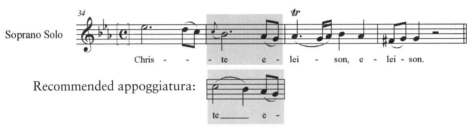

Example J
W. A. Mozart, *Requiem* K626, Agnus Dei, measures 11–14

The following examples illustrate appoggiaturas that should take the place of the first part of a tied note, with the resolution occurring on the second part of the tie. In these instances, the length of the appoggiatura is critical to the expressive spirit of the music. An unusual occurrence is illustrated in Example L, where the soprano appoggiatura is written out, while the bassoon part, which is *colla parte* to the soprano part, has the ornament (the obvious intent being that the bassoon would apply the appoggiatura in the same manner as the soprano).

Example K
W. A. Mozart, *Vesperae solennes de Confessore* K339,
Laudate Dominum, measures 17–19

Recommended appoggiatura:

Example L
W. A. Mozart, *Vesperae solennes de Confessore* K339,
Laudate Dominum, measures 35 and 36

Even though the preponderance of primary source information reinforces the rule of considerable length for appoggiaturas, the practice has been challenged (see *Ornamentation and Improvisation in Mozart* by Frederick Neumann), and upon inspection of musical context this challenge seems reasonable. For instance, in the Gloria of the Mozart *Mass in C Minor*, appoggiaturas are indicated as seen in Example M. Recommending long application of these, which would be in accordance with conventional guidelines, is in conflict with the orchestral material, seen reduced under the vocal parts. In a similar instance, long treatment of the appoggiatura seen in measure 4 of the vocal part of Example N is in seeming conflict with the orchestral accompaniment. Yet another striking example can be seen in Example O. Here, however, the appoggiaturas in measure 20 of the tenor part are indicated by quarter notes, even though the first violin part seems to suggest that the tenor ought to perform the appoggiaturas as eighth notes. The notation of a quarter-note appoggiatura is quite unusual, but also quite important. It could be that in this example, as well as in Examples M and N, the appoggiaturas in the vocal parts should be long, thus creating a dissonance with the orchestral material. In other words, it could be that conforming the parts is undesirable—that the expression of the music would be heightened by the momentary conflict between the parts. Since dissonance is a prime attribute of appoggiaturas, the application of long appoggiaturas could be desirable since performing the appoggiaturas short would seem to make the music unusually tame and unexpressive. The ultimate decision regarding the lengths of these and similar appoggiaturas, as well as of all other appoggiaturas, should be determined by the expressive content of the music. It is this determining factor that is articulated time and time again in the primary source material of the era.

Example M
W. A. Mozart, *Mass in C Minor* K427, Gloria, measures 22–26

Example N
W. A. Mozart, *Missa Solemnis in C* K337, Sanctus, measures 4–7

Example O
W. A. Mozart, *Requiem* K626, Tuba mirum, measures 18–23

The following quotations all address the lengthy application of the appoggiatura.

Geminiani, violin treatise (1751), "Of the Superior Appoggiatura"

The Superior Appoggiatura is supposed to express Love, Affection, Pleasure, etc. It should be made pretty long, giving it more than half the Length or Time of the Note it belongs to, observing to swell the Sound by Degrees. . . . If it be made short, it will lose much of the aforesaid Qualities, but will always have a pleasing Effect, and it may be added to any Note you will.

Quantz, flute treatise (1752), Chapter 8
"Of the Appoggiaturas and the Little Essential Graces Related to them"

Accented appoggiaturas, or appoggiaturas that fall on the downbeat, are found before a long note on the downbeat following a short one on the upbeat (see Fig. 11).

Fig. 11

Here the appoggiatura is held for half the value of the following principal note, and is played as illustrated in Fig. 12.

Fig. 12

If the note to be ornamented by the appoggiatura is dotted, it is divisible into three parts, with the appoggiatura receiving two of these parts and the note itself only one part, that is, the value of the dot. Therefore, the notes in Fig. 13 are played as illustrated in Fig. 14.

Fig. 13   Fig. 14

If in six-eight or six-four time two notes are tied together upon the same pitch and the first is dotted, as occurs in gigues, the appoggiaturas are held for the value of the first dotted note (see Figs. 15 and 17).

Fig. 15   Fig. 17

They are played as illustrated in Figs. 16 and 18.

Fig. 16   Fig. 18

If a rest follows a note, the appoggiatura receives the time of the note and the note the time of the rest, unless the need to take a breath makes this impossible. The three kinds of notes in Fig. 23 are thus played as illustrated in Fig. 24.

Fig. 23   Fig. 24

C. P. E. Bach, clavier treatise (1753), Part 1, Chapter 2 "Embellishments"

The usual rule of duration for appoggiaturas is that they take from a following tone of duple length one-half its value (Figure 73, Example (a)), and two-thirds from one of triple length (b). In addition, the examples of Figure 74 and their executions should be carefully studied.

Figure 73

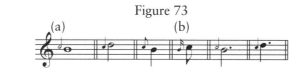

Figure 74

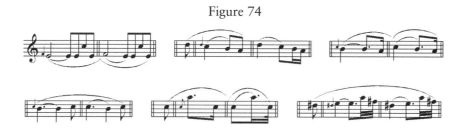

The examples under Figure 75 are frequent occurrences. Their notation is not the most correct, since in performance the rests are filled in. Dotted or longer notes should be written instead.

Figure 75

L. Mozart, violin treatise (1756), Chapter 9
"Of the Appoggiaturas and some related Embellishments"

There are two kinds of long appoggiatura, one which is longer than the other. If the appoggiatura stands before a quarter, eighth, or sixteenth note, it is worth half the value of the note following it. The appoggiatura is therefore sustained the length of time equivalent to half the note and is slurred smoothly on to it. What the note loses is given to the appoggiatura. Here are examples:

Thus is it written:

So is it played:

The second kind of long appoggiatura . . . is held longer. With dotted notes the appoggiatura is held the same length of time as the value of the note. In place of the dot, however, the written note is taken first, and in such fashion as if a dot stood after it.

Thus is it written:

So is it played:

If, however, one desires to play a half note with an appoggiatura, then the appoggiatura receives three parts of the half note, and only at the fourth part is the note of the half taken. For example:

Thus is it written:

So is it played:

There are yet other cases in which the longer appoggiatura is used, but these all belong to the same subject of how to play dotted notes. For example, in 6/4 and 6/8 time, two notes are often tied together as one note, of which the foremost has a dot after it. In such cases the appoggiatura is held out the whole value represented by the note together with the dot. For example:

Thus is it written:

So is it played:

In the same manner, the appoggiaturas in the following example are sustained throughout the whole of the first quarter note, and only at the second quarter note are the principal notes taken, the remaining notes being then played immediately after it.

Thus is it written:

So is it played:

Sometimes a rest or even a pause occurs when the note should surely still be heard. If now the composer has overlooked this, the violinist must be more clever and must sustain the appoggiatura as long as the value of the following note, and only at the pause bring in the written note. For example:

Thus should it be written and also thus played.

Above all things . . . the accent in the long and longer appoggiaturas must always be on the appoggiatura itself, the softer tone falling on the melody note. . . . In the long appoggiatura, of which we speak here, it is quite easy to accent somewhat gently, letting the tone grow rapidly in strength and arriving at the greatest volume of tone in the middle of the appoggiatura, but then so diminishing the strength, that finally the chief note is slurred on to it quite piano [messa di voce].

Agricola, singing treatise (1757), Chapter 2 "Concerning the Appoggiatura"

All appoggiaturas are sung at the time when the main note to which they belong should be performed, and also as part of its written value, whether with the bass or any other accompanying parts. Thus, they belong to the time value of the note that they precede and not to the note that they follow, and consequently, whatever time is allotted to the appoggiatura is taken from the main note. The singer, as a result, must abide by the following very important rule: when a syllable falls on a main note, which itself is notated with an appoggiatura or any other ornament, then it (the syllable) must be pronounced on the appoggiatura. . . .

Other appoggiaturas that are longer than these have their own specific rules, since they are not always of the same value as the note before which they stand. Because of the changeability of their duration, Bach, in his clavier treatise, calls these appoggiaturas variable. He calls the short ones by the name invariable appoggiaturas. I shall adopt this nomenclature because it is very clear.

The variable appoggiaturas ordinarily last half the time of the main note. I will continue to indicate them by means of the smaller notes according to exact value, thus:

If the main note is dotted, the appoggiatura takes the time of the main note, which itself in turn will receive the value of the dot. For example:

This example   is performed

An analogous situation often occurs before notes followed by a rest where, in like manner, the appoggiatura takes the time of the entire main note, but the main note is not sounded until the time of the rest. . . .

gli af - fet - ti a mo - de - rar,   quest'

This is performed as though it were written:

If the main note is tied to an even shorter note, the appoggiatura takes all the time of the main note, which is not sung until the time of the short note. For example:

is sung thus:

The expression of the Affect also demands occasionally that the appoggiatura be held longer than half the note value. For example:

is performed thus:

Binns (Hoyle), dictionary (1770)

APPOGGIATURA, is a small note inserted by the practical Musician between two others. The Superior Appoggiatura is supposed to express love, affection, pleasure, etc. It should be made pretty long, giving it more than half the length of time of the note it belongs to, and observing to swell the sound by degrees.

Tartini, ornamentation treatise (1771), Part 1 "The Appoggiatura"

The time value of a long grace note should equal that of the main note to which it is added; that is, it should take half the value of this main note.

If the main note is dotted, it is worth half its value more than without a dot:

Here, the grace note is worth two thirds and the main note the remaining third. For instance, if the main note is a dotted quarter note, the grace note will be worth two eighth notes and the main note only one eighth. In the next example, we see the grace note written small, and underneath written large to show its value:

The effect of such grace notes is to give the expression melodiousness and nobility. Thus, they suit all slow, mournful tempos. If they were used in gay, quick tempos, known as the "Lombard style," their brilliance would be dimmed and the liveliness of such tempos would be weakened.

J. C. Bach and F. P. Ricci, pianoforte treatise (c.1788), Part 7

The Appoggiatura, when attached to a note whose division is binary, or has two counts, takes half the value of that note, but if it is attached to a note of three counts, it assumes two-thirds of that note's value.

**Türk, clavier treatise, (1789), Chapter 3, Part 2
"Concerning Variable Appoggiaturas"**

Durations of common variable long appoggiaturas can be determined by the following three rules.

Rule No. 1: The appoggiatura receives half the value of the following note when that note can be divided into two equal parts (halves). . . .

Rule No. 2: Before dotted (compound) notes, the appoggiatura receives two-thirds of the complete value of the note and consequently, the main note itself receives only one-third of its full value (or the value of the dot). For example:

Arrangement of note values:

In certain cases, the following execution in (a) is also not unusual, for example, in a slow tempo for a very affect-laden musical idea. Composers who are more precise, however, notate as in (b) should they desire this manner of distributing the note values.

Arrangement of note values:

Often, for the sake of uniformity (or for a reason to be given [below]), one must deviate from this second rule and give an appoggiatura before a dotted note only a third of its value, leaving two-thirds to the main note, as in this example.

Arrangement of note values:

Rule No. 3: An appoggiatura receives the full value of the following note if this note is tied to another note (generally shorter) of the same pitch. For example:

That is:

The above rule is also followed when the first of the two notes is dotted. Examples of this type occur very frequently in 6/8, 6/4, 9/8, 12/8, etc. meter, namely:

Arrangement of note values:

Since the third rule is violated very frequently, I recommend it to all students most urgently.

For appoggiaturas before notes that are followed by rests, some teachers would follow the rule in the preceding paragraph. In so doing, they restrict themselves to passages of gentle character, and the appoggiatura would receive the complete value of the main note and this note would then fall during the value of the rest, for example:

That is:

Anonymous, *New Instructions for Playing the Harpsichord, Piano-forte or Spinnet* (c.1790), "Of the Graces"

An Apogiatura is a small Note placed occasionally before a Larger one, as thus ♪ or thus ♩. When a small Note is put before a Minim [half note], it is to be played the length of a Crotchet [quarter note], and the Minim to be made no longer than another Crotchet, that the Time may not be broken: when put before a Crotchet it is to be played as a Quaver [eighth note], and the Crotchet as another Quaver: and so on for the rest of the Notes, as it may be placed before, except when put before a dotted Note, then the little Note is most commonly played two thirds of the Time, and the remaining third part only used by the principal Note.

Tromlitz, flute treatise (1791), Chapter 10 "The Ornaments"

The value of the long appoggiatura can vary: when it stands before a single note, it is worth half this note (see (e)).

If there is a dot after the note, the appoggiatura takes up the value of the note, and only the dot is played and slurred to the long appoggiatura (f).

You proceed in the same manner when a rest instead of a dot follows the note (g).

These appoggiaturas are played as in example (h).

Where the rest is, should there be a second voice that does an imitation or plays a whole passage, or should you have to use this time to take a breath, then the rest is not played. It is better that such examples are written out in regular notes so there is no error and no unpleasant sounds.

[Above] I said that an appoggiatura, when it comes before a dotted note, is worth the length of the note itself, and only the dot is played, as you can see in the examples. However, in 6/8 or 6/4 time, this rule allows an exception. For example, if you have a passage such as the second measure of (m), the appoggiatura is not determined according to the dotted note.

The two tied notes are treated like a beat consisting of two equal parts, and you therefore divide these notes in two equal parts through the appoggiatura, so that the first part (the dotted quarter note) becomes the appoggiatura and the quarter note following it is slurred to it (see (n)).

(n)

Altenburg, trumpet and kettledrum treatise (1795)

Because the *accent* or the *appoggiatura* is one of the most common ornaments, I would like to begin with it. It is applied to rising and falling [notes] progressing in steps, and to leaping notes. It is usually indicated by small notes that take their value from the following principal note. The duration of an appoggiatura varies greatly, depending on the nature of the [afore]mentioned principal note and certain other circumstances. Principally, one must observe the following three main rules:

1) If the principal note can be divided into two equal parts, the appoggiatura receives half [the value] thereof.

2) In front of a dotted note, the appoggiatura receives two parts of the principal note, leaving only the third part for the latter.

3) If a shorter [note] of equal pitch is tied to [another] note, the appoggiatura usually receives the full value of the first principal note.

Notation:

Application:

Clementi, pianoforte treatise (1801)

The length of the appoggiatura is taken from the following note, and, in general, is half its duration, more or less, however, according to the expression of the passage.

**Garcia, singing treatise (1840–1847), Part 1, Chapter 7, Section 12
"Appoggiaturas and Little Notes"**

Of all the ornaments in singing, the appoggiatura is the easiest to perform and at the same time the most frequent and most necessary.

The appoggiatura, as its Italian name indicates, is a tone on which the voice leans. . . . It can be above or below the chord tone; if it is above, one takes it as the scale offers it, whether by whole tone or by half tone; if it is below, one nearly always does it by a half tone. . . . Here are some examples:

Rossini, *Tancredi,* Act 1 recitative "Oh Patria"

Gluck, *Orfeo,* Act 2 aria "Che farò"

Mozart, *Le Nozze di Figaro,* Act 3 duettino "Sull aria"

The duration of the appoggiatura is quite flexible. If the measure is even, the appoggiatura assumes one half the value of the tone it is intended to embellish. If the principal note is dotted, or if the measure is uneven, the appoggiatura borrows two thirds of the value of the principal tone. The appoggiatura absorbs the entire value of the principal tone when the duration of the latter is prolonged by a tie. Finally, the appoggiatura can be extremely rapid.

The requirements of the situation and the nature of the melody will determine the choice from these different applications more surely than any precepts could.

SHORT APPOGGIATURAS

Appoggiaturas to be given a short duration are considerably less common than those to be treated with a long application. This no doubt has to do with the fact that the inherent "leaning" quality of the appoggiatura is difficult to achieve on a short note. Short appoggiaturas are also generally attached to specific musical characteristics (light, vivacious, spirited) and specific melodic constructions (descending thirds). Unlike the long appoggiatura, which can have a variety of durations and always begins on the beat, the short appoggiatura has only one duration but can begin on or before the beat. This latter element of performance practice was controversial during the Classical era; some authors held the belief that all appoggiaturas, short or long, must begin on the beat, while other authors were more flexible in their opinions. The following quotations will address this inconsistency. It should become clear, however, that, as with all decisions regarding the application of ornaments, the mood or sentiment of a musical composition should determine the duration and point of commencement of all appoggiaturas.

Geminiani, violin treatise (1751), "Of the Inferior Appoggiatura"

The Inferior Appoggiatura has the same qualities as the Superior Appoggiatura, except that it is much more confined, as it can only be made when the Melody rises the Interval of a second or third, observing to make a Beat on the following Note.

Quantz, flute treatise (1752), Chapter 8 "Of the Appoggiaturas and the Little Essential Graces Related to them"

Passing appoggiaturas occur when several notes of the same value descend in leaps of thirds (see Fig. 5).

Fig. 5

When performed, they are expressed as illustrated in Fig. 6.

Fig. 6

The dots are lengthened, and the notes on which the slurs begin (the second, fourth, and sixth) are tipped. Notes of this kind must not be confused with those in which a dot appears after the second note, and which express almost the same melody (see Fig. 7).

Fig. 7

In this figure the second, fourth, and following short notes fall on the downbeat, as dissonances against the bass; when performed, they are executed boldly and briskly, while the appoggiaturas discussed here require, on the contrary, a flattering expression. Were the little notes in Fig. 5 lengthened and tipped in the time of the following principle notes, the melody would be completely altered and would sound as illustrated in Fig. 8.

Fig. 8

Often two appoggiaturas are found before a note, the first marked with a small note, but the second by a note reckoned as part of the beat; they occur at phrase pauses (see Fig. 9).

Fig. 9

Here the little note is again tipped briefly and reckoned in the time of the previous note in the upbeat. Thus the notes in Fig. 9 are played as illustrated in Fig. 10.

Fig. 10

C. P. E. Bach, clavier treatise (1753), Part 1, Chapter 2 "Embellishments"

It is wholly natural that the invariable short appoggiatura should appear most frequently before quick notes (Figure 76, Example (a)). It carries one, two, three, or more tails and is played so rapidly that the following note loses scarcely any of its length. It also appears before repeated (b) as well as unrepeated (c) long notes. Further, it is found in cadences before a rapid note (d), and in syncopated (e), tied (f), and slurred passages (g). In all such cases, the character of the notes remains unchanged. Example (h) with an ascending appoggiatura is better when the ornament is played as an eighth. For the rest, the short appoggiatura remains short even when the examples are played slowly.

Figure 76

Marpurg, clavier treatise (1755), Chapter 9 "Concerning Ornaments"

All appoggiaturas—that is, all notes which comprise them, no matter what the type of progression—fall exactly on the beat, as do all irregular substitution notes . . . *and not on the beat of the note preceding the two.* . . . Therefore, it is not correct if the examples in Figs. 28 and 29 are played as in Figs. 30 and 31, or even as in Figs. 32 and 33 (which is usually quite all right, but not here).

On the contrary, they must be played as in Figs. 34 and 35.

L. Mozart, violin treatise (1756), Chapter 9
"Of the Appoggiaturas and some related Embellishments"

There are short appoggiaturas with which the stress falls not on the appoggiatura but on the principal note; it is made as rapidly as possible and is not attacked strongly, but quite softly, and is used: 1) when several half notes follow each other, of which each is marked with a little appoggiatura note; 2) or if at times only one half note is present which, however, occurs in such a passage as is imitated immediately by a second voice in the fourth above, or in the fifth below; 3) or else if it is foreseen that the regular harmony, and therefore also the ear of the listener, would be offended by the use of a long appoggiatura; 4) and even in thirds, each being preceded by an appoggiatura, in which case the appoggiatura is played quickly in order not to rob the piece of its liveliness by the long-sustained appoggiatura. For example:

Without embellishment.   Thus could it be written.

down up down

But they are played thus, and are better written so.

Agricola, singing treatise (1757), Chapter 2 "Concerning the Appoggiatura"

Invariable appoggiaturas serve mainly to increase the brilliance or luster of a melody . . . and occur quite frequently in fast tempos.

When two descending leaps of a third occur consecutively, the appoggiaturas between them are generally invariable. Should a third one occur, it becomes variable.

Some famous performers want the appoggiaturas that occur between descending leaps of a third to be taken from the time of the previous note, in the French manner, giving the appoggiatura a gentle aspiration in order to distinguish it from the termination of the previous note. In all other respects it is treated like another appoggiatura. Consequently, they perform the following example:

In doing so, they intend to differentiate these appoggiaturas from the expression of another commonly written-out figure in which the first note is shorter than the second, and which is particularly common to the so-called Lombardian Taste.

But they acknowledge that in the above figure, the first note must be performed louder and sharper than if it were an appoggiatura. Other famous performers, however, treat this situation according to the general rule for appoggiaturas, so that the appoggiatura derives its time from the time of the note which follows it. They intend that these appoggiaturas, especially when occurring on long notes or in the Adagio, should not be too short, but rather that they occupy one-third of the note which follows, or have the length of the first note of a triplet into which the main note is mentally subdivided. The above example would thus be performed in the following manner:

Binns (Hoyle), dictionary (1770)

The Inferior Appoggiatura has the same qualities with the Superior, only that it is more confined, as it can be made only when the melody raises the interval of a Second or Third, observing always to make a Beat on the following note.

Tartini, ornamentation treatise (1771), Part 1
"A General Rule for Using Long Grace Notes"

Short or passing descending grace notes are suitable only in descending leaps of a third. . . . In descending leaps of a third the grace notes fill in the intervals and form a scale with the main notes. They should pass very lightly and in such a manner that one hears the main notes more strongly. Thus, the accent of the bow or voice should lie much more on the main notes than on the grace notes.

In the following example, which is in eighth notes, the length of the grace notes is indeterminate; they appear to be worth about half the eighths:

Grace notes may be used not only in descending leaps of a third, but also in other places, even in descending runs, and in any tempo, whether in common or triple time.

The effect of short, passing grace notes is to sharpen and brighten the expression. It is very different from that of long grace notes, which merely make it sing more. Short, passing grace notes should therefore not be used in slow, mournful pieces, but only in allegros, or at most in those marked *andante cantabile*.

Türk, clavier treatise (1789), Chapter 3
"Concerning Invariable Appoggiaturas"

Invariable short appoggiaturas are those that always have only a very short duration, whether the following note is long or short. Invariable appoggiaturas occur more commonly before those notes that come on weak beats of unaccented beat divisions. Besides, it goes without saying that *variable* appoggiaturas are used more before long notes and *invariable* appoggiaturas more before short notes.

All appoggiaturas are invariable, or of short duration, which occur:
1.   Before a note repeated several times. . . .
2.   Before a note after which others of the same value follow. . . .
3.   Before detached (staccato) tones. . . .
4.   Before interval skips. . . .
5.   At the beginning of a movement, of a single idea, as well as after a
      rest. . . .

6. Before notes which are displaced (syncopated notes). . . .
7. When a similar distribution of note values has been required before. . . .
8. Before dotted notes in a rapid tempo, particularly between skips. . . .
9. Before a break in the melody, especially when monotony would result because of a somewhat longer appoggiatura. . . .
10. When the melody ascends one step and then immediately returns to the preceding tone. . . .
11. Before several slurred ascending or descending seconds. . . .
12. Before thirds in descending motion. . . .
13. Before duple figures. . . .
14. Before triplets and other ternary figures. . . .
15. Before a note followed by two notes which are half its value. . . .
16. When intervals, which are notated in small notes, are not contained in the diatonic scale of the key of the composition or the key to which the composer has modulated. . . .
17. When freely entering appoggiaturas are more than a step removed from the main note, or approach it by skip.

Tromlitz, flute treatise (1791), Chapter 10 "The Ornaments"

There are short appoggiaturas, called *passing appoggiaturas*, which take their value not from the next note, but from the previous one; however, they are slurred to the next. They are usually used in sequences of descending thirds, as here at (t), which is played as at (u):

Not everybody agrees about this; Quantz wants them played as at (u), but to me the example he gives does not seem to express the rule properly, since these little appoggiaturas are only supposed to be placed between descending runs in thirds, though he has used them otherwise. The step from the last quarter note of the first bar to the first quarter note of the second is not a third, and it is the same with the two last quarter notes, so it cannot be played in this way. Here is his example (w), which is supposed to be played as at (x):

The first appoggiatura takes its value from the first quarter note, the second from the second quarter note, and the first in the next bar should take its value from the third quarter note of the previous bar, though this step is not a third. Setting aside the peculiarity that the appoggiatura in the next bar should take its value from the previous beat, I think that this first appoggiatura should be left out of the second bar altogether, for it cannot take its value from the next note either, because the next appoggiatura takes its value from it. The appoggiatura before the last quarter note, which is just the same kind, must therefore either be left out, or must be changed into a long one; see (y):

Quantz seeks to affirm this way of playing by citing as a precedent its inventors, the French; he gives it as a rule, but does not use it himself. Marpurg disapproves of them because he asserts that all short appoggiaturas must fall right on the beat, just like the long ones, and he requires therefore that the example at (z) be played as at (a):

He supports this by citing the French author *Boivin*, who in his book on the organ published in 1690 says *that these little notes must fall exactly on the harmony notes in the bass*, and who provides this example; see (b):

So who is right? The melody is good in both, but the effect is different. I hold more with Marpurg. Would it not be better for the composer to write out such a melody in ordinary notes and not leave so much to chance? Doing so would remove all doubt. But if such cases do occur in the way described above, I do not know any other way than to study the content of the melody and choose the decoration suitable to it. Both kinds are suitable in slow movements, but for quick ones the second kind is more fitting.

This is also to be observed in sequences of rising thirds, as at (c), played as at (d), or also as at (e):

There is another kind of short appoggiatura that also takes its value from the preceding note. It occurs at caesuras, where there is already an appoggiatura written out in the melody, and so there are two appoggiaturas, one as a little note, the other as an ordinary note counted in the bar, as at (f):

These are played as at (g):

These appoggiaturas can be played on the beat, but it has a different effect, and not such a good one. Since everybody plays differently, and the contents of each piece must be taken into consideration, everyone must choose according to his feeling. Short appoggiaturas are used more in lively tempos and long ones in slow or *cantabile* ones. Only employ them sparingly. . . . This use of discretion is really the province of the player of concertos and solos; in pieces with many parts, where several people are playing one part, one must play as written, so that the additions will not cause confusion, for one person would certainly not make the same additions as another.

Altenburg, trumpet and kettledrum treatise (1795), Chapter 13 "On Trumpet Ornaments"

The rules for the duration of long appoggiaturas tolerate various exceptions, which in the interest of brevity cannot all be pointed out here. Nonetheless, I would like to single out some very common cases in which the appoggiaturas are played very rapidly, without regard to the following note. This [exception] occurs mainly when several notes (a) of equal duration, or (b) of equal pitch follow immediately after one another. Furthermore, [such a case may be observed] before skips (c), before staccato notes (d), at the beginning of a piece (e), after rests (f), and in many other instances.

In all these cases, therefore, the appoggiaturas do not receive half the value of the succeeding principal note, but only a very small part of it.

Clementi, pianoforte treatise (1801)

Sometimes appoggiaturas are indicated to give emphasis to other notes.

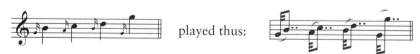

N.B. – the finger or thum must be taken off immdiately from the lower notes.

Example

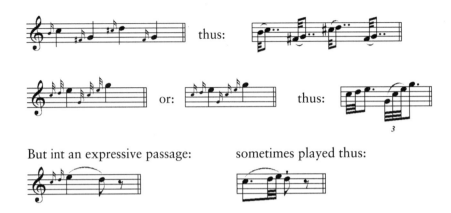

thus:

or:

thus:

But int an expressive passage:

sometimes played thus:

Garcia, singing treatise (1840–1847), Part 1, Chapter 7, Section 12 "Appoggiaturas and Little Notes"

Among the appoggiaturas, it is necessary to distinguish the *acciaccatura*. This is a lively little note that precedes, at a distance of a whole tone or a semitone, a second note as short as itself. The voice abruptly precipitates these two notes, so to speak, and stops only on the third. Examples:

Written:

Performed

Good.

Good.

Bad.

APPOGGIATURAS IN RECITATIVE

The addition of appoggiaturas in recitative was a continuation of the practice common during the Baroque era. However, there is very little primary source material from the Classical era that addresses this subject, perhaps because composers began to notate the melodic lines more specifically. Nevertheless, there are instances in Classical-era music that warrant the insertion of appoggiaturas as an expressive element of performance. These instances generally involve repeated notes and are invariably located at the ends of phrases, especially at cadence points. In Example A, the penultimate note would likely be changed to create an appoggiatura.

Example A
Joseph Haydn *The Creation*, And the heavenly host

Uriel

And the heav-en-ly host pro-claim'd the third day, prais-ing God and say-ing:

Basso Continuo

6   6   3   6   #
         5

Agricola, signing treatise (1757)

Custom has it that in all three kinds of recitative some notes are changed, while additions are made to others, and this applies more frequently to church and chamber than to theater recitatives.

1) Recitative cadences are usually written thus (a): but the note before the last is sung a fourth higher, thus repeating the preceding note (b). Some composers habitually write them as they are sung. But if such a cadence ends with a single long syllable, one inserts before the last note only an appoggiatura from the fourth above (c).

e non a-mo-re   e non a-mo-re   cam - biato an-cor sa-rà   sa - rà.

2) Before the second note of a downward leap of a third, when that note occurs on a strong beat, especially when it is followed by a brief rest, representing a comma or other punctuation mark, it is customary either to introduce an appoggiatura from the second above, even adding to this, in tender passages, a light Pralltriller [an inverted mordent, or *schneller*] (d), or else, particularly when another note on the same pitch follows, in passages that are not expressive, simply to substitute the appoggiatura for the first of the two identical notes (e). The same things can be done, in similar instances, when the downward melodic interval is only a second, instead of a third (f).

co-me s'ar-da e s'agghiac-cia unpun-to sol tu m'in-se   co-me   s'ar - da   a un pun-to   sol

troppo à il suo cor av - vol-to.   av - vol-to.

d'ogn' al-ma ina-mo - ra-ta   mo - ra-ta   mo-ra-ta

Haydn, preface to *Applausus* (1768)

Above all I recommend that the two boy soloists have good enunciation, slow in the recitatives, so that every syllable may be understood. Likewise, the style of singing a recitative, for example,

Quae   me - ta - mor - pho - sis

must be as follows

Quae   me - ta - mor - pho - sis

and not:

Quae   me - ta - mor - pho - sis

Otherwise the note before the last, the penultimate G, would be completely suppressed. And this style is applicable to all the other similar cases. In this regard I have confidence in the expertise of the principle tenor who will give all the directions about it to the boys.

TRILLS

Trills, along with their component appoggiaturas, were the most frequently applied ornaments during the Classical era. Considered important elements of refinement that added interest to music, trills were viewed with such consequence, they were considered to be indispensable ingredients of performance. Referred to by a number of different terms (typically "trill" and "shake,") and indicated by a variety of symbols (most commonly *tr* , *ᴧ* , + , and ⌇⌇⌇⌇⌇⌇), their construction depended upon their desired expressive effect and their placement in a score. Trills could be fast or slow, and they could have various endings (also referred to as terminations).

The symbols that were used did not specify certain types of trills, except for the extended wavy line, which obviously indicated a long trill. As mentioned above, the construction or type of trill depended upon its desired expressive effect. Most trills, because of their ornamental nature, were short; the long trill, common during the Baroque era, had declined in popularity.

In almost every instance, a Classical-era trill began with an appoggiatura—which could be either an upper or lower neighboring note. In music of a cheerful nature or in a fast tempo, the appoggiatura would be from above. However, in music that was sad and slow, the appoggiatura could be from below. Whether from above or below, the appoggiatura generally followed rules for its application: it was held for half the value of the note before which it stood if that note was divisible by two, or two-thirds the value of the note if that note was divisible by three (see Long Appoggiaturas above). The trill was simply an added decoration, as illustrated below.

This type of trill, sometimes referred to as an "appoggiatura trill" because of the prominence of the appoggiatura, was most frequently employed at cadences. The general trill, with minimal length to the appoggiatura, was frequently used at non-cadential points.

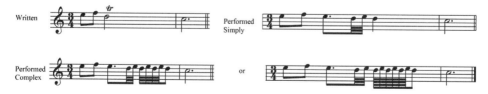

Trills, unlike appoggiaturas, are dependent upon skill levels of performers; appoggiaturas do not require technical facility or performer dexterity as do trills. In addition, trills can be extremely varied, with just a few alternations of notes or with many, and performed rapidly or slowly. Consequently, it is challenging (and perhaps unwise) to recommend precise applications of trills; recommendations may be too difficult for some performers, too easy for others, or appropriate for some voices/instruments while being inappropriate for others. Furthermore, there are factors of tempo, volume, and place of performance to consider. The following examples, therefore, are limited to basic applications, with minimal alternations of notes within the trills. Performers, if capable, can always add more notes.

Trills most commonly occur at cadences as embellishments to the penultimate note, which often leads to the tonic note of the cadence. The soprano part in measure 26 of Example A illustrates this typical cadential pattern. An appoggiatura with a trill may also connect other parts simultaneously, especially when they are in parallel thirds or sixths. Consequently, it would be appropriate to also decorate the tenor of measure 26 with an appoggiatura trill.

In numerous occasions appoggiaturas are already written into the melodic lines of cadences. In these instances, as seen in Examples B and C, one simply decorates the end of the appoggiatura and either resolves it on the following beat or continues trilling, as technical capacity permits.

Example A
W. A. Mozart, *Missa Solemnis in* C K337, Sanctus, measures 25–27

Recommended trills and appoggiaturas:

Example B
W. A. Mozart, *Missa Solemnis in* C K337, Sanctus, measures 4–6

Recommended trills and appoggiaturas:

Example C
Joseph Haydn, *Missa Sancti Nicolai*, Gloria, measures 38–48

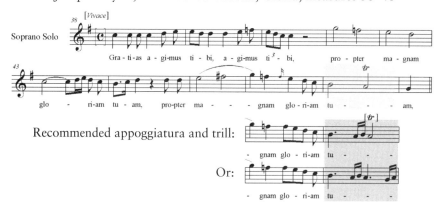

To serve its purpose in creating harmonic dissonance in need of resolution, an appoggiatura generally occurs at the beginning of a metric beat. As such, beat three in measure 49 of Example D should begin with the note c, and, as well as with most cadential trills, the appoggiatura should take the majority of beat, with the trill decorating only the end. Examples E and F illustrate further typical applications of appoggiatura trills, and Example G illustrates an application to a note of considerable length. Observe here that the appoggiatura receives almost the entire first half of the measure.

Example D
W. A. Mozart, *Requiem* K626, Benedictus, measures 47–50

Example E
Joseph Haydn, *Missa Sancti Nicolai*, Credo, measures 33–36

Example F
W. A. Mozart, *Te Deum* K141, measures 101–105

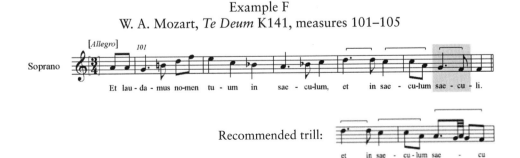

Example G
W. A. Mozart, *Mass in C Minor* K427, Et incarnatus est, measures 22–24

Although the majority of cadences require long appoggiaturas, some cadences, because of the relative brevity of the trilled note and the rapidity of the marked tempo, require that the appoggiatura receive only a short duration. In most of these instances, as seen below, the appoggiatura receives half the value of the note, with the trill receiving the other half.

Example H
W. A. Mozart, *Regina coeli*, K276, measures 147–151

Example I
Joseph Haydn, *Missa in Angustiis* (Nelson Mass), Kyrie, measures 140–143

While appoggiatura trills—especially those in which the appoggiaturas receive considerable duration—are common at cadences, they are not common at other locations in melodic lines. Generally, trills in the context of an ongoing melody have short beginning notes. This is especially true when the character, texture, and tempo of a musical passage make performance of an appoggiatura cumbersome or awkward. In these instances, as seen in Example J, the trill should most likely begin immediately on the written note (i.e., not on the note above). In Example K, the trill should probably begin before the beat.

Example J
W. A. Mozart, *Regina coeli* K276, measures 16–18

Example K
W. A. Mozart, *Missa Solemnis in* C K337, Credo, measures 82–89

Recommended trills:

The long trill, seen only in music for soloists, is extremely rare and often indicated in the score by a lengthy wavy line after the *tr* sign.

Example L
W. A. Mozart, *Missa Solemnis in* C K337, Agnus Dei, measures 27–30

Example M
W. A. Mozart, *Mass in* C *Minor* K427, Laudamus te, measures 108–117

Geminiani, violin treatise (1751),
"Of the Plain Shake and Of the Turned Shake"

The plain Shake is proper for quick Movements; and it may be made upon any Note, observing after it to pass immediately to the ensuing Note. . . .

The turn'd Shake being made quick and long is fit to express Gaiety; but if you make it short and continue the Length of the Note plain and soft, it may then express some of the more tender Passions.

Quantz, flute treatise (1752), Chapter 9 "Of Shakes"

Shakes add great polish to one's playing, and, like appoggiaturas, are quite indispensable. If an instrumentalist or singer were to possess all the skill required by good taste in performance and yet could not strike good shakes, his total art would be incomplete. . . .

All shakes do not have to be struck with the same speed; in this matter you must be governed by the place in which you are playing, as well as by the piece you are performing. If playing in a large place with long reverberation, a somewhat slower shake will be more effective than a quicker one, for too rapid an alternation of notes confuses notes through the reverberation and this makes the shake indistinct. In a small room, or one with tapestries, on the other hand, where the listeners are close by, a quicker shake will be better than a slow one. In addition, you must be able to distinguish the character of each piece you play, so that you do not mistake those of one sort with those of another, as many do. In melancholy pieces the shake must be struck more slowly, in gay ones, more quickly.

Slowness or quickness, however, must not be excessive. The very slow shake is customary only in French singing, and is of as little use as the very quick, trembling one, which the French call *chevroté* (bleating). You must not be misled even if some of the greatest and most celebrated singers execute the shake chiefly in the latter fashion. Although many, from ignorance, indeed consider this bleating shake a special merit, they do not know that a moderately quick and even shake is much more difficult to learn than the very fast trembling one, and that the latter must therefore be considered a defect. . . .

To fix precisely the proper speed of a good regular shake is rather difficult. Yet I believe that a *long* shake which prepares a cadence will be neither too slow nor too quick if it is so struck that the finger makes not many more than *four* movements in the time of a pulse beat, and thus makes *eight* notes, as illustrated in Fig. 1.

Fig. 1

Each shake begins with the appoggiatura that precedes its note, and the appoggiatura may be taken from above or below. The ending of each shake consists of two little notes that follow the notes of the shake, and are added to it at the same speed (see Fig. 2). They are called the *termination*.

Fig. 2

This termination is sometimes written out with separate notes (see Fig. 3).

Fig. 3

If, however, only a plain note is found (as in Fig. 4), both the appoggiatura and termination are implied, since without them the shake would be neither complete nor sufficiently brilliant.

Fig. 4

C. P. E. Bach, clavier treatise (1753), Part 1, Chapter 2 "Embellishments, The Trill"

Trills enliven melodies and are therefore indispensable. In earlier times they were introduced chiefly after an appoggiatura (Figure 90, Example (a)) or on the repetition of a tone (b). The first is called the enclosed trill. Today trills are used in both stepwise and leaping passages, immediately at the beginning of a movement, in succession, at cadences, and, in addition, on held tones (c), fermatas (d), and phrase endings without (e) as well as with (f) an introductory appoggiatura. Thus, this embellishment has become versatile with the passing of time.

Figure 90

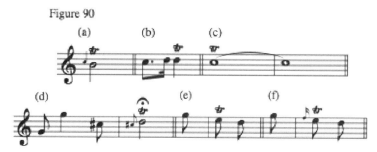

The normal trill has the sign of an ⚬ (Figure 91, Example (a)), which is extended over long notes (b). Its execution is illustrated in Example (c). Since it always begins on the tone above the principal note, it is superfluous to add a small note (d) unless this note stands for an appoggiatura.

Figure 91

At times two short notes from below are appended. These are called the suffix, and they serve to make a more rapid trill (Figure 92, Example (a)). The suffix is often written out (b) as well as indicated through an addition to the symbol (c). However, since the long mordent has almost the same symbol, I think it better to retain the ⚬ and avoid confusion.

Figure 92

Trills are the most difficult embellishments, and not all performers are successful with them. They must be practiced industriously from the start. Above all, the finger strokes must be uniform and rapid. A rapid trill is always preferable to a slow one. In sad pieces the trill may be broadened slightly, but elsewhere its rapidity contributes much to the melody. With regard to the amount of pressure, the performer must be guided by the nature of the passage, be it forte or piano, in which the trill appears. . . .

The half or short trill, which is distinguished from the others by its acuteness and brevity, is notated for the keyboard in the manner of Figure 113. Included in the figure is an illustration of its execution. . . .

Figure 113

The short trill adds life and brilliance to a performance. It is possible, when necessary, to omit any other ornament, even the other trills, and arrange matters so that easier ornaments may be substituted for them. But without the short trill no one can play successfully. Even if all other ornaments were correctly performed, no one could be happy in the absence of this one.

L. Mozart, violin treatise (1756), Chapter 10 "On the Trill"

The trill is a common and pleasing alternation of two neighboring notes which are either a whole-tone or a half-tone apart. . . .

The beginning and the end of a trill can be made in various ways. It can begin at once from the upper note downwards. For example:

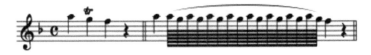

All short trills are played with a quick appoggiatura and a turn. For example:

One must know how to apply the appoggiatura both before and after the trill, in the right place, and of appropriate length or brevity. If a trill occurs in the middle of a passage, for example:

then not only is an appoggiatura made before the trill, but the appoggiatura is held through half the value of the note, while the trill [with the turn] is not begun till the other half, as given here:

But if a passage begins with a trill, the appoggiatura is hardly heard. For example:

Agricola, singing treatise (1757), Chapter 3 "Concerning Trills"

He who can produce a beautiful trill, though he has no store of other ornaments, always has the advantage of acquitting himself with honor. He who can produce no trill or only a faulty one will never become a great singer, no matter how much else he might understand.

Since the trill is so indispensable to singers, the teacher must take pains through oral instruction, through reflection, and through the aid of one or another instrument to bring the student to the point that he can produce a trill, equally beaten, clear, flexible, and moderately quick, for these are the principal qualities of the trill. . . .

To be beautiful, the trill must be prepared. However, it does not always require an appoggiatura, for at times, neither time nor good taste permits it. It [the trill] requires an appoggiatura in almost all final cadences and at various other places, the tonality prescribing whether a whole or half step is required above the main note.

There are many defects of the trill to be avoided. The very long sustained trill not infrequently [used] at the wrong time, was very popular in the past, just as the divisions are today. Since the art of singing has become refined, it [the long trill], however, has been left to trumpeters, or to those singers who dare to risk exploding in order to wrest shouts of approval from the plebes. Employed too often, the trill does not please, regardless of its beauty. The trill beaten with an uneven speed pleases even less. . . .

Terminations of two notes . . . occur after fairly long trills, no matter whether the following notes ascend, descend, or leap. . . .

The proper, or long, trill should take up the full duration of the note on which it occurs, especially when right before a cadence. In this case, the termination should occur preferably later rather than earlier, joining [directly] to the final note. If one were to end the trill at the midpoint of the penultimate note of the cadence, as some singers do, the brilliance, which is the purpose here of the trill, would be totally lost.

Often the time allotted to the trill does not permit the addition of a termination. Short written notes that follow the main note and take the place of the termination, as it were, prohibit it, as in this example:

In tender and sad pieces and above slurred notes, one must be especially cautious in adding a trill because a careless accumulation of trills can easily express the opposite of that which was intended.

The *half* or *short trill* is distinguished from the normal trill not merely by its shortness and clarity but in particular by the fact that when it occurs on a rather long note it does not occupy the entire duration of the long note. It occurs only before a descending second and may be generated from a written-out note or an appoggiatura.

When descending appoggiaturas occur before long notes, especially when followed by either a pause, a fermata, or a cadence, it is customary to gently slur the sustained and louder appoggiatura together to the short trill.

No termination is permitted after the short trill. Those that have terminations, however, should be properly included among the category of turns.

Holden, musical essay (1770), Chapter 5 "Of Several Marks and Terms relating to particular Passages, and to larger sections"

The shake or *trill* is marked by *tr*, put over a plain note: this is by far the finest grace in music, and generally costs the performer the most pains to acquire it. It may, with sufficient propriety, be called a quick, alternate repercussion of two sounds, whereof the lower is represented by the note itself, and the upper is the next superior degree of the scale. The singer, who would attain this capital qualification of executing a shake, must begin with sounding two contiguous degrees of the scale alternately, and *slowly*, increasing the quickness of succession as the voice grows more flexible. . . .

Sometimes the note next below that marked with the trill is inserted, just before the end of the shake, as shewn, Ex. 30, and then it is called a turned shake. At other times, none but the two principal notes are used, as in Ex. 31, and then it is called a plain shake. Sometimes the shake is not begun till one half of the note be sung plain. These and other such varieties are generally left to the performer's choice.

Ex. 30   A turn'd Shake explain'd.   Ex. 31   A plain Shake explain'd.

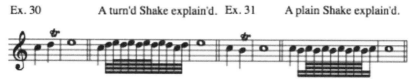

Mancini, singing treatise (1774), Article 10 "Of the Trill and of the Mordent"

Among the most necessary qualities and beautiful embellishments of the art with which every singer should be furnished, there is, it seems to me, no quality more interesting, nor embellishment sweeter than that which is commonly called the trill: when done, this produces in the ears and in the souls of the audience the increase and the summit of tenderness, of pleasure, and of love. Let a singer have a beautiful voice, let him have facile execution, and let him have good taste, nonetheless his singing, if not united to the sweet grace of a trill, will ever be imperfect, arid, and dry. Put on display a professor [artist or teacher] who is industrious in joining together a good style, perfect cadenzas, perfect held notes, and the most perfect execution, but without a trill; display another, who lacks these qualities, but possesses alone a perfect portamento of the voice, method, understanding, and direction of all of this, but who has a beautiful trill; ask the public to pass judgment on the two singers. . . . The second, they say loudly, is preferred, pleases, is honored, because the perfection, the beauty, and the final polish of singing is, in a word, the trill. To assert that a cadenza composed of two notes alone, that is, a messa di voce . . . and a trill, is enough, and remains perfect, complete, and believable; but if it has only an appoggiatura, if it races toward the final note without a trill, everything falls apart, and remains imperfect. O trill! Sustenance, decoration, and life of singing!

Burney, account of performances in Westminster Abbey (1785) "Air in Richard the First, Composed 1727. Miss Cantelo"

Nothing can prove more clearly the difference of style in singing this species of Air, fifty years ago, than the shake which Cuzzoni made on the first note, and almost always on the word *caro*, wherever it occurred. A good shake, well applied, is certainly one of the first embellishments of good singing; but when injudiciously used, it is pert and unmeaning. Shakes are now sparingly used by the few who are able to make them, except at a close [cadence], and in old-fashioned French singing.

J. C. Bach and F. P. Ricci, pianoforte treatise (c.1788), Part 9

The trill, called in Italian TRILLO, and in French TREMBLEMENT, sometimes improperly CADENCE, is a grace note placed ordinarily on the penultimate note of a musical phrase, although it can be played on any note of the scale, be it ascending or descending in succession. It is marked with the sign *tr* written above or below the note, and it is produced by touching alternately and rapidly the note that lies immediately above in the scale, or it is suitable to the note that carries the trill sign. . . . Some composers mark them plainly, others . . . take them for granted.

Türk, clavier treatise (1789), Part 3
"Concerning Essential Ornaments Indicated by Fixed Signs"

Concerning the Trill

Four main classes of trills are generally distinguished, namely: 1) the common or proper (long, complete) trill (a) without and (b) with termination; 2) the trill from below; 3) the trill from above; and 4) the short, half trill or *Pralltriller*. (Some persons are also accustomed to increasing the number of trills by adding mordents to them, which they term inverted trills.) Each of the trills named above has its own sign, nevertheless, some composers indicate either one or the other by *tr* and also by +. . . .

Concerning the Trill Without Termination

This trill is commonly indicated by the sign shown at (a). The aforementioned and somewhat uncertain sign shown at (b) or the one at (c) are also not unusual. If the trill is to be played through several measures without interruption, it is customary to indicate this by a prolonged ⁓⁓⁓ as shown at (d) and (e). The sign at (f) has the same meaning, however, it is not as clear. . . .

Every common trill is usually begun with the auxiliary note (a), consequently the execution in (b) is incorrect. . . .

Concerning the Trill with a Termination

In order for a trill to become more spirited, it is often concluded with a short embellishment, which most of the time consists of two tones, as in (a). This is called a termination, whether it is notated by notes of usual size (a) or by small ones (b). A termination is also indicated by a small hook at the end of the ⁓⁓⁓ (c). The sign at (d) has the same meaning, but because a mordent is notated almost in the same manner, an incorrect realization can easily result from its use.

Instead of the usual termination, it is often customary to prescribe only the following main note, as in (e) and (f). In this case the above-mentioned termination is omitted.

If the termination is to fulfill its purpose, which is, above all, to give a trill an even livelier character, then it should not be played slowly and feebly. Most music teachers would therefore have it played as fast as the trill itself (a). A few require the termination to have an even shorter value (b). Others, however, prescribe the execution in (c) and (d). These last two types, at least in a composition of lively character, do not have a good effect on me. The execution shown in (e) appears to me to be even less suitable.

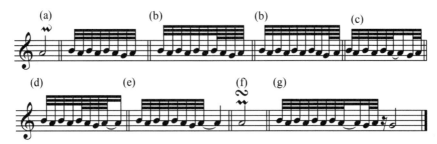

Since the trill is bound even more closely to the following tone by the termination, among other things, then the realization in (g) would be poor, also from the standpoint of performance.

Concerning the Trill with Prefix from Below

The so-called trill from below receives, in addition to the notes of the trill, a prefix of two notes or appoggiaturas, namely the lower auxiliary tone and the main tone itself. For this reason some call it the trill with appoggiatura, but this is too vague. At (a) I have shown the formation of this trill broken down into its individual parts and at (b) the required uninterrupted execution.

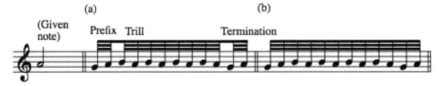

Concerning the Trill with Prefix from Above

The trill from above has the sign shown at (a); it is also indicated by three (b) or four (c) small notes. The prefix consists of two tones more than the trill from below. Thus it begins with the first auxiliary tone followed by the main tone (as in the common trill), with the prefix already mentioned inserted immediately afterward. At (d) the composition of this trill is shown, and at (e) its proper continuous execution is noted.

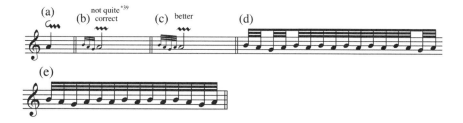

Concerning the Half or Short Trill

    The half or short trill (*Pralltriller*) is a very agreeable and necessary, but by no means easy ornament, for much dexterity and elasticity of the fingers is required in order to play a short trill with the requisite clarity and speed. The usual sign for this ornament is shown at (a); its execution is at (b).

    In a number of textbooks, one finds the execution in (c) and (d) prescribed. The fact that in (b), the (first) auxiliary tone e (which is tied to the preceding note) will not be heard, as well as the final d, has unquestionably given rise to the abridged notation in (c), which is easier to read. When one considers, however, that this ornament is basically only a shortened trill without termination, then the notation in (b) or (+) will be found more correct than that in (c), because the common trill begins with the auxiliary tone. At (d), the first note is too markedly prolonged by the dot, therefore this realization is not to be recommended.

Anonymous, *New Instructions for Playing the Harpsichord, Piano-forte or Spinnet* (c. 1790), *Of the Graces*

The most usual and elegant Graces are the following:

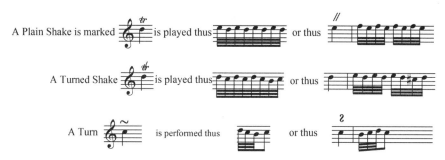

Note, this Character, *tr*, is commonly used instead of either of the above, and may be played either as a plain Shake, or a Turn only, at the Discretion of the Performer.

Tromlitz, flute treatise (1791), Chapter 11 "The Trill"

Since the trill is one of the most splendid ornaments, but also one of the most difficult, . . . it is important to . . . learn it; for since the melody is very much enhanced by it, it is a great disadvantage for instrumentalists as well as for singers to be unable to make correct and beautiful trills, or even any at all. No matter how beautifully an instrumentalist or singer performs, his performance will lose a great part of its beauty if this ornament is missing, especially if he ends cadences without trills or with bad ones.

The sign found at (3) is placed over the note that should be changed into a trill on the flute. These notes can be of any kind (i.e., whole notes, half notes, quarter notes, eighth notes, or sixteenth notes, and the trill takes the value of the note above which it is written; but it is actually not yet exactly defined how many little notes (which make up the trill) such a note should be divided into, although there is agreement that there must be trills of different speeds. . . . So the notes of the trill look like this; see (4): . . .

The trill, when it appears in the course of a melody, is always dependent on an appoggiatura from above or below, or on a preceding note taking the place of an appoggiatura; see (7):

But if the melody begins with a trill, either at the beginning [of the piece] or in the course of it, it can take an appoggiatura, though a very short one; see (8) – however, it can also be made without an appoggiatura; see (9):

When the appoggiatura precedes a trill, it takes its time as usual, that is, half from the note in front of which it stands, and the other half is trilled; or it takes two thirds if the note is dotted, and the third part or dot is trilled, in such a way that the trill begins right after the appoggiatura on the note over which it is written; see (10):

Frequently there is a note written instead of the appoggiatura; see (11):

Two little notes must be attached to the end of each trill, the first of which is a semitone or whole tone below the main note, and the second sounds the main note once again. This is called the *termination*, and every trill must have one; see (8), (9), (10), (11). Sometimes the two little notes of the termination are written out in ordinary notes; see (8), (9). The termination is also made in other ways, however; some people do it as in (12), others as in (13):

The first way is too simple and no longer very common; the second is too gay, but is used by many people. The two straightforward notes I mentioned previously are always the best, for singers and instrumentalists.

Some people think the trill should begin from above and consider the upper notes at this fast speed as simple appoggiaturas, consequently putting the weight on them. They, then, treat the second note, which is supposed to be the main note, as the passing note, on which, for my feeling, the weight ought to come. Anyone who wants to do it like this may do so; for me it is impossible and unnatural to my feeling; the note over which the trill is written is the main note, and this must be clearly heard for the sake of good and expressive melody just as if the trill were not there.

**Altenburg, trumpet and kettledrum treatise (1795), Chapter 13
"On Trumpet Ornaments"**

The *trill*, which is the best known but also the most difficult ornament, is
properly a rapid alternation between two adjacent tones. There are two
principal [kinds of] trills: 1) the common or long and 2) the half or so-
called inverted mordent (*Pralltriller*). The former is indicated by *tr* or ᵕᵕ,
and when performing it one must take care mainly to see that it is played
evenly. Moreover, the trill always has the note a whole or half step above the
prescribed note as a so-called auxiliary note.

**Clementi, pianoforte treatise (1801),
"Style, Graces, and Marks of Expression, etc."**

Corri, singing treatise (1810),
"Dialogue. Introductory. Requisites for Vocal Music"

The Shake is the quick alternate repetition of two notes, not exceeding the distance of a semitone or tone, and is effected by the flexile motion of the larynx; its power of articulating the Shake is chiefly derived from the natural construction, which is more or less pliable in different persons. . . .

There are various opinions respecting the manner of executing the shake. Some are for a close rapid shake, giving a brilliancy and shortness to the upper note, others prefer both notes of equal length and force. From the instructions I received from the preceptor Porpora and from my own observation of almost all the best singers Europe has produced within these last 50 years, I find that the qualifications necessary to form a perfect shake are: *Equality of Notes Distinctly Marked Easy and Moderately Quick.* Also that the note which bears the shake ought to be the most predominant, being the note belonging to the melody.

There are several sorts of shakes, but all spring from the same root, and the different manner of executing them will be shown in the following Example. The long shake should begin with the note on which the shake is to be made. The short shake should begin with the upper note. Begin the Note on which you mean to shake piano, swell it to forte, and return to piano; and begin the shake very slow, increasing in speed by degrees until it becomes rapid, and at the conclusion let the principal note be heard again distinctly before proceeding to the next note, or to the turn. . . .

In general, at the conclusion of a Shake, a Turn is added, the nature of which being so various, it is scarcely possible to ascertain it by any fixed rule [and], therefore must be left to the judgment of the Singer; this circumstance evinces the advantage possessed by those Singers who have acquired a knowledge of the rules of harmony.

Busby, musical grammar (1818), "Shake"

This ornament, both in vocal and instrumental practice, ought to be one of the earliest objects of attainment, not only because its use is more general than that of any other, but that its perfect execution is peculiarly delicate and difficult. Nothing in musical performance is more common than a shake, nothing more rare than a fine one. The shake consists of the alternate and rapid reiteration of two notes, bearing to each other the relation of a tone, or semi-tone. Its sign is formed of the first two letters of the word, *trill*, and is placed over the note upon which the shake is to be executed.

Of the *Shake*, there are six kinds: the *Open Plain Shake*, the *Close Plain Shake*, the *Prolonged Shake*, the *Passing Shake*, the *Open Turned Shake*, and the *Close Turned Shake*.

The *Open Plain Shake* is limited in its celerity and distinct in its alternations; but both powerful and mellifluous in its effect and terminates without a *turn*.

The *Close Plain Shake* is unbounded in its rapidity, approaches to a tremulation, and is less energetic, as well as less sweet than the open shake, and, like the Open Plain Shake, closes without a *turn*.

The *Prolonged Shake* has no specific character; it may be open or close according to the pleasure, judgment, or ability of the performer. Its introduction properly occurs upon holding notes, at the terminations of pauses, and at the closes of strains and final cadences of melodies.

The *Passing Shake* is necessarily close, because it is transient. Its time of execution is, indeed, so exceedingly short, that a sufficient number of alternations would be impracticable unless they were rapid.

The *Open Turned Shake* is an open Shake that terminates with the embellishment of a *turn*.

The *Close Turned Shake* is a close Shake that finishes with the embellishment of a *turn*.

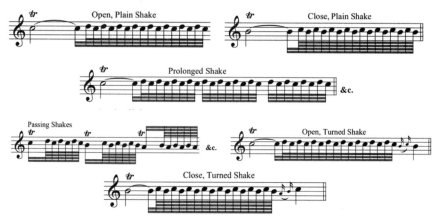

Tulou, flute treatise (1835), "Trills (Cadences)"

Never play trills without terminations. I will give examples of four types of terminations.

1. That in which the cadence is resolved on the same note
2. That which ascends to the note above
3. That which descends to the note below
4. And that in which the resolution occurs on some other degree.

In the first example, the termination is played with only one little note.

Example 1

In the second, third, and fourth examples, the termination is played with two little notes.

Example 2

Example 3

Example 4

For the final trill, that is to say the one that ends the entire phrase, it is better to play it using three little notes.

Example 5

Sometimes, instead of three notes, four notes are played.

Example 6

Carefully avoid playing four notes; this termination is in bad taste.

**Garcia, singing treatise (1840–1847), Part 1, Chapter 7, Part 13
"The Trill"**

The trill is an alternating, striking, rapid, and equal succession of two contiguous tones at an interval of a semitone or a whole tone. It is indicated by the letters *tr*. When this sign is placed on a note, it signifies that the trill should be composed of that note and the note a semitone or a whole tone above, according to the key. The note which bears the trill sign is called the principal note, and it is never combined in a trilled succession with the lower tones. The upper note is called the auxiliary note. . . .

The major or minor trill, if one accounts for all the different manners by which the celebrated singers have always used it, offers the following varieties:

Either it can belong to a single tone, or it can be used in the body of a phrase in a *measured succession*; if the trill is isolated, it can take the character of the *trillo mordente* (trill with a turn), the *trillo radoppiato* (redoubled trill), or, finally, the *trillo lento* or *trillo molle* (slow or soft trill).

The isolated trill, major or minor

If the trill is free, all good singers attack it and leave it by a regular preparation and termination, which make the effect of it very pleasant. The preparation consists of having the two tones which comprise the trill preceded by a tone which is a semitone or a whole tone below the principal tone. Those two tones, by a gradual but short acceleration, lead to the effect of the oscillation. The trill so begun is developed following the rules for sustained tones or the *messa di voce*. The termination is done softly, as is the preparation, and consists in placing immediately after the abruptly stopped trill the note below the principal note, which is itself followed by a final note or by a final passage. Example:

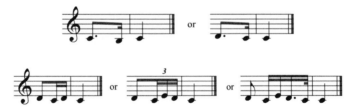

This preparation and these terminations are the most simple; one can vary them infinitely. . . . The pupil should remain free to stop the trill according to his own taste, and he will invariably stop it on the principal note.

The trill in a diatonic progression

When trills are placed in the body of a phrase in measured succession, ascending or descending, one generally does not prepare them at all because one usually does not have the time to do so. Then one attacks them abruptly by the upper note, and only the final trill receives termination. Example:

MORDENTS, TURNS, SLIDES, AND GRACE NOTES

Ornaments other than appoggiaturas and trills were in the minority during the Classical era. Mordents and turns were generally presented in the treatises of the time as miscellaneous embellishments, and slides were mentioned occasionally as an ornament one might find notated or might wish to perform. Grace notes were not included in discussions or presentations of ornaments until the very late years of the era. Before then, any quick single-note ornament that was to be executed before the time value of the note to which it was attached was treated as a short or invariable appoggiatura. At that, circumstances for short before-the-beat ornaments were limited, and they were not commonly applied (see Short Appoggiaturas). During the main part of the Classical era, the time value of almost all ornaments was taken from the notes following them.

The mordent, indicated by the sign ✹ and referred to as a *grupetto* or *gropetto*, was used as an interesting diversion from the short trill. Performed by quickly playing or singing the printed note along with its lower neighbor and the printed note again, the mordent provided variety and contrast. Its counterpart, the inverted mordent (✹), was identical to the *Pralltriller* of the Baroque era and was performed with the upper neighbor note. The turn, indicated by the sign ∾, was a reduction and simplification of the extemporaneous passage-work common in the Baroque and was a way of adding ornamentation in the form of momentary melodic interest. The slide, indicated by two or three stepwise appoggiatura-like notes either ascending or descending, was an altogether different ornament from the others. It was generally executed with quick panache before the note it graced.

Mordents were almost exclusively utilized by soloists; they are rarely seen in music to be performed by multiple singers (choral) or players (orchestral strings) per part. Examples A, B, and C illustrate three typical applications. Example D illustrates the inverted mordent.

Example A
Joseph Haydn, *Missa brevis St. Joannis de Deo*, Benedictus, measures 1–6

Example B
Joseph Haydn, *The Creation*, In native worth, measures 33–40

Examples C-1 and C-2
Joseph Haydn, *Missa Sancti Nicolai*, Benedictus, measures 12–13 and measures
19–20

Example C-1

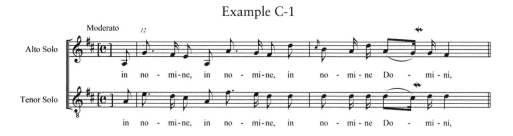

Example C-2

Example D
Joseph Haydn, *The Creation*, On mighty pens, measures 186–195

Turns—which were performed by singing or playing in quick succession the printed note, its upper neighbor note, the printed note, its lower neighbor note, and the printed note again—were not always able to be performed within the allotted time of the notated rhythm or with equal time given to every note of the turn. Because there are five notes to be accommodated, either the beginning or ending note becomes longer than the others or time is taken from the note following the turn. Examples E and F illustrate.

Example E
Joseph Haydn, *The Creation*, On mighty pens, measures 97–100

Example F
Joseph Haydn, *The Creation*, With verdure clad, measures 5–8

Slides, unlike mordents and turns, were performed before the time value of the notes they embellished. The time value they occupy, therefore, is taken from the previous note or rest. Example G illustrates a two-note slide approached from below. Example H illustrates a three-note slide approached from above. Grace notes (as seen in Example I) were consistently marked with a slash or line intersecting the flag or stem of an eighth note and were also performed before the time value of the notes they embellished.

Example G
W. A. Mozart, *Mass in C K257*, Credo, measures 80–88

Example H
Joseph Haydn, *The Creation*, The heavens are telling, measures 1–4

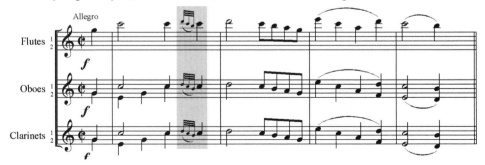

Example I
Joseph Haydn, *Missa in Tempore Belli* (Paukenmesse), Sanctus, measures 1–4

Quantz, flute treatise (1752), Chapter 8
"Of the Appoggiaturas and the Little Essential Graces Related To Them"

Several little embellishments stemming from the appoggiaturas, such as the *half-shake* (see Figs. 27 and 28), the *pincé* (the mordent, see Figs. 29 and 30), and the *double* or *turn* (see Fig. 31) are customary in the French style for giving brilliance to a piece.

Fig. 27   Fig. 28   Fig. 29   Fig. 30   Fig. 31

The half-shakes are of two kinds (see Figs. 27 and 28), and may be added to upper appoggiaturas in place of the simple *Abzug*. The *pincés* are also of two sorts and, like the *doubles*, may be added to lower appoggiaturas.

The *battemens* (see Figs. 32 and 33) may be introduced in leaps, where appoggiaturas are not permitted, to enliven the notes and make them brilliant.

Fig. 32   Fig. 33

C. P. E. Bach, clavier treatise (1753), Part 1, Chapter 2
"Embellishments; The Turn; The Mordent; The Slide"

The turn is an easy embellishment that makes melodies both attractive and brilliant. Its symbol and execution are shown in Figure 118.

Figure 118   **Adagio**   **Moderato**   **Presto**

While discussing this matter, I must point out an exception in slow tempos where, because of the affect, a trill may be replaced by a soft turn, the last tone of which is held until the following note enters. As illustrated in Figure 120, this may occur in cadences and also after an ascending appoggiatura (a).

The mordent is an essential ornament that connects notes, fills them out, and makes them brilliant. It may be either long or short. The symbol of the long mordent is shown in Figure 140. Its execution may be lengthened (a) if necessary, but the symbol remains the same. The short mordent and its execution are illustrated in Example (b).

Although it is customary to play the long mordent only over long notes and the short over short notes, the symbol of the long ornament is often found over quarters or eighths, depending on the tempo, and that of the short mordent over notes of all values and lengths.

The slide appears both with and without a dot. Its execution is suggested by its name. Melodies are made flowing through its use.

The undotted slide consists of either two or three small notes that are struck before a principal tone. When it consists of two notes, they are notated as small thirty-seconds in the manner shown in Figure 156. In an *alla breve* they may also appear in the form of sixteenths, as in the asterisked example. Occasionally the slide is indicated in the manner of Example (*a*), and frequently it will be found in large notation (*b*).

The two-toned slide is distinguished from the three-toned in that 1) it is always used in a leap which it helps to fill in, as in Figure 156; the three-toned slide, as we shall see presently, performs other duties in addition to this one; 2) the two-toned slide is always played rapidly (*b*), the three-toned is not.

Figure 157 illustrates the execution of the three-toned type. Its pace is determined by the character of a movement and its tempo. Inasmuch as there is no generally accepted symbol for this ornament and, also, because its pattern is an exact inversion of the turn, I find it more convenient to use the symbol of Example (*b*) than to follow the occasional practice of writing out the notes in small notation. The eyes can more easily assimilate our indication of the ornament, and it takes up less space.

Figure 157

L. Mozart, violin treatise (1756), Chapter 11
"Of the Tremolo, Mordent, and some other improvised Embellishments"

The mordent [is made up of] two, three, or more little notes which quite quickly and quietly, so to speak, grasp at the principal note and vanish at once, so that the principal note only is heard strongly.

The mordent is made in three different ways. Firstly, it comes from the principal note itself. Secondly, from the two next higher and lower notes. Thirdly, it is made with three notes when the principal note falls between the two neighboring notes. Here are all three:

The third kind of mordent can be used in two different ways, namely, ascending and descending. If the last note before the mordent is lower than the one following, where the mordent occurs, then it is played upwards; but if the note stands higher, it is played downwards. For example:

But the notes must not be overloaded with this kind of mordent, and there are only a few special cases where an up stroke can begin with a mordent. For example:

Here it is good.   But, here it is bad.

Above all, the mordent must only be used if it is desirable to give special emphasis to a note, for the stress of the tone falls on the note itself, while the mordent, on the contrary, is slurred quite softly and very quickly on to the principal note; otherwise, it would no longer be called a mordent. It makes the note lively; it makes it different from the others and gives to the whole style a different aspect. It is therefore generally used for unequal notes, mostly at the beginning of an eighth note, for it is here that the emphasis really belongs. For example:

Finally, it must be remembered that, as with appoggiaturas, the descending mordent is always better than the ascending, and indeed for the same reasons that we have applied to appoggiaturas. Moreover, the good performance of a mordent consists in its rapidity: the more rapidly it is played, the better it is. But rapidity must not be driven to the point of unintelligibility. Even in the quickest performance the notes must be expressed comprehensibly and very crisply.

Agricola, singing treatise (1757), Chapter 3 "Concerning Trills"

The mordent serves as a pleasant ornament of song, but is taught more by nature than by art. It arises with greater speed than the other [ornaments] but is over as soon as it is begun. Knowing how to introduce it occasionally into the divisions is a great advantage to the singer. And he who understands the art will seldom omit [the mordent] immediately after an appoggiatura. Ignorance has no right to disdain it.

The Italians always confuse the mordent with the short trill. The mordent proper, called *pincé* by the French, is executed in the following manner:

The following sign is used by the keyboardists: ✶ . Except for the first note, it is simply a *short trill* executed from below. When preceded by an appoggiatura, however, it becomes the inversion of a brief trill that in turn also has a preceding appoggiatura. The only difference between them is that the mordent in this instance requires an appoggiatura from below, whereas the short trill requires an appoggiatura from above. For example:

In most cases when a main note (preceded by an appoggiatura) is followed by a rest, a mordent or brief trill is permitted on the main note, [and it] must be executed more softly than the appoggiatura and slurred together with it.

The mordent can be continued on a long note when space permits. In this instance it is [no different than] a trill that simply takes the lower note instead of the upper as an auxiliary note. For example:

The keyboardists usually indicate it thus ✶ .

The turn is an ornament related to the trill. It deserves special attention and study because of its great usefulness. In a strict sense, it consists of an invariable appoggiatura, a main note, and a termination, all of which are connected. In the execution of the turn, one follows the rules for the performance of appoggiaturas and terminations, in that one strikes the appoggiatura more sharply but slurs the main note onto it and the main note to the termination. The first and second notes must always be in quick succession. The last two notes of the turn that constitute the termination can, however, be performed at various speeds. This engenders three main types of execution. . . .

Once in a while the first two notes of the turn are repeated very fast and with a sharp snap. For example:

At this speed, this kind of turn takes the place of a short trill with a termination. Nevertheless, because the last two notes are not always beaten at the same speed and not slurred quickly to the following note—both of which are important qualifications for the termination of a trill—Bach classifies this ornament more precisely as a *turn* in his keyboard treatise.

Thus, two main types of turns exist: the *simple turn* and the *short turn*.

**Mancini, singing treatise (1774), Article 10
"Of the Trill and of the Mordent"**

The mordent is born from the trill. It differs from the trill, however, because the trill is composed of one real note and a real and equal vibration with another note a tone above, while the mordent is composed of a true note with the beating of another false note a half-tone below; this false note should be struck more slowly and with less strength and less value than the real note, but even so, the mordent, like the trill, should always end equally.

The mordent has the singular advantage of being able to blend anywhere in the art and is apt for any style of singing; therefore, it is appropriate to use it any time that it can be put in its proportionate niche. He whose fate it is to acquire the trill, let him hope to acquire the mordent as well, and I assure him that although the mordent ought to be closer and faster than the trill, the student will acquire it easily if he will exercise often on a solfeggio of agility, with notes fixed in various places.

J. C. Bach and F. P. Ricci, pianoforte treatise (c.1788), Part 9

The mordent (in Fr. *Pincé*, in It. *Mordente*) is a grace note proper for certain instruments, particularly the Clavecin. It is marked by a certain sign very similar to the one of the trill. The difference between the mordent and the trill is that the latter begins with the upper note and is executed faster and louder than the mordent, which is not only slower and softer, but starts and ends on the main note.

Türk, clavier treatise (1789), Part 3
"Concerning Essential Ornaments Indicated by Fixed Signs"

The mordent (*Pincé, Mordant, Kraüsel, Beisser*) is played in two ways: long and short. The customary sign for a short (half) mordent is this: ♦, and the execution must always be very fast (even for larger note values) as in (a) and (b)

When a short mordent comes after a suspension—which is very often the case— then it is played softly (*a*). In order to give this ornament greater sharpness, one often takes the note a half-step below as auxiliary, possibly even without indication (*b*); however, this is rather not done when the preceding or following note lies a whole tone lower, as in (*c*).

The long mordent can naturally be used only for a somewhat longer tone. It is customarily indicated by a [somewhat lengthened regular mordent] sign. The duration of a long mordent depends on the length or the brevity of the ornamented note and may not be more precisely defined. It should be noted, however, that the auxiliary tone must be played at least two times (*a*). For notes of longer duration, this tone should be repeated several times (*b*); nevertheless, the mordent may never, as the trill, take the full value of the ornamented note. Thus the realization in (*c*) is incorrect, and that in (*d*) can be permitted only in compositions of a very fiery character.

The turn (*Doublé*) is without doubt one of the most beautiful and usable ornaments, by means of which the melody is given uncommon charm and animation. For this reason the turn can be used in compositions of a tender as well as of a lively character and on legato or detached notes. In itself, its execution is easy but rather varied, and only in this regard is it difficult. It is customary to use the turn mainly in four ways: 1) by itself, in which case it can simply be called the turn; 2) with a small note often added (on the same step), which then is called a quick turn; 3) at times preceded by two small notes, from which it has received the name ascending or slurred turn; 4) when it is combined with a short trill, and is then customarily called a trilled turn.

The turn itself is usually indicated by the sign shown in (*a*) or (*b*). Various composers are also accustomed to write it out as three small notes, (*c*), or as in (*d*). I have shown the realization, which most of the time must be played rapidly, in (*e*), (*f*), and (*g*).

Tromlitz, flute treatise (1791), Chapter 10 "The Ornaments"

The slide consists of two little notes that are slurred from the distance of a third either above or below to the following note; see (m):

It is very similar to the passing appoggiatura. The slide, though, falls on the beat, while the passing appoggiatura belongs in the time of the previous note and takes its value from it. . . .

The grupetto [turn] *sometimes consists of three and sometimes four notes, and is either played freely or in time if there is a note at the same pitch preceding, or attached to a long rising appoggiatura, or between two notes of equal value, or also if the first is dotted. It is made from above and from below. The first kind is indicated by the sign* ∾ *and the other kind by the sign inverted.* When it is attacked freely, or when a short note precedes it, there are only three short notes, and the fourth is the main note; see (u):

and it is played as at (w):

When it is attached to a long appoggiatura, or placed between two equal notes of which the second makes a step up, or of which the first is dotted, all four little notes are heard; see (x):

When it is between two equal notes; see (y):

When the first note is dotted; see (z):

The mordent or mordant consists of two little notes, like the short trill, only backwards. The *short trill* begins on the main note, continues with the one above, and comes back to the main note. The *mordent* starts off on the main note as well, but goes on to the one *below*, and returns to the main note. It is done very quickly and the weight falls on the main note. It is *short* or *long*, or as they say, *single* or *double*, according to the demands of the circumstances. The *short* one comes simultaneously with the note; the *long* one, consisting of four notes, takes its value from the note [above] which it stands; see (t), and is played as at (u):

It is used freely, without an upbeat, or with an upbeat in leaps, as in (x):

Quantz calls this short mordent a *battement,* and he uses long mordents after an appoggiatura from below; see (y):

How it should be played and divided into the beat are to be found at (z):

**Altenburg, trumpet and kettledrum treatise (1795), Chapter 13
"On Trumpet Ornaments"**

The inverted mordent is merely indicated by this sign ⹌ and is performed in the following manner:

Clementi, pianoforte treatise (1801),
"Style, Graces, and Marks of Expression, etc."

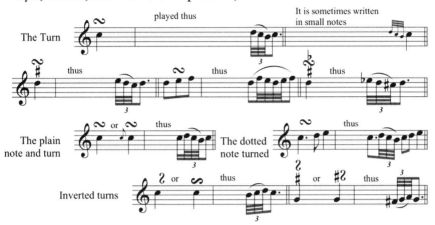

Forkel, letter to Hoffmeister and Kühnel (1801)

The ornaments included herein must be carefully differentiated. . . . The ～ is a Pralltriller, and is used in descending melodies, like the *short Mordent* ～ in ascending melodies. Both ornaments consist of only two tones, the former employing the tone above and the latter the tone below the principal tone. The ～ means a simple trill, the ～ a trill approached from below, and the ～ a trill approached from above.

Corri, singing treatise (1810),
"The Practical Part. Lesson 9, The Turn"

The use of this ornament is to prevent monotony, but should be used sparingly, and only where the melody requires relief. The student must be cautious not to grow too fond of it, lest he acquire the habit of teasing every note with it.

The turn may be used more frequently in quick music than in any other style and is particularly applicable to those notes where the language is animated; turns are also of great use to those singers who do not possess a mellow and sweet tone of voice, as they help to cover the want of this gift.

The turn consists of the addition of two notes, one higher and one lower than the note of the composition, not exceeding the distance of a tone. . . . All turns must be well articulated and quickly executed.

**Busby, musical grammar (1818),
"Turn, Slide, and Mordent"**

Of the *turn* there are three kinds: the Full, or Double Turn; the Partial Turn; and the Back Turn. The *Full Turn* follows the note upon which it is made, consists of four distinct Appoggiaturas, and forms an embellished repetition of the note to which it is applied. The *Partial Turn* forms an ornamented commencement of the note upon which it is constructed, and consists of that note preceded by three Appoggiaturas, the first of which is a whole tone, or semi-tone, above the note embellished. The *Inverted Turn* forms an ornamented commencement of the note upon which it is constructed, and consists of that note, preceded by three Appoggiaturas, the first of which is a semi-tone below the note embellished.

The *Slide*, a grace in very frequent use, generally consists of two notes gradually ascending or descending to the note it is intended to ornament. . . .

The *Mordente*, or, according to the Germans, the *Spring*, consists of two notes preceding the note to be graced, the first of which is the same as the principle, and the second, one note higher than the principle.

Tulou, flute treatise (1835), "Turns"

The ascending turn, or *groppetto*, consists of four little notes.

Garcia, singing treatise (1840–1847)

The mordent is placed at the beginning, in the middle, or at the end of a tone. It is used to call attention to a note or a detail, and most often in these forms:

This ornament, the most unspared of all, follows the character of the music. It is lively for sentiments which require verve and energy, and it is slow in the tender and melancholy sentiments; these modifications it has in common with the trill.

The mordent which does not begin the tone is made after having well placed the note to which it belongs. Examples:

Don Giovanni

CADENZAS

Cadenzas—extemporaneous melodic flourishes added by solo performers at cadential points and fermatas in genres such as operas, sonatas, and concertos—were very much a feature of Classical-era performance, both in repertoire from the Baroque era that continued to be performed throughout the Classical era, and also to newly composed Classical-era repertoire. Singers and instrumentalists were expected to demonstrate their virtuosity at the ends of arias and concertos by adding displays of melodic invention, and as long as these displays were tasteful (i.e., in the style of the composition being sung or played) and not too long (i.e., not longer than could be sung in one or two breaths by singers or not played longer than a minute or so by instrumentalists), the cadenzas were lauded by composers, critics, and other musically sophisticated observers. Primary source quotations only complain about distasteful and excessively lengthy cadenzas.

The application or insertion of cadenzas is important for a number of reasons: they add balance to compositional structures by extending and heightening the effect of cadences; they allow the tension of harmonic dissonance to be relieved over a period of time; and, of course, they allow the performer to demonstrate particular qualities of his or her voice or instrument.

Example A illustrates a cadenza written by W. A. Mozart himself. Involving the interplay of three instruments and voice, it is not representative of the improvised cadenzas performed by a single singer or instrumentalist. However, it does indicate the degree of importance (especially considering its length) given to a cadenza, and it illustrates appropriate melodic figurations.

Example B illustrates a fermata appropriate for elaboration and a relatively simple illustration of an applied cadenza. Since this fermata is located not at the end of the vocal solo, but eight measures before it, it does not warrant the length or degree of closure of fermatas located at a solo's end.

Example A
W. A. Mozart, *Mass in C Minor* K427, Et incarnatus est, measures 89–113

ctus est.

Example B
Joseph Haydn, *Missa Brevis St. Joannis de Deo*, Benedictus, measures 39–42

Quantz, flute treatise (1752), "Of Cadenzas"

By the word cadenza I understand here neither the closes and stops in a melody, nor the shakes which some Frenchmen call *cadence*. I address here that extemporaneous embellishment created, according to the fancy and pleasure of the performer, by a concertante part at the close of a piece on the penultimate note of the bass, that is, the fifth of the key of the piece.

It was perhaps less than half a century ago that these cadenzas became fashionable among the Italians, and were subsequently imitated by the Germans and others who devoted themselves to singing and playing in the Italian style. The French, however, have always abstained from using them. Presumably, cadenzas were still not the mode when *Lully* left Italy; otherwise he might also have introduced this ornament among the French. It is more probable that cadenzas first came into use after the time *Corelli* published his twelve solos for the violin, engraved in copper. In any event, several years before the end of the previous century, and in the first ten years of the present one, the close of a concertante part was made with a little passage over a moving bass, to which a good shake was attached; between 1710 and 1716, or thereabouts, the cadenzas customary at present, in which the bass must pause, became the mode. Fermatas, in which one pauses *ad libitum* in the middle of a piece, may well have a somewhat earlier origin. . . .

The object of the cadenza is simply to surprise the listener unexpectedly once more at the end of the piece, and to leave behind a special impression in his heart. To conform to this object, a single cadenza would be sufficient in a piece. If, then, a singer makes two cadenzas in the first part of an aria, and yet another in the second part, it must certainly be considered an abuse, for doing so, because of the da capo, five cadenzas appear in one aria. Such an excess is not only likely to weary the listeners, especially if all the cadenzas are alike, as is very often the case, but also may cause a singer not too rich in invention to exhaust himself all the more quickly. If the singer makes a cadenza only at the principal close, he retains his advantage, and the listener retains his appetite.

It is indeed undeniable that cadenzas serve as an adornment if they fit the requirements of the piece and are introduced at the right place. . . . It would be difficult to circumscribe with rules ideas which are extemporaneous. . . . Yet [knowledge of] the art of composition provides some useful benefits. . . .

Cadenzas must stem from the principal sentiment of the piece and include a short repetition or imitation of the most pleasing phrases contained in it. At times, if your thoughts are distracted, it is not immediately possible to invent something new. The best expedient is then to choose one of the most pleasing of the preceding phrases and fashion the cadenza from it. In this manner you not only can make up for lack of inventiveness, but can always confirm the prevailing passion of the piece as well. This is an advantage that is not too well known which I would like to recommend to everyone.

Cadenzas are of one or two parts. Those of one part are chiefly extemporaneous, as stated above. They must be short and fresh and surprise the listeners like a *bon mot*. Thus they must sound as if they have been improvised spontaneously at the moment of playing. Hence you must not be too extravagant, but must proceed economically, especially if you often have the same listeners before you.

Since the compass [of cadenzas] is very narrow and is easily exhausted, it is difficult to keep them from sounding the same. Thus you must not introduce too many ideas.

Neither the figures nor the simple intervals with which a cadenza is begun and ended may be repeated more than twice in transpositions or they will become disagreeable. I shall give two cadenzas in a similar style as an illustration of this point (see Tab. 20, Figs. 1 and 2). In the first, to be sure, there are two kinds of figures. But since each figure is heard four times, the ear is wearied. In the second, on the other hand, the figures are repeated only once and are then interrupted with fresh figures. In consequence, it is preferable to the first, for the more the ear can be deceived with fresh inventions, the greater the pleasure it feels. The figures must therefore always alternate with one another in different ways. In the first cadenza another error is found: from beginning to end it employs the same meter and the same division of the notes. And this also is contrary to the nature of the cadenza.

If you wish to reduce the second cadenza to simple intervals, take the first note of each figure (as in Fig. 3); the latter will then be suitable for an Adagio, the former for an Allegro.

C. P. E. Bach, clavier treatise (1753), Part 1, Chapter 2
"Embellishments, The Elaboration of Fermatas"

Fermatas are often employed with good effect, for they awaken unusual attentiveness. Their sign is a slur with a dot under it, which denotes that a tone is to be held as long as required generally by the nature of the composition.

At times a note without the sign may be held for expressive reasons. Aside from this, there are three places at which the *fermata* appears: over the next to the last, the last, or the rest after the last bass note. To be used correctly, the sign should be written at the beginning and again at the end of an elaborated *fermata*.

Fermatas over rests occur most frequently in allegro movements and are not embellished. The two other kinds are usually found in slow, affettuoso movements and must be embellished if only to avoid artlessness. In any event, elaborate decoration is more necessary here than in other parts of movements.

With this in mind I have illustrated both types of *fermatas* with their elaborations in Figure 164 [partially shown here].

Figure 164

**Agricola, singing treatise (1757), Chapter 8
"Concerning the Cadenzas"**

Formerly, the main endings—*literally called cadences*—were performed
in rhythm just as they were written. A trill was made on the middle note.
Later, a small improvised embellishment began to be attached to the note
before the trill if there was time for it without disturbing the rhythm. From
this point on, the last measure of the voice part began to be sung more slowly
and to be held back somewhat. Finally, there was an attempt to adorn this
delay with all kinds of improvised divisions, runs, drags, leaps—in short,
all the possible figures that the voice is capable of executing. These are still

in use today and are now *preferably* called *cadenzas*. They are said to have originated between the years 1710 and 1716. . . .

Every aria has at least three cadences, all of which are final. The singers of our day usually try to discharge a running fire of improvised divisions at the end of the first part while the orchestra waits. With the cadence of the second part, the throat is doubly loaded and for the orchestra, time stands still. When finally the fermata arrives with the third cadence, the whole fusillade, painstakingly loaded to bursting, explodes with so many divisions that the orchestra is almost driven to swearing from impatience. Why deafen the world with so many divisions? I beg the modern gentlemen to forgive me if I take the liberty of saying, in the best interest of music, that good taste does not lie in the continuous speed of a voice wandering about without guidance or purpose, but rather in the fact that it expresses itself in a manner appropriate to singing: by the sweetness of the *portamento*, by the appoggiaturas in artistic and evenly improvised ornamentation, and by seeking to move from one note to another with unusual and unexpected rubato, *which, however, must be tailored to the exact movement of the bass. . . .*

A singer should pay attention to the following rules:
1) Cadenzas must not be too long or too frequent. 2) They must always be related to the main Affect [character] of the aria. It is so much the better, if possible, to include some of the most beautiful individual phrases or periods [from the aria]. Furthermore, this similarity is a means by which one may always have good ideas in reserve. 3) Similar figures should not be repeated or transposed too often; rather, one should seek to connect different figures and skillfully alternate them. Yet the cadenza must not be an actual arioso melody, but only a skillful weaving together of broken phrases that are not enlarged upon. Therefore, 4) no meter is to be observed therein. It must seem as though the singer has been overcome by passion in such a way that he could not possibly be thinking of being limited by a meter. 5) Though one is very likely to touch some tones that are outside the [indicated] scale, one must still not stray too far into distant keys; and the foreign tones, which would be dissonances in an ordinary melody if the bass were provided, must be given their proper resolution. 6) The cadenza of a lively and fiery aria may consist of large leaps, trills, triplets, runs, etc., but that of a sad and pathetic aria prefers the slurred and dragged manner intermixed with some dissonant intervals. 7) The more unexpected elements that can be brought into a cadenza the more beautiful it is. 8) One may not breathe in a cadenza that is sung by the singer alone; therefore, it may not be held longer than is possible in one breath, and some breath must be left over for a sharp trill.

Double cadenzas, especially those that are executed either by two voices or by a voice and an accompanying instrument, must, of course, comply with everything that has been said above about cadenzas, but they are 1) more closely bound to the laws of harmony and correct imitation. They must 2) not always consist of figures entirely in thirds and parallel sixths, since one soon tires of these; but instead, they must contain properly connected and resolved figures and especially adroit imitations, since one imitates that which another has sung, though this may occur in various intervals. Whoever is desirous of inventing such double cadenzas must well understand the rules of preparing and resolving dissonances and of imitations. Though they are also 3) not bound to any specific beat, it is nevertheless self-evident that a beat must be maintained during the imitation of those figures that the other singer has performed. 4) Those figures that have been presented for imitation must be crafted in such a way that the second [other] performer is able to imitate them equally well with his voice and with his instrument, with regard to both skill and range. Consequently, it is necessary that one singer yield to the other and adapt his voice to the other's capabilities. It is especially important that the instrumentalist not perform something that is impossible for a singing voice, nor a singer, something that is impossible for many an instrument. 5) It is permissible to take a breath in the double cadenzas, since it is difficult to craft them in such a way that one breath will suffice; and this is true also, since while one is singing, the breathing of the other is not so easily noticed. However, both singers must not take a breath at the same time. 6) To invent double cadenzas on the spur of the moment without prior agreement is rarely successful, because it is seldom that two people possess the same insight into the harmony, the same mental adroitness, and the same patience and courtesy. In Italy, many absurd disputes have risen over this matter. It is better, therefore, that the musicians understand each other very well beforehand; if this is not possible, they must leave the invention of the cadenza to the composer and adhere exactly to what he has written. He will arrange it in such a way that it will not be apparent to the listener that it has been memorized.

Burney, account of music in France and Italy (1770), "Rome, Sunday, November 11"

I went . . . to the Chiesa Nuova to hear . . . the oratorio of Abigaille set by Signor Casali. . . . Signor Cristofero sung the principal part very well, in Guarducci's smooth and polished manner—he made 2 or 3 excellent closes, tho' rather too long. This fault is general all over Rome and Naples;

a long winded licentiousness in all their cadences, which very much wants curtailing and correction. A few select notes with a great deal of meaning and expression given to them is the only expedient which can render a cadence desirable, as it should consist of something superiour to what one has heard before in the air, or it becomes impertinent. This abuse is not of very ancient standing, for in a serious opera of old Scarlatti composed in 1717 there is no place for a cadenza ad libitum to be found.

Mancini, singing treatise (1774), Article 11
"Of Cadenzas"

I know that [there are those] of the opinion that in order to close a cadence perfectly it is sufficient to have a mass of notes circulating from the lower notes through the middle to the acute, and enough to finally bring it to an end with a single trill. I also know that these same persons suppose that there is nothing easier in the whole art than the making of a cadenza. Yes, I have noted that many think thus, but I know better, that they deceive themselves greatly. And I do not shiver to assert that the cadenza is usually a part of the most scabrous and thorny problems of vocal music, because it is necessary to overcome many difficulties in order to arrive at forming it perfectly.

To know that I speak the truth, let me tell you how many things are required to perfect a cadenza. . . .

First, it must be free and secure in modulation; without this freedom one runs the risk of beginning the trill in another key. Second, it is necessary to know how to rule and measure the breath. Third, it would be a great advantage to be gifted with a creative mind (and these are the traits of the unexpected genius, improvised, parts of the creative mind, which suddenly distinguish a man, and carry him to the stars with acclaim). And for this, one must have a straightforward judgment, which is necessary to regulate every note to its perfection.

Burney, account of music in Germany, the Netherlands,
and United Provinces (1775), "1 October 1772"

I was conducted to one of the interior apartments of the palace [Sans-Souci], in which the gentlemen of the king's [Frederick II of Prussia] band were waiting for his commands. This apartment was contiguous to the concert-room, where I could distinctly hear his majesty practising solfeggi [exercises] on the flute.

The concert began by a German-flute concerto, in which his majesty executed the solo parts with great precision; his *embouchure* was clear and even, his finger brilliant, and his taste pure and simple. I was much pleased, and even surprised with the neatness of his execution in the *allegros*, as well as by his expression and feeling in the *adagio*; in short, his performance surpassed, in many particulars, any thing I had ever heard among *Dilettanti*, or even professors. His majesty played three long and difficult concertos successively, and all with equal perfection. . . . The cadences [cadenzas] which his majesty made, were good, but very long and studied.

Rousseau, musical dictionary (1779)

CADENZA, an Italian word, by which we denote a point d'orgue, or sign of a pause, not written, and which the author [composer] leaves to the will of him who performs the principle part, for the purpose of his making, relatively to the character of the air, the passage most suitable to his voice, his instrument, or his taste.

J. C. Bach and F. P. Ricci, pianoforte treatise (c.1788), "Part 9"

When next to the *Fermata* the word ARBITRIO is written into the principal part, it is a call for improvising certain passages, written or not written, in measured or not measured time, in a succession of harmonies that have to pass over a single sustained bass note.

If the word CADENZA appears, it also means POINT-D'ORGUE, whose realization is left to the performer so that he may improvise in the character of the piece, with passages most suited for his instrument and to his taste, and that he makes the penultimate note of his cadence a trill and finishes on the tonic.

Regarding their length, *Arbitrio* and *Cadenza* have no fixed measures. Voices and wind instruments are limited to the duration of one single breath; the other instruments, to the duration of two breaths. This length, or pause, is not prescribed. The musician with fire, genius, and soul can extend it, especially when the *Arbitrio* or *Cadenza* is connected with the principal part whereby he can keep the attention alive and prevent boredom. It is always desirable to retain the proper and perceptible relationship between such cadenzas and the character of the piece. In such cases practice demands less study and more talent.

**Türk, clavier treatise (1789), Chapter 1, Part 6
"Concerning Various Other Signs and Terms"**

The pause (hold) ⌢ is used in two ways, namely 1) as a fermata, that is a lingering, a holding or, as is also said, a stop, with or without extemporaneous embellishments. . . . The fermata sign can also be used 2) to indicate places where an embellished cadenza can be suitably placed, as here:

Those who would not desire a cadenza wait a little on the note with a and close with a trill about once again as long as the prescribed value of the held note.

———. Chapter 5, Part 2 "Concerning Embellished Cadences"

The word cadence is used chiefly with two meanings. The first is any musical conclusion, whether it occurs at the end or in the middle of a composition. In a narrower sense, the word cadence especially means the extemporaneous embellishments which are found before a full cadence in the main voice and which conclude immediately before the final tone with a trill. These so-called cadenzas, in which the meter and the accompaniment cease, I would like to discuss in this part.

I would not be saying anything new but would simply be repeating an often heard complaint in declaring myself against the very great misuse of embellished cadences. For it is not seldom that a concerto or the like seems to be played merely because of its cadenzas. The performer goes to excess not only with regard to the suitable length of the composition, but in addition to this even incorporates all sorts of ideas that do not have the least relationship to what has gone before in the composition. The result is that the good impression left on the listener by the composition has for the most part been *cadenzaed* out of him. Notwithstanding this misuse, there have been many advocates of the cadenza and there still are. Even refined composers often write such embellishments or at least indicate where cadenzas might be played. Moreover, even sagacious philosophers, for reasons against which there are few arguments, justify the use of these embellishments; consequently it is probably not the thing itself as much as its misuse which should be censured. In order to assist in setting limits to this misuse wherever possible, I will attempt to describe below the most important requirements of a good cadenza by means of rules.

Embellished cadences can be divided into two main classes. In the first class are the simple or single-voiced cadenzas and in the second are cadenzas with two or more voices.

The places where cadenzas are to be played are for the most part indicated by composers themselves through the use of the fermata. If the cadenza has been added by the composer (as often happens for good reasons), then it should be played by the performer more according to feeling rather than strictly in time. For even in such a case, the notes should not be played exactly according to their specific values. But what is chiefly of concern in simple cadenzas, or how they are to be composed, may be found specified in the following rules.

1. The cadenza, among other things, should reinforce the impression the composition has made in a most lively way and present the most important parts of the whole composition in the form of a brief summary or in an extremely concise arrangement. . . .

2. The cadenza, just as every extemporaneous embellishment, must consist not so much of intentionally added difficulties as of such thoughts which are most scrupulously suited to the main character of the composition. . . .

3. Cadenzas should not be too long, especially in compositions of a melancholy character. In singing or on a wind instrument, a cadenza should last only as long as the breath of the performer permits. On stringed instruments this principle need not be followed too strictly, but this notwithstanding, enormously long cadenzas which sometimes last several minutes are in no way excusable.

4. Modulations into other keys, particularly to those which are far removed, either do not take place at all—for example, in a short cadenza—or they must be used with much insight and, as it were, only in passing. In no case should one modulate to a key which the composer himself has not used in the composition. . . .

5. Just as unity is required for a well-ordered whole, so also is variety necessary if the attention of the listener is to be held. Therefore, as much of the unexpected and surprising as can possibly be added should be used in the cadenza. . . .

6. No thought should be often repeated in the same key or in another, no matter how beautiful. . . .

7. Every dissonance, even in single-voiced cadenzas, must be resolved. . . .

8. A cadenza does not have to be erudite, but novelty, wit, an abundance of ideas and the like are so much more its indispensable requirements.

9. The same tempo and meter should not be maintained throughout the cadenza; its individual fragments (those parts which are incomplete in themselves) must be skillfully joined to one another. For the whole cadenza should be more like a fantasia which has been fashioned out of an abundance of feeling, rather than a methodically constructed composition. . . .

10. From what has been said, it follows that a cadenza which perhaps has been learned by memory with great effort or has been written out before should be performed as if it were merely invented. . . .

    If I include a number of cadenzas of varying character at this point, it is merely to show the arrangements of cadenzas in more detail through these examples [partially shown here]. It follows from the above rules that it is impossible to design patterns which can be used or imitated in all cases. . . .

Tromlitz, flute treatise (1791), Chapter 12
"Fermatas and Cadenzas"

Now we come to cadenzas. Just as one has more freedom to branch out here, more care is also required. However, this freedom is abused these days; especially on stringed and keyboard instruments, [the cadenza] is often made as long as the entire movement up to that point and one gets so far away from the subject that when the *ritornello* returns one has to recollect whether or not it belongs to this movement. So ideas are heaped on ideas, or to be more accurate, notes upon notes, which do not manifest the slightest feeling of the main subject; just as long as the cadenza is very long-winded, people cry: *bravissimo*! If he performs the most beautiful concerto in the clearest and most correct manner, and makes no rubbishy fantasy at the end, or only a short one, whether suitable or not, his whole performance will be worthless. . . .

The wind player and the singer cannot do as they wish, but are limited by the length of their breath, because no cadenza should be longer than the breath lasts. But there can be an exception to this under certain circumstances.

A cadenza is a surprising discretionary embellishment appropriate to the main passion of the piece or movement, on a note before the final trill with a fermata sign; or it is an artificial, decorative, surprising lead-in appropriate to the main sentiment, from the note with the fermata sign to the cadential trill. Cadenzas are of *two* kinds, either with *one part* or with *two parts*. The discussion here is about the ones with *one part*. The movement and melody of such a cadenza and the arrangement of its figures are discretionary, but the treatment of the intervals occurring in it and the regulation of the figures and their connections are subject to rules. Since these cadenzas are free fantasies composed of all kinds of figures and ideas, and are mostly without meter, their movement and melody cannot really be determined, neither can they well be written down for another person in notation. Sometimes it does seem as though they had meter, but it does not last long before this disappears again. For these reasons it is difficult, if not quite impossible, to give examples of them, since the pupil will not get what the master has imagined in any case, because they are unmeasured. Nonetheless I will give a little illustration here, from which one will be able to perceive their movement and how they are arranged; see (1 and 2):

**Kollmann, composition essay (1799), Chapter 4 "Of Concertos,"
Section C of Part 1 "The fancy cadences"**

The grand Cadence towards the end of the first movement . . . is commonly set with a Pause [fermata] over the leading note, and it is usual to introduce a *Fancy* [cadenza] between the chord of the sixth and fourth, which suspends the leading chord on that note and the leading chord itself. In regard to the said fancy, I have given three Rules. . . .

Rule I. The whole can properly consist of no other *harmony* than what may be introduced as a continued cadence or an Organ Point between the suspending chord (or chord of the sixth and fourth) and the leading chord, on the leading note. For, the suspending chord creates a desire to hear its resolution in the leading chord. This suspension therefore may be *continued*, by letting the harmony go several unexpected but regular ways, in the same manner, as the resolution of the Essential Seventh may be suspended; but the whole must remain *one continued* cadence, like an Organ Point, and no satisfactory conclusion must be made in it before the suspended final resolution.

Yet the following *liberties* are allowable in the cadence in question, viz: *first*, the Bass note need not be continued, as in a real Organ Point, if only the harmony is of such a nature as to admit the same note when supposed under it; *secondly*, the harmony may take even such turns as to oblige the supposed holding note to quit its station for a few chords. But this last must be done with great discretion and under the limitations of what I have said in explanation of the rule in question.

Rule II. No other *passages* must be introduced in a fancy cadence, than what are conformable to the Style, Movement, and Measure of the piece in which it is made, though without confining it to one fixed *movement* or *measure*, which would be against the following rule.

Rule III. The more *novelty*, *richness of modulation*, and *variety* a fancy cadence contains without trespassing against the two foregoing rules, or without making it too long, the better it is.

Spohr, musical diary (1860–1861), "The Journey to St. Petersburg, 1802–1803"

On May 23 we met Tietz, the famous mad violinist, at Senator Teplon's weekly musicale. He played a concerto of his own composition, repeating the first allegro and the rondo, presumably because his performance the first time failed to please him. . . . The difficult passages went better the second time. In all three movements he interpolated improvised cadenzas according to the old custom. They were quite attractive, and in the repeated movements wholly different from what had gone before.

Corri, singing treatise (1810), "The Nature of Cadenzas"

Cadenzas are an extemporary fancy, or, as it were a spontaneous melody, not limited to any number of notes. They should be consonant with the style of the air to which they belong, also, of whatever combination those notes may consist, they must be regulated by the rule of modulation. . . .

On the first note of the Cadenza, extemporary fancies are to be introduced. The instruments are then silent, and after the uttering of the final shake note, the piano forte must strike the 2nd Chord, the turn is then executed, falling on the concluding note together with all the other parts.

When cadenzas were first introduced in the practice of vocal music, the taking of a breath in the midst of them was deemed treason. But our modern cadenzas having become so widely excursive, more than human breath can execute with ease, the taking of a breath before the final shake may be admissible.

Busby, musical grammar (1818)

The *Cadenza* is a flourish, or flight of notes, introduced at the end of a melody, or movement; and the matter and style of which is generally left to the performer.

Busby, musical manual (1828)

CADENCE, or *Reprise*. A graceful extempore embellishment with which a singer closes his performance. The term *Cadence* is also sometimes applied to the pause made at the end of an air, previous and preparatory to a *Cadence*.

CADENZA. (Ital.) The spontaneous ornament with which a singer closes his song. See *Cadence*.

**Czerny, improvisation treatise (1836), Chapter 3
"Concerning Cadenzas, Fermatas, and More Extended Elaborations"**

Prolonged pauses appear very frequently in the midst of a piece over the six-four or seventh chord (over the latter, especially, as transition into another subject or tempo as well as into the principal theme), where either the composer has actually inscribed above, "Cadenza ad libitum"— or at least a fermata, which would not be superfluous— or finally where a cadenza that has actually been written out but is much too brief can be nicely extended.

These elaborations in music, just as in other arts, are a measure of good taste; they arouse the attention of the listeners and direct it towards the following material. Moreover, through these the performer can display the refinement of his feelings just as much as his strength and prowess when necessary.

Naturally, only the more cultivated taste and broad experience of the performer can determine their suitable application. In works of profound content and serious character (for example, Beethoven's Sonata, D Minor, op. 29), employing any kind of additional material would be very ill advised. On the other hand, preferably in compositions intended for a glittering, delicate, or sentimental manner of playing—in variations, potpourris, arrangements of vocal works, or whatever products of popular taste, there are abundant opportunities where just such little impromptus are appropriate, indeed are often a necessity, in order to adorn a rather dull and dragging passage.

Apropos of these, the performer has to observe the following:

A. The cadenza must be fully compatible with the content and spirit of the piece in general, as with the preceding and subsequent material in particular. Therefore, following an energetic delivery, similarly brilliant passagework should be introduced; on the other hand, gentle material should be followed by correspondingly light and delicate elaborations.

B. The cadenza must be neither too long nor too rhapsodic so as not to impede the continuity and momentum of the whole.

C. The performer may modulate neither into other keys nor into remote harmonies, but must always retain the chord of prolongation (which is the dominant seventh most of the time) as the underlying harmony.

D. He must enter into the following subject with melodic propriety and in a manner that is pleasing and suitable which, for the most part, occurs by means of diminuendo, and rallentando into the *tempo di adagio*. Should the subsequent theme be of a lively and dynamic nature, then the transition can also at times be accomplished through a lively passage, crescendo, and accelerando.

Here are several examples for practice which must be executed similarly or imitated in all keys (ex. 24 and 25).

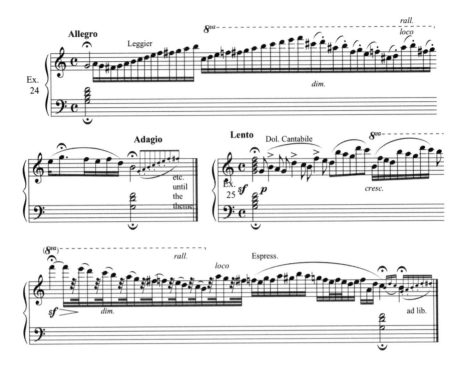

**Garcia, singing treatise (1840–1847),
"Ornaments and Changes"**

Q. What is a cadenza?

A. The cadenza is either a momentary suspension of musical meaning or it is final.

Q. On what chords do you find the momentary suspensions?

A. The momentary suspensions are chiefly found on the two triads (major and minor), their first inversion, the dominant seventh, the two ninths, the first inversion or the three last chords, and the augmented sixth.

Q. And the final cadenza?

A. On the formula

or simply the last dominant chord alone.

Q. What other observations on the cadenza can you offer?

A. The ornaments give the singer opportunity to display taste and wealth of resources. But whatever his imagination and facility may be, his cadenza must remain exclusively within the chord that bears it; the cadenza should never occur except on a long syllable; or if this be not convenient, on the exclamation "ah!" The cadenza ought to be performed, as far as possible, on a single syllable, and in a single breath.

The rule that the cadenza should be performed in a single breath can be avoided by composing it of several words, the breath being taken between them, thus:

Syllabic cadenzas acquire greater effect by the power of the word.

Chapter 7

EXPRESSION

EXTRA-MUSICAL FACTORS

Expression is not a term generally associated with music of the Classical era, but instead, is usually applied to music of the Romantic era. Because of this latter association, which is quite significant, and because the eras are often contrasted, Classical-era music is often thought to be expressionless. Ideals of structure, simplicity, order, restraint, and formality (which the term "classicism" connotes) are thought to preclude the involvement of expressivity. However, romanticism and expressivity are not exclusive to each other, and expression was exceedingly important to composers and performers of the Classical era.

Expression of a subjective nature was at the heart of Classical-era thinking. Composers had, or were supposed to have, highly developed expressive characteristics that motivated the rhythms, melodies, and harmonies of their compositions—even those that were purely instrumental. And performers were expected to discern, feel, and portray these expressive characteristics so that their listeners could be emotionally moved. All composition and performance were to be motivated by affects (i.e., characteristic emotions), and the conveyance of these affects was analogous to spoken oratory, with ebbs and flows, rises and falls, and moods and sentiments. This is why there were so many expressive terms attached to or associated with tempo indications—why an allegro, for instance, was not merely fast, but gay and spirited. It is also why singing was the model of all instrumental performance, why wind players articulated by pronouncing different syllables, and why rhythms were altered and beats of measures had varying stresses. Every aspect of performance practice had its reason for being because of the desire to portray expression in composition and to manifest it in performance. In the words of Georg Sulzer, "The most important, if not the only, function of a perfect musical composition is the accurate expression of sentiments and passions with all their particular shadings. . . . Every composition, whether it is vocal or instrumental, should possess a definite character and be able to arouse specific sentiments in the minds of listeners. . . . Expression is the soul of music."

The following quantity of primary source material is reflective of the amount of attention the topic of expression received throughout the era. Although most of the quotations merely state fundamental precepts quite similar to each other, the preponderance of the quotes testifies to the universal understanding and belief in the subject.

Such emphasis on expression during the Classical era in no way implies unbridled freedoms of crescendo and decrescendo, variations of tempo, diversified weights of emphasis, and degrees of articulation; composers and performers of the Classical era were unaware of the degrees of volume, ranges of coloristic textures, and expansion of forces that were to be standard in later eras. Nor does expression negate ideals of simplicity, order, restraint, and formality. Expression serves these ideals. Consequently, the performer should exhibit expression by understanding the underlying affect or sentiment of each composition and then by varying all the components of performance practice (including tempos, articulations, metric accentuations, dynamics, rhythmic and phrase shapes, and ornaments) within the confines of Classical-era ideals of taste and sensibility.

C. P. E. Bach, clavier treatise (1753), Part 1, Chapter 3 "Performance"

Keyboardists whose chief asset is mere technique are clearly at a disadvantage. A performer may have the most agile fingers, be competent at single and double trills, master the art of fingering, read skillfully at sight regardless of the key, and transpose extemporaneously without the slightest difficulty; a performer may be able to play tenths, even twelfths or runs, cross the hands in every conceivable manner and excel in other related matters, and yet he may be something less than a clear, pleasing, or stirring keyboardist. More often than not, one meets technicians, nimble keyboardists by profession, who possess all of these qualifications and indeed astound us with their prowess without ever touching our sensibilities. . . . A mere technician, however, can lay no claim to the rewards of those who sway the ear in gentle undulation rather than the eye, the heart rather than the ear, and lead it where they will. . . .

Good performance occurs when one hears all notes and their embellishments played in correct time with fitting volume produced by a touch which is related to the true content of a piece. Herein lies the rounded, pure, flowing manner of playing which makes for clarity and expressiveness. . . .

In general, the briskness of allegros is expressed by detached notes and the tenderness of adagios by broad, slurred notes. The performer must keep in mind that these characteristic features of allegros and adagios are to be given consideration even when a composition is not so marked, as well as when the performer has not yet gained an adequate understanding of the affect of a work. I use the expression, "in general," advisedly, for I am well aware that all kinds of execution may appear in any tempo. . . .

A musician cannot move others unless he too is moved. He must of necessity feel all of the affects that he hopes to arouse in his audience, for the revealing of his own humor will stimulate a like humor in the listener. In languishing sad passages the performer must languish and grow sad. Thus will the expression of the piece be more clearly perceived by the audience. Here, however, the error of a sluggish, dragging performance must be avoided, caused by an excess of affect and melancholy. Similarly, in lively, joyous passages, the performer must again put himself into the appropriate mood. . . . Above all, he must discharge this office in a piece that is highly expressive by nature, whether it be by him or someone else. In the latter case he must make certain that he assumes the emotion that the composer intended in writing it.

Chapter Seven

Algarotti, opera essay (1755), Preface

It seems that our composers behave like those writers who, paying no attention to word order or to how speech is organized, aim only at stringing together beautiful words. However harmonious and full-sounding they may be, the ensuing oration will only prove vain and ineffectual. The same is true for music, if the composer does not aim at portraying some image or expressing some emotion.

L. Mozart, violin treatise (1756), Chapter 12
"Of Reading Music correctly, and in particular, of Good Execution"

The good performance of a composition according to modern taste is not as easy as many imagine, who believe themselves to be doing well if they foolishly embellish a piece out of their own heads, and who have no sensitivity whatever for the affect which is to be expressed in the piece. And who are these people? They are mostly those who, hardly at ease with time, get immediately to work on concertos and solos in order (in their foolish opinion) to force themselves straight into the company of virtuosos. Many succeed so far that they play with uncommon dexterity the most difficult passages in various concertos or solos they have practiced with great industry. These they know by heart. But should they have to perform only a couple of minuets melodiously according to the instructions of the composer, they are unable to do so; yea, this is to be seen even in their studied concertos. For so long as they play an allegro, all goes well; but when it comes to an adagio, there they betray their great ignorance and bad judgment in every bar of the whole piece. They play without method and without expression; the piano and forte are not differentiated; the embellishments are in the wrong place, too overloaded, and mostly played in a confused manner; and often the notes are far too bare and one observes that the player knows not what he does. For such people there is rarely any hope of improvement, for they, more than anyone, are taken up with self-esteem. . . .

To read the musical pieces of good masters rightly according to the instructions, and to play them in keeping with the outstanding characteristics of the piece, is far more artistic than to study the most difficult solo or concerto. For the latter, but little sense is necessary. And if one has enough wit to think out the appoggiaturas, one can learn the most difficult passages for oneself if energetic practice be added. The former, on the contrary, is not so easy. For, not only must one observe exactly all that has been marked and prescribed and not play it otherwise than as written, but one must

416

throw oneself into the affect to be expressed and apply and execute in a certain good style all the ties, slides, accentuation of the notes, the forte and piano—in a word, whatever belongs to tasteful performance of a piece, which can only be learned from sound judgment and long experience. . . .

Before beginning to play, the piece must be looked at well and considered. The character, tempo, and kind of movement demanded by the piece must be sought out and carefully observed as to whether a passage occurs which often at first sight seems of little importance, but on account of its special style of execution and expression is not quite easy to play at sight. Finally, in practicing, every care must be taken to find and to render the affect that the composer wished to have brought out; and as sadness often alternates with joy, each must be carefully depicted according to its kind. In a word, all must be so played that the player himself be moved thereby.

Alembert, music treatise (1759), Chapter 38

We [French] have much less to reform in our symphonies [instrumental music] than in our songs. . . . In this regard, not even the Italians can match our wealth. I completely discount the prodigious amount of sonatas they have given us. All this purely instrumental music, without design, without purpose, speaks neither to the mind nor to the soul. . . . The composers of instrumental music will make nothing but an empty noise as long as they do not have in their heads, like the celebrated Tartini, as they say, an action or an expression to be represented.

Löhlein, clavier treatise (1765)

Performance on the clavier depends on the touch, so you have to let the fingers act in like manner to the soul or feeling in order to place the listener in the mood that the composer has sought to arouse. . . . Because all on the clavier depends upon the stroke, you must consider foremost adjusting this to the piece suitably. So as an example: the gay, through using a light, flying, but also pithy and meaningful touch. The playful kind also requires such an expression. The dreary, on the contrary, must be carried entirely phlegmatic, well held, and, likewise, one tone joined to the other.

Chapter Seven

Verri, essay on music (1765)

By music I mean what others call melody, that is, a particular style in which one sound follows another, which varies either in terms of tempo, discontinuity, the distance from one voice to another, or the varying techniques of holding back or projecting the voice itself with greater energy. In short, by music I mean a succession of sounds that awakens in music lovers various emotions, such as tenderness, daring, compassion, pride, and all the other emotions that, as if by magic, are aroused by sounds. . . .

I have listened to voices that could not be reproached for being in any way defective, and yet my heart hurled against them the greatest of reproaches, because it felt nothing.

Gluck, *Alceste* (1769), Preface

When I undertook to write the music for Alceste, I determined to strip it completely of all those abuses, whether introduced by the mistaken vanity of singers or by the excessive obligingness of composers who have long been disfiguring Italian opera and have turned the most magnificent and beautiful of all spectacles into the most ridiculous and boring. I determined to restrict music to its true function, namely, to enhance poetry in terms of expression and the situations it relates, without interrupting the action or numbing it with useless and superfluous ornaments. And I thought music ought to do for the poetry what lively colors and the contrast of light and shadow do for a correct and well-ordered drawing, animating the figures without modifying their contours. Therefore, I have taken care not to halt a singer in the heat of his dialogue to make him wait through a boring ritornello, nor stop him in mid-word on a favorable vowel, either to display the agility of his beautiful voice in a long melisma or to wait for the orchestra to give him time to catch his breath for a cadenza. I did not think it necessary to rush through the second part of an aria, when this second part was the most impassioned and important, just to allow time regularly to repeat the words of the first part four times, and to end the aria where perhaps the meaning does not end in order to give the singer more leeway to show how he can vary a passage in so many different ways according to his whim. In short, I have attempted to do away with all those abuses against which common sense and reason have been crying out in vain.

I have felt that the overture should inform the listeners beforehand of the nature of the action that is about to be represented, to sum up, as it were, its subject; that the instrumental passages should be used in proportion to interest and emotion, above all to avoid that sharp break in the dialogue between aria and recitative; and that they should not cut off the sentence illogically or interrupt the heat and power of the action inopportunely.

Finally, I have deemed it my greatest task to seek the beauty of simplicity, and I have avoided making a display of complexities at the expense of clarity. I have not judged any novelty estimable unless it immediately and naturally flows from the situation and the expression; and there is no convention that I have not felt free to sacrifice for the sake of effect.

Binns (Hoyle), dictionary (1770), "Expression"

EXPRESSION, is to express well the author's intention; and as the intention of Muisck is not only to please the ear, but to express sentiments, strike the imagination, affect the mind, and command the passions; and every piece is to be executed with exactness, propriety, and delicacy of expression, according to the true intent of Musick.

Sulzer, general theory of music (1771–1774), Chapter 1 "Aesthetic foundations"

The most important, if not the only, function of a perfect musical composition is the accurate expression of sentiments and passions with all their particular shadings. Any work that fills our imagination full of harmonious tones but without touching our heart can be compared to a painting of the sky at twilight. We may be entranced by the pleasing mixture of differing colors, but we certainly will not see anything in the patterns formed by the clouds which will touch our heart. Now, if we hear in a song not just the most perfect succession of notes, but also a speech that seems to be the outpourings of a sensitive heart, the pleasing engagement of the ear serves as a kind of inducement to the soul by which it can succumb to all the sentiments brought forth through the expressiveness of the song. . . .

Expression is the soul of music. Without it, music is but an entertaining diversion. But with it, music becomes the most expressive speech overpowering the heart. It compels us to be tender, then to be resolute and steadfast. It can quickly bring forth our pity, and just as quickly, admiration. At times it ennobles and elevates our soul, while at other times it enfeebles it with effeminate emotions. . . .

Every composition, whether it is vocal or instrumental, should possess a definite character and be able to arouse specific sentiments in the minds of listeners. It would be foolish of the composer to begin composing without having established the character of his work. He must know whether the language he will set down is that of a man who is proud or humble, courageous or timid, master or servant, tender or tempestuous. Even if he stumbles upon his theme by chance or he arbitrarily selects it, he must still examine its character carefully so that he can sustain it while composing.

Having established the character of the piece, the composer must next place himself in the emotional state to which he would wish to bring others.

———. Chapter 3 "Musical issues"

Instrumental music employs tones, not words, to make comprehensible what it is expressing. It is to be understood in opposition to vocal music, in which comprehensible words are sung. All music is rooted in the energy contained in simple tones in order to express various passions. . . . And no music would be possible if one could not speak the language of sentiment. . . .

Some genres of music have a particular character, such as the ballet, dance, and march, and the composer has a plumb-line as to their character by which he may proceed in its composition. The more precisely he observes the character of each art, the better his work will appear. In the cases of overtures and symphonies that will serve to open a play, the composer already has to a certain extent something by which to base his invention, since his music must express the main character of the play for which it is made. But the invention of a concerto, trio, solo, sonata, and the like, all of which have no specific purpose, is left almost entirely to chance. One can understand how a man of genius may arrive at some invention when he has something in front of himself that he can hold on to. But where it is not possible to say what he is to create, or what he should have in mind, then he seems to work only by good luck. Thus it happens that most pieces of this kind are nothing other than pleasant-sounding noise that strikes the ear either violently or gently. In order to avoid this, the composer would do well to imagine some person, or a situation or passion, and exert his fantasy to the point where he can believe that this person is ready to speak. He can help himself by seeking out poetry that is pathetic, fiery, or tender in nature, and declaim it in an appropriate tone, and after that sketch out his composition following this sentiment. He must never forget that music that expresses no kind of passion or sentiment in a comprehensible language is nothing but sheer noise.

C. P. E. Bach, letters from and to Heinrich Wilhelm von Gerstenberg (1773)

I found myself at a gathering a few evenings ago, where among other things, certain concertos by the old Tischer that he set on biblical passages were being played and judged. . . . He carried out that which he undertook to carry out without particular genius. On the other hand, any attempt to give to the clavier expression and meaning appeared to me to be worthy of praise, even if it failed. . . . The more I think about it . . . the greater seem the advantages that the expressive quality of the clavier would gain through a collection of sonatas for which, for example, some of the most moving Psalms would serve as the basis. . . . I imagine a pastorale on passages from the Song of Solomon—a maestoso on Isaiah—an oratorio on the Passion assembled from biblical passages just for the clavier, as Handel put together his *Messiah* for voices. . . . And now I will confess to you that I have already corresponded with your brother in Bückeburg last winter on the same subject, the expressiveness of the clavier. But no further word about it until I see your answer.

Your Honor is completely correct when you say that devout feelings are precisely those which are expressed most properly in music, and I, as a clavier player, dare to claim that one can actually say a great deal on our instrument with a good performance. I exclude here the mere tickling of the ears and demand that the heart should be moved. Such a clavier player, especially if he has a highly inventive genius, can do a great deal.

Eximeno (y Pujades), music history treatise (1774), Preface

Music is only prosody, the purpose of which is to imbue language with gracefulness and expression. . . . Music evolves from those modifications of language that enable it to delight the ear and touch the heart. These modifications concern both the stress and the quantity of the syllables, which no philosopher ever thought should be regulated by means of mathematical rules. The more observations I have made on the common speech of humans, and especially on that of women, the more I have become convinced of this truth. I have often set myself to speaking while playing the harpsichord, and, noting the variations of my voice, I subsequently have found them in the strings of that instrument. Above all, I have had no hesitations at all regarding music's identity with prosody when, upon examining the prosodies of the most cultivated languages, which were once Greek and Latin, I have seen that the rules on accents generally tend to produce, in ordinary speech, a series of musical cadences, and that the entire variety of tempos and notes that music uses are the same as the feet in Greek and Latin poetry. Since these things have a common origin in language, it follows that language, prosody, and music must all proceed from a common source.

Burney, account of music in Germany, the Netherlands, and United Provinces (1775), "Vienna"

I went to Mr. L'Augier's concert, which was begun by the child of eight or nine years old, whom he had mentioned to me before, and who played two difficult lessons of Scarlatti, with three or four by M. Becke, upon a small, and not good Piano forte. The neatness of this child's execution did not so much surprise me, though uncommon, as her expression. All the *pianos* and *fortes* were so judiciously attended to; and there was such shading of some passages and force given to others as nothing but the best teaching, or greatest natural feeling and sensibility could produce.

Manfredini, harmony treatise (1775), Part 3, Chapter 1

Many singers, believing that singing in style consists in variations, vary so often and so badly, that they ruin everything. But how they deceive themselves! Singing in style means nothing other than singing with feeling, with spirit, sustaining and shading the voice, and above all else expressing every piece of music according to its true sense and character.

Marmontel, essay on music in France (1777)

Why should we not practice in music what has been done in poetry? Passions are expressed with cries, howls, wrenching, and terrible sounds; but these accents, if they are not embellished when imitated, will, as in nature, create only an impression of suffering. If we simply wished to be moved, we could go among the common people to hear a mother who has lost her son, or children who have lost their mother; here, no doubt, the expression of grief is artless, and here too it is most forceful. But what pleasure would these wrenching emotions give us? The sharp point of grief that moves us in the theater must leave some balm in the wound. This balm is the pleasure of the mind, or of the senses; and the cause of this pleasure, in poetry, is the sublimity of thoughts, of sentiments and images, the noble elegance of expression, the charm of beautiful verse. In music, the same pleasure must combine with impressions of grief; and the reason for this is in the musician's art, as in that of the poet—in the art of giving to musical expression a charm that the airs, the laments, and the dire or grievous accents of passion do not possess in nature. . . . In a word, melody without expression is worth little; expression without melody is something, but not enough. Expression and melody, each to the highest degree to which they may rise together, is the challenge of art.

Rousseau, dictionary (1779), "Expression"

EXPRESSION. A quality by which the musician has a lively feeling, and renders with energy all the ideas which he should utter and all the sentiments which he should express. There is one expression in composition and another in execution, and it is from their concurrence that the most musical and most agreeable effect results.

To give expression to his works, the composer should seize and compare all the connections which may be found between the strokes of his object and the productions of his art; he ought to know or feel the effect of every character so that he may convey that which he has chosen to a degree suitable to it: for as a good painter does not give an equal light to all his objects, an ingenious musician should neither give the same energy to all his sentiments or the same force to all his paintings, and should fix each part in its convenient place, not so much to give powers to it alone, as to afford a greater effect to the whole. . . .

The melody, harmony, movement, and choice of instruments and voices are the elements of musical language; and the melody, by its immediate connection with the grammatical and oratorical account, is that which gives the character to all the rest. Wherefore, it is always from the air that the principal expression should be drawn, as well in instrumental as vocal music.

It will be useless for the composer to have a knowledge of animating his work, unless the fire which ought to reign therein is transmitted to the soul of those who execute it. The singer who only sees the notes of his part is not in a condition of catching the expression of the composer, or to give any to what he sings, unless he has a true idea of the sense. We must understand what we read to give a true idea of the sense. We must understand what we read to give a true comprehension of it to others, and it is not sufficient to be sensible in general, unless we are particular also in regard to the energy of the language in which we speak.

W. A. Mozart, letter to his father (1781), "26 September"

In the original libretto [of *Die Entführung aus dem Serail*], Osmin has only a little song to sing and nothing else except the trio and the finale. Now, however, he has another aria in the first act, and he will get yet another one in the second. . . . You only have the beginning and the ending, which must make a good effect. To turn Osmin's rage comical, it is set to Turkish music. In the composition of the aria, I let his beautiful low tones gleam (in spite of the Salzburg Midas). The section "drum beim Barte des Propheten," etc., is set in the same tempo, but with fast notes. Since his rage keeps growing, and one thinks the aria is already at an end, the allegro assai—in a completely different tempo and another key—is bound to make the best effect: a man in such a vehement state of rage exceeds all order, measure, and intention; he doesn't know himself, and so the music must not know itself anymore. Since the passions, however, whether vehement or not, must never be expressed to a point that disgusts; and since the music must never offend the ear, even in the most horrible situations, but must still please it—in short, always remain music—I have not chosen a remote key to accompany F, the key of the aria, but a related one—not the key most closely related, D minor, but one further removed, A minor. Now comes Belmonte's aria in A major, "O wie ängstlich, o wie feurig"; you see how it is expressed—the affectionately beating heart is already indicated, with the two violins in octaves. This is the favorite aria of everybody who has heard it – mine, too. . . . You see trembling and shaking, you see the swelling of his throbbing breast, portrayed by a crescendo. You hear the whispering and sighing, expressed by the first violins with mutes and a flute in unison.

——. letter to his father (1784)

I must write in a hurry. Herr Richter, the clavier-player, is making a tour on his way back to Holland, his native country. . . . He plays well so far as execution goes, but, as you will discover when you hear him, he is too rough and labored and entirely devoid of taste and feeling.

Türk, organ in worship treatise (1787), Chapter 1
"Chorales" Section 2

Since one of the main aims of the worship service as such, and also of its musical constituent, is the fostering of devotion and religious feeling, etc., the organist cannot permit himself to forget for an instant that he is playing in church and is accompanying solemn hymns that are directed toward the Supreme Being. . . .

Therefore, the organist is advised in these instances to play solemnly and devotionally, appropriate to the locality, and to refrain carefully from musical word- and subject-painting that is inappropriate, definitely misguided, disturbing to the service, and often ludicrous. . . .

If the organist does not wish to fall prey to such inappropriate musical painting, he should not try to express everything that is in the text. . . .

Even serious subjects represented by a hymn should not be "painted" by the organist. It would be disturbing and childish if he were to attempt to express sin by crude errors in the harmony, heaven and hell by high and low notes respectively, or the barking of a dog as in nature. . . .

However, with hymn texts of completely contrasting content, for which only one melody is known or used, the organist can at least contribute to a more satisfying interpretation if he does not play one stanza just like the next, according to a certain routine. Therefore, depending on the circumstances, the same melody can and must often be treated in a very different and completely contrasting manner.

The tempo (rate of speed) in which a hymn is played can greatly reinforce the expression, but can also weaken it immensely. In general, the chorale requires a slow and solemn tempo; still, because of its various sentiments, it can support minor variations in tempo, since penitential and funeral hymns should rightly be played even more slowly and movingly than those in which the theme is joyful and merry. But the chorale should never be performed rapidly since it loses all dignity as soon as one chooses an only slightly faster tempo. Here, too, the organist must take into consideration where is he playing and to whom the hymns are directed. . . .

Variation, when appropriate to the place and purpose, can likewise contribute much to expressing the sentiment. With long hymns, particularly, when the content changes, [variation] is necessary to some degree, for when there are thirteen verses in which, moreover, the first two lines of the melody must be repeated, who can listen to the very same bass twenty-six times without a feeling of revulsion? Therefore, the organist can feel free to introduce variations.

———. Chapter 3 "Accompaniment"

The strength of the accompaniment depends to a large extent on the number and type of voices. . . . The organist must take all sorts of circumstances into consideration.

The ritornellos and interludes in arias, duets, etc. require a relatively stronger accompaniment than solo passages; that is, when a ritornello is marked *forte*, this *forte* must be played more strongly than a *forte* in a vocal passage. . . . The same applies to the indication piano in the reverse situation. Since the organist himself does not always have enough time, while playing, to pull out several stops or to retire others, he must arrange the registration beforehand so that the ritornellos, the choruses, the appearance[s] of the fugue theme, the loud passages in unison, etc. can be played on the great keyboard, but the medium-loud or quite soft solo passages, etc. on one of the other keyboards in proportionate strength.

If the organist has only one manual and in addition must play the bass alone, he should, on the whole, register the manual with only moderate strength; or he could allow one hand to rest at the ends of the ritornellos, for example, even if no rests occur in the piece itself, and meanwhile continue playing the bass with only the pedal and the other hand until he has retired several stops; for it is always preferable to accompany only a few measures imperfectly, than to accompany the greatest part of a composition poorly.

Choosing to accompany in two, three, or more voices can likewise contribute much to a suitable performance. If, for example, *forte* and *piano* alternate so quickly that it is not possible to play each on a different manual, then one should play very full chords for the *forte*, but only two- or three-voiced ones for the *piano*. Moreover, the employment or omission of the pedals is also beneficial in [achieving] quick changes of loud and soft.

J. C. Bach and F. P. Ricci, pianoforte treatise (c.1788), Part II

The ENSEMBLE, (IL COMPLESSO), depends not only on the skill to read music with precision, but also on the intelligence to sense the particular character and the binding element of the whole, be it in the exact phrasing, correct grasping of the succession of movements, and nuances of loud and soft, and finally, in realizing among the marks of ornaments those which are so obviously meant by the composer that nobody can possibly omit them.

Without loss of character, the same composition can be performed in different ways. Unless one compares the performances with the rules, it is difficult to determine why one is more pleasing than the other. But the genius finds them, the heart senses them, and the whole art consists of knowing how to light one's heart fire and carry it into the heart of others.

Forkel, music history treatise (1788), "Introduction"

The surest guide in this investigation (i.e., the gradual progression of music from its first beginning to the highest perfection) may be offered by the similarity traceable between man's language and his music, which reaches back not only to their origins but extends throughout their complete development from their beginning to their highest perfection. In its origin, music, just like language, is nothing but the vehement tonal expression of a feeling. Both spring from a common source: sensation. Although they separated subsequently, each in its own way grew into what it was capable of becoming—one the language of the mind, the other the language of the heart—and yet both retained so many characteristics of their common ancestry that even at their greatest distance they still speak in similar manner to mind and heart.

———. "The Third Age of Music"

If music . . . had to be for feelings what language is for the mind, then its proper expressions had to be extended and determined in the same measure as those of language. Nothing has contributed more to this extension and to a more exact determination of musical expressions than harmony in its present state. Only through harmony could music become what it is today, namely a true and proper language of emotion.

Manfredini, defense of modern music (1788), "Conclusion"

There is general agreement about instrumental music . . . that it is in a lofty position now, and that ancient music did not achieve so much. But what else does this kind of music contain, if not vocal lines or melodies that are more spirited, more pleasing, and more meaningful than the ancient ones? They are melodies almost all of which derive from vocal music, whose follower and companion instrumental music has been and always will be. It is simply true that instrumental music is for the most part a copy and imitation of the vocal. When it doesn't sing, it doesn't express—that is, it says nothing and it is worth nothing at all. So while instrumental music has greatly improved, it first had to be made into vocal music, and whoever denies this can deny anything.

Türk, clavier treatise (1789), Chapter 1, Part 5
"Concerning the Tempo and the Character of a Musical Composition"

Every good composition has a certain (predominant) character; that is, the composer has expressed in his composition a certain degree of joy or sorrow, jest or seriousness, anger or composure, etc.

——. Chapter 6, Part 3
"Concerning the Expression of the Prevailing Character"

The most essential part of good execution in performance is expression of music's prevailing character. Without this no listener can be moved to any great degree. This effect, which is the highest goal of music, can only be induced when the artist has the capacity to become infused with the predominant affect and to communicate his feelings to others through the eloquence of music. Expression is therefore that part of a good execution in which the true master, full of genuine feeling for his art, distinguishes himself noticeably from the average musician. Mechanical skill can ultimately be learned by much practice; only expression presupposes—other than mechanical facility—a broad range of knowledge, and above all things, a sensitive soul. . . .

The words: will he come soon? can merely through the tone of the speaker receive a quite different meaning. Through them a yearning desire, a vehement impatience, a tender plea, a defiant command, irony, etc., can be expressed. The single word: God! can denote an exclamation of joy, of pain, of despair, the greatest anxiety, pity, astonishment, etc., in various degrees. In the same way tones, by changes in the execution, can produce a very different effect. It is therefore extremely necessary to study the expression of feelings and passions in the most careful way, make them one's own, and learn to apply them correctly.

Tromlitz, flute treatise (1791), Chapter 5
"Time-signatures, and how the notes are divided and counted in them; the beat itself, or counting time according to an appointed tempo"

A means of lighting upon the tempo indicated by the superscription [Italian tempo term] must indeed exist. I know of none other than feeling. But if one is to find out the correct tempo for a movement by feeling, one must first of all be familiar with the content of the piece. To be governed solely by the superscription is in my opinion a mistake, or at best a very vague expedient. Often a composer superscribes a movement *Allegro*, but not merely with the meaning fast. Rather, he has attempted thereby to convey a particular degree of joy and happiness. Now if the performer is guided by the bare meaning *fast*, as very often happens, then he will certainly, or at least most of the time, mistake the composer's intention, for he will not be in accordance with the content, the substance, on which his aim should be quite set and on which everything depends.

——. Chapter 15 "Summary of the whole, together with a few remarks for pupils and masters"

Musical expression must resemble a skillful discourse; just as it can be lifted up by a good delivery and spoiled by a bad one, so also can a piece of music. It can happen that a bad piece gains much from a good performance. . . .

Since light and shade are brought into a performance by the waxing and waning of sound, by weakening and strengthening it by degrees, . . . one should be particularly careful not to play always in one color, as they say, plodding on flat and shapeless. . . .

Every piece, no matter how limited by rules, is nothing other than a fantasy in which lively, joyful, flattering, sad, and suchlike ideas appear by turn according to the various passions.

Kollmann, composition essay (1799), Chapter 1
"Of the Plan for a Piece to be Composed"

A piece may be composed either in a certain prescribed character or its character may be optional. But in both cases it ought to have some general character, which receives its shades and lights from particular characteristics. . . .

The means by which prescribed as well as other characteristics may be brought into a musical piece are: Time, Rhythm, Subjects, Modulation, Imitation, Variation, the nature and management of Voices or Instruments, and anything else which can produce strong characteristics of various sorts. Particularly when words are set to music, they may be rendered expressive, not only of anything that is conceivable by Sound or Motion, but even of many passions of the soul.

——. Chapter 3, Part 1 "Of Symphonies in General"

In regard to their *particular character*, Symphonies may be either characteristic or free. By characteristic Symphonies I mean those which are to express a certain *prescribed* character. . . . Of Free Symphonies I comprehend all those that have *no prescribed* Character, though I have said before that every Musical Piece ought to have *some* general character.

Allgemeine Musikalische Zeitung (1799), review of Beethoven op. 13 *Sonate Pathétique*

The admirable sonata is well named *pathétique*, for it is indeed deeply emotional. A noble melancholy is introduced with the smoothly modulated Grave in C Minor that recurs from time to time to interrupt the strongly expressive, fiery mood of the Allegro.

Streicher, remarks on the fortepiano (1801), Chapter 2 "On tone"

A true musical artist . . . knows how to permit his instrument to express the noble sentiments befitting the gentleness or melancholy of the *adagio*. If his sentiments are good—familiar with the action of his instrument and capable of communicating profound feelings, he will know how to make his notes flow like oil and not creep along. His *piano* [soft volume] is so prepared that it must hold our attention. For the expression of sorrow, he never plays in a shrill or coarse manner, but rather expresses it gently, because sorrow, if it is beautified and nobly expressed, arouses in each listener, as in the observer, then, the opposite feeling.

Thayer, biography of Beethoven (1866–1879), Volume 2 "Reflecting on the period 1801–1805"

When I [Ferdinand Ries, piano student of Beethoven] made a mistake in a passage, or struck wrongly notes or leaps which he often wanted specially emphasized, he [Beethoven] seldom said anything; but if my fault was in expression, or a crescendo, etc., or in the character of the piece, he became angry, because, as he said, the former was accidental, while the latter showed a lack of knowledge, feeling, or attention. He himself very often made mistakes of the former kind, even when playing in public.

Spohr, musical diary (1860–1861), "Review of performances during a German tour, 1804–1805"

What we think of as correctness in playing in its widest significance is with Herr Spohr, as a solid foundation, only a point of departure. Perfect purity, security, precision, the most brilliant finish, every type of bowing, all varieties of violin tone, the most natural ease in the execution of all such things, even in the most difficult passages—these render him one of the most skillful of virtuosos. But the soul that he breathes into his playing, the flight of fantasy, the fire, the tenderness, the intimacy of expression, the good taste, the insight into the spirit of the most varied compositions, and his ability to present them each in its own style and spirit—all this makes him a true artist.

Momigny, harmony and composition treatise (1806), Chapter 30 "On Composition, Strict or Free, in Four Parts, Analysis of a Quartet [in D Minor, K421] by Mozart, About the Musical Style of this Piece"

The style of this *Allegro Moderato* is noble and pathetic. I decided that the best way to have my readers recognize its true expression was to add words to it. But since these verses, if one can call them that, were improvised, as it were, they ought not to be judged in any other regard that that of their agreement with the sense of the music.

I thought I perceived that the feelings expressed by the composer were those of a lover who is on the point of being abandoned by the hero she adores: *Dido*, who had had a similar misfortune to complain of, came immediately to mind. Her noble rank, the intensity of her love, the renown of her misfortune—all this convinced me to make her the heroine of this piece. She should be made to speak in a manner worthy of herself, but this is the task of a great lyric poet. It is sufficient to my task that the feelings of this unhappy queen be recounted and carefully set to music that renders them faithfully. . .

DIDO'S LAMENT
Reprise II, Part I

Hélas! mes larmes, mes appas	Alas! my tears, my charms
Ne te touchent pas.	do not touch you.
Tu veux me donner le trépas.	You want me to die.
Monstre indigne du jour,	O monster unworthy of the light,
Voilà le prix de tant d'amour!	this is my reward for such a love!
Fuis, malheureux! Non! reste	Fly away, you wretch! No! stay
encore.	here.
(*à part, avec espoir*) Il paraît	(*Aside, hopefully*) He seems to
s'attendrir!	be moved!

Reichardt, letters (1810), "17th letter [1808]"

[On the 22nd of December] the local [Viennese] musicians gave the first of this season's great performances at the Burgtheater . . . while on the same day Beethoven also gave at the great suburban theater a concert for his benefit, at which only his own works were played. . . . [Included was] a new concerto for fortepiano [#4, op. 58], terribly difficult, which Beethoven played astonishingly well in the fastest possible tempos. The Adagio, a masterpiece of beautiful sustained melody, he actually sang on his instrument with a deep melancholy feeling which awakened its response in me.

Schindler, biography of Beethoven (1840), Second Period, Section 2 "1804 to 1805"

The admiration that Beethoven had felt for Napoleon was no more; it had changed into hatred, and not until the emperor met his tragic end on St. Helena was the composer able to forgive him. . . . He pointed out that he had already composed the music appropriate to such a catastrophe, namely the Funeral March in the *Eroica*. He went even further in describing the symbolism of this movement, for the theme of the middle section in C major was supposed to represent a new star of hope in Napoleon's reversed fortunes (his return to the political stage in 1815), and finally the great hero's powerful decision to withstand fate until, at the moment of surrender, he sinks to the ground and allows himself to be buried like any other mortal.

———. Second Period, Section 4 "1809 to 1813"

Why in some catalogues, including the Breitkopf & Härtel *Thematic Index*, is [the piano sonata op. 81a "Les Adieus, l'Absence, et le Retour"] designated by the term "characteristic." Are we to suppose that all the other Beethoven sonatas are not characteristic simply because they bear no title by which the emotions of the hearer are led in a certain direction? One day this author heard the master lament that he had ever added the designation pathétique to the opus 13 sonata. "The whole world," he complained, "seizes upon a single sonata because it has a name that the pianists can exploit." When we look at the general meaning of this word: That which is truly pathetic expresses a strong emotion earnestly and with dignity, we realize that it is a word that summarizes the fundamental character of all of Beethoven's music.

———. Third Period, Section 1 "1815 to 1820"

When we consider the medium and nature of the compositions directly preceding the 7th and 8th symphonies, the *Battle* symphony opus 136, and the cantata *Der glorreiche Augenblick*, we are seized with amazement at the deep tenderness and intimacy of this newest composition [piano sonata opus 90 in E minor] in contrast to its predecessor's energy and power. . . . The sensitivity of Count Lichnowsky, to whom this sonata was dedicated, made it possible for him to know the work and grasp its particular significance. When he asked the composer about it, Beethoven replied that he had set the Count's love-story to music, and if he wished to have names for the movements, the first would be, *Conflict Between Head and Heart*, and the second, *Conversation with the Beloved*.

———. Musical Section, Part 1

If Beethoven's sonatas contain passages of pathos or lyricism that rise to heights of rhetoric, then the methods of the orator must rise to express them. A performance will then result which, without the aid of a written or spoken word, will achieve the appearance of artistic truth. Rhetoric in musical writing differs from performance in the same way that rhetoric in verbal expression differs from public speaking. Freedom with regard to the rhythm, together with a deep insight into the inner meaning of specific passages, is the first requisite of good performance in both categories.

Corri, singing treatise (1810),
"On Expression. Rules to be observed"

This Qualification [expression] being so important and indispensable to Vocal Music, which in a skillful Performer directs and guides the utterance of every Tone and Word, I have thought it expedient by some farther [sic] observations to enforce on the mind of the Scholar the absolute necessity of its attainment.

Busby, musical grammar (1818)

On the introduction of *Graces*, it is indispensable that we should be constantly governed by one sovereign rule: that of not deviating from the character of the music we perform. There are more styles than one in which some compositions may very properly be rendered; but there is no composition to which some methods of giving them will not be wholly unsuitable. All hearers have not organs equally refined, all are not blessed with natural taste, all are not alike endowed with a quick sensibility and delicate discernment; but most can judge of general consistency, feel the discordance of opposing qualities, and distinguish between the expressions appropriate to contrary emotions.

Genius is an attribute of the composer, taste of the performer; genius conceives and embodies, taste judges and adorns; genius produces the subject matter, but confides in taste for its just and becoming display. The composer does not leave to the performer this province only; sometimes he does more; sometimes the fire of imagination, too rapid to receive the cold, tardy admonitions of judgment, resigns to the taste of others the task of correcting or palliating discrepancy. We see then how much depends upon just performance. The performer is never altogether in the *composer's* power; the composer, less or more, ever in that of the performer. How important, therefore, that the performer should be sedulous in cultivating a chaste and genuine style! that he should be capable not only of understanding what a composition really is, but of feeling what it ought to be! that he should be able to catch and transfuse the spirit of his author! be at once susceptible of all his warmth and vivacity, and have the full possession of his own cool and matured judgment!

Among the various qualifications of a good musical performer, there are many which cannot be communicated by the press, because, more easily felt than defined, they exist but in their own exercise, and are themselves their only intelligible interpreters.

Parke, musical memoirs (1830)

1787. On the 24th of April, "Nina," with original music by Dalyrac, was produced at Covent Garden. Mrs. Billington sang the music of the part of "Nina" with great feeling and expression, and was loudly and deservedly applauded.

1789. The professional concert commenced in Hanover Square on Monday the 2nd of February. Marchesi and Mrs. Billington were the singers, and Cramer led the band. The concerto players were Dance on the *pianoforte,* who displayed great taste and power of execution, and Cervetto on the violoncello, who, though he did not play with the fire and rapidity of Crosbill, could not be exceeded in delicacy and expression.

1801. The singers at the King's Theatre this year were the same as in the preceding, till the 5th of May, when Madame Vinci made her first appearance in this country in Andreozzi's fine comic opera "La Principessa Filiosa." Madame Vinci displayed a pleasing figure, an agreeable countenance, and a sweet and powerful voice. She had the skill of expressing a perfect crescendo and diminuendo in her singing, which was new and highly effective.

1827. The Philharmonic concert at the Argyll Rooms on the 19th of February . . . opened with Beethoven's fine symphony, "L'Ernica" (Eroica), the middle movement of which is a "Marcia funebre," highly descriptive of a departed hero.

**Nathan, singing treatise (1836), Chapter 9
"Expression"**

Judicious expression is the very acme of the art and is the charm that leads us to the highest estimation of the singer, the finishing stroke to the works of the painter, poet, and musician—and can only be the result of natural feeling, the child of innate sensibility, instructed by the Muses and the Graces, without whose aid the most perfect voice and rapid execution, though they may astonish for a time, can never reach the heart. An insipid singer who has not sufficient judgment to vary his expression, may with propriety be compared to a marble statue, the symmetrical proportions of which please the eye, but, wanting the animation of existence, compel us to turn, after a while, tired by its inanity, to contemplate a less beautiful object of life.

Marx, general music instruction book (1839)

Besides technical skill, a perfect acquaintance with and observance of the written expression marks is indispensable for proper performance. We also hold, however, that in addition to these, sensitivity and insight into those matters that cannot be completely expressed in words are just as necessary. As for the meaning and purpose of the whole work and all its sections, they may be written down and defined or they may be filled out from our personal feelings. At the same time, we must keep in mind that every feature takes its direction from the central idea and purpose of the whole work, and that we too, when we seek to understand, study, and perform a work, must proceed from its central idea. To understand and present a work perfectly, starting with this central idea and following it through all of its parts: this is the objective of artistic performance.

VOLUME

Most of the quotations about expression deal with its importance and general requirement as a component in composition and performance. Specific characteristics of expression, such as tempo and rhythmic alteration, for example, are dealt with as separate subjects and are presented throughout this book. Variation of volume—the adjustment of dynamic levels by performers—has also been mentioned in many quotations that deal with other subjects. However, the subject of volume as a specific characteristic of expression was given some individual attention in writings of the Classical era, and excerpts from these writings are presented here.

Quantz, flute treatise (1752), Chapter 10 "What a Beginner Must Observe in his Independent Practice" Paragraph 3

With regard to force of tone, one must take special care never to play a piece so loudly or so softly that the player cannot, if it should be necessary, play a *Fortissimo* after a *Forte,* and a *Pianissimo* after a *Piano.* This can be done only by increasing or by moderating the wind. Playing always on the same level would soon become tedious.

——. Chapter 17 "Of the Duties of Those Who Accompany or Execute the Accompanying or Ripieno Parts Associated with a Concertante Part" Section 6 "Of the Keyboard Player in Particular"

It is true that on the harpsichord, especially if it has only one keyboard, volume of tone cannot be augmented or diminished as well as upon the instrument called the *pianoforte*, in which the strings are not plucked with quills, but struck with hammers. Nevertheless, on the harpsichord the manner of playing is most important. Thus passages marked *Piano* on this instrument may be improved by moderating the touch and by decreasing the number of parts, and those marked *Forte* by strengthening the touch and by increasing the number of parts in both hands.

L. Mozart, violin treatise (1756), Chapter 12
"Of Reading Music Correctly, and in particular, of Good Execution"

One must know how to change from *piano* to *forte* without directions and of one's own accord, each at the right time; this means, in the well-known phraseology of the painters, Light and Shade. The notes raised by a ♯ and ♮ should always be played rather more strongly, the tone then diminishing again during the course of the melody. For example:

In the same way a sudden lowering of a note by a ♭ and ♮ should be distinguished by *forte*. For example:

It is customary always to accent half notes strongly when mixed with short notes, and to relax the tone again. For example:

Many a quarter note is played in the same manner. For example:

Just as the slurring and detaching, the *forte* and *piano*, according to the demands of expression, must be observed in the most exact manner; so one must not play continuously with a lagging, heavy stroke, but must accommodate oneself to the prevailing mood of each passage.

Rousseau, dictionary (1779), "Forte Piano"

FORTE PIANO. The *forte piano* is the art of sweetening and enforcing the sounds in imitative melody, as we do in the words which it ought to imitate. . . . We do not always express ourselves in the same tone and we do not always speak even with the same degree of force. Music, by imitating the variety of the accents and tones, ought also to imitate the intense or remiss degrees of the words.

J. C. Bach and F. P. Ricci, pianoforte treatise (c.1788), Part 10

The term, NUANCE DES FORTS ET DES DOUX, the grading of loud and soft sounds, is used here figuratively to express the manner in which shades of loud and soft are produced, reinforced, reduced, maintained, and modified on the instrument with the best possible taste and art.

When we speak with ardor, we do not express ourselves always with the same degree of intensity or force. Music, imitating the variety of accents and meanings of words, must, therefore, also imitate their degrees of intensity and relaxation, articulating at times soft, at times loud, and at times in a whisper.

These different gradations, to which sounds of the *Forte-Piano* are very adaptable, must always be drawn out from the melodies; without them all music, no matter how harmonious it may be, will soon tire the ear and will leave the heart cold.

Türk, clavier treatise (1789), Chapter 6, Part 3
"Concerning the Expression of the Prevailing Character"

The composer often specifies the main degree of loudness or softness by the words *sempre forte* or *sempre piano* which are placed at the beginning of the composition. The *sempre*, however, should not be taken too literally, for the composer is only saying that the execution should be generally loud or soft. Certain musical thoughts, in spite of this, must be suitably modified according to the affect (played stronger or weaker). . . .

To specify whether a specific passage must be played somewhat louder or softer than the preceding and following is utterly impossible; nevertheless, one can generally assume that the livelier parts of a composition can be played louder and the tenderly singing parts can be played softer, even if in the first case no forte, and in the second, no piano has been indicated. When a musical thought is repeated, then it is customary to play it softly the second time, provided it has been played loudly the first. On the other hand, a repeated passage may also be played louder, especially when the composer has made it livelier through elaborations. In general, one must even play single tones of importance with more emphasis than the others.

Tromlitz, flute treatise (1791), Chapter 10 "The Ornaments"

Since the alternation of loud and soft is a chief component of good performance, I include it among the essential ornaments. Both are indicated by the following words retained from the Italian, or their initial letters:

forte, strong, *f*
poco forte, rather strong, *poco f*
mezzo forte, moderately strong, *mf*
piu forte, stronger, *piu f*
fortissimo, very strong, *ff*
fortissimo assai, very strong indeed, *fff*
piano, weak, *p*
poco piano, rather weak, *poco p*
mezzo piano, moderately weak, *mp*
piu piano, weaker, *piu p*
pianissimo, very weak, *pp*
pianissimo assai, very weak indeed, *ppp*

The other degrees lying between these are *nuances* which can really only be decided by feeling. They are therefore applied according to rules by few people, and cannot even be applied at all on every instrument. The *forte* and *piano* always begin on the note under or over which the letter *f* or *p* stands. They are used both on single notes and on whole passages, especially those which have already appeared once. Loud and soft are such that they form a contrast with one another, that is to say: they do not always flow into one another, like *crescendo* or *decrescendo*. . . . I do not give an example here, because I would make the *f* and *p* according to my feelings, and another might prefer to make them according to his feelings. In performance one should seek out the places where these alternations or shadings have the greatest effect, and one will find the right way.

Altenburg, trumpet and kettledrum treatise (1795), Chapter 11 "On Clarino Playing and the Style of Execution Required Thereby. Some Rules"

Do not always play with the same loudness or softness, but rather [in a manner] appropriate to the expression or character [of a] given [movement], and [in the case of vocal music], of its accompanying text.

BIBLIOGRAPHY

Agricola, Johann Friedrich. *Allgemeine deutsch Bibliothek* (general German reference). 1769.

_____. *Anleitung zur Singekunst* (singing treatise). Berlin, 1757.

Aitken, John. *A Compilation of the Litanies and Vespers Hymns and Anthems* (Litanies). Philadelphia, 1787.

Albrechtsberger, Johann Georg. *Gründliche Anweisung zur Composition . . . mit einem Anhange von der Beschaffenheit und Anwendung aller jetzt üblichen musikalischen Instrumente* (composition treatise). Leipzig, 1790.

Alembert, Jean le Rond d'. *De la liberté de la musique* (music treatise). Paris, 1759.

Algarotti, Francesco. *Saggio sopra l'opera in musica* (opera essay). Venice, 1755.

Allgemeine Musikalische Zeitung, ed. Friedrich Rochlitz. Leipzig, 1769–1842.

Altenburg, Johann Ernst. *Versuch einer Anleitung zur heroisch-musikalischen Trompeter-und Pauker-Kunst* (trumpet and kettledrum treatise). Halle, 1795.

Anonymous. *New Instructions for Playing the Harpsichord, Piano-forte or Spinnet*. London, c.1790.

Antoniotto, Giorgio. *L'Arte armonica* (composition treatise). 1760.

Avison, Charles. *An Essay on Musical Expression*. London, 1753.

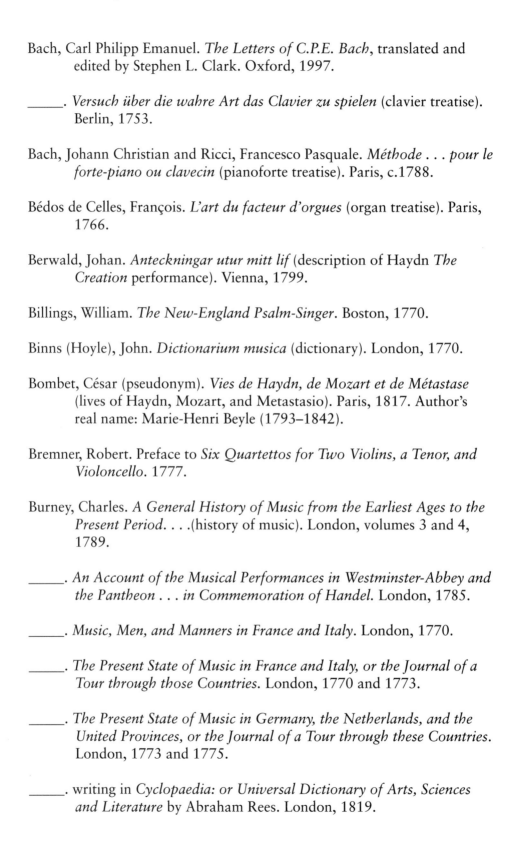

Bach, Carl Philipp Emanuel. *The Letters of C.P.E. Bach*, translated and edited by Stephen L. Clark. Oxford, 1997.

_____. *Versuch über die wahre Art das Clavier zu spielen* (clavier treatise). Berlin, 1753.

Bach, Johann Christian and Ricci, Francesco Pasquale. *Méthode . . . pour le forte-piano ou clavecin* (pianoforte treatise). Paris, c.1788.

Bédos de Celles, François. *L'art du facteur d'orgues* (organ treatise). Paris, 1766.

Berwald, Johan. *Anteckningar utur mitt lif* (description of Haydn *The Creation* performance). Vienna, 1799.

Billings, William. *The New-England Psalm-Singer*. Boston, 1770.

Binns (Hoyle), John. *Dictionarium musica* (dictionary). London, 1770.

Bombet, César (pseudonym). *Vies de Haydn, de Mozart et de Métastase* (lives of Haydn, Mozart, and Metastasio). Paris, 1817. Author's real name: Marie-Henri Beyle (1793–1842).

Bremner, Robert. Preface to *Six Quartettos for Two Violins, a Tenor, and Violoncello*. 1777.

Burney, Charles. *A General History of Music from the Earliest Ages to the Present Period. . . .*(history of music). London, volumes 3 and 4, 1789.

_____. *An Account of the Musical Performances in Westminster-Abbey and the Pantheon . . . in Commemoration of Handel*. London, 1785.

_____. *Music, Men, and Manners in France and Italy*. London, 1770.

_____. *The Present State of Music in France and Italy, or the Journal of a Tour through those Countries*. London, 1770 and 1773.

_____. *The Present State of Music in Germany, the Netherlands, and the United Provinces, or the Journal of a Tour through these Countries*. London, 1773 and 1775.

_____. writing in *Cyclopaedia: or Universal Dictionary of Arts, Sciences and Literature* by Abraham Rees. London, 1819.

Burney, Susannah. Letter to her sister. London, 1779.

Busby, Thomas. *A Complete Dictionary of Music* (musical dictionary). London, c.1801.

_____. *A Grammar of Music*. London, 1818.

_____. *A Musical Manual, or Technical Directory: Containing Full and Perspicuous Explanations of All the Terms, Ancient and Modern* (musical manual). London, 1828.

Callcott, John Wall. *A Musical Grammar* (musical grammar). London, 1806.

Clementi, Muzio. *Introduction to the Art of Playing on the Piano Forte* (pianoforte treatise). 1801.

Corri, Domenico. *The Singer's Preceptor* (singing treatise). London, 1810.

Cramer, Johann Baptist. *Anweisung das Pianoforte zu spielen* (pianoforte treatise). London, 1810.

Czerny, Carl. *Briefe über den Unterricht auf dem Pianoforte* (letters on playing the pianoforte). New York, c.1837–1841.

_____. *Die Schule des Fugenspiels und des Vortrags mehrstimmiger Sätze und deren besonderer Schwierigkeiten auf dem Piano-Forte* (improvisation treatise). Vienna, 1836.

_____. *Erinnerungen aus meinem Leben* (memories of my life). Manuscript, 1842.

_____. *Vollständiges Lehrbuch der musikalischen Composition* (composition treatise). Vienna, 1834.

_____. *Vollständige theoretisch-praktische Pianoforte-Schule,* op. 500 (pianoforte treatise). Vienna, 1839.

Diderot, Denis. *Le neveu de Rameau* (Rameau's nephew dialogue). Manuscript. c.1760.

Ellis, Alexander. *On the History of Musical Pitch*. Journal of the Society of Arts, xxviii, 1880.

Eximeno (y Pujades), Antonio. *Dell'origine e delle regole della musica* (music history treatise). Rome, 1774.

Forkel, Johann Nicolaus. *Allgemeine Geschichte der Musik* (music history treatise). Leipzig, 1788.

_____. *The Forkel-Hoffmeister and Kühnel Correspondence* (letter to Hoffmeister and Kühnel). New York, 1990.

Garcia, Manuel. *Traité complet de l'art du chant* (singing treatise). Paris, 1840–1847.

Geminiani, Francesco. *The Art of Playing on the Violin* (violin treatise). London, 1751.

Glover, Sarah Anna. *Scheme for Rendering Psalmody Congregational* (psalmody treatise). London and Norwich, 1835.

Gluck, Christoph Willibald Ritter von. *Alceste*. Vienna, 1769.

Grimm, Friedrich Melchior. *Encyclopédie*. Paris, 1763.

Hastings, Thomas. *Dissertation on Musical Taste*. Albany, 1822.

Hawkins, Sir John. *A General History of the Science and Practice of Music* (history of music). London, 1776.

Haydn, Joseph. *Applausus*. 1768.

_____. *Die Schöpfung (The Creation)*. Vienna, 1798.

Heck, John Gasper. *The Art of Playing the Harpsichord* (harpsichord treatise). London, c.1770.

Hiller, Johann Adam. *Anweisung zum musikalisch-richtigen Gesange* (singing treatise). Leipzig, 1774.

Holden, John. *An Essay Towards a Rational System of Music* (musical essay). Glasgow, 1770.

Hook, James. *Guida di musica, Being a Complete Book of Instructions for Beginners on the Harpsichord or Piano Forte* (keyboard treatise). c.1785.

Hummel, Johann Nepomuk. *Ausführlich theoretisch-practische Anweisung zum Piano-forte Spiel* (pianoforte treatise). Vienna, 1829.

Jenks, Stephen. *Harmony of Zion*. Dedham, 1818.

Junker, Carl Ludwig. *Einige der vornehrnsten Pflichten eines Kapellmeisters oder Musikdirectors* (handbook for church music directors). Winterthur, 1782.

Kirnberger, Johann Philipp. *Die Kunst des reinen Satzes in der Musik, aus sicheren Grundsätzen hergeleitet und mit deutlichen Beyspielen erläutert* (composition treatise). Berlin, 1771.

Koch, Heinrich Christoph. *Versuch einer Anleitung zur Composition* (composition treatise). Rudolstadt and Leipzig, 1782 (Volume 1), 1787 (Volume 2), 1793 (Volume 3).

Kollmann, Augustus Frederic Christopher. *An Essay on Practical Musical Composition*. 1799.

Kullak, Franz. *Beethoven's Piano-Playing*. New York, 1901.

Law, Andrew. *Harmonic Companion*. Philadelphia, 1807.

Löhlein, Georg Simon. *Clavier-Schule, oder Kurze und gründliche Anweisung zur Melodie und Harmonie* (clavier treatise). Leipzig and Züllichau, 1765.

Mancini, Giovanni Battista. *Pensieri, e riflessioni pratiche sopra il canto figurato* (singing treatise). Vienna, 1774.

Manfredini, Vincenzo. *Difesa della musica moderna* (defense of modern music). Bologna, 1788.

_____. *Regole armoniche, o sieno Precetti ragionat* (harmony treatise). Venice, 1775.

Marmontel, Jean François. *Essai sur les révolutions de la musique en France* (essay on music in France). Paris, 1777.

Marpurg, Friedrich Wilhelm. *Anleitung zum Clavierspielen der schönen Ausübung der heutigen Zeit gemäss* (clavier treatise). Berlin, 1755.

Marx, Adolf Bernhard. *Allgemeine Musiklehre* (general music instruction book). Leipzig, 1839.

Mason, Lowell. *Manual of the Boston Academy of Music for Instruction in the Elements of Vocal Music* (vocal manual). Boston, 1839.

Milchmeyer, J.P. *Die wahre Art das Pianoforte zu spielen* (pianoforte treatise). Dresden, 1797.

Momigny, Jérôme-Joseph de. *Cours complet d'harmonie et de composition* (harmony and composition treatise). Paris, 1806.

Mozart, Leopold. *Versuch einer gründlichen Violinschule* (violin treatise). Augsburg, 1756.

Mozart, W.A. *The Letters of Mozart and his Family* (letters), translated by Emily Anderson. London, 1966.

Nathan, Isaac. *Musurgia vocalis* (singing treatise). London, 1836.

Parke, William Thomas. *Musical Memoirs* (musical memoirs). 1830.

Petri, Johann Samuel. *Anleitung zur practischen Musik, vor neuangehende Sänger und Instrumentspieler* (musical guide). Lauban, 1767.

Porges, Heinrich. *Die Bühnenproben zu den Bayreuther Festspielen des Jahres 1876* (commentary on Wagner rehearsing *The Ring*). Leipzig, 1881.

Quantz, Johann Joachim. *Versuch einer Anweisung die Flöte traversiere zu spielen* (flute treatise). Berlin, 1752.

Reichardt, Johann Friedrich. *Vertraute Briefe geschrieben auf einer Reise nach Wien und den österreichischen Staaten zu Ende 1808 und zu Anfang 1809* (letters). Amsterdam, 1810.

Rellstab, Johann Carl Friedrich. *Anleitung für Clavierspieler, den Gebrauch der Bachschen Fingersetzung, die Manieren und den Vortrag betreffend* (clavier treatise). Berlin, 1790.

Rossini, Gioachino (written by E. Michotte). *Souvenirs: une soirée chez Rossini à Beau-Séjour* (account of an evening at Villa Rossini). Passy, 1858.

Rousseau, Jean-Jacques. *Dictionnaire de musique* (dictionary). Paris, 1768. English translation, 1771 and 1779.

_____. *Lettre sur la musique française* (letter on French music). Paris, 1753.

Schindler, Anton Felix. *Biographie von Ludwig van Beethoven* (biography of Beethoven). Münster, 1840.

Schröter, Christoph Gottlieb. *Deutliche Anweisung zum Generalbass* (figured bass treatise). Halberstadt, 1772.

Spohr, Louis. *Selbstbiographie* (musical diary). Kassel, 1860–1861.

Streicher, A. *Kurze Bemerkungen über das Spielen, Stimmen und Erhalten der Fortepiano* (remarks on the fortepiano). Vienna, 1801.

Sulzer, Johann Georg. *Allgemeine Theorie der schönen Künste* (general theory of music). Leipzig, 1771–1774.

Tartini, Giuseppe. *Lettera del defonto Signor Giuseppe Tartini alla Signora Maddalena Lombardini* (letter to Signora Maddalena Lombardini). Venice, 1770.

_____. *Regole per arrivare a saper ben suonar il violino* (violin treatise). Paris, 1771.

_____. *Traité des agréments de la musique* (ornamentation treatise). Paris, 1771.

Tenducci, Giusto Ferdinando. *Instruction of Mr Tenducci to his Scholars* (singing treatise). London, 1782.

Thayer, A.W. *Ludwig van Beethovens Leben* (biography of Beethoven). Berlin, 1866–1879.

Tromlitz, Johann Georg. *Ausführlicher und gründlicher Unterricht die Flöte zu spielen* (flute treatise). Leipzig, 1791.

Tulou, Jean-Louis. *Méthode de flûte* (flute treatise). 1835.

Türk, Daniel Gottlob. *Clavierschule, oder Anweisung zum Clavierspielen für Lehrer und Lernende* (clavier treatise). Leipzig and Halle, 1789.

_____. *Von den wichtigsten Pflichten eines Organisten in Beytrag zur Verbesserung der musikalischen Liturgie* (organ in worship treatise). Halle, 1787.

Verri, Pietro. "*La Musica*" (essay on music), in *Il Caffè* 2. Milan, 10 August 1765.

Wagner, Richard. *Über das Dirigieren* (conducting treatise). 1869.

Weber, Carl Maria von. Article in the *Berliner Musik-Zeitung* (comments about tempo). Berlin, 1827.

Wragg, J. *The Oboe Preceptor, or the Art of Playing the Oboe* (oboe treatise). London, 1792.

AUTHOR INDEX

ABOUT THE AUTHOR

Dennis Shrock is author of *Music for Beginning Conductors* and *Performance Practices in the Classical Era* (GIA) as well as *Choral Repertoire* and *Choral Scores* (Oxford University Press). In addition, he is Interim Director of Choral Activities at Texas Christian University and a frequent lecturer, guest conductor, and clinician – serving as Artist-in-Residence and member of the Conducting Institute at Westminster Choir College (2010), Guest Lecturer and Conductor at Yale University (2009–2010), Guest Conductor of the Dallas Symphony Chorus (2010), and lecturer at American Choral Directors National Conferences (2009 and 2011).

Past positions have included Visiting Professor of Music at Boston University (2009–2010), Artistic Director of the Santa Fe Desert Chorale (1999–2004), Director of Choral Activities and Graduate Choral Studies at the University of Oklahoma (1978–2006), Artistic Director of Canterbury Choral Society (1981–1999), and Assistant Conductor and Choral Director of the Oklahoma City Philharmonic (1990–1998).

He has been called one of the very top choral scholars in the United States, and for his exceptional work the City of Santa Fe declared December 22, 2003 "Dennis Shrock Day," Westminster Choir College granted him an "Alumni Merit Award," the state of Oklahoma conferred on him a citation for "Contributions of Excellence," and the University of Oklahoma granted him two "Distinguished Lectureships" and named him a "Presidential Professor."

Dr. Shrock received a bachelor's degree in music education from Westminster Choir College and both master's and doctoral degrees in choral conducting from Indiana University.